THE PENGUIN GOOD AUSTRALIAN
WINE GUIDE

Huon Hooke is one of Australia's most experienced and best qualified wine writers and judges. He is a wine-marketing graduate from Roseworthy Agricultural College and a qualified journalist. His wine-writing career began with the *Australian Financial Review* in 1983 and he's had a weekly column in a Fairfax paper ever since. He has a weekly column in the *Sydney Morning Herald*'s 'Good Living' section, and the *Herald*'s and the *Age*'s *Good Weekend* magazine; he is contributing editor of *Australian Gourmet Traveller WINE* magazine and writes for many other publications. He began judging in wine competitions in 1987 and has judged in most wine shows in Australia, doing about 10 shows a year in Australia and overseas. He is a senior judge and chairman of several shows including (in 2005) the Barossa, Mudgee, Adelaide Hills, Mount Barker and the Boutique Winery Awards. His favourite pastimes, when not up to his nose in wine, are fly fishing, bushwalking, skiing, sailing, music and reading almost anything except wine books.

Ralph Kyte-Powell has more than 30 years' experience in the wine business and hospitality industry. His first wine job was with Seppelt during university vacation. Since then he has worked in marketing and sales for some of Australia's leading wine merchants, managed wine stores, been sommelier at a couple of Melbourne's best restaurants, worked in vineyards and wineries in Australia and France, and lectured on wine at a TAFE college. He's also owned a successful small hotel, and managed a restaurant. He started writing about wine 11 years ago and has a regular column in Melbourne's *Age*. He contributes to other publications including Tourism Victoria's *Wine Regions of Victoria* guide, chairs the imported-wine panel and writes regularly for *Cuisine* in New Zealand, judges at Australian regional wine shows, and at Le Concours des Vins du Victoria. A list of Ralph's favourite wines would be encyclopaedic and variable, but would always include champagne, great pinot noir, Rutherglen liqueur muscat and the best Italian sangiovese – and when it all gets too much, he loves a good beer.

D0227166

THE PENGUIN GOOD AUSTRALIAN
WINE GUIDE
2005 | 2006

Huon Hooke & Ralph Kyte-Powell

Penguin Books

PENGUIN BOOKS

Published by the Penguin Group
Penguin Group (Australia)
250 Camberwell Road, Camberwell, Victoria 3124, Australia
(a division of Pearson Australia Group Pty Ltd)
Penguin Group (USA) Inc.
375 Hudson Street, New York, New York 10014, USA
Penguin Group (Canada)
90 Eglinton Avenue East, Suite 700, Toronto, ON M4P 2Y3, Canada
(a division of Pearson Penguin Canada Inc.)
Penguin Books Ltd
80 Strand, London WC2R 0RL, England
Penguin Ireland
25 St Stephen's Green, Dublin 2, Ireland
(a division of Penguin Books Ltd)
Penguin Books India Pvt Ltd
11 Community Centre, Panchsheel Park, New Delhi – 110 017, India
Penguin Group (NZ)
Cnr Airborne and Rosedale Roads, Albany, Auckland, New Zealand
(a division of Pearson New Zealand Ltd)
Penguin Books (South Africa) (Pty) Ltd
24 Sturdee Avenue, Rosebank, Johannesburg 2196, South Africa

Penguin Books Ltd, Registered Offices: 80 Strand, London WC2R 0RL, England

First published by Penguin Group (Australia), a division of Pearson Australia Group Pty Ltd, 2005

10 9 8 7 6 5 4 3 2 1

Cover design by Elizabeth Dias © Penguin Group (Australia)
Cover illustration by Elizabeth Dias
Authors photograph by Kevin O'Daly/Aspect Photographics
Photograph on p.310 by photolibrary.com
Typeset in Stone Sans by Post Pre-Press Group, Brisbane, Queensland
Printed and bound in Australia by McPherson's Printing Group, Maryborough, Victoria

ISBN 0 14 300273 2.
ISSN 1038–6467.

www.penguin.com.au

Contents

Penguin Wine Awards 2005

This year has been a great year for new Australian wines: more wineries, more labels, more brands; it's all go. That means more choice than we really need, and indeed the jungle of products is probably confusing for many wine-drinkers. The good news is that many of the new wines are very good, and we can't afford to ignore the new brands and producers.

At the business end of things, there's still a lot of good-value wine at the price-levels where most Australians buy their wine – that is, below $20 a bottle. Most of these wines are from the bigger companies, and while a lot of their sub-$12 white wines are tasting decidedly bland and boring, our Penguin Wine of the Year is anything but. It's a humble $12 semillon chardonnay that sells as low as $9.99. Inexpensive, yes, but modest, no! It's chock-full of flavour and character.

The humble sem-chard blend has died out somewhat in this age of obsession with mono-varietals, and we're sorry to see it decline. We believe a little semillon would improve a lot of chardonnays by lending them some steeliness, backbone, length and nerve. It would also help them go better with food, and handle some bottle-age. On the other hand, a dose of chardonnay enriches the leaner profile of semillon and adds appealing peachy fruit flavours and aromas, generosity and mid-palate fullness. Like its red equivalent, the cabernet shiraz, the sem-chard is an Aussie tradition that is worth continuing. But that's not why we chose our wine of the year: it's simply a damn good drink at an amazingly low price.

We could easily choose our award winners each year exclusively from the best of the best – the great wines of Australia. But inevitably, that would mean we were filling the pages with super-expensive wines that are beyond most people's pocket, making this guide of limited use to most Australians, and we don't want that!

So our awards are selected with an eye on several criteria: quality, certainly, but also price and value for money, quantity and availability (always a problem with a book that's prepared some months before it actually goes on sale). A reasonable quantity has to have been produced. We are a little tired of discovering fabulous wines that ring all our bells, only to find in the fine print that just 100 cases or so were made. That goes nowhere. People have to be able to buy the stuff. We're confident this year's wine of the year is widely available in Australia and overseas.

THE PENGUIN WINE OF THE YEAR
BEST-VALUE WHITE WINE

Peter Lehmann Semillon Chardonay 2004

There are many wines in the Lehmann portfolio that offer extraordinary value for money but this tasty little blend takes the cake. Both authors independently rated it gold-medal quality, and it's under $12! Not only that, it's a great drink. Another thing: the bottle-variation of some of Australia's better known cheap wines concerns us (batch bottling is often suspected), but Lehmann wines are very consistent. They're as honest as the day is long. (See page 149.)

BEST WHITE WINE
BEST CHARDONNAY

Hardys Eileen Hardy Chardonnay 2002

Is this Australia's best value in super-premium chardonnay? Quite possibly: it's a great wine and delivers real excitement for half the cost of the price-leaders. (See page 79.)

BEST RED WINE
BEST SHIRAZ

Shaw & Smith Shiraz 2003

We loved the spicy varietal intensity of this Adelaide Hills shiraz combined with its rich, ripe, full body; we also like the way it doesn't parade the fact there's a lick of viognier in it. (See page 282.)

BEST ROSÉ WINE

Willow Creek Pinot Saignée 2004

Pinot noir can make beautiful rosé. While more delicate than many Australian rosés, this has great flavour and balance, and that all-important but hard to quantify attribute – slurpability! (See page 172.)

BEST SPARKLING WINE

Brown Brothers Whitlands Patricia 1999

Browns were a late entrant in the premium fizz biz, but their high-altitude Whitlands vineyard has helped them make up for lost time – fast. This is a tremendous, rich, multi-faceted tilt at champagne. (See page 46.)

BEST SWEET WINE

Lillypilly Noble Sauvignon Blanc 2002

Robbie Fiumara's impressive range of stickies are second to none in Australia, although not as feted as some in the Riverina. This is the best of a terrific range. (See page 302.)

BEST FORTIFIED WINE

Seppelt Para Liqueur Single Vintage Tawny 1984

Seppelt has so many beaut fortifieds it's hard to choose a 'best', but for ultra-complex aged wine at a remarkable price, this is a winner. Take a bow, James Godfrey! (See page 320.)

PICKS OF THE BUNCH

BEST RIESLING

Delatite Riesling 2004

Rosie Ritchie turns out some of the best riesling in the land year after year, and not being in a big region like Clare, she's probably under-sung. This is riesling of great purity and finesse. (See page 107.)

BEST SAUVIGNON BLANC AND BLENDS
TK Adelaide Hills Sauvignon Blanc 2004

Tim Knappstein is a perfectionist: an outstanding white winemaker who delivers sauvignon with properly ripe fruit and impeccable balance, without resorting to showiness or sugar. (See page 138.)

BEST SEMILLON AND BLENDS
Ferngrove Frankland Semillon Sauvignon Blanc 2004

Young Kim Horton is doing good things across the board at Ferngrove: his '04 showed real intensity of classic varietal fruit in a high-cropping year that produced many weak sem savs. (See page 143.)

BEST OTHER WHITES AND BLENDS
Petaluma Viognier 2004

Petaluma has managed to get marvellously intense, complex varietal fruit without the excessively apricotty aromas and hot alcoholic finish that unbalances many Aussie viogniers. (See page 157.)

BEST CABERNET SAUVIGNON AND BLENDS
Balnaves Cabernet Sauvignon 2001

Balnaves' top wine, The Tally, is one of the best cabernets in the land but their regular bottling is much cheaper and almost as good. The Balnaves family are top viticulturists and Pete Bissell is a great winemaker. Serendipity! (See page 174.)

BEST PINOT NOIR
Stonier Reserve Pinot Noir 2003

Stonier is a class producer which makes some lovely easy-drinking pinots, none better than the 2003. We even preferred it over their new single-vineyard releases. (See page 233.)

⚘ BEST OTHER REDS AND BLENDS

Charles Melton Nine Popes 2002

The 2002 season was excellent for grenache-based Rhône blends in the Barossa, and while the Nine Popes is a perennial favourite, the '02 rang our bells a bit louder than usual. (See page 211.)

BEST-VALUE PICKS

⚘ BEST-VALUE SPARKLING

Lindemans Bin 25 Brut Cuvée

For a sub-$10 bubbly this is as much as you could wish for, and more. It's clean, well-made and full of simple, fresh fruit with a refreshing finish. (See page 52.)

⚘ BEST-VALUE RED WINE

Preece Cabernet Sauvignon 2003

The quality of all Preece wines impressed us this year, none more so than this cabernet sauvignon, which is loaded with flavour and personality. (See page 199.)

⚘ BEST-VALUE FORTIFIED

Grant Burge Aged Tawny

The big companies tend to hog the cheap fortified wine field, but Burge's modestly priced tawny port is more than competitive, and the latest bottling seems to have a bit of extra depth and character. (See page 314.)

⚘ BEST NEW PRODUCER

Toolangi

With two releases of wines on the market to date, this Yarra Valley producer has impressed us deeply. The Hounsell family have a vineyard at Dixons Creek in the Yarra Valley, neighbouring the Toolangi State Forest. Being intent on producing the best wines they can, they've enlisted Tom Carson at Yering Station to make chardonnay and pinot noir, and Rick Kinzbrunner at Giaconda to make the stunning Reserve chardonnay. They also buy in some grapes from the Coldstream area. The three Toolangi chardonnays – Reserve,

Estate and regular – are all exemplary wines that well suit their price-points. Artefact – or winemaker induced complexity – increases progressively with the price of the wines. The regular $20 wine is fruit-driven but certainly not simplistic; the Reserve is simply outstanding and seldom do we find a new brand, supplied by relatively young vines, turning out such nectar. The hand of Kinzbrunner is of course very significant, but silk purses cannot be made from sow's ears. The pinot noir is not quite of the calibre of the chardonnays, but we are optimistic for the future. Shiraz and cabernet are still to make their debut. These are exciting, rewarding wines.

The Year in Review

What's happened in Aussie wine in the last 12 months? Oh, nothing much. General drought, over-production, too many wineries, retail chains dominating the market and putting the screws on wine producers, cellar-door trade in the doldrums, two big investment companies collapse owing millions of bucks, cleanskin sales going berserk, etc., etc. Oh, and Foster's swallowed up Southcorp (yawn). Just another day at the office, really.

CLEANSKIN MANIA

The biggest phenomenon in Australian wine in the past year has been the massive acceptance of so-called cleanskins – bottles of wine without labels, or, at best, a very rudimentary label. These 'no frills' wines have become a very significant force in the wine market, so much so they are cannibalising sales of inexpensive, mass-branded wines and causing hardship for the larger wine producers and wholesalers. No sales figures exist but you just have to walk into one of the larger supermarket-chain liquor stores and be confronted by a wall of cleanskins to realise they are big business. One major wholesaler told us unhappily: 'I wish I could wave a magic wand and make cleanskins disappear.'

Originally, a cleanskin was usually a 'bin end' (a quick way of quitting the last of a vintage to make way for the next one) or a distressed sale (a winery or wholesaler with cash-flow problems needing to sell wine quickly, by dropping its price). As a cleanskin, the true brand name is not revealed, and so the brand's credibility is protected. But now, big operators such as Coles and Woolworths engage wineries to produce cleanskins especially for them – and the surplus wine sloshing around in the wine industry's tanks means it's a buyer's market for this material. Even smaller retailers are doing the same thing: contracting wineries to make cleanskins especially for them. The evidence shows cleanskins are pulling sales away, not only from branded wines in retail outlets, but also from wineries – indeed, every facet of the wine business is probably losing sales to cleanskins.

The big question on wine drinkers' lips is: are cleanskins good value? Our answer to that: some are; some aren't. Cleanskins vary just like any other category of wine. The widespread belief is that these wines are hidden bargains: they're either 'bin ends' being specialled off to make way for the next vintage, or they're distressed sales from cute boutiques that are having a cash-flow crisis. Sometimes that's exactly what they are, but that doesn't mean they're any good. A lot of them are just plain bad wines that cannot be sold under their normal label, so they're being dumped. And often when you buy a cleanskin from retailer X, take it home, like it, decide to buy a case and go back a few days later, that cleanskin contains an entirely different wine. As there are no distinguishing marks on the bottle, you never know till you get it home that you don't like it. Caveat emptor! But there are some very good buys: as always, the only rule is – if you can – try before you buy.

IS RETAILING GOING TO THE DOGS?

There's a widespread assumption that there is a dire threat to diversity in the retailing of wine. This is supposedly caused by the increasing concentration of retailing power in the hands of the two biggest supermarket chains, Coles and Woolworths. Coles with its Liquorland, Vintage Cellars and Quaffers shops (and lately its new brand, First Choice); Woolies with its Dan Murphy's, First Estate, BWS, Safeway and Woolworths Liquor shops. The chains have been aggressively taking over independent liquor stores and placing them under collective banners, then standardising the product ranges in look-alike shops.

The cry is that this is leading to a boring same-ishness of their offering; that small wineries can no longer find an outlet for their wines; and that independent shops which give some diversity are being squeezed out by the aggressive pricing of the chains.

We agree that too much power in the hands of the few is innately bad; we agree that the range stocked by the likes of Liquorland, BWS and Woolworths Liquor shops is same-ish and boring and limited. But the truth is, that's probably all that most of the customers who shop there want. Research conducted for Southcorp this year showed that 77 per cent of shoppers were intimidated when shopping for wine and found it an unpleasant experience, largely because of the baffling array of wines. The research showed they would be happier, and more likely to return, if the range of choice was smaller. This was dreadful news for those who want more choice in shops, not less! If shoppers want more choice and a bigger range, or if they're interested in wine and want to dig deeper, they can always go to other shops, especially the better independents. There is no danger of these dying out altogether.

The competitiveness of retailing, largely stimulated by the chains, has led to a climate of very low prices, and that's great for customers like you and us, although it is damaging the profitability of some wineries. But we believe that, far from squeezing independent retailers out of business, it's encouraging them to be more thoughtful and creative and seek new ways of selling. They can specialise in the service that the chains find so hard – if not impossible – to deliver. To provide that service, they have better staff: very few good staff remain working in the chains for very long. They get bored and frustrated by the lack of freedom. If you love wine and love diversity, and want to learn and be challenged and stimulated when you go to buy wine, you'd go to a good independent every time.

Finally, the complaint that small wineries can no longer get their wines listed in the shops. This is correct: the chains rarely fiddle around with small-lot wines, phoning boutique wineries and placing small orders. They want to rationalise: make one phone call and order by the truckload. Or see one sales person from one big wholesaler and order right across their range. This is natural and predictable.

If the 101 new boutiques that opened their doors for trading in 2004–5 can't get their wine into a retail shop, it's not the fault of the chains. The number of small wineries in Australia has doubled in the last seven years, from around 1000 to 2000. Obviously, they can't all have their wines in Liquorland. A lot of their wines aren't much good anyway (this is heresy!) and no decent retailer would want to stock them. A lot of boutiques, especially new ones, are amateurish and their wines are poor value: small is not necessarily beautiful. The truth is, there is a surfeit of small wineries, and the world doesn't owe them a living; likewise the trade doesn't owe them a place on a shop shelf. A lot of them are in the wine business for questionable motives in the first place.

No matter how often the wine industry leaders and analysts warn that there are too many wineries, and that there's little chance of profit in starting a winery, still more than 100 new winemaking enterprises start up every year. No one can stop lemmings rushing off cliffs.

CHAINS PUT SCREWS ON

A disturbing side to all this is that the liquor chains are now so powerful that they are dictating prices at the supply end. Their buyers say to winery people: 'Sell us X quantity of this wine at Z price, or else we will go to one of the other big companies and they will.' The end-result is that there is less and less profit in producing wine. Listed wine companies are on the nose, their share prices have plunged and no one recommends buying their shares. And at the end of the line is the poor old grapegrower, who is being screwed the hardest. When grapes are in over-supply, prices fall and demand slackens off. Result: growers on the poverty line and at least 20 000 tonnes of grapes left on vines around the nation after the (record) 2005 vintage. The buck always stops with the primary producer, it's always the mum-and-dad farmers who have the bum out of their pants.

The good news is that even though the currency exchange rates have not been in our favour, exports continue to grow. If they didn't, our wine industry would be in a disastrous position. ('Thank God for Yellow Tail!' is the refrain heard around the country.) Problem is: most of our exports – and virtually all of the growth in exports – are at the cheap end. For reasons of image and profit, Australia needs to export more high-value wine.

INVESTMENT COMPANIES COLLAPSE

First Wine Orb and then Heritage Fine Wines collapsed, owing $1 million and $2.4 million respectively. In addition, investors stand to lose a lot of money because some of their wine will be sold to pay expenses. Wine Orb apparently lacked any proper record-keeping, so most of its investors will never get their wine: it'll be sold by the receivers to pay the secured creditors. In a chaotic situation, millions of bottles of wine are stored on behalf of these two companies in a number of professional cellarage facilities in Sydney and Melbourne, and the Heritage stocktake alone (counting and identifying the bottles) was expected to cost $1 million and take several months. The liquidator planned to pay for this by imposing a levy of $1 a bottle on the investors.

What amazes us is the continued gullibility of people who willingly throw large sums of hard-earned cash at salesmen who have no credentials in either the wine or investment businesses, who make rash promises about the potential of wine to grow in value. (We use the present tense because even though these two companies have folded, the same scenario has happened many times before and will happen again.) One truly high-quality wine retailer in Sydney told us: 'Heritage apparently sold $90 million worth of wine in five years. Just imagine how that would have boosted all the fine wine retailers in town if they'd been able to share out that business.' Yep, and the investors would still have their wine and the suppliers would have been paid . . .

We have always maintained that very few wines make worthwhile investments. You either need to know a lot about this quite specialised area yourself, or employ someone who does. Much of the wine these two companies sold as 'investment wine' was no such thing. Heritage in fact created brands and labels especially for Heritage clients, with no track-record, and hence no real investment potential. If you wanted good advice on how to invest your money in the stock exchange, you'd go to a qualified professional, wouldn't you? Why treat wine investment any differently?

(Anyone interested in following this story can read an archive of articles at www.cellarit.com; and anyone still keen to invest in wine should have a look at www.investdrinks.org, and click on Down Under first.)

DROUGHT BITES

It's ironic that Australia has had two successive record wine-grape harvests at a time when most of the country has suffered either drought or prolonged dry periods. By winter 2005, most of South Australia had enjoyed replenishing rains (floods, in fact), and Western Australia had done quite well, too, but all of New South Wales west of the Great Dividing Range and much of Victoria was still struggling with various degrees of drought. New South Wales country towns were running out of water and minor top-up rains were just a tease, distracting attention from the real problems – of depleted aquifers and restrictions on irrigation water. Sustained soaking rains with follow-ups were needed to wet the deeper soil layers and prevent masses of beautiful, century-old eucalyptus trees dying. Some wit was heard to remark: 'They should take all the surplus wine, and the juice of the unwanted grapes, and use it all for irrigation.' A new kind of recycling? Just joking.

FOSTER'S SWALLOWS SOUTHCORP

Foster's paid zillions for what was formerly Australia's biggest wine company, Southcorp, and the new company, created by rolling Beringer Blass Wine Estates and Southcorp together, will be the world's biggest wine company. It's called Foster's Wine Estates. Paul Hogan might have wisecracked: 'Foster's. That's Australian for wine, mate!'

What will it mean for wine drinkers? Probably nothing, or very little. Foster's would be crazy to meddle with the good things about Southcorp. The key winemakers will probably stay where they are, and any scuttlebutt about Fosterising Grange would be ridiculous. Foster's will need to save money somewhere – by streamlining, combining operations and cutting costs, and no doubt some heads will roll, but it's to be hoped they keep the best people and the best resources.

Inevitably, there will be speculation about winery closures. Both companies are South Australian based with Beringer's biggest winery now the new Wolf Blass pile at Nuriootpa, the same town that houses Southcorp's biggest premium-quality winery, the former Penfolds. We can't see them closing either of those. But Seppeltsfield, also in the Barossa and looking increasingly 'surplus to requirements', will surely be on the chopping block again.

As far as wine quality goes, we don't foresee too many changes. Both Beringer and Southcorp have been serving up some pretty dire stuff in their cheapest bottles, and we hope they address that. It's not that the wines are bad in quality terms, they are just bland and same-ish. Raw reds sold at less than a year old are sweetened up with juice to hide their green astringency, and boring characterless whites are now the norm in Rosemount split-label, Lindemans cheapies, Queen Adelaide and even Rawson's Retreat is looking pretty ordinary. The Hardy group is serving up the best cheap wines of the big companies today, and Orlando Wyndham is also delivering the goods.

ARE CORKS SCREWED FOR GOOD?

Alternative closures for wine bottles continue to gain ground over the humble cork. We're strongly in favour of screw-caps, and believe they will continue to be adopted more and more widely. They're mainly intended to overcome the twin scourges of cork-sealed wine: TCA cork-taint and random oxidation. Correctly applied, they do overcome those taints. And there is another benefit: screw-caps ensure bottles of the same wine stored in the same conditions will be as close to identical as it's possible to be at this time. We reckon a screw-cap equates to the best cork. Both stop air getting in and wine leaking out. Problem is, the best corks are probably only 10–20 per cent of any given batch.

Like all wine-nuts, we go to dinners where people bring treasured bottles of wine, sometimes expensive French stuff, often quite old, and invariably we find some bottles are either damaged or completely ruined by faulty cork. The loss runs into hundreds of dollars, and frankly everyone is very sick of that. We're also tired of the wine industry (especially France's) being in a state of denial about it all. They seem to be quite happy for the vulnerable public to wear the cost of cork-tainted wine, which runs into billions of dollars worldwide every year.

Synthetic 'corks' – or more correctly, plastic stoppers – are a very different subject. Whereas screw-caps are great for ageing, synthetics have a limited shelf-life. Their problem is that they let air in, and eventually the wine starts to oxidise. Depending on the type of plastic stopper, their useful life can be very short, i.e. drink it within a year of bottling, while the best synthetics are guaranteed for up to three years from bottling date. Among the best is Nomacorc (used in the lower-priced Lindemans and Rosemount wines). This is a two-piece stopper with a soft outer sleeve enclosing a harder cylinder. The latest generation Nomacorcs, due to be released in late 2005, will be guaranteed for five years from bottling date.

But how do you know when the wine was bottled? There's nothing that tells you that on the package. A rough rule of thumb: whites are bottled about three to twelve months after the harvest (early autumn of the year on the label) and reds, say, between a year and two years of harvest.

Maybe one day the wine companies will let us into the secret and actually put a packing date or use-by date on the bottle. That would be a big help.

Screw-caps are not without their problems, too, and reductive smells, i.e. sulphides, are the main debating point right now. We'd much rather find a hint of hydrogen sulphide in some wines (which most drinkers don't even notice) than cork taint ruining 5 or 6 per cent. However, there are three other alternative closures that provide promising alternatives to screw-caps: Diam, Procork and Zork.

Zork is a soft plastic Australian-made invention that seems to do a very good job. You tear a tab like you do with a champagne foil to release it, then pull it out like a stopper. Procork, also an Aussie invention, is a conventional cork with a polymer membrane applied to either end. This is supposed to prevent wine coming into direct contact with cork, and thereby cancel out cork taints. Finally, the French Diam cork may be the best of all. It looks like a genuine cork, but is assembled from ground cork powder that has been subjected to a super-critical CO_2 treatment that is said to remove any TCA. The powder is then reassembled into a cylinder with glues. We have yet to see a faulty wine with a Diam cork in it. And it has the advantage of being made from real cork.

OUR NEW FORMAT

This edition of *The Penguin Good Australian Wine Guide* is a slightly slimmer volume than previous editions. The reason is that we have culled some of the lower-rated wines and thereby reduced the total number reviewed. It has gone from just over 1000 in past editions to more than 750. On the other hand, we have allocated more space to each review, and increased the cover size of the book slightly. We take the attitude that our readers are mostly interested in quality and value, so the new yardstick is the number '4'. Nearly all the wines between these two covers have scored at least four out of five, either for absolute quality (wine glasses), or value-for-money (stars) – or both. We hope you enjoy the new-look *Guide*.

Happy drinking!

The Heartland of Modern Australian Wine

A couple of years ago, one of us asked a colleague whether he'd ever visited the vineyards and wineries of the New South Wales Riverina. 'Why would I want to do that?' he replied. While it's an amazing response from a wine commentator, it does reflect the position that Australia's warm hinterland vineyards have occupied in public consciousness for much of their existence. People are happy to swan around the Yarra Valley, Margaret River or the Hunter, but the Riverina . . . forget it.

The Riverina, and similar vast flat tracts of vineyard along the Murray, the Darling, and the Murrumbidgee rivers, have occupied the bottom end of the Australian wine hierarchy for most of their history with vines. Until the wine boom of the 1960s and '70s the produce of these vineyards was mostly used for distillation or inexpensive fortified wine, then as Australians embraced table wine these hot vineyards became the source of our *vin ordinaire* – everyday wine slurped unceremoniously from flagons and cardboard winecasks.

Back in those early wine boom days, these regions were grouped together in the trade as 'irrigated vineyards', an unofficial title and one with truly derogatory connotations. The general belief was that better quality wines came from regions that depended on natural rainfall, and irrigated vineyards made lacklustre wines at best. This perception of low quality was generally on the mark, and the nature of viticulture in the irrigated regions didn't encourage production of the best grapes.

Growers of irrigated grapes were usually paid by the wineries according to yield, so the temptation to over-crop was very strong. And when an increased quantity of fruit from the vines was as easy as turning on the tap, growers did so. The result was washed out, yet sometimes curiously harsh reds, and watery whites. Their saving grace was that they were cheap. These vineyards have always represented a remarkably efficient way to produce lots of wine. To start with, vineyard land is cheaper and easier to obtain than it is in less remote regions. This allows very large vineyards to be planted, and these dimensions mean great economies of scale. The vineyards are flat and easy to mechanise, the climate is benign, and high yields come easily with the controlled ready availability of water.

Thankfully the standing of the traditional irrigated regions has been on the rise for the last decade or two. Winemakers now cringe when their vineyards are called 'irrigated'. Regional names are being used more often to define them, and Riverina, Murray Valley and Riverland are becoming names to be proud of. These areas have become the heartland of Australian wine. What's happened to change things?

Slowly the stigma attached to irrigation has disappeared. Australia is a very dry continent and grapevines need water. Even in cool areas with high annual rainfall there can be dry periods, so it's not only growers in the 'irrigated' regions who occasionally give their vines a drop to drink in difficult times. The difference is that in cooler regions irrigation is generally used to help vines survive drought and the like, while in traditional irrigated regions the vines rely on irrigation as their principal source of water to produce a crop.

The culture in these heartland regions has changed, too. A large part of production still goes into the cheap bulk market, but a generational shift has taken place that's led to a new crop of well-educated, quality-oriented, young winemakers taking the reins of many enterprises. Add to this the quality emphasis that's taken hold in our bigger wine companies, and you have an environment that has encouraged growers and producers alike to lift their sights above the inexpensive generic market, opting more and more to sell the region's wines with a quality regional identity, or under a recognised quality label. They've learnt that it's much better long-term for buyers to choose your wine for its identity and quality, rather than just its modest price. The scale of things has kept prices low, but the quality approach has meant tighter yield controls in the vineyard, the replacement of poor, bulk-oriented grape varieties with grapes for fine wine, better viticulture, bonuses for the best grapes, the identification of better sites, and the employment of better techniques for handling grapes in warm climates. Marketing techniques attuned to the modern wine scene have helped, and some growers are now able to sell wines that stand comparison with very good wines from the traditional quality areas.

All this has added up to some of the best-value table wine in the world, a fact that's been at the heart of Australia's runaway export success. Labels that use the produce of these heartland regions as the foundation of their top-selling wines include some of Australia's best known. Household names like Jacob's Creek, Yalumba Oxford Landing, Yellow Tail, McWilliams, De Bortoli, Rosemount Estate and Lindemans are among them. Foreign markets have fallen in love with the 'bottled sunshine' type of Aussie wine, especially new wine drinkers who choose these friendly drops ahead of traditional European styles at similar price points.

Grape varieties that figure large in the modern story of these regions are chardonnay, shiraz, cabernet sauvignon and merlot, and it's these that fuel the thirst of local and export markets. Other grapes show promise, with petit verdot looking to have found its true home in the Murray Valley, a world away from its origins in Bordeaux. Most other grape varieties are present in the vineyards, but those with more delicate personalities like riesling, sauvignon blanc and pinot noir aren't as successful as they are in cooler climes. Semillon is important in the Riverina where it makes the best wine of this region.

Riverina semillon produces the one truly 'great' wine type to come from these warm inland vineyards. Each year the heat of summer fades away, the leaves on the vines turn autumnal gold, and while the mornings remain comfortably mild, mist cloaks the vines. Conditions are perfect for one of wine's minor miracles as the green–gold bunches of semillon grapes shrivel, turn brown and become covered with a downy grey mould called *botrytis cinerea*. The mould's spores leach moisture from the grapes, shrivelling them and concentrating sugar, acids and flavour components, yet preventing spoilage. It's a high-risk strategy but when everything clicks into place the grapes make wine of incomparable lusciousness and sweetness.

Botrytis plays a principal part in the production of the great sweet wines of Sauternes in France and the best German sweeties. In the Riverina it was pioneered with spectacular success by De Bortoli. Now this 'Riverina gold' is produced from semillon, and sometimes other white varieties, by many of the region's wineries with consistent quality standards that would be the envy of those making similar wines in France and Germany. The advent of this luscious elixir has given the Riverina an excellent flagship wine to add prestige to its growing reputation.

Vintage Round-up 2001–2005

The best-quality table wines nearly always have the year the grapes were harvested noted on the label. This information isn't only an indication of age, freshness, and relative maturity, like a sort of vinous use-by date, it's also a clue to the sort of wine inside the bottle. Knowing the vintage gives you a chance to sort the tart, green wines from chilly years, from the robust, potent products of years that were roasting hot, and all points in between.

In Europe, where dramatic swings could occur from year to year, this was always important, but here in Australia it was less vital; although the widely held European belief that Australia had little vintage variation was also wrong. The diversification of late-twentieth-century Australian wine, as cooler, more marginal vineyards were explored, made vintage more relevant here than ever before. Knowing the year is important, so each year the *Guide* brings you an independent, five-year, region-by-region vintage overview. This year we look at the vintages 2001–2005, those most likely to be found on the shelves of your local wine shop, or on a restaurant wine list.

2005 VINTAGE

Evaluating the new vintage for the *Guide* each year is a difficult task, especially as the definitive wines from most regions aren't yet available, or even in bottle. So we listen, observe, ask questions, and taste what we can to make a preliminary assessment. This year we had time to scan the regions for some general overviews, but bear in mind that these are only initial impressions; we'll have more definite opinions about the 2005 wines when we prepare next year's edition. Happily, indications so far are that '05 is a very good year just about everywhere.

NEW SOUTH WALES

Hunter Valley: scattered hailstorms caused problems but it looks a very good year generally, particularly for whites.

Riverina: a very good vintage.

Orange/Hilltops: a high-quality vintage.

Mudgee: looks to be a good middle-of-the-road vintage.

Cowra: hail made for some difficulties, but the wines should be good.

Canberra: early tastings indicate a very good vintage.

VICTORIA

Rutherglen: an excellent year.

Murray Valley: a very good year.

Pyrenees/Grampians: looks to be excellent.

Bendigo/Heathcote: an excellent vintage. Great balance.

Yarra Valley: an excellent year.

Mornington Peninsula: a late harvest that looks to be very good.

Geelong: an excellent vintage.

SOUTH AUSTRALIA

Barossa/Eden Valley: an early vintage of good yields that should produce some excellent wines across the board. Although it's early days, 2005 looks to be a year of similar high quality to 2002. The best reds will be worth waiting for.

McLaren Vale: an excellent year.

Clare Valley: an excellent vintage for both whites and reds.

Adelaide Hills: a first-class vintage.

Coonawarra/Limestone Coast: a very good year.

Riverland: a very good year.

WESTERN AUSTRALIA

Margaret River: an outstanding vintage across the board.

Great Southern/Pemberton: an excellent year.

TASMANIA

Looks to be a very good year, at the least.

2004 VINTAGE

NEW SOUTH WALES

Hunter Valley: another of those Hunter vintages where rain intervened with similar results to 2002: great whites, reds pretty ordinary.

Riverina: generally good despite very, very hot conditions.

Orange/Hilltops: a mixed vintage with the Orange area faring best. Generally good wines from the best producers.

Mudgee: generally a good vintage.

Cowra: a warm vintage and generally good wines.

Canberra: a very good vintage with excellent pinot noir and chardonnay. Other wines are less consistent, but the best growers succeeded admirably.

VICTORIA

Rutherglen: a very good vintage.

Murray Valley: heatwave conditions presented some difficulties but quality was generally very good.

Pyrenees/Grampians: an excellent all-round vintage with some ageworthy reds that are generally less formidable than the '03s.

Bendigo/Heathcote: very good wines across the board, with reds standing out.

Yarra Valley: an excellent year, especially for chardonnay and cabernet sauvignon.

Mornington Peninsula: possibly the best vintage for some years. Time will tell.

Geelong: an excellent vintage.

SOUTH AUSTRALIA

Barossa/Eden Valley: one of the worst droughts in history meant a mixed Barossa vintage, but there are still some good wines. Eden Valley did much better, producing consistently good-quality whites and reds.

McLaren Vale: a very good vintage.

Clare Valley: this was a mixed vintage with some very hot weather. The best makers' wines look very promising.

Adelaide Hills: an excellent year, especially for reds from the best makers, but yields were very high, which was a handicap.

Coonawarra/Limestone Coast: a very good vintage for the best estates, but yields were on the high side.

Riverland: a hot vintage, something like 2001. Good quality though, especially for the new darling of the region, petit verdot.

WESTERN AUSTRALIA

Margarer River: excellent vintage for stylish refined reds and whites, better than 2003.

Great Southern/Pemberton: a very good year.

TASMANIA

Patchy weather meant a very mixed vintage. As usual, the name of the maker may be more important than the region.

2003 VINTAGE

NEW SOUTH WALES

Hunter Valley: a small, early vintage that produced very good wines across the board.

Riverina: a very good vintage

Orange/Hilltops: a good vintage.

Mudgee: the rain returned mid-vintage to upset things a bit. Whites were good, reds less impressive.

Cowra: as in other parts of central and southern New South Wales, good whites, so-so reds.

Canberra: good whites, variable reds.

VICTORIA

Rutherglen: drought and nearby bushfires affected many northern Victorian regions. Rutherglen reds were very concentrated, quality was mostly fair to good.

Murray Valley: small yields of middling quality.

Pyrenees/Grampians: a low-yielding drought year that produced some massive reds for long keeping, as well a few more elegant wines.

Bendigo/Heathcote: similar results to Pyrenees/Grampians.

Yarra Valley: excellent vintage for both whites and reds.

Mornington Peninsula: a warm, dry vintage that produced some out-standing chardonnays and pinot noirs.

Geelong: an excellent vintage.

SOUTH AUSTRALIA

Barossa/Eden Valley: there was drought followed by rain which wasn't ideal for reds; whites were another matter with great, ageworthy rieslings.

McLaren Vale: a very good, smallish vintage.

Clare Valley: as in most southern Australian regions, drought meant very small yields. Good reds and whites, although the rieslings don't have quite the richness of the '02s.

Adelaide Hills: a very good year.

Coonawarra/Limestone Coast: very good wines from a smaller than usual vintage.

Riverland: a good year.

WESTERN AUSTRALIA

Margaret River: a very good year.

Great Southern/Pemberton: a mixed bag but many respectable wines, and some very good.

TASMANIA

A vintage of two parts due to rain mid-vintage: early-picked whites and pinot noir did well, other wines less so.

2002 VINTAGE

NEW SOUTH WALES

Hunter Valley: rain split this vintage in two: early-picked varieties like semillon and most other whites were good; later-picked varieties like shiraz were much less satisfactory.

Riverina: cool, dry conditions gave Riverina wineries their best vintage in memory. The best wines really do show some class.

Orange/Hilltops: cool conditions made very good whites. Reds were variable.

Mudgee: an outstanding year, made even more welcome by the series of lousy vintages 1999–2001 that had preceded it. Outstanding reds that combine power with finesse.

Cowra: cool, dry conditions made very good wines.

Canberra: a problematic year due to cool temperatures.

VICTORIA

Rutherglen: mild conditions provided a chance for more elegant editions of Rutherglen's red table wines, although not all took the opportunity. Warm, dry autumn conditions proved ideal for fortified wines.

Murray Valley: an excellent year.

Pyrenees/Grampians: a tiny harvest and cool conditions. Better whites than reds.

Bendigo/Heathcote: another Victorian region to produce a much smaller than usual crop. Reds are good.

Yarra Valley: a tiny crop with pinot noir and chardonnay performing best.

Mornington Peninsula: variable quality but some excellent pinot noir.

Geelong: a difficult year but the most skilled winemakers produced very good wines.

SOUTH AUSTRALIA

Barossa/Eden Valley: a cooler vintage that produced much more elegant wines than usual. The best reds are great and Eden Valley rieslings are classical, if a little less concentrated than the '03s.

McLaren Vale: excellent reds that drink beautifully in youth, but they should age well. Cool summer weather and a mild autumn gave them an unusual elegance.

Clare Valley: generally excellent reds and outstanding rieslings.

Adelaide Hills: early ripening varieties, such as most whites and pinot noir, fared well, other reds less impressive.

Coonawarra/Limestone Coast: cool conditions favoured whites. Reds were generally less convincing. Tiny yields helped.

Riverland: an outstanding year in all hot hinterland regions. Great value reds.

WESTERN AUSTRALIA

Margaret River: refined reds of less concentration than 2001 but still pretty good. Whites were excellent.

Great Southern/Pemberton: early ripening whites and pinot noir were the pick of the crop. Other reds were a mixed bag.

TASMANIA

An Indian summer made for a good vintage.

2001 VINTAGE

NEW SOUTH WALES

HunterValley: the Lower Hunter had heavy rains ahead of a heatwave, resulting in very concentrated semillons which weren't subtle but good nevertheless. Reds were variable. By contrast the Upper Hunter did very well.

Riverina: a good vintage.

Orange/Hilltops: a variable vintage with good white wines and merlots.

Mudgee: this was a difficult vintage due to a combination of rain, hail and tropical heat. White wines were the pick but most are past it.

Cowra: a wet year that favoured white wines, but they are getting long in the tooth now.

Canberra: a mixed bag with one or two superb wines from the best makers.

VICTORIA

Rutherglen: an excellent vintage with outstanding fortified material.

Murray Valley: a very good year.

Pyrenees/Grampians: an outstanding vintage with some ageworthy reds of classic personality.

Bendigo/Heathcote: excellent reds worth cellaring.

Yarra Valley: excellent wines from the best makers and more mature vineyards.

Mornington Peninsula: similar conditions to the Yarra Valley but with less consistency.

Geelong: outstanding.

SOUTH AUSTRALIA

Barossa/Eden Valley: torrid temperatures gave some problems, and some commentators have been less than complimentary, but we've found the wines generally of good quality. Riesling from the cooler highlands was very concentrated and excellent.

McLaren Vale: a roasting hot year with similar problems to the Barossa, but the reds were generally better. Whites are forgettable.

Clare Valley: the best region in South Australia in 2001. It was very hot but the reds were excellent. These heavily extracted wines are now coming into their own with age. Riesling excelled too.

Adelaide Hills: an excellent year.

Coonawarra/Limestone Coast: a good vintage, especially for reds.

Riverland: oven-like heat made for some raisiny, over-ripe wines. An average year.

WESTERN AUSTRALIA

Margaret River: one of the best vintages ever. The reds have impeccable balance and concentration, they are worth long ageing.

Great Southern/Pemberton: a great year.

TASMANIA

Outstanding wines were produced in Tasmania's northern vineyards, but rain and frosts created problems in other corners of the island. Choose carefully.

The Top-quality Wines (♟♟♟♟♟)

Among the 750-odd wines reviewed in this book, there are some that made a special impression. These wines represent, to us, the acme of quality, character and style. Not surprisingly, some are quite pricey, but many are not, and in fact some of them are terrific bargains.

This list includes only our five-glass rated wines, so you can see at a glance which wines really rang our bells. Each one is accompanied by its price and value-for-money star-rating. All the five-glass wines are included, right down to the lowest value-for-money rating – because if you want the very best and can afford it, you'll still want to know that we loved it, despite its price tag!

If there seem to be rather a lot of red wines, especially shirazes, that's because there are a disproportionate number of shirazes on sale. It's simply a reflection of the market. The industry harvests significantly more tonnes of red grapes these days than white (around 55 per cent to 60 per cent, depending on vintage conditions) and more red wine than white is produced. In turn, there is more shiraz wine being made than anything else.

Finally, a word of warning: the best of anything is usually in short supply, so grab 'em while you can!

Wine	Price	Value
SPARKLING WINES		
Hardys Sir James Vintage Pinot Noir Chardonnay 2001	$24.00	★★★★★
Brown Brothers Whitlands Patricia 1999	$39.00	★★★★★
Yarrabank Cuvée 2000	$35.00	★★★★﹢
Chandon Blanc de Blancs 2001	$33.95	★★★★
Clover Hill 2000	$37.20	★★★★

Stefano Lubiana Brut NV	$32.00	★★★›
Chandon Vintage Brut 2001	$33.95	★★★›
Yarrabank Crème de Cuvée 2000	$30.00	★★★

WHITE WINES

Chardonnay

Forest Hill Chardonnay 2003	$20.00	★★★★★
Bannockburn Chardonnay 2002	$49.00	★★★★★
Hardys Eileen Hardy Chardonnay 2002	$50.00	★★★★★
Rosemount Orange Vineyard Chardonnay 2003	$28.00	★★★★›
Evelyn County Estate Black Paddock Chardonnay 2002	$30.00	★★★★›
Coldstream Hills Reserve Chardonnay 2003	$43.95	★★★★›
Leeuwin Estate Art Series Chardonnay 2002	$80.00	★★★★›
Carlei Green Vineyards Chardonnay 2003	$33.00	★★★★
Yabby Lake Vineyard Chardonnay 2003	$38.50	★★★★
Cape Mentelle Chardonnay 2003	$38.90	★★★★
Giant Steps Sexton Bernard Clones 95 & 96 Chardonnay 2003	$39.75	★★★★
Lake's Folly Chardonnay 2003	$50.00	★★★★
By Farr Chardonnay 2003	$53.00	★★★★
Toolangi Reserve Chardonnay 2003	$62.00	★★★★
Shaw and Smith M3 Chardonnay 2003	$38.00	★★★›
Stonier Reserve Chardonnay 2003	$39.00	★★★›
Picardy Chardonnay 2004	$40.00	★★★›
Giaconda Nantua Les Deux 2004	$49.00	★★★›
Cullen Chardonnay 2003	$55.00	★★★›
Grosset Piccadilly 2003	$49.00	★★★
Penfolds Reserve Bin 03A Chardonnay 2003	$85.00	★★★

Penfolds Yattarna Chardonnay 2002 $115.00   ★★⫟

Petaluma Tiers Chardonnay 2001 $150.00   ★★

Riesling

Richmond Grove Watervale Riesling 2004	$16.00	★★★★★
Orlando Jacob's Creek Reserve Riesling 2004	$17.00	★★★★★
Leo Buring Eden Valley Riesling 2004	$18.00	★★★★★
Delatite Riesling 2004	$20.00	★★★★★
Frankland Estate Isolation Ridge Riesling 2004	$23.00	★★★★★
Henschke Julius Riesling 2004	$23.50	★★★★★
Howard Park Riesling 2004	$25.00	★★★★★
Houghton Museum Release Riesling 1995	$26.00	★★★★★
Heggies Museum Reserve Riesling 1999	$27.00	★★★★★
Penfolds Reserve Bin Eden Valley Riesling 2004	$27.80	★★★★★
Pewsey Vale The Contours Riesling 1999	$28.00	★★★★★
Pikes The Merle Reserve Riesling 2004	$32.00	★★★★★

Heggies Riesling 2004 $20.50   ★★★★⫟

Twofold Riesling 2004 $25.00   ★★★★⫟

Neagles Rock Frisky Filly Reserve Riesling 2004 $28.00   ★★★★⫟

Geoff Weaver Riesling 2004 $23.80   ★★★★

Knappstein Single Vineyard Watervale Riesling 2004 $26.00   ★★★★

Mesh Riesling 2004 $27.00   ★★★★

Bay of Fires Tasmania Riesling 2004 $29.00   ★★★★

Pauletts Antonina Riesling 2004 $38.00   ★★★★

Sauvignon blanc and blends

TK Adelaide Hills Sauvignon Blanc 2004 $22.00   ★★★★★

Cape Mentelle Walcliffe 2002 $35.00   ★★★

Cullen Sauvignon Blanc Semillon 2004 $35.00   ★★★

Semillon and blends

Peter Lehmann Semillon Chardonnay 2004	$12.00	★★★★★
Mount Pleasant Lovedale Semillon 1999	$44.00	★★★★
Mount Horrocks Semillon 2004	$27.50	★★★┤

Viognier

Petaluma Viognier 2004	$38.00	★★★★
By Farr Viognier 2003	$55.00	★★★★
Clonakilla Viognier 2004	$50.00	★★★┤

ROSÉ WINES

Pepperjack Grenache Rosé 2004	$24.00	★★★★┤
Willow Creek Pinot Saignée 2004	$20.00	★★★★

RED WINES

Cabernet sauvignon and blends

Balnaves Cabernet Sauvignon 2001	$31.00	★★★★★
Wyndham Estate Show Reserve Cabernet Merlot 1998	$24.00	★★★★┤
Leconfield Cabernet Sauvignon 2002	$32.00	★★★★┤
Arlewood Reserve Cabernet Sauvignon 2001	$33.00	★★★★┤
Flying Fish Cove Upstream Reserve Cabernet Sauvignon 2003	$35.00	★★★★┤
Voyager Estate Cabernet Sauvignon Merlot 2001	$40.00	★★★★┤
Reynell Basket Pressed Cabernet Sauvignon 1998	$56.00	★★★★┤
Juniper Estate Cabernet Sauvignon 2001	$33.00	★★★★
Charles Melton Cabernet Sauvignon 2002	$40.00	★★★★
Wynns Harold Vineyard Cabernet Sauvignon 2001	$40.00	★★★★
Ladbroke Grove Killian Vineyard Cabernet Sauvignon 2001	$42.00	★★★★

John's Blend Cabernet Sauvignon No. 28 2001	$45.00	★★★★
Jamiesons Run Winemakers Reserve Cabernet Shiraz 2001	$57.00	★★★★
Seville Estate Reserve Cabernet Sauvignon 2003	$36.50	★★★⁺
Coldstream Hills Reserve Cabernet Sauvignon 2001	$48.00	★★★⁺
Lindemans St George Cabernet Sauvignon 2001	$55.00	★★★⁺
Tahbilk Reserve Cabernet Sauvignon 1999	$70.00	★★★⁺
Jamiesons Run Rothwell Cabernet Sauvignon 2001	$75.00	★★★⁺
Balnaves The Tally Reserve Cabernet Sauvignon 2001	$80.00	★★★⁺
Orlando Jacaranda Ridge Cabernet Sauvignon 1999	$56.50	★★★
Cullen Diana Madeline Cabernet Sauvignon Merlot 2003	$90.00	★★★
Penfolds Bin 707 Cabernet Sauvignon 2002	$155.00	★★★
Barons of Barossa WHS Cabernet Shiraz 2002	$375.00 (4-pack)	★★★

Grenache and blends

Charles Melton Nine Popes 2002	$45.00	★★★⁺

Merlot and blends

Murdock Merlot 2001	$28.00	★★★★
Capel Vale Howecroft Merlot 2002	$50.00	★★★⁺

Pinot noir

Port Phillip Estate Pinot Noir 2003	$35.00	★★★★
Stonier Reserve Pinot Noir 2003	$39.00	★★★★
Bannockburn Stuart Pinot Noir 2002	$65.00	★★★★
Picardy Tête de Cuvée Pinot Noir 2002	$45.00	★★★⁺
Seville Estate Reserve Pinot Noir 2003	$45.00	★★★⁺

Shiraz

Edwards Shiraz 2003	$26.00	★★★★⬩
McWilliams Rosehill Shiraz 2000	$32.00	★★★★⬩
Seppelt Chalambar Shiraz 2003	$23.95	★★★★
Stella Bella Shiraz 2003	$26.00	★★★★
Cape Mentelle Shiraz 2003	$36.00	★★★★
Shaw and Smith Shiraz 2003	$38.00	★★★★
Robert Johnson Vineyard Shiraz Viognier 2003	$41.00	★★★★
Craiglee Shiraz 2003	$45.00	★★★★
Heathcote Estate Shiraz 2003	$45.00	★★★★
Petaluma Shiraz 2003	$48.00	★★★★
Wirra Wirra RSW Shiraz 2003	$48.00	★★★★
Seppelt St Peters Shiraz 2001	$52.00	★★★★
Jeanneret Denis Shiraz 2002	$55.00	★★★★
Penfolds St Henri Shiraz 2001	$70.00	★★★★
Henschke Mount Edelstone Shiraz 2002	$76.00	★★★★
Sheep's Back Old Vine Shiraz 2002	$39.75	★★★⬩
Spinifex Indigene 2003	$44.00	★★★⬩
Charles Melton Shiraz 2002	$46.00	★★★⬩
Capel Vale Kinnaird Shiraz 2002	$51.00	★★★⬩
Mount Langi Ghiran Langi Shiraz 2000	$56.30	★★★⬩
Saltram No.1 Barossa Shiraz 2001	$66.00	★★★⬩
Rosemount Balmoral Syrah 2000	$70.00	★★★⬩
Tahbilk Reserve Shiraz 1999	$70.00	★★★⬩
Seppelt St Peters Shiraz 2002	$55.00	★★★
Seppelt St Peters Shiraz 2003	$55.00	★★★
Yering Station Reserve Shiraz Viognier 2003	$58.00	★★★
Penfolds Magill Estate Shiraz 2002	$90.00	★★★
Penfolds RWT Barossa Shiraz 2002	$150.00	★★★
Wolf Blass Platinum Label Shiraz 2002	$180.00	★★★
Saltram The Eighth Maker Shiraz 2001	$1500.00 (8 bottles)	★★⬩

Other reds and blends

Brown Brothers Cellar Door Release Heathcote Durif 2003	$18.90	★★★★★
Wood Park Zinfandel 2003	$30.00	★★★★

SWEET WINES

Lillypilly Noble Sauvignon Blanc 2002	$22.50	★★★★★
Lillypilly Noble Blend 2002	$27.30	★★★★⸱
Margan Botrytis Semillon 2004	$23.50	★★★★
De Bortoli Noble One Botrytis Semillon 2002	$26.00	★★★★
Brown Brothers Patricia Late Harvested Noble Riesling 2000	$49.00	★★★★
Southern Highland Wines Golden Vale Botrytis 2003	$35.00	★★★⸱

FORTIFIED WINES

Seppelt Vintage Fortified GR27 1997	$13.00	★★★★★
Noon Winery Tawny	$18.00	★★★★★
Seppelt Show Amontillado DP116	$20.95	★★★★★
Seppelt Show Oloroso DP38	$20.95	★★★★★
Seppelt Grand Rutherglen Muscat DP63	$28.50	★★★★★
Morris Old Premium Liqueur Muscat	$57.00	★★★★★
Morris Old Premium Liqueur Tokay	$57.00	★★★★★
Chambers Grand Rutherglen Muscat	$52.15	★★★★⸱
Morris Old Premium Amontillado Sherry	$45.70 (500 ml)	★★★★
Campbells Grand Rutherglen Muscat	$60.00	★★★★
Seppelt Rare Rutherglen Muscat GR113	$65.95	★★★★
Seppelt Rare Tawny DP90	$65.95	★★★★
Campbells Merchant Prince Rare Rutherglen Muscat	$113.00	★★★★

All Saints Classic Rutherglen Muscat	$30.50	★★★
Penfolds Grandfather Liqueur Tawny	$90.00	★★★
Seppelt Para 100-Year-Old Vintage Tawny 1905	$528.50 (375 ml)	★★★
All Saints Museum Release Rare Muscat	$434.50 (500 ml)	★★⊣
All Saints Museum Release Rare Tokay	$434.50 (500 ml)	★★⊣

Best-value Wines under $15

Each year there are more and more high-ticket wines flooding onto the market, but still the question we're most often asked when the *Guide* comes out each year is: 'What's the best value?' or 'Which are the best wines under $15?' So, to make it easier for you to find the best-value wines, we list them using $15 as the cut-off point. The wines are sequenced in descending order of value-for-money, using our star ratings (from five down to four), and in ascending order of price, so that you can easily spot the best buys. To save space, we've left out the quality ratings (out of five glasses) but you can easily check these by turning to the review pages.

The prices quoted here are full retail prices, but don't forget that many of these wines can often be found discounted. You will very likely find them substantially cheaper if you shop around, especially if you buy by the dozen. Retailers commonly charge around 10 per cent less for a case purchase, as an incentive to buy more. That discount is usually for both unbroken and mixed dozens. Theoretically, you should be able to buy 11 bottles of Queen Adelaide for Auntie Merle and one bottle of deluxe Champagne for yourself, at the case price! So take advantage!

Wine	Price	Value
SPARKLING WINES		
Seaview Sparkling Shiraz	$9.60	★★★★★
Orlando Trilogy Pinot Noir Chardonnay Pinot Meunier	$15.00	★★★★★
Lindemans Bin 25 Brut Cuvée	$10.00	★★★★⁺
Seppelt Fleur de Lys	$12.80	★★★★⁺
Minchinbury Private Cuvée Brut de Brut	$7.50	★★★★
Seppelt Great Western Imperial Reserve	$8.60	★★★★

Eaglehawk Cuvée Brut	$10.50	★★★★
Killawarra Brut	$10.50	★★★★
Savy Sparkle	$11.00	★★★★
Cockatoo Ridge Sparkling Red	$11.25	★★★★
McWilliams Hanwood Sparkling Shiraz	$12.00	★★★★
Rosemount V Chardonnay Pinot Noir Brut	$13.00	★★★★
Yellowglen Pink	$14.00	★★★★
Seaview Special Reserve Chardonnay Pinot Noir	$14.40	★★★★
Hardys Sir James Sparkling Pinot Noir Shiraz	$15.00	★★★★

WHITE WINES

Chardonnay

Cheviot Bridge CB Adelaide Hills Chardonnay 2004	$13.50	★★★★）
Preece Chardonnay 2004	$15.00	★★★★）
Simon Gilbert Chardonnay 2004	$15.00	★★★★）
Terra Felix Chardonnay 2004	$15.00	★★★★）

Penfolds Rawson's Retreat Chardonnay 2004	$10.00	★★★★
Deakin Estate Chardonnay 2004	$10.75	★★★★
Yalumba Oxford Landing Chardonnay 2004	$10.80	★★★★
Fiddlers Creek Chardonnay 2003	$11.00	★★★★
The Little Penguin Chardonnay 2004	$11.00	★★★★
Trentham Murphy's Lore Chardonnay 2004	$11.00	★★★★
Kirrihill Companions Chardonnay 2003	$12.99	★★★★
Hungerford Hill Fish Cage Chardonnay Viognier 2004	$14.00	★★★★
Two Rivers Wild Fire Unwooded Chardonnay 2004	$14.40	★★★★
Lindemans Reserve Chardonnay 2003	$14.50	★★★★
Gapsted Victorian Alps Chardonnay 2004	$15.00	★★★★
Padthaway Estate Unwooded Chardonnay 2004	$15.00	★★★★
Rosemount Diamond Label Chardonnay 2004	$15.00	★★★★

Riesling

| Penfolds Rawson's Retreat Riesling 2004 | $10.00 | ★★★★★ |
| Yalumba Y Series Riesling 2004 | $12.95 | ★★★★★ |

Chrismont Riesling 2004	$15.00	★★★★★
Peter Lehmann Eden Valley Riesling 2004	$15.00	★★★★★
Wynns Coonwarra Riesling 2004	$15.00	★★★★★
Bellarmine Pemberton Dry Riesling 2004	$15.00	★★★★⁺
Bellarmine Pemberton Riesling 2004	$15.00	★★★★⁺
De Bortoli Windy Peak Victoria Riesling 2004	$14.00	★★★★
Brown Brothers Victoria Riesling 2004	$14.40	★★★★
Goundrey Homestead Riesling 2004	$15.00	★★★★

Sauvignon blanc and blends

The Long Flat Wine Company Adelaide Hills Sauvignon Blanc 2004	$14.00	★★★★★
Tobacco Road Sauvignon Blanc Semillon 2004	$11.00	★★★★⁺
Zilzie Buloke Reserve Sauvignon Blanc 2004	$10.00	★★★★
Beelgara Estate Woorawa Sauvignon Blanc 2004	$12.00	★★★★
The Rothbury Estate Orange Sauvignon Blanc 2004	$13.00	★★★★
Beresford Highwood Sauvignon Blanc 2004	$15.00	★★★★
Preece Sauvignon Blanc 2004	$15.00	★★★★

Semillon and blends

Peter Lehmann Semillon Chardonnay 2004	$12.00	★★★★★
Classic McLaren Semillon Sauvignon Blanc 2003	$14.00	★★★★★
Ferngrove Frankland Semillon Sauvignon Blanc 2004	$15.00	★★★★★
Grant Burge Barossa Vines Semillon Sauvignon Blanc 2004	$12.00	★★★★⁺
De Bortoli Black Creek Semillon 2004	$14.00	★★★★⁺
McGuigan Bin 9000 Semillon 2004	$15.00	★★★★⁺
De Bortoli Montage Semillon Sauvignon Blanc 2004	$9.00	★★★★

Pepperton Estate Rascals Prayer Semillon

    Sauvignon Blanc 2004 $10.00   ★★★★

Penfolds Rawson's Retreat Semillon Chardonnay 2004 $11.50   ★★★★

Peter Lehmann Barossa Semillon 2003 $12.00   ★★★★

Rosemount Semillon Chardonnay 2004 $12.00   ★★★★

Rosemount Semillon Sauvignon Blanc 2004 $12.00   ★★★★

Tatachilla Growers Semillon Sauvignon Blanc 2004 $13.00   ★★★★

Tulloch Semillon 2003 $15.00   ★★★★

Other white and blends

Meerea Park Verdelho 2004 $12.95   ★★★★★

Hardys Voyage Colombard Semillon Sauvignon Blanc 2004 $6.00   ★★★★

Angoves Butterfly Ridge Colombard Chardonnay 2004 $7.00   ★★★★

Fox Creek Shadow's Run The White 2004 $12.00   ★★★★

McWilliams Hanwood Verdelho 2004 $12.00   ★★★★

Terra Felix Marsanne Roussanne 2004 $14.95   ★★★★

Simon Gilbert Verdelho 2004 $15.00   ★★★★

ROSÉ WINES

Lindemans Bin 35 Rosé 2004 $10.00   ★★★★★

Tobacco Road King Valley Rosé 2004 $11.00   ★★★★★

Orlando Jacob's Creek Shiraz Rosé 2004 $9.95   ★★★★

Moondah Brook Cabernet Rosé 2004 $14.00   ★★★★

RED WINES

Cabernet sauvignon and blends

Kirrihill Companions Cabernet Merlot 2002 $13.00   ★★★★★

Preece Cabernet Sauvignon 2003 $15.00   ★★★★★

Tobacco Road Cabernet Sauvignon 2002 $11.00   ★★★★★

Grant Burge Barossa Vines Cabernet

    Sauvignon Merlot 2002 $14.90   ★★★★★

Long Flat Cabernet Merlot 2003	$10.00	★★★★
Penfolds Rawson's Retreat Cabernet Sauvignon 2004	$11.50	★★★★
Rosemount Cabernet Merlot 2004	$12.00	★★★★
Yalumba Y Series Cabernet Sauvignon 2002	$13.50	★★★★
Lindemans Reserve Cabernet Merlot 2002	$14.50	★★★★
Barossa Valley Estate Epiphany Cabernet Merlot 2002	$15.00	★★★★
Heath Wines Southern Roo Cabernet Shiraz 2002	$15.00	★★★★
Leasingham Bastion Cabernet Sauvignon 2003	$15.00	★★★★
Orlando Trilogy 2002	$15.00	★★★★

Grenache and blends

St Hallett Gamekeeper's Reserve 2004	$13.95	★★★★┥

Merlot and blends

Peter Lehmann Merlot 2003	$15.00	★★★★★
Yalumba Y Series Merlot 2002	$13.50	★★★★
Lindemans Reserve Merlot 2003	$14.50	★★★★

Petit Verdot

Angoves Stonegate Limited Release Petit Verdot 2003	$8.99	★★★★
Kingston Estate Petit Verdot 2002	$12.90	★★★┥

Pinot noir

Clos Saint Pierre Pinot Noir 2004	$14.99	★★★★

Sangiovese and blends

Rosemount Diamond Label Sangiovese 2003	$15.00	★★★★

Shiraz

Willandra Estate Leeton Selection Shiraz 2004	$8.00	★★★★★
Rosemount Diamond Label Shiraz 2003	$15.00	★★★★★
Three Brothers Reunion Shiraz 2003	$15.00	★★★★★

Orlando Jacob's Creek Shiraz 2002	$10.00	★★★★½
Simon Gilbert Central Ranges Shiraz 2003	$15.00	★★★★½
Angoves Butterfly Ridge Shiraz Cabernet 2003	$7.75	★★★★
Outback Chase Shiraz 2003	$9.50	★★★★
Rosemount Shiraz Cabernet 2004	$12.00	★★★★
Kirrihill Companions Shiraz 2002	$13.00	★★★★
Plantagenet Hazard Hill Shiraz 2003	$13.00	★★★★
Hungerford Hill Fish Cage Shiraz Viognier 2004	$14.00	★★★★
Lindemans Reserve Shiraz 2003	$14.00	★★★★
Grant Burge Barossa Vines Shiraz 2003	$15.00	★★★★

SWEET WINES		
Brown Brothers Moscato 2004	$13.70	★★★★½
Trentham Murphy's Lore Spatlese Lexia 2004	$11.00	★★★★
Two Hands Brilliant Disguise Moscato 2004	$13.50	★★★★
De Bortoli Windy Peak Spatlese Riesling 2004	$14.00	★★★★

FORTIFIED WINES		
Seppelt Vintage Fortified GR27 1997	$13.00	★★★★★
Grant Burge Aged Tawny	$13.25	★★★★★
Queen Adelaide Fine Old Tawny Port	$8.00	★★★★½

The Penguin Rating System

The rating system used in this *Guide* is designed to give you an immediate assessment of a wine's attributes, as they will affect your purchasing decision. The symbols provide at-a-glance information, and the written descriptions go into greater depth. Other wine guides are full of numbers, but this one places importance on the written word.

The authors assess quality and value; provide an estimate of cellaring potential and optimum drinking age; and give notes on source, grape variety, organic cultivation where applicable, decanting, and alcohol content. We list previous outstanding vintages where we think they're relevant.

We assess quality using a cut-down show-judging system, marking out of a possible 10. Wine show judges score out of 20 points – three for nose, seven for colour, 10 for palate – but any wine scoring less than 10 is obviously faulty, so our five-glass range (with half-glass increments) indicates only the top 10 points. When equated to the show system, three glasses is roughly equivalent to a bronze medal, and five glasses, our highest award, equals a high gold medal or trophy-standard wine.

Value is arrived at primarily by balancing absolute quality against price. But we do take some account of those intangible attributes that make a wine more desirable, such as rarity, great reputation, glamour, outstanding cellar-ability, and so on. We take such things into account because they are part of the value equation for most consumers.

If a wine scores more for quality than for value, it does not mean the wine is overpriced. As explained below, any wine scoring three stars for value is fairly priced. Hence, a wine scoring five glasses and five stars is extraordinary value for money. Very few wines manage this feat. And, of course, good and bad value for money can be found at $50 just as it can at $5.

If there are more stars than glasses, you are looking at unusually good value. We urge readers not to become star-struck: a three-glass three-star wine is still a good drink.

Where we had any doubt about the soundness of a wine, a second bottle was always sampled.

Quality

🍷🍷🍷🍷🍷	The acme of style: a fabulous, faultless wine that Australia should be proud of.
🍷🍷🍷🍷🍷	A marvellous wine that is so close to the top it almost doesn't matter.
🍷🍷🍷🍷	An exciting wine that has plenty of style and dash. You should be proud to serve this.
🍷🍷🍷🍷	Solid quality with a modicum of style; good drinking.
🍷🍷🍷	Decent, drinkable wine good for everyday quaffing. You can happily serve this to family and friends.
🍷🍷🍷	Sound, respectable wines, but the earth won't move.
🍷🍷	Just okay but, in quality terms, starting to look a little wobbly.

(Lower scores are not usually included.)

Value

★★★★★	You should feel guilty for paying so little: this is great value for money.
★★★★✦	Don't tell too many people because the wine will start selling and the maker will put the price up.
★★★★	If you complain about paying this much for a wine, you've got a death adder in your pocket.
★★★✦	Still excellent wine, but the maker is also making money.
★★★	Fair is fair, this is a win–win exchange for buyer and maker.
★★✦	They are starting to see you coming, but it's not a total rip-off.
★★	This wine will appeal to label drinkers and those who want to impress their bank manager.
★✦	You know what they say about fools and their money . . .
★	Makes the used-car industry look saintly.

Grapes

Grape varieties are listed in order of dominance; percentages are cited when available.

Region

Where the source of the grapes is known, the region is stated. If there is more than one region, they are listed in order of dominance. Many large commercial blends have so many source regions that they are not stated.

Cellar

Any wine can of course be drunk immediately, but for maximum pleasure we recommend an optimum drinking time, assuming correct cellaring conditions. We have been deliberately conservative, believing it's better to drink a wine when it's a little too young than to risk waiting until it's too old.

An upright bottle 🍾 indicates that the wine is ready for drinking now. It may also be possible to cellar it for the period shown. Where the bottle is lying on its side ➖ the wine is not ready for drinking now and should be cellared for the period shown.

🍾 Drink now: there will be no improvement achieved by cellaring.

🍾 3 Drink now or during the next three years.

➖ 3–7 Cellar for three years at least before drinking; can be cellared for up to seven years.

➖ 10+ Cellar for 10 years or more; it will be at its best in 10 years.

Alcohol by Volume

Australian labelling laws require that alcohol content be shown on all wine labels. It's expressed as a percentage of alcohol by volume, e.g. 12.0% A/V means that 12 per cent of the wine is pure alcohol.

Recommended Retail Price

Prices were arrived at either by calculating from the trade wholesale using a standard full bottle-shop mark-up, or by using a maker-nominated recommended retail price. In essence, however, there is no such thing as RRP because retailers use different margins. The prices in this book are indicative of those in Sydney and Melbourne, but they will still vary from shop to shop and city to city. They should only be used as a guide. Cellar-door prices have been quoted when the wines are not available in the retail trade.

[$] Special

The wine is likely to be 'on special', so it will be possible to pay less than the recommended retail price. Shop around.

⊛ Organic

The wine has passed the tests required to label it as 'organically grown and made'.

⬗ Decant

The wine will be improved by decanting.

⧢ Screw-cap

This wine is available with a screw-cap seal. Some of these wines are also available with a cork finish, but at least part of the production has a screw-cap. We recommend them, as a guarantee against cork-taint and random oxidation.

Sparkling Wines

The best Aussie sparklers are being made increasingly from cold-climate grapes grown in Tasmania and high-altitude and/or southerly parts of Victoria. These wines often stand comparison with good non-vintage Champagne, albeit with a decidedly Aussie character. Our cheapie bubblies are remarkable value, especially if you can ensure you're buying a fresh bottle. This is hard to guarantee, as there's no vintage or other indication of age on the label, and these wines get stale quickly. All you can do is try to buy from a shop with a high turnover of that kind of wine. The fizz market is dominated by big company brands, such as Seppelt, Seaview, Yellowglen, Domaine Chandon and Hardys.

Bay of Fires Pinot Noir Chardonnay

The Hardy Wine Company's range of sparkling wines is vast these days. The base wines for Bay of Fires bubblies are made in Tassie by Fran Austin, and the wines are 'champanised' in the main Hardys bunker in McLaren Vale. CURRENT RELEASE 2001   The colour is very light yellow, and the wine is restrained and backward in development, tasting younger than it is. There are some earthy, slightly rubbery aromas from lees-contact and the palate is austere and very, very lively, with lemony acidity that coats the lips and seems a little disjointed. The finish is very firm. It needs food, such as pan-fried fish with a buttery meunière sauce.

Quality	♥♥♥♥
Value	★★★
Grapes	pinot noir; chardonnay
Region	Tasmania
Cellar	🍾 4+
Alc./Vol.	12.5%
RRP	$30.00 Ⓢ

Bindi Macedon Multi–Vintage Cuvée IV

Michael Dhillon picks the grapes from the slowest-ripening parts of the original vineyard. The components are aged in barriques for several years; the blend is bottle-fermented and aged on yeast lees for four years. This cuvée is based on the '93 to '98 vintages.
CURRENT RELEASE non-vintage   An unusual approach yields a very eccentric wine! The colour is brassy deep yellow and it smells more like a dry flor sherry than a bubbly, with lots of aldehydes, major yeast autolysis giving hints of Vegemite, plus bottle-age and oak influence. It's a very deep, multi-layered wine with concentration and length, finishing very dry but rich. Try it with chicken liver pâté on toasts.

Quality	♥♥♥♥
Value	★★★
Grapes	chardonnay; pinot noir
Region	Macedon Ranges, Vic.
Cellar	🍾 1+
Alc./Vol.	12.0%
RRP	$35.00

Blue Pyrenees Vintage Brut

Quality	🍷🍷🍷🍷
Value	★★★½
Grapes	chardonnay; pinot noir; pinot meunier
Region	Pyrenees, Vic.
Cellar	🍾 4+
Alc./Vol.	12.0%
RRP	$25.00 [$]

We tasted this in the same line-up as the Bindi. You could not find a bigger style difference than these two! They are polar opposites. Winemaker these days is Andrew Koerner.

CURRENT RELEASE 2000 The colour is very light yellow and it looks, smells and tastes young, chardonnay-driven and underdeveloped. The aroma is clean, fresh and youthful without much apparent yeast influence, with hints of straw and toast. It's frothy in the mouth, and tastes dry and crisp almost to the point of austerity. It has decent length and needs food. It makes a serious aperitif style. Try it with crab timbale.

Brown Brothers Whitlands Patricia

Quality	🍷🍷🍷🍷🍷
Value	★★★★★
Grapes	pinot noir; chardonnay; pinot meunier
Region	King Valley, Vic.
Cellar	🍾 3+
Alc./Vol.	12.0%
RRP	$39.00

PENGUIN BEST SPARKLING WINE

This won gold medals at both Sydney and Melbourne in 2002, which is a feather in its cap as the bubbly classes in those shows are quite competitive. The wine is named after family matriarch the late Patricia Brown, mother of today's senior generation: John, Ross and Peter Brown. Maker: Terry Barnett.

CURRENT RELEASE 1999 This is a great Australian sparkling wine. It has a bright mid-yellow colour and the bouquet suggests creamy vanilla, candy and meringue: fresh and subtle yet very complex and inviting. It's a wine of real character: deep and mouth-filling, multi-faceted and yet retaining great finesse. The finish is very long and dry but has a trace of richness and avoids austerity. It suits quail canapés.

Chandon Blanc de Blancs

Quality	🍷🍷🍷🍷🍷
Value	★★★★
Grapes	chardonnay
Region	Yarra, Goulburn, & King Valleys, Vic.; Coonawarra, SA; Central Victoria
Cellar	🍾 2
Alc./Vol.	13.0%
RRP	$33.95 [$]

We often find this chardonnay-based sparkler to be the pick of Chandon's standard range. In style it seems to show a little more of the influence of French owners Moet et Chandon than other wines in the range.

CURRENT RELEASE 2001 Chandon B de B shows the customary finesse and freshness that's made it one of our favourites over recent editions of the *Guide*. The '01 is an excellent example with an elegant nose of delicate intensity. Citrus, apple and stone-fruit aromas are seasoned with a little nutty, biscuity complexity, and the palate has true finesse with a long silky feel and a clean, lingering finish. Very more-ish. Enjoy it with shellfish.

Chandon Cuvée Riche

Cuvée Riche is a doux style of sparkling, with a higher level of sweetness than the other Chandon wines. It naturally finds its place as an interesting dessert wine, but it has enough of a clean tang to make it a good 'anytime' drink.
CURRENT RELEASE *non-vintage* An unusual style, and when you first sniff and taste it, it's a real surprise. The nose has mellow stone-fruit, patisserie and nutty aromas, and the palate has a lush layer of sweetness that leads through a clean smooth finish. The sweetness, although it isn't over the top, does mask other complexities the wine may or may not have, but it does fill a unique role. It suits lighter desserts when something with a bit of light, jolly effervescence is called for, and it's a very convivial thing to serve in such circumstances.

Quality 🍷🍷🍷🍷
Value ★★★
Grapes pinot noir 55%; chardonnay 40%; pinot meunier 5%
Region Yarra, Goulburn & King valleys, Vic.; Coonawarra, SA; Tasmania
Cellar 🍾 2
Alc./Vol. 12.7%
RRP $33.95 [$]

Chandon NV

Chandon Non-vintage was launched a few years ago, and to be frank the early wines didn't quite do justice to the Chandon name. Now it's been remodelled slightly into a finer, more elegant style.
CURRENT RELEASE *non-vintage* A bright-looking wine with a clean aroma reminiscent of citrus and stone fruit. It's an appealing tangy introduction that's driven by fruit rather than bottle-ferment secondary characters. The palate is smooth and fresh with a long, crisp finish. A good style that shows a lot of improvement over the first Chandon NVs we tasted. Try it as a party starter.

Quality 🍷🍷🍷🍷
Value ★★★
Grapes chardonnay 50%; pinot noir 45%; pinot meunier 5%
Region Yarra, Goulburn & King valleys, Vic.; Coonawarra, SA; Tasmania
Cellar 🍾 1
Alc./Vol. 13.0%
RRP $23.95 [$]

Chandon Sparkling Pinot Shiraz

Chandon sparkling red fits a less robust image than most other sparkling red, probably due to the influence of the inclusion of one-third pinot noir. It still has plenty of personality though.
CURRENT RELEASE *non-vintage* A wine that treads a middle road between the fuller characters of shiraz and the less powerful pinot noir component. It smells of blackberries and mocha with a foresty note in the mix. The palate has good flavour intensity, a touch of sweetness, and a supple texture, with a slightly stemmy firmness behind it. Serve it with a country-style terrine.

Quality 🍷🍷🍷🍷
Value ★★★
Grapes pinot noir 69%; shiraz 31%
Region Rutherglen, Goulburn & Yarra valleys, Vic.; McLaren Vale, SA
Cellar 🍾 2
Alc./Vol. 14.0%
RRP $26.50 [$]

Chandon Vintage Brut

Quality	🍷🍷🍷🍷🍷
Value	★★★⁺
Grapes	pinot noir 47%; chardonnay 44%; pinot meunier 9%
Region	Yarra, Buffalo, Goulburn & King valleys, Vic.; Coonawarra, SA; Tumbarumba, NSW
Cellar	🍾 2
Alc./Vol.	13.0%
RRP	$33.95 Ⓢ

Chandon's Yarra Valley operation is part of a sparkling-wine empire that encompasses California, Argentina, Brazil and Spain, and, of course, the Moet et Chandon headquarters in France. Rumour has it the French bosses think the Aussie product is the best outside France.

CURRENT RELEASE 2001 Chandon's Vintage Brut has been getting more elegant in style in recent years, more like the Blanc de Blanc, although it still has a higher proportion of red grapes than white. The '01 is pale with a steady creaming foam, and it smells delicately complex with white-peach, citrus and light biscuity aromas that are clean and appetising. In the mouth it is fine textured with a light, soft mid-palate, balanced by a crisp tang at the end. Enjoy as an aperitif with cheese gougères.

Clover Hill

Quality	🍷🍷🍷🍷🍷
Value	★★★★
Grapes	chardonnay; pinot noir; pinot meunier
Region	Northern Tasmania
Cellar	🍾 2
Alc./Vol.	13.0%
RRP	$37.20

Clover Hill is one of Tasmania's flagship sparkling wines. The island state is fast making a name for itself as one of Australia's premier sources of top-quality fizz, and Clover Hill is always at the top of the tree. It gets better every vintage and we think this is the best yet.

CURRENT RELEASE 2000 This is very fine indeed. The appetising nose is very complex, yet it has the subtlety that one most often finds in champagne, rather than Australian sparkling wine. The nose has subtle bready/yeasty notes woven through white peach-like fruit and hints of white flowers. The palate has super-clean flavour of great length with a creaming texture and a sherbetty tang. Superb with cured salmon blinis.

Cockatoo Ridge Sparkling Red

Quality	🍷🍷🍷
Value	★★★★
Grapes	not stated
Region	not stated
Cellar	🍾 2
Alc./Vol.	13.0%
RRP	$11.25 Ⓢ

A sparkling red has joined the Cockatoo Ridge range relatively recently, but it's an obvious inclusion for such a dinky-di group of wines.

CURRENT RELEASE non-vintage This has an attractive deep colour of good density. On the nose it smells of blackberries and earth, and a touch of oak maturation adds dimension. In the mouth there's good depth of juicy berry flavour, with nicely controlled sweetness that gives a mellow, generous mid-palate feel. Soft tannins round things out well. Try it with sweet and sour Chinese dishes.

Cofield T XIII Sparkling Shiraz

In 2005 Cofield became the first quality sparkling wine producers to put all their bubblies under the humble crown seal. This durable closure promises an end to cork taint in Cofield's wines. It doesn't pop, but what would you prefer, a popping cork or a guarantee of good, fault-free wine every time you open a bottle? Maker: Damien Cofield.

CURRENT RELEASE *non-vintage* This crimson-foamed wine has an attractive nose of raspberries and blackberries, with some complex aged touches. The palate is smooth and friendly with good depth of rich fruit and some underplayed sweetness. It has red wine structure with ripe, fine balanced tannins backing it up, making it a more 'serious' wine than some of the sparkling red competition. Try it with a roast, prune-stuffed loin of pork.

Quality	🍷🍷🍷🍷½
Value	★★★
Grapes	shiraz
Region	Rutherglen, Vic.
Cellar	🍾 4
Alc./Vol.	14.5%
RRP	$29.99

Eaglehawk Cuvée Brut

When is a brut not a brut? It's common enough for sparkling wines labelled brut to have a dab of sweetness mid-palate, but some take the sugar a wee bit far for our liking. Eaglehawk Cuvée Brut is a case in point.

CURRENT RELEASE *non-vintage* This has a simple grapey nose, suggestive of riesling, or perhaps a muscat variant. There's also a fresh hint of citrus. The palate continues with a fruity theme, and a touch of sweetness takes it well out of the dry territory of a true brut. That said, it finishes with a clean tang, and the finish is reasonably long. An inexpensive refresher that's really pretty good value for around 10 bucks. A party wine.

Quality	🍷🍷🍷
Value	★★★★
Grapes	not stated
Region	not stated
Cellar	🍾 1
Alc./Vol.	11.5%
RRP	$10.50 [$]

Gartelmann Vintage Brut

Jorg and Jan Gartelmann bought an established vineyard, formerly Oliver Shaul's George Hunter Estate on the Lovedale Road, in the mid-'90s. The wines, made by Jim Chatto at Monarch, are of a consistently high standard.

CURRENT RELEASE 2001 Okay, so the varieties are not classic Champagne grapes, but the result is pretty good. The bouquet is all toasty straw-hay developed semillon characters, and the profile is lean and dry with straw-like semillon flavour and a finish that's pleasingly low on liqueur sweetness. It's not terribly complex but has plenty of flavour and a clean, crisp finish. It would suit a fishy entrée.

Quality	🍷🍷🍷🍷
Value	★★★★
Grapes	semillon; chenin blanc
Region	Hunter Valley, NSW
Cellar	🍾 2+
Alc./Vol.	12.5%
RRP	$22.00

Grant Burge Pinot Noir Chardonnay Brut

Quality 🍷🍷🍷🍷
Value ★★★
Grapes pinot noir; chardonnay
Region not stated
Cellar 🍾 2
Alc./Vol. 12.0%
RRP $22.00 [$]

The packing here is quite glitzy with plenty of shiny gold trimming. Whether you like it or not is a matter of taste, but the quality of the wine inside is pretty good.
CURRENT RELEASE *non-vintage* As usual this is a flavoursome style, light on for subtlety, but with plenty of personality and body. Colour is fairly deep, probably reflecting the pinot noir component, and the nose has stone-fruit and smoky aromas of some intensity. In the mouth it's rich and round in texture with a faint whisper of sweetness that enhances its full flavour. Serve it with little chicken pies.

Hardys Arras Chardonnay Pinot Noir

Quality 🍷🍷🍷🍷½
Value ★★★
Grapes chardonnay; pinot noir
Region mainly Tasmania
Cellar 🍾 4
Alc./Vol. 13.0%
RRP $53.00 [$]

The '99 is the fifth release of Arras, and it's been based on Tasmanian grapes since the beginning. Occasionally some Yarra Valley grapes from the high-altitude Hoddles Creek vineyard are included. Maker Ed Carr reckons six years on lees is a pretty good target for Tassie fizz.
CURRENT RELEASE 1999 This is a puzzling wine: the bouquet reveals a lot of malolactic derived creamy/milk powder aromas, together with smoky and toasted-bread characters, while the palate has a lot of natural acidity giving a tangy, zingy tartness that doesn't quite fit the broader structure of the palate. It certainly has flavour and finishes clean and dry, with a particularly long carry. But the malo character is a bit excessive. A superior kind of bubbly, nevertheless. Drink with Tassie Pacific oysters and Tetsuya's dressing.

Hardys Sir James Sparkling Pinot Noir Shiraz

Quality 🍷🍷🍷½
Value ★★★★
Grapes pinot noir; shiraz
Region not stated
Cellar 🍾 3
Alc./Vol. 14.0%
RRP $15.00 [$]

Judging from the number of wines on sale now, there must have been an explosion of interest in sparkling red. We find most of the cheaper ones very raw, sweet and simple – the best of the style have some aged character. Maker: Ed Carr.
CURRENT RELEASE *non-vintage* This one is undoubtedly young, but has attractive flavour, good drinkability and isn't overdone in the alcohol, tannin, oak or liqueur departments. It has sweet prune, raisin and jam aromas, while the palate is lighter than expected and all the better for it. It finishes with some soft tannin and the sweetness is well balanced. Try it with devils-on-horseback.

Hardys Sir James Vintage Pinot Noir Chardonnay

While Arras is a more austere wine, and perhaps more ageworthy, it's more than double the price of Sir James Vintage, which consistently offers the best value in the Hardy repertoire. Maker Ed Carr is doing us a great favour supplying fizz of this calibre at an affordable price. CURRENT RELEASE 2001   Sir James Vintage is a perennial favourite and gob-smacking value. The straw/herbal and citrusy aromas are pleasant, but it's on the palate where this wine impresses. The key words are intensity and persistence. Lively acidity gives a clean, dry finish. It's a model of finesse and power. Best with fresh oysters

Quality	♥♥♥♥♥
Value	★★★★★
Grapes	pinot noir; chardonnay
Region	mainly Tasmania & Macedon Ranges, Vic.
Cellar	🍶 2+
Alc./Vol.	13.0%
RRP	$24.00 Ⓢ

Heemskerk Tasmania Pinot Noir Chardonnay

Heemskerk, which began as a vineyard and winery established by a syndicate of wine lovers including veteran winemaker Graham Wiltshire in the '70s, and sold to Pipers Brook at one stage, is now a brand owned by the Cellarmasters direct-marketing organisation. You can order this from their web site www.cellarmasters.com.au CURRENT RELEASE 2002   This is a youthful Tassie fizz that could have repaid longer time on its lees. The aromas are fruit driven, shy and not terribly complex; the palate is very crisply acidic and citrusy, dominated by lemon and lime flavours, and the finish is tangy, frisky and very clean. It makes a good pre-dinner drink with buttery mushroom puffs.

Quality	♥♥♥♥
Value	★★★⬧
Grapes	pinot noir; chardonnay
Region	Tasmania
Cellar	🍶 4
Alc./Vol.	12.0%
RRP	$28.00

Killawarra Brut

The Killawarra name is purely a brand within the Southcorp portfolio, without vineyards or winery. Once upon a time it was used on red wines, but now it's reserved solely for sparklers. It may be a manufactured thing, but don't get snooty about it, these sparklers are invariably good value. CURRENT RELEASE non-vintage   This has a little more depth than most of Southcorp's cheap fizz, and the nose shows more richness and development. It's not exactly delicate, with tropical-fruit and apple-sauce aromas that are pleasantly clean and fruity, along with a slight eggy touch. In the mouth it's very pleasant with good texture and surprising length, characteristics that lift it above much of the competition in the sub-$10 stakes. A good party wine that won't poison your guests.

Quality	♥♥♥♦
Value	★★★★
Grapes	not stated
Region	not stated
Cellar	🍶 1
Alc./Vol.	12.0%
RRP	$10.50 Ⓢ

Killawarra Reserve Pinot Noir Chardonnay Pinot Meunier

Quality	♟♟♟♟
Value	★★★⁴
Grapes	pinot noir; chardonnay; pinot meunier
Region	not stated
Cellar	▮1
Alc./Vol.	12.0%
RRP	$16.50 Ⓢ

This is Killawarra's more upmarket bubbly, but it should still give you change out of $15 when it's on special.
CURRENT RELEASE 1999   This well-priced sparkling wine has some depth and complexity on the nose. It smells of peach, red fruit, and cracked yeast with a nutty touch. In the mouth it has some real style that comes from its smooth creaming texture, rich bready flavour and length of finish. Serve it well chilled. It suits Balinese fried chicken well.

Lindemans Bin 25 Brut Cuvée

Quality	♟♟♟❘
Value	★★★★⁴
Grapes	not stated
Region	not stated
Cellar	▮1
Alc./Vol.	12.0%
RRP	$10.00 Ⓢ

It would be churlish to expect a better glass of fizz than this for a measly tenner (less on discount). It's a member of the ubiquitous Lindemans Bin range and we can't help but observe it tastes a bit like Bin 65 chardonnay with bubbles in it!
CURRENT RELEASE *non-vintage* It's bright medium yellow with a good mousse, and smells of peachy chardonnay with a lacing of green herbs, perhaps parsley. There's no yeast or bottle-age influence. The taste is soft, round and fruity, again peachy and chardonnay-like, quite simple and a touch short, but it's not tart or sweet and they've got the balance perfect for easygoing drinkability. Serve it with pretzels and nuts.

PENGUIN BEST-VALUE
SPARKLING WINE

McWilliams Hanwood Sparkling Shiraz

Quality	♟♟♟❘
Value	★★★★
Grapes	shiraz
Region	Riverina, NSW
Cellar	▮2
Alc./Vol.	13.0%
RRP	$12.00 Ⓢ

Sparkling reds now feature in many budget-priced wine ranges, reflecting growing interest in this unorthodox type of Australian bubbly. McWilliams Hanwood employs Riverina shiraz to good effect in this example.
CURRENT RELEASE *non-vintage*   An honest, earthy style of red fizz, this has spices, licorice and dark-berry aromas with a whisper of sweet oak in the background. The palate is smooth with good structure and some supporting firmness. More of a food wine than a celebratory sipper; try it with Chinese BBQ pork.

Miceli Michael Méthode Champenoise

The Miceli operation is a family affair, with the wines being named after members of the family. Owner is Dr Anthony Miceli, a medico, who took the trouble to gain a degree in wine science from Charles Sturt University. His wines are as distinctive as they are impressive. This won the trophy for the best sparkling wine at Cowra in 2004.

CURRENT RELEASE 2001 This is a head-turning bubbly, loaded with toasty, smoky, yeast-derived complexities as well as tart appley, straw-like fruit. The acidity is a touch challenging, and the liqueur sweetness is not perfectly integrated, but this is hair-splitting. It's a thoroughly enjoyable glass of bubbly. Try it with cheese puffs.

Quality 🍷🍷🍷🍷½
Value ★★★★
Grapes chardonnay; pinot noir; pinot gris
Region Mornington Peninsula, Vic.
Cellar 3+
Alc./Vol. 12.0%
RRP $39.00

Minchinbury Private Cuvée Brut de Brut

This name was once a significant one in Australian wine, but the Minchinbury vineyard on Sydney's outskirts has long gone, Penfolds role in it is never mentioned, and the range of once relatively prestigious sparkling wines has been reborn down in the bargain basement.

CURRENT RELEASE *non-vintage* This is our pick of the Minchinbury sparkling range. Okay, so it ain't Dom Perignon, but it does offer an honest fault-free fizz experience, while other sub-$8 sparklers struggle. It has a good foamy bubble, and it smells fresh and succulent. There are grapey, clean flavours that are just off dry, and it finishes pleasantly crisp.

Quality 🍷🍷🍷
Value ★★★★
Grapes not stated
Region not stated
Cellar 1
Alc./Vol. 11.5%
RRP $7.50 (\$)

O'Leary Walker Hurtle Chardonnay Pinot Noir

Hurtle Walker was the grandfather of Nick Walker, one half of the O'Leary Walker team. Born in 1890, Hurtle was one of Australia's most famous sparkling winemakers, responsible for Wynns' high-quality Romalo range and many other bubblies until his death in 1975.

CURRENT RELEASE 2002 A worthy memorial to Hurtle Walker, this sparkling wine is smooth and complete. It is straw-coloured with a fine bead, and the nose has smoky hints along with subtle peach, wild-strawberry and creamy notes. The palate is mellow and clean, without being particularly complex. The finish is dry with comparatively soft acidity. Try it with pan-fried fish.

Quality 🍷🍷🍷🍷
Value ★★★
Grapes chardonnay; pinot noir
Region Adelaide Hills, SA
Cellar 1
Alc./Vol. 12.0%
RRP $31.00

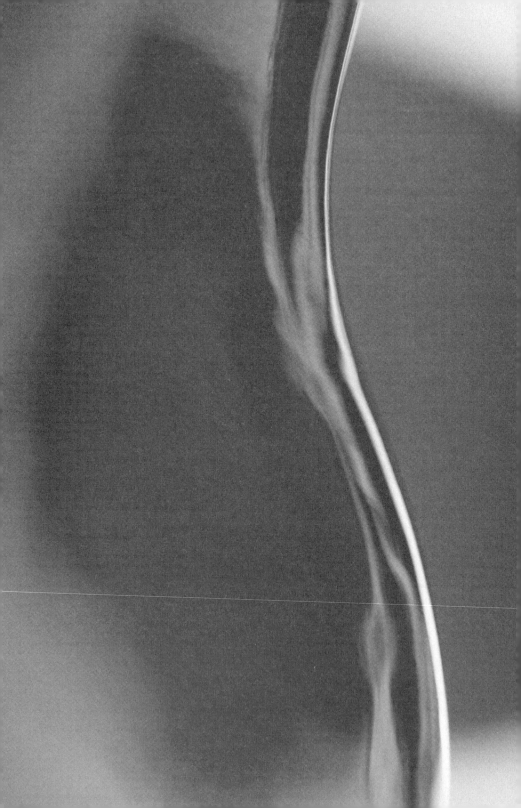

Top 20 Restaurant Wine Lists

Australian Capital Territory

Anise Restaurant
20 West Row
Melbourne Building
Canberra ACT 2601
(02) 6257 0700

New South Wales

Aria
1 Macquarie St
Sydney NSW 2000
(02) 9252 2555

Bathers Pavilion
4 The Esplanade
Balmoral NSW 2088
(02) 9969 5050

Buon Ricordo
108 Boundary St
Paddington NSW 2021
(02) 9360 6729

Marque
355 Crown St
Surry Hills NSW 2010
(02) 9332 2225

Seven Mile Cafe
41 Pacific Pde
Lennox Head NSW 2478
(02) 6687 6210

Queensland

Cru Bar & Cellar
22 James St
Fortitude Valley Qld 4006
(07) 3252 2400

The Downs Club
15 Mylne St
Toowoomba Qld 4350
(07) 4632 3532

Sails Beach Restaurant
75 Hastings St
Noosa Heads Qld 4567
(07) 5447 4235

South Australia

Blake's Restaurant
Hyatt Regency Hotel
North Terrace
Adelaide SA 5000
(08) 8238 2381

The Apothecary 1878
118 Hindley St
Adelaide SA 5000
(08) 8212 9099

Tasmania

Franklin Manor
The Esplanade
Strahan Tas. 7468
(03) 6471 7311

Stillwater River Cafe
2 Bridge Rd
Launceston Tas. 7250
(03) 6331 4153

Victoria

Asiana
181 Victoria Ave
Albert Park Vic. 3206
(03) 9696 6688

Circa, The Prince
2 Acland St
St Kilda Vic. 3182
(03) 9536 1122

The Deanery
13 Bligh Place
Melbourne Vic. 3000
(03) 9629 5599

Lake House
King St
Daylesford Vic. 3460
(03) 5348 3329

Melbourne Supper Club
161 Spring St
Melbourne Vic. 3000
(03) 9654 6300

Oscar W's Wharfside
101 Murray Esplanade
Port of Echuca Vic. 3564
(03) 5482 5133

Western Australia

Must Wine Bar
519 Beaufort St
Highgate WA 6003
(08) 9328 8255

Orlando Trilogy Pinot Noir Chardonnay Pinot Meunier

Quality 🍷🍷🍷🍷½
Value ★★★★★
Grapes pinot noir; chardonnay; pinot meunier
Region not stated
Cellar 🍾 1
Alc./Vol. 12.0%
RRP $15.00 [$]

This is an excellent offering from Orlando. It might not have the profile of some other mid-priced sparklers, but it gives plenty of bang for your buck. We're not sure how they do it at the price.

CURRENT RELEASE *non-vintage* Pale with a fine bead, this smells truly appetising. There are aromas of citrus and pear with some smoky pinot-noir and yeast-extract touches. It really has an extra dimension over most of the competition. The palate is smooth with attractive richness in the middle, pleasant vanilla-cream flavour, some yeast-lees influence and a long crisp finish. A bargain at the price and it's often on special too. Try it as an aperitif.

Radenti Chardonnay Pinot Noir

Quality 🍷🍷🍷🍷½
Value ★★★★
Grapes chardonnay; pinot noir
Region East Coast, Tas.
Cellar 🍾 2
Alc./Vol. 12.0%
RRP $45.00 (cellar door)

This is the bubbly of the Freycinet winery on Tasmania's east coast, where Claudio Radenti is the chief winemaker. They were stopped from using the Freycinet name on anything fizzy by the Spanish Cava giant, Freixenet. Work that out, if you can.

CURRENT RELEASE 1998 A very complex, fully mature style of sparkling that shows its extended lees-ageing time. The colour is still medium-light yellow but the bouquet is strong on smoky, toasted-bread, and straw/hay-bale characters that we find typical of Tasmanian sparkling. The palate has broadened out a little, and has some wilder flavours plus noticeable liqueur sweetness. It's an entertaining, character-filled style which would suit Chinese gow gees and dumplings.

Rosemount V Chardonnay Pinot Noir Brut

Quality 🍷🍷🍷
Value ★★★★
Grapes chardonnay; pinot noir
Region not stated
Cellar 🍾 1
Alc./Vol. 12.5%
RRP $13.00 [$]

Nice packaging goes a long way towards success in the world of wine, especially at the lower-price levels. This one looks snappy, with its yellow diamond label and the big red tick that could be a V, or is it a tick of approval?

CURRENT RELEASE *non-vintage* There was a lot of development on the bottle we tasted: full-yellow in colour with a somewhat rubbery bouquet of slightly underripe herbal, parsley-like chardonnay fruit overlain by bottle-age. It doesn't pretend to be bone-dry: the sweetness level is both appropriate and well balanced. It's a pleasant easy-drinking bubbly at its price. It suits smoked oysters.

Rymill The Bee's Knees Sparkling Red

We have to deduce from the name that this wine is the Rymill team's idea of heaven. Well, if you don't believe in your product, who else will? Chief winemaker is John Innes. CURRENT RELEASE *non-vintage* We liked the softness and harmony of this wine in the mouth. It has a deep red–purple hue and the bouquet is dominated by smoky, leathery, almost charcoal aromas, together with licorice/aniseed and fruitcake scents. The sweetness is well balanced and the tannins are soft. The cabernet character is noticeable (which may irk some purists) but the natural grip and firmness of Coonawarra cabernet is cleverly avoided. It goes with pork spare ribs and plum sauce.

Quality	♥♥♥♥
Value	★★★⅃
Grapes	cabernet sauvignon; merlot; cabernet franc
Region	Coonawarra, SA
Cellar	▬ 2+
Alc./Vol.	14.5%
RRP	$22.00

Savy Sparkle

Do you savvy the name? We don't, but we imagine this is an attempt to grab a slice of a youth market that's addicted to alcoholic soft drinks. We reckon anything that steers 18–21-year-olds in the direction of wine drinking instead of those abominations is a good thing.
CURRENT RELEASE *non-vintage* The nose is very grapey and muscaty, floral and sweet. In the mouth it follows suit exactly, with grapey flavour and soft texture. With a little more sweetness it would approach the much maligned spumante style. All in all, it's pleasant enough and well priced. Serve it at a party.

Quality	♥♥♥
Value	★★★★
Grapes	not stated
Region	not stated
Cellar	▬ 1
Alc./Vol.	11.5%
RRP	$11.00 Ⓢ

Scarpantoni Black Tempest

These days there are so many sparkling reds on the market that it's hard to believe the style came within a whisker of disappearing in the 1970s, due to public apathy. Now it's one of Scarpantoni's specialities, with Black Tempest enjoying something of a cult following among red fizz fans.
CURRENT RELEASE *non-vintage* This well-made red bubbly has a medium-depth ruby colour and a creaming persistent mousse. The nose is deliciously ripe and rich with aromas of blackberries, bitter chocolate and a touch of oaky spice. In the mouth it has intense dark-berry flavour and chocolatey richness with a savoury whisper of mint. Sweetness is well-controlled and at a level below many commercial examples, and it finishes with soft furry tannins and great balance. Try it with Chinese roast duck and crispy pork.

Quality	♥♥♥♥
Value	★★★
Grapes	shiraz
Region	McLaren Vale, SA
Cellar	▬ 3
Alc./Vol.	13.5%
RRP	$38.30

Seaview Blanc de Blancs Chardonnay

Quality 🍷🍷🍷🍷
Value ★★★★
Grapes chardonnay
Region not stated
Cellar 🍾 1
Alc./Vol. 12.0%
RRP $21.30 [$]

The hilltop Seaview winery was once the source of some of Australia's most highly regarded McLaren Vale cabernet sauvignons. After a couple of decades of help from brand managers, marketing gurus and assorted Southcorp regimes, it's now just a brand name for a range of oft-discounted sparkling wines. Why can't they leave well enough alone?

CURRENT RELEASE 2001 There's no great subtlety here, but it does have plenty of flavour and drinkability. It smells of stone fruits and custard with a hint of green herbs and some leesy complexity. The palate is flavoursome with smooth texture, good length, and some attractive dosage sweetness but an admirably dry finish. A crowd-pleaser. Good with fresh chicken sandwiches at the races.

Seaview Sparkling Shiraz

Quality 🍷🍷🍷🍷
Value ★★★★★
Grapes shiraz
Region not stated
Cellar 🍾 2
Alc./Vol. 13.5%
RRP $9.60 [$]

Inexpensive sparkling shiraz has been a surprise packet for the authors. It's a wine category that's evolved in recent years and general quality has been very good indeed. They are usually better value than their white equivalents.

CURRENT RELEASE *non-vintage* This has good depth of colour and an interesting, attractive nose of ripe loganberries and spices with a vague hint of pepper and some earthy richness. In the mouth it has a smooth texture with ripe flavour and well-controlled sweetness. A clean tangy finish balances it well, there's good length of flavour, and it finishes with fine tannins. Great buying. Serve with roast pork and a fruity stuffing.

Seaview Special Reserve Chardonnay Pinot Noir

Quality 🍷🍷🍷🍷
Value ★★★★
Grapes chardonnay; pinot noir
Region not stated
Cellar 🍾 1
Alc./Vol. 13.0%
RRP $14.40 [$]

This is a relatively recent addition to the Seaview sparkling wine family, and it's a welcome one given its impressive quality and good price. Shop around for the best buy, it's often discounted.

CURRENT RELEASE *non-vintage* This is a crowd-pleasing sparkling wine with plenty of flavour. In fact it's a bit like a chardonnay with bubbles, despite the inclusion of pinot noir in the blend. The nose has ripe-peach and melon-fruit aromas with a little touch of nuttiness to add interest. It has a very smooth mouth-feel and finishes soft and dry. A good drop that tastes as though it should cost more. Drink it with seafood fritto misto.

Seppelt Fleur de Lys

Fleur de Lys NV is a cut above the standard Seppelt sparkling wines, but be sure to buy wine that hasn't been on the shelf for too long. Freshness is the key to enjoying wines like this, so look for them in shops with a high turnover.
CURRENT RELEASE *non-vintage*   This has a rather plain nose, but it's not unpleasant. There's some ripe stone fruit and a hint of raspberry pastille aroma, probably from pinot noir. In the mouth it's flavoursome and satisfying, with a slight biscuity touch in the mouth that adds dimension. A whisper of sweetness deepens the mid-palate and it finishes pleasantly dry. Drink it at a picnic.

Quality	♀ ♀ ♀ ♀
Value	★ ★ ★ ★ ↓
Grapes	chardonnay; pinot noir; pinot meunier
Region	not stated
Cellar	▮ 1
Alc./Vol.	12.5%
RRP	$12.80 Ⓢ

Seppelt Great Western Imperial Reserve

Seppelt's fizz factory at Great Western is a wondrous thing, responsible for oceans of sparkling wine that ranges from the really special to the cheap-and-cheerful. Despite its grand name, Imperial Reserve is one of the latter.
CURRENT RELEASE *non-vintage*   This has a pleasantly fruity, clean nose reminiscent of apples and grapes. In the mouth it's simple, light and fresh with soft mid-palate fruit and a pleasantly soft dry finish. Despite its commonplace reputation, this isn't bad at all. Serve it at a twenty-first birthday party.

Quality	♀ ♀ ♀ ♀
Value	★ ★ ★ ★
Grapes	not stated
Region	not stated
Cellar	▮ 1
Alc./Vol.	11.5%
RRP	$8.60 Ⓢ

St Leonards Wahgunyah Sparkling Shiraz

We all know how well Rutherglen's warm climate suits the production of great fortified wines, but the region also has an affinity with sparkling shiraz. The first-class sparkling reds like this are well worth seeking out.
CURRENT RELEASE *non-vintage*   The colour shows some maturity, and the nose has slightly jammy, very plummy-fruit aromas. The palate is creamy-smooth with plum and spice flavours that are long and satisfying. Sweetness is there but it's subtle and well-integrated, and a lightish thread of tannin gives the palate an attractively dry foundation. Good with Cantonese roast duck.

Quality	♀ ♀ ♀ ♀
Value	★ ★ ★
Grapes	shiraz
Region	Rutherglen, Vic.
Cellar	▮ 2
Alc./Vol.	14.1%
RRP	$27.50

Stefano Lubiana Brut NV

Quality	🍷🍷🍷🍷🍷
Value	★★★⁴
Grapes	pinot noir 95%; chardonnay 5%
Region	Southern Tasmania
Cellar	🍾 1
Alc./Vol.	12.5%
RRP	$32.00

These Tassie sparkling wines were once the subject of much huffing and puffing by a certain giant French champagne house over the use of the colour yellow on Stefano Lubiana's labels! To avoid hassles the yellow label was dropped in favour of a bright red one. Wine quality of this non-vintage blend is consistently good.

CURRENT RELEASE *non-vintage* This is a surprisingly complex drop of bubbly. The colour has a slight pink tinge, and it smells very inviting (and dare we say it, a bit 'French'), with patisserie, bready-yeast and nutty-aged characters. The palate shows good body and depth of bottle-developed flavour, with attractive richness ahead of a long, dry finish. It has the substance to work well with little brioches filled with sautéed kidneys.

Stonier Pinot Noir Chardonnay

Quality	🍷🍷🍷🍷
Value	★★★
Grapes	pinot noir; chardonnay
Region	Mornington Peninsula, Vic.
Cellar	🍾 2
Alc./Vol.	12.5%
RRP	$28.00

This was originally made in 1999 to give the winery team something to sip after vintage . . . well, that's not entirely true, but the Stonier crowd are known to enjoy it enthusiastically themselves. It rounds off the Stonier range of wines very nicely. Maker: Geraldine McFaul.

CURRENT RELEASE 2002 A lively bubbly with a nose of candied stone fruits and red-berry patisserie. In the mouth it's smooth with fine texture and a persistent line of acidity that carries a long appetising finish. A little bit of firmness gives structure to the palate, and there's a mouth-watering quality that makes it a good pre-dinner appetiser with some shellfish.

Yarra Burn Pinot Noir Chardonnay Pinot Meunier

Quality	🍷🍷🍷🍷🍷
Value	★★★
Grapes	pinot noir; chardonnay; pinot meunier
Region	mainly Yarra Valley, Vic.
Cellar	🍾 2
Alc./Vol.	12.5%
RRP	$25.00

David Fyffe, who established Yarra Burn in the 1970s, was a pioneer of Yarra Valley sparkling wine, converting cool-climate chardonnay and pinot into very refined fizz. Now Yarra Burn is owned by Hardys, and this very good sparkler is under the creative control of Hardys' guru Ed Carr.

CURRENT RELEASE 2001 A pale wine with a persistent fine bubble. The delicate, appetising nose has smooth aromas of red apple, citrus and lightly creamy lees influence. The palate is tangy, fresh and light with plenty of clean delicate flavour and a very long, crisp finish. An excellent aperitif

Yarrabank Crème de Cuvée

Crème de Cuvée is Yarrabank's sweeter sparkler. It's set apart by a soft, sienna pink label that mirrors the colour of the wine inside. A good choice as a festive dessert wine.

CURRENT RELEASE *non-vintage* A coppery pink-tinged sparkling wine with a subtle nose that hints at strawberries and shortbread. The palate has a soft thread of sweetness through it, but it's gentle, still leaving the wine fresh and appetising. It finishes long and restrained with a whisper of red-berry fragrance lingering in the mouth. Try it with a fruit tart.

Quality	🍷🍷🍷🍷½
Value	★★★
Grapes	chardonnay; pinot noir
Region	Yarra Valley & other cool Victorian vineyards
Cellar	🍾 2
Alc./Vol.	12.0%
RRP	$30.00

Yarrabank Cuvée

Yarrabank is a cooperative effort between Yarra Valley winery Yering Station and Champagne house Devaux. This vintage-dated Cuvée is always among Australia's very best sparkling wines.

CURRENT RELEASE 2000 Yarrabank's 2000 is right on song. It's pale in colour with a fine, persistent bubble, and the nose is elegant with subtle fragrances of apple, wildflowers and buttered brioche. In the mouth it's a clean, harmonious type with very restrained flavours, creamy texture and a long dry finish. Subtle and classy, it goes well with the freshest oysters.

Quality	🍷🍷🍷🍷🍷
Value	★★★★½
Grapes	pinot noir; chardonnay
Region	Yarra Valley & Mornington Peninsula, Vic.
Cellar	🍾 2
Alc./Vol.	12.0%
RRP	$35.00

Yellowglen Bella Vintage

This prettily presented new Yellowglen sparkling wine comes with a glittery silver and very pale copper-pink label. In style it's a little like an Italian moscato but with more effervescence.

CURRENT RELEASE 2005 This has a delicate rose-pink colour and a creamy bubble. The nose has a clean, light, muscaty fruitiness, with appealing touches of flowers and Turkish delight. In the mouth it's fruit-juicy flavoured with a light, frothy texture. Clean tasting, sweet and grapey, this is a delicious, low-alcohol moscato style, with a little more froth and bubble than you'd expect. A fun wine for a warm afternoon. Try it with fruit salad.

Quality	🍷🍷🍷🍷
Value	★★★★
Grapes	frontignac
Region	not stated
Cellar	🍾 1
Alc./Vol.	7.0%
RRP	$16.00 [$]

Yellowglen Pink

Quality	♟♟♟♟
Value	★★★★
Grapes	not stated
Region	not stated
Cellar	🍷 1
Alc./Vol.	12.0%
RRP	$14.00 Ⓢ

Red, yellow, pink. This range of Yellowglen sparklers is a colourful lot. Quality is good for not that many dollars. CURRENT RELEASE *non-vintage* A light fresh drop of fizz with an aroma of red fruits that's pleasantly direct and unfussed. The palate is soft and easy with a thread of gentle sweetness in good balance with zesty acidity. Drink it outdoors at a summertime get-together.

White Wines
Chardonnay

Chardonnay is the world's favourite white varietal. Despite various knockers, the ABC (anything but chardonnay) reactionaries and the anti-oak brigade, its rise continues. In 1982 our winemakers harvested just over 4000 tonnes of chardonnay grapes; this year 416 000 tonnes! Twenty-two per cent of the national crush is now chardonnay; and most of our top-selling white wines are chardonnays. A number of unwooded chardonnays, a less-expensive style Australians have taken to their hearts, are reviewed in the *Guide*. Chardonnay to our minds should be balanced, without excessive oak, residual sweetness or alcohol. We value finesse, flavour persistence and complexity, the last being one of chardonnay's key assets.

Ainsworth & Snelson Chardonnay

Brett Snelson and Gregg Ainsworth aim to produce wines that typify classic Australian regional types from vineyards in Coonawarra, the Barossa and the Yarra Valley.
CURRENT RELEASE 2003   Although it's been barrel-fermented, 25 per cent in new French oak, this is a more subtle chardonnay than most. The nose has fine fruit characters, reminiscent of nectarines, grapefruit and green lime. There's also a honeyed touch and oak is a restrained dressing. In the mouth it's smooth and silky in texture with very fine fruit and minerally flavours that last long and fragrant. A welcome alternative to the big sunshiny chardonnays, this suits steamed scampi with Chinese seasonings well.

Quality	🍷🍷🍷🍷
Value	★★★
Grapes	chardonnay
Region	Yarra Valley, Vic.
Cellar	3
Alc./Vol.	13.0%
RRP	$29.00

Alexander Park Chardonnay

Alexander Park is a label of Dominion Wines, an ambitious vineyard development with a large winery attached, in Victoria's Strathbogie Ranges, about 140 kilometres north of Melbourne. Maker: Travis Bush.
CURRENT RELEASE 2003   This is a bright yellow–green colour and the nose shows citrus, herb and nutty aromas, with a veneer of slightly resinous oak. The medium-weight palate has good texture and length, with intense peach, herb and oak flavours ahead of a dry finish. Try it with grilled prawns.

Quality	🍷🍷🍷🍷
Value	★★★
Grapes	chardonnay
Region	Strathbogie Ranges, Vic.
Cellar	2
Alc./Vol.	14.0%
RRP	$17.00 (cellar door)

Ambleside Chardonnay

Quality	♥♥♥♥
Value	★★★
Grapes	chardonnay
Region	Adelaide Hills, SA
Cellar	🍷 2
Alc./Vol.	13.5%
RRP	$22.00 🍷

The Adelaide Hills town of Hahndorf changed its name to Ambleside during World War I to avoid the stigma of a German name. It reverted to its original name in 1935. The vineyards this wine hails from are close by.
CURRENT RELEASE 2003   A bright lemon–yellow-coloured chardonnay, this has a nose of fig and pineapple dressed in well-integrated nutty oak and creamy nuances. The palate is full-flavoured and rich. An up-front oaked chardonnay with plenty of smooth flavour that finishes dry and smooth. Try it with soft cheeses.

Annvers Adelaide Hills Chardonnay

Quality	♥♥♥♥
Value	★★★★
Grapes	chardonnay
Region	Adelaide Hills, SA
Cellar	🍷 2+
Alc./Vol.	14.0%
RRP	$20.00

This got a run in last year's *Guide* but is still available and has come up a little since last year, earning a slightly higher rating. It was barrel fermented in 50 per cent new French oak and spent nine months on lees.
CURRENT RELEASE 2003   The colour is still light to medium yellow, showing a slow rate of ageing. The nose is a touch shy but it tastes good, with balance and subtlety. The flavours are intense and gathering some complexity, while the texture is refined. It has some of the typical Adelaide Hills' delicacy.

Austin's Barrabool Ellyse Chardonnay

Quality	♥♥♥♥♥
Value	★★★★
Grapes	chardonnay
Region	Geelong, Vic.
Cellar	🍷 3
Alc./Vol.	13.5%
RRP	$28.00

Austin's started out as a pocket handkerchief-sized operation, but now it's one of the most significant Geelong area producers. Chardonnay has been very successful over recent years.
CURRENT RELEASE 2003   A bright-looking chardonnay with a smooth nose combining attractive vanilla bean, dried fig, cream and subtle nutty oak in real harmony. The palate is full of ripe fruit and balanced oak flavours with smooth texture, good concentration and a long, nutty finish. A good match for scallops in a creamy sauce.

Balnaves Hand Picked Chardonnay

Balnaves winemaker Pete Bissell is one of the most talented in Coonawarra. He also makes the Parker Estate, Punter's Corner and Murdock wines. Of course, the winemaker can't improve on the quality of the raw materials, and Doug Balnaves' vineyard is impeccably managed.
CURRENT RELEASE 2002   This is a very good chardonnay but would be even better with a touch less new oak. The barrel is most evident in the bouquet; it's much better balanced to taste. The palate is refined and combines delicacy with fruit intensity, and the acid is frisky and freshening. There is no oak hardness on the finish. A lovely chardonnay to drink with chicken and mushroom pie.

Quality	♟ ♟ ♟ ♟ ♟
Value	★ ★ ★ ★
Grapes	chardonnay
Region	Coonawarra, SA
Cellar	▮ 3
Alc./Vol.	14.0%
RRP	$28.00 (cellar door)

Bannockburn Chardonnay

This was made and finished off by Gary Farr, who departed Bannockburn Vineyards in late 2004. It shows the man's distinctive winemaking style. It will be interesting to see if that style continues with other winemakers in charge.
CURRENT RELEASE 2002   This has quite a deal of age-development in its medium to deep yellow colour, and it's very complex with smoky/toasty apricot and meaty/mealy complexities. It's not unlike a good burgundy in its mysteriously feral, slightly funky profundity. The palate is concentrated and powerful, with penetrating complex flavour and formidable persistence. A magic wine that entertains to the last drop. It suits satay chicken.

Quality	♟ ♟ ♟ ♟ ♟
Value	★ ★ ★ ★ ★
Grapes	chardonnay
Region	Geelong, Vic.
Cellar	▮ 2
Alc./Vol.	14.5%
RRP	$49.00

Bay of Fires Tigress Chardonnay

Tigress is the 'second label' of Bay of Fires, which is Hardys' Tasmanian brand. Like Cascade's beer labels, it pays homage to a creature made extinct by humans: the thylacine or Tasmanian tiger.
CURRENT RELEASE 2002   The wine is still very youthful and fresh, with typically zingy Tasmanian acidity running the full length of the palate. The bouquet is full of complex oak-fruit interactions, some tropical-fruit and malolactic characters, and very good palate intensity. It's delicate and subtle at three years and could still age happily. Try Tassie scallops here.

Quality	♟ ♟ ♟ ♟ ♟
Value	★ ★ ★ ★ ﹢
Grapes	chardonnay
Region	various, Tasmania
Cellar	▮ 3
Alc./Vol.	13.0%
RRP	$26.00 Ⓢ

Bindi Chardonnay

Quality 🍷🍷🍷🍷½
Value ★★★★
Grapes chardonnay
Region Macedon Ranges, Vic.
Cellar 🍾 4+
Alc./Vol. 13.5%
RRP $35.00

Bindi is a very small vineyard – just six hectares – but winemaker Michael Dhillon is very focused and is dedicated to producing the very best that he can from his piece of land. He's accomplished a great deal in a short time.
CURRENT RELEASE 2003 With a cropping level of well under one tonne per acre, this has concentrated fruit, as well as the trademark cool-climate bracing acidity of chilly Macedon. There are strong buttery/milk-powder aromas from a vigorous malolactic, and the palate is tautly structured and refined, with terrific focus and length. It would suit grilled prawns.

Blue Pyrenees Chardonnay

Quality 🍷🍷🍷🍷
Value ★★★★
Grapes chardonnay
Region Pyrenees, Vic.
Cellar 🍾 2
Alc./Vol. 13.0%
RRP $18.00 [$] 🔩

Blue Pyrenees Estate was established in the 1960s by Remy Martin, the French brandy people. They finally sold it, and current owner is John Ellis (not the Hanging Rock one). Winemaker is Andrew Koerner.
CURRENT RELEASE 2004 There's a lot of flavour and weight here for a relatively moderate outlay. The bouquet has some malolactic buttery, butterscotch aromas plus peachy chardonnay fruit, and the palate is big-boned and fairly warm from alcohol, which unbalances it slightly. This all results in a soft, rounded, slightly viscous mouth-feel, and it would go well with a creamy chicken dish.

Bridgewater Mill Chardonnay

Quality 🍷🍷🍷🍷
Value ★★★½
Grapes chardonnay
Region Adelaide Hills, Coonawarra & Clare Valley, SA
Cellar 🍾 2
Alc./Vol. 14.0%
RRP $23.00 [$]

The Bridgewater Mill style has been built on deliberately different principles to the regular Petaluma wines. While the latter are single-region, these are three-region blends. This approach probably smooths out vintage variation a little, but theoretically results in more consistent wines year to year.
CURRENT RELEASE 2002 The first bottle was corked; the second more than made up for it. It's a soft, rounded wine with up-front nougat and caramel developed characters, with some complexity and not too much bottle-aged toastiness. Indeed, it has good freshness for its age, is clean and alive in the mouth, with appealing softness and balance. It suits chicken with cashew nuts.

By Farr Chardonnay

Don't look for any screw-caps on Gary Farr's wines, he doesn't believe in them. The day Chateau d'Yquem comes with a screw-cap he might consider it, he's been heard to remark.
CURRENT RELEASE 2003   The Farr touch is alive and well here: this is a stunner of a chardonnay, as long as you enjoy the big, complex, heavily worked style. Marzipan, nougat, vanilla and smoky, toasty barrel aromas fill the bouquet and reappear on the very powerful, rich, concentrated palate. The flavour builds to a breathtaking crescendo as the wine flows across the tongue. It's very, very long. Pair it with stuffed roast chook.

Quality	🍷🍷🍷🍷🍷
Value	★★★★
Grapes	chardonnay
Region	Geelong, Vic.
Cellar	🍾 3+
Alc./Vol.	13.5%
RRP	$53.00

Cape Mentelle Chardonnay

Margaret River produces some of Australia's best chardonnay. Some pundits hold that it's our supreme region for this variety and, based on performance over many years and the general standard of wines, they have some justification. Cape Mentelle is among Margaret River's finest.
CURRENT RELEASE 2003   Excellent integration of fruit, oak and winemaking input makes this a lovely drink. The nose has peach, melon, grapefruit and vanilla-cream aromas of richness and finesse. The palate is full of flavour and seamless in mouth-feel, with very good varietal richness, a perfectly reserved seasoning of classy oak, and a long, elegant aftertaste. Works well with poached salmon.

Quality	🍷🍷🍷🍷🍷
Value	★★★★
Grapes	chardonnay
Region	Margaret River, WA
Cellar	🍾 3
Alc./Vol.	14.5%
RRP	$38.90

Carlei Green Vineyards Chardonnay

Serge Carlei is a passionate, dedicated winemaker, whose adventurous nature has resulted in some cutting-edge chardonnays that incorporate technique, inspiration and intuition in equal measures. When it all comes together the results are very impressive.
CURRENT RELEASE 2003   This looks brilliant, a bright youthful yellow–green. The nose has citrus and melon aromas with a syrupy fruit character that's very attractive. There are also complex touches of butter/cream and nutty, leesy elements. The palate is medium in body with lovely texture and length, and a chalky-dry finish. Try it with a creamy chicken dish.

Quality	🍷🍷🍷🍷🍷
Value	★★★★
Grapes	chardonnay
Region	Yarra Valley, Vic.
Cellar	🍾 3
Alc./Vol.	14.0%
RRP	$33.00

Cassegrain Fromenteau Reserve Chardonnay

Quality	▼▼▼▼⸮
Value	★★★★
Grapes	chardonnay
Region	Sydney, Tumbarumba, Hunter Valley & Cowra, NSW
Cellar	▮3
Alc./Vol.	13.0%
RRP	$26.95

Although Cassegrain's main source of fruit is their large vineyard on the New South Wales northern coast, they do seek material elsewhere. This chardonnay employs various sources, including the Sydney region, in a blend of some distinction.
CURRENT RELEASE 2003   Chardonnay of generous build, this yellow–green wine has an elaborate nose offering syrupy, candy-like fruit immersed in rich nutty, buttery complexities. Oak is subtle and not out of whack with everything else. In the mouth it's smooth and long-tasting, with fine structure. It should develop well short-term. A flavoursome wine to serve with pan-fried scallops.

Centennial Vineyards Reserve Chardonnay

Quality	▼▼▼▼⸮
Value	★★★★⸮
Grapes	chardonnay
Region	Orange, NSW
Cellar	▮2
Alc./Vol.	14.0%
RRP	$25.00 (cellar door)

Orange in the New South Wales Central Highlands is a true cool-climate region that shows a lot of promise. The explosion in viticulture in many parts of New South Wales has been incredible in recent years, with a lot of the emphasis on finding cooler climes.
CURRENT RELEASE 2003   A very attractive young chardonnay that in many ways fits into the modern Australian style, but it has a touch of elegance as well. The nose is ripe and complex with aromas of pineapple, honey, citrus and nuts. In the mouth it's intense, yet with finesse that keeps it light and fresh in the mouth. A long, fragrantly nutty finish completes the picture. A name to watch. Serve it with salmon cakes.

Centennial Vineyards Woodside Chardonnay

Quality	▼▼▼▼
Value	★★★★
Grapes	chardonnay
Region	Southern Highlands, NSW
Cellar	▮2
Alc./Vol.	13.0%
RRP	$22.00 (cellar door)

The Centennial Vineyards operation at Bowral is a significant one with a large winery, a vineyard and a restaurant to cater for a growing number of visitors. This historic part of New South Wales is an easy drive from Sydney.
CURRENT RELEASE 2003   Less subtle than Centennial's Reserve Chardonnay, this wine has fig and citrus aromas robed in nutty, lightly spicy oak. The palate has good flavour intensity and texture, leading to a dry, fairly austere finish. It's a good safe type of chardonnay that will match fried chicken well. Reasonably priced too.

Chapel Hill Reserve Chardonnay

Chapel Hill's Reserve Chardonnay was once an oaky blockbuster style, but it's become much more refined over the years. These days it's a multi-regional blend, rather than straight McLaren Vale.
CURRENT RELEASE 2003   As usual, this is an early-drinking type of oaked chardonnay, and there's a hint of earthiness that hasn't been there before. Smoky oak dresses it up well, and peachy fruit has a lightly nutty lees influence to it. The palate is quite full and long flavoured with a dry, slightly edgy finish. Drink it with roast chicken.

Quality	▼▼▼▼
Value	★★★
Grapes	chardonnay
Region	McLaren Vale, Adelaide Hills & Padthaway, SA
Cellar	▮ 2
Alc./Vol.	13.0%
RRP	$24.00 ⌸

Cheviot Bridge CB Adelaide Hills Chardonnay

Although based on a Yea Valley vineyard, under Hugh Cuthbertson's direction Cheviot Bridge is able to find parcels of quality fruit here and there across the country. The result is a very well-priced range of high-quality wines.
CURRENT RELEASE 2004   Paler than a lot of young chardonnays, this is a succulent early-drinking style. The nose has stone-fruit and grapefruit aromas with a very understated dusting of oak. In the mouth it's a light middleweight of good intensity, attractively clean-tasting, with a long, dry, tangy finish. Try it with barbecued prawns.

Quality	▼▼▼▼
Value	★★★★✦
Grapes	chardonnay
Region	Adelaide Hills, SA
Cellar	▮ 2
Alc./Vol.	13.0%
RRP	$13.50 ⌸

Classic McLaren La Testa Chardonnay

Tony De Lisio is the winemaker and general frontman at Classic McLaren. He's a large, affable chap who's very proud of his Italian ancestry. He's more noted for his big regional reds, but his chardonnay has pleasantly surprised us two years in a row.
CURRENT RELEASE 2002   De Lisio has again fielded a remarkably fine, complex, structured chardonnay from a region not really noted for same. The cooler year would have helped in '02. It has a bright, full-yellow colour and smells subtly complex, with a whiff of classy high-toast oak. The palate is rich and beautifully textured, with honey, silage and buttery flavours which are as appealing as they are penetrating. The finish is long and satisfying. It suits grilled lobster.

Quality	▼▼▼▼▽
Value	★★★★
Grapes	chardonnay
Region	McLaren Vale, SA
Cellar	▮ 2+
Alc./Vol.	14.5%
RRP	$31.00

Coldstream Hills Chardonnay

Quality	🍷🍷🍷🍷½
Value	★★★½
Grapes	chardonnay
Region	Yarra Valley, Vic.
Cellar	3
Alc./Vol.	13.5%
RRP	$25.95

Originally Coldstream Hills chardonnays were bottled as individual-vineyard wines, sometimes from outside growers. As the estate vineyards matured, the range became centred on this very good standard wine, and the excellent Reserve.

CURRENT RELEASE 2004 Another good Coldstream Hills Chardonnay, this has ripe melony fruit at the heart of things, and there's a layer of smoky, nutty characters, and minerally lees influence that lifts the wine into 'serious' territory. Everything combines in silky harmony and the palate has real finesse, freshness and length. It finishes with a chalky dry aftertaste that's pleasantly appetising. Good with roasted snapper.

Coldstream Hills Reserve Chardonnay

Quality	🍷🍷🍷🍷🍷
Value	★★★½
Grapes	chardonnay
Region	Yarra Valley, Vic.
Cellar	3
Alc./Vol.	14.0%
RRP	$43.95

Under the joint tutelage of the Southcorp team of winemaker Andrew Fleming and founder James Halliday, the Coldstream Hills Reserve Chardonnay just keeps getting better. The '03 is one of the best yet.

CURRENT RELEASE 2003 A complex wine of great character, this is more 'New World' in style than Burgundian, but that's not to denigrate it at all. The nose is very inviting with deep melon and peach fruit, a yeasty, leesy richness and beautifully integrated nutty oak. In the mouth it's complex, full, and multi-layered with a lovely creamy texture and an ultra-long, superfine finish.
A luxurious accompaniment to char siew ocean trout.

Cookoothama Chardonnay

Quality	🍷🍷🍷½
Value	★★★½
Grapes	chardonnay
Region	Riverina, NSW
Cellar	1
Alc./Vol.	13.5%
RRP	$16.95 ($)

The last decade has seen the New South Wales Riverina throw off much of its reputation as a source of cheap plonk, in favour of a more quality-oriented direction. Nugan Estate, via its Cookoothama range, is one of the significant players.

CURRENT RELEASE 2003 If you like chardonnays to have a fair whack of oak, this is for you. It's a bright yellow–green wine with a rich nose of vanillin oak and peachy fruit. The palate follows the theme with lush texture, syrupy fruit character and plenty of nutty wood influence. Serve it with Malaysian chicken curry.

Craig Avon Chardonnay

Craig Avon's plain-Jane label conceals some pretty good chardonnay. It has a lower profile than some Mornington Peninsula chardonnays, but it's always worth trying. Maker: Ken Lang.
CURRENT RELEASE 2003   This wine improves with air in the glass, evolving subtle melon-rind and stone-fruit aromas that are interwoven with restrained smoky oak in fine harmony. In the mouth it's attractively put together with welcome finesse and smooth, subtle flavours that are nicely lingering and clean. Serve it with vitello tonnato.

Quality	♟♟♟♟
Value	★★★
Grapes	chardonnay
Region	Mornington Peninsula, Vic.
Cellar	▮ 2
Alc./Vol.	13.5%
RRP	$36.00

Cullen Chardonnay

Vanya Cullen's chardonnay doesn't quite enjoy the accolades of her outstanding red wines, but it should. We think it's one of the two or three best Margaret River chardonnays, and one of the very best in Australia.
CURRENT RELEASE 2003   A tight, subtle chardonnay that gets better and better with time in the glass. Australian chardonnay rarely comes as complex as this, nor as subtly seductive. It challenges our vocabulary of descriptors, but here goes: grapefruit, nectarine, apricot, minerals, spices, nuts, fig syrup, wheatmeal, cedar . . . what the heck, it's bloody good. The mouth-feel is a little more angular than usual, with a firm backbone and a tangy, clean finish. It really needs time in bottle to come together, but we think it will reward patience well. Try it with grilled marron.

Quality	♟♟♟♟♟
Value	★★★⸸
Grapes	chardonnay
Region	Margaret River, WA
Cellar	➥1–5+
Alc./Vol.	14.0%
RRP	$55.00 ⬧

D'Arenberg The Olive Grove Chardonnay

Like many others in the Vale, D'Arenberg has shifted its focus for its best chardonnay grapes from McLaren Vale up into the Adelaide Hills. This is their one remaining Vale chardonnay; their top wine, Lucky Lizard, is a Hills wine.
CURRENT RELEASE 2004   This shows the deficiencies of McLaren Vale chardonnay as well as offering a decent drink at a fair price. It's fairly developed, with a mid-yellow colour; a rich bouquet of peach, cashew and apricot; and a soft, broad, almost fat palate which pulls up a trifle short. It's a decent wine that will appeal to those who like soft, up-front chardonnay. Serve with chicken satays.

Quality	♟♟♟⸴
Value	★★★⸸
Grapes	chardonnay
Region	McLaren Vale, SA
Cellar	▮ 1
Alc./Vol.	14.5%
RRP	$18.90 Ⓢ ⬧

De Bortoli Gulf Station Chardonnay

Quality 🍷🍷🍷🍷½
Value ★★★★★
Grapes chardonnay
Region Yarra Valley, Vic.
Cellar 🍾 2+
Alc./Vol. 13.5%
RRP $19.00 [$]

Gulf Station is De Bortoli's second-label Yarra Valley wine, the name being taken from a distinguished old grazing property on the Melba Highway near Yarra Glen. This won a gold medal at the 2005 Sydney Royal Wine Show. Chief winemaker is Stephen Webber.

CURRENT RELEASE 2003 Restrained power and refined intensity are bywords for the best Yarra Valley chardonnays, and this one captures those features well. It's an understated but subtly complex creamy, smoky, suave chardonnay with delicate oak, fine texture and a seamless, flowing structure. It would go well with lightly grilled scampi.

Deakin Estate Chardonnay

Quality 🍷🍷🍷
Value ★★★★
Grapes chardonnay
Region Riverland, Vic.
Cellar 🍾 1
Alc./Vol. 14.5%
RRP $10.75 [$] 🔩

Deakin Estate is part of the Wingara Group that also owns Katnook and it's one of the bigger operations in the Riverland. Maker: Phil Spillman.

CURRENT RELEASE 2004 This is a light, simple dry white that does have vestiges of chardonnay character, but is a bit lean and hollow. Possibly the rather hot, high-alcohol finish helps give this impression of hollowness: it's more a lack of balance, perhaps. The wine is fair value when (often) discounted and goes with chicken skewers.

Diamond Valley Blue Label Chardonnay

Quality 🍷🍷🍷🍷
Value ★★★½
Grapes chardonnay
Region Yarra Valley, Vic.
Cellar 🍾 3
Alc./Vol. 13.5%
RRP $23.00 [$] 🔩

Diamond Valley – the vineyard and brand – was recently bought by Graeme Rathbone, whose brother Doug owns Yering Station. The founders, the Lance family, retain a small piece of the vineyard and Jamie Lance continues as winemaker.

CURRENT RELEASE 2004 This is a lighter wine than the estate chardonnay and made for early drinking. The '03 is quite intense, though, and has some attractive bready sur-lie characters over peachy fruit and rather obvious oak. There's a touch of phenolic grip on the palate from the oak. The aftertaste is long and dry, and it would suit barbecued garlic prawns.

D'Meure Chardonnay

Dirk Meure renamed the tiny 1-hectare Flowerpot vineyard, at Birch's Bay in the Channel Country, after himself when he bought it in 2000. The vines were 14 years old in the '05 vintage. Sydney buyers can find this wine at Porters Liquor, Randwick.

CURRENT RELEASE 2004   We love the subtle, refined flavours that seem to distinguish D'Meure wines. This one has a light-yellow hue and smells predominantly of buttery malolactic characters, although it's fine and balanced with lovely fruit flavour as well, which dominates on the palate. It has lively, zippy Tasmanian acidity that tastes seamless and integrated. Oak is very restrained but adds extra complexity. A lovely drinking wine, to enjoy with fish and seafood.

Quality	▼▼▼▼▼
Value	★★★★
Grapes	chardonnay
Region	Channel Country, Tas.
Cellar	4+
Alc./Vol.	12.1%
RRP	$25.00 (cellar door)

Elderton Unwooded Chardonnay

Unwooded chardonnay is often a pretty ho-hum sort of wine, simple and unexciting. But the good ones can fill a need for a soft, fruity dry white that you don't need a doctorate to understand.

CURRENT RELEASE 2004   This is a forward type of unoaked chard with enough juiciness and interest to lift it a little above the ruck. It also has a whisper of what almost seems like oak, probably due to lees influence we suppose. It smells of honeydew melon and stone fruit, and the palate, although a tad short, is soft and clean with reasonable presence. A gluggable no-wood chardonnay to have with chicken sandwiches.

Quality	▼▼▼▼
Value	★★★
Grapes	chardonnay
Region	Barossa Valley, SA
Cellar	1
Alc./Vol.	13.0%
RRP	$13.40

Evans & Tate Margaret River Chardonnay

The Evans & Tate concern has become bigger than Ben-Hur in recent years. It's grown to become a public company, the biggest producer in the Margaret River region, and it's expanded to include Oakridge in Victoria's Yarra Valley and Cranswick in the New South Wales Riverina.

CURRENT RELEASE 2004   The nose has melon, tropical-fruit and grapefruit aromas that are intense, yet rather delicate at the same time. Oak is admirably restrained throughout, and it tastes smooth and round while staying at the lighter end of the Margaret River chardonnay style. The palate has a long tangy finish that leaves a crisp fresh impression. Try it with steamed marron.

Quality	▼▼▼▼
Value	★★★★
Grapes	chardonnay
Region	Margaret River, WA
Cellar	3
Alc./Vol.	14.0%
RRP	$21.00

Evelyn County Estate Black Paddock Chardonnay

Quality	♟♟♟♟♟
Value	★★★★↓
Grapes	chardonnay
Region	Yarra Valley, Vic.
Cellar	▮ 3+
Alc./Vol.	14.0%
RRP	$30.00

There's a very good restaurant at Evelyn County, and we can recommend the food. The building design alone makes it worth a visit. The wines are made on contract by Jamie Lance at Diamond Valley Vineyards.
CURRENT RELEASE 2002   This is a humdinger of a chardonnay, depleted grape yields resulting in great concentration. It's jammed with grapefruit, tropical-fruit and roast hazelnut aromas, and there are touches of malo-butter and toasty, smoky oak showing. For all that power, it is fine and subtle with a lively acid spine. Most impressive and goes well with grilled lobster.

Ferngrove Unwooded Chardonnay

Quality	♟♟♟♟
Value	★★★★
Grapes	chardonnay
Region	Frankland River, WA
Cellar	▮ 2
Alc./Vol.	13.0%
RRP	$18.00 Ⓢ ⧢

Ferngrove's Kim Horton was one of the people nominated for The Wine Society's young winemaker of the year award, and we reckon that's a good call. He's doing a sterling job.
CURRENT RELEASE 2004   Passionfruit, tropical aromas burst from the glass, unencumbered by oak. In the mouth it is clean, soft and very pleasant to quaff. The finish is clean and dry, with some alcohol warmth. There's a touch of richness and it's not propped up by sugar. It's one of the better unwoodeds doing the rounds. Try it with chicken kebabs.

Fiddlers Creek Chardonnay

Quality	♟♟♟♟
Value	★★★★
Grapes	chardonnay
Region	not stated
Cellar	▮ 1
Alc./Vol.	13.5%
RRP	$11.00 Ⓢ

Fiddlers Creek is one of the sous-marques of Blue Pyrenees Estate. It's positioned above the cheapie, Ghost Gum. The company has a very substantial 177 hectares of vineyards in the Pyrenees region.
CURRENT RELEASE 2003   This is a nicely turned-out commercial style of chardonnay at a more than fair price. The colour is bright, medium-deep yellow, while the bouquet has some greenness of the parsley/herbal kind. It's medium-bodied and well-balanced, with plenty of flavour and style, a core of peachy fruit, a lick of sweetness and a clean finish. It goes with san choy bow.

Forest Hill Chardonnay

Entered under its company name of Passchendaele Ridge Pty Ltd, this won a gold medal in very strong company in the 2005 Sydney Royal Wine Show where HH was judging. Forest Hill was the first vineyard planted at Mount Barker and now has 120 hectares of vines. Larry Cherubino, ex-Houghton, was chief winemaker for a while, in 2003–4.
CURRENT RELEASE 2003 The light-yellow colour marks this as a wine that's developing appropriately slowly. It's a pristine wine with a very gentle oak influence, and both bouquet and palate show subtle complexities and terrific freshness. The palate has fine texture, great mouth-feel and flavour, with a juicy (but not sugar-sweet) quality from ripe grapes. It would suit braised calamari.

Quality	♟♟♟♟♟
Value	★★★★★
Grapes	chardonnay
Region	Great Southern, WA
Cellar	🍾 4
Alc./Vol.	13.5%
RRP	$20.00

Foxeys Hangout Chardonnay

The name comes from a big old tree, from whose branches fox hunters used to hang their catch in days gone by. The label depicts a stylised Reynard. Quirky, if nothing else!
CURRENT RELEASE 2003 A restrained, delicate style of Peninsula chardonnay that has some finesse and therefore drinkability. We prefer it to the heavier styles of chardonnay. There's a slight reductive aroma to start with, while the palate is light and citrusy, with a lemony tang, and lean and almost narrow profile. It has good length and is likely to keep well for a couple of years. Drink it with sautéed scallops.

Quality	♟♟♟♟
Value	★★★★
Grapes	chardonnay
Region	Mornington Peninsula, Vic.
Cellar	🍾 3
Alc./Vol.	13.5%
RRP	$24.00

Freycinet Chardonnay

Freycinet is one of the leading wineries in Tasmania and has occupied an exalted position there for around 20 years. Its pinot noir is its flagship wine, but chardonnay is a regular performer, too. Winemaker is Italo-Taswegian Claudio Radenti.
CURRENT RELEASE 2003 This is not as pristine on the nose as most Freycinet chardonnays, with a slightly matty character along with nutty and lemon-butter aromas. It's intensely citrusy on the palate with lemon and grapefruit flavours. The structure is soft and round with a clean dry finish. A good but not great example of the label. Try it with Tassie crayfish.

Quality	♟♟♟♟
Value	★★★⭒
Grapes	chardonnay
Region	East Coast, Tas.
Cellar	🍾 3
Alc./Vol.	13.5%
RRP	$33.00

Fuse Adelaide Hills Chardonnay

Quality	🍷🍷🍷🍷
Value	★★★★
Grapes	chardonnay
Region	Adelaide Hills, SA
Cellar	🍾 2
Alc./Vol.	13.5%
RRP	$19.00 ⊗

Fuse is a new range of wines, created by Neil Pike at Pike's winery in the Clare Valley. There are some good-value wines among them. This is one such.

CURRENT RELEASE 2004 A delicious young, fresh, possibly unwooded chardonnay that relies on exuberant primary fruit for its charm. Aromas of grapefruit and passionfruit lead into a fruity, uncomplicated but quite stylish palate which carries a trace of sweetness. It's a good wine, a cut above your average quaffer. It goes well with chicken caesar salad.

Gapsted Victorian Alps Chardonnay

Quality	🍷🍷🍷
Value	★★★★
Grapes	chardonnay; verdelho
Region	Alpine Valleys, Vic.
Cellar	🍾 2
Alc./Vol.	13.5%
RRP	$15.00 ⊗

Few Australian vineyards are sited in such a lovely landscape as Gapsted. The forests, pastures and mountains of the Victorian High Country are food for the soul.

CURRENT RELEASE 2004 A fruit-driven chardonnay offering succulent tropical-fruit aromas with hints of dry herbs, minerals and cashew. The palate is smooth and satisfying with juicy, fruit-sweet flavour in the middle and a clean, persistent finish. A crowd-pleasing type of wine, this should appeal to those who aren't too keen on oaky chardonnays. Try it with cold chicken.

Garlands Reserve Chardonnay

Quality	🍷🍷🍷🍷
Value	★★★★⟩
Grapes	chardonnay
Region	Mount Barker, WA
Cellar	🍾 2
Alc./Vol.	13.0%
RRP	$22.00

The small Garlands vineyard and winery at Mount Barker quietly goes about the business of crafting some excellent wines in this cooler corner of Western Australia. Their focus on quality is admirable; they say they are constantly striving to 'improve the breed'. Prices are very reasonable relative to quality.

CURRENT RELEASE 2003 A well-priced chardonnay of generous proportions. The nose has syrupy-peach and balanced spicy-oak aromas, with a nicely underplayed touch of buttery richness. In the mouth, ripe fruit is at the core with good oak woven through seamlessly. It's smooth and full-flavoured with a suggestion of sweetness in the middle leading through to a dry finish. Serve it with roast chicken.

Giaconda Nantua Les Deux

Previously labelled as a blend of chardonnay and roussanne, this 2004 edition only lists chardonnay. There's still a little roussanne in it; the change is for international labelling requirements. Giaconda now offers buyers the choice of reliable screw-cap or iffy cork to seal their wines.
CURRENT RELEASE 2004   As befits a Giaconda chardonnay-based wine, this is a subtle, creamy and refined wine. In youth it shows a little more new oak influence than we've come to expect, but the complex Frenchy elements are still there, giving savoury-nutty, burnt match, herbal and earthy traits that transcend simple fruit. There are also hints of butterscotch and minerals. The palate is rich and mouth-filling with great depth and length, finishing fine and long. For a second-string wine, this is superb. Serve it with salmon.

Quality	🍷🍷🍷🍷🍷
Value	★★★⬦
Grapes	chardonnay 93%; roussanne 7%
Region	Beechworth, Vic.
Cellar	🍾 4+
Alc./Vol.	13.5%
RRP	$49.00 🍷

Giant Steps Sexton Bernard Clones 95 & 96 Chardonnay

Clonal selection in the vineyard is one of the secrets of success and Giant Steps proprietor Phil Sexton has been doing his homework in that area. This topnotch chardonnay is made using high-quality Bernard clones from France.
CURRENT RELEASE 2003   This is an elaborate, 'worked' style of chardonnay that offers plenty of the secondary complexities that can make French burgundy so distinctive. This has savoury, nutty, leesy and matchsticky elements taken to the fore, while subtle citrus and apple/pear fruit fill the gaps with great flair. The result is a long-tasting, creamy, nutty palate of great distinction that finishes with savoury, dry austerity. Quite special. Great with roasted poussin.

Quality	🍷🍷🍷🍷🍷
Value	★★★★
Grapes	chardonnay
Region	Yarra Valley, Vic.
Cellar	🍾 3
Alc./Vol.	14.0%
RRP	$39.75 🍷

Goundrey Reserve Selection Chardonnay

This 2003 vintage chardonnay won one of 64 Gold Medals from 1090 wines exhibited at the Chardonnay-du-Monde competition in Burgundy, France.
CURRENT RELEASE 2003   A flavoursome chardonnay that stands out in a line-up, this has tons of personality. Concentrated buttery stone-fruit and tropical aromas lead the way, and oak is applied sympathetically, although it's still a tad edgy. Six months in bottle should harmonise the wood. The palate has tons of flavour that's long, rich and round. Tangy fruit/acid/oak balance is excellent, and it finishes with a long toasty signature. Serve it with pot-roasted chicken and chestnuts.

Quality	🍷🍷🍷🍷⬦
Value	★★★⬦
Grapes	chardonnay
Region	Mount Barker, WA
Cellar	🍾 2
Alc./Vol.	14.0%
RRP	$30.00 🍷

Gramp's Chardonnay

Quality 🍷🍷🍷🍷
Value ★★★½
Grapes chardonnay
Region Barossa Valley, SA
Cellar 🍾 2
Alc./Vol. 13.5%
RRP $18.50 [$]

Gramp's is a good example of the flavoursome style that's made chardonnay such a hit with Australians in the last 20 years.

CURRENT RELEASE 2003 A bright-coloured wine with a smooth nose, and like the '02 it's good value, especially as it's usually discounted well below the RRP listed here. The nose has plenty of nutty, complex secondary character, rather than simple fruit and oak. Yeast lees, brazil nut, cashew and spicy oak are worked into nectarine-like fruit character. The palate is plump and somewhat oaky. Tart acidity underlines creamy mid-palate texture and it has a long, toasty finish. Ideal with chicken satays.

Grant Burge Summers Chardonnay

Quality 🍷🍷🍷🍷½
Value ★★★★★
Grapes chardonnay
Region Eden Valley & Adelaide Hills, SA
Cellar 🍾 2
Alc./Vol. 13.5%
RRP $19.85 [$]

This has been one of our picks of the chardonnay crop in recent years, able to stand up well in tasting line-ups with wines of twice the price and more. And it's often on special.

CURRENT RELEASE 2004 This has a brilliant yellow–green colour that looks the goods. It's not quite the wine the '03 was, but it still has a surprisingly complex nose with cashew, white peach, earth and lightly nutty-barrel ferment aromas that are smooth and rich. The palate has tons of rich flavour, but there's refinement too. It finishes long, dry and tangy. Try it with sautéed chicken breasts and grapes.

Green Point Chardonnay

Quality 🍷🍷🍷🍷½
Value ★★★★
Grapes chardonnay
Region Yarra Valley, Vic.
Cellar 🍾 2+
Alc./Vol. 13.0%
RRP $23.95 ➰

The Green Point label is reserved for the still wines produced at Chandon's Yarra Valley sparkling-wine centre. They are getting better all the time, and wines like this chardonnay are keenly priced relative to quality.

CURRENT RELEASE 2003 Another winner under the Green Point banner, this young chardonnay is very fragrant with green melon-like varietal fruit of great purity in the middle of things. Some nutty, creamy and savoury notes add subtle complexity, and restrained oak adds its understated spice. In the mouth it's silky and quietly complex with a long, chalky, bone-dry finish. A very elegant drop to enjoy with delicately flavoured cheeses.

Grosset Piccadilly

Piccadilly in the Adelaide Hills is consistently one of South Australia's best places for high-quality chardonnay. Jeff Grosset is one of the high-profile, high-quality producers to proudly give the region name top billing.

CURRENT RELEASE 2003 This is a deliciously complex and complete Adelaide Hills chardonnay. It has melon and citrus aromas with the added dimension of sensitively handled nutty, earthy lees and oak influence. The palate is silky smooth with subtle creamy fruit and oak flavours that lead to a very fine, very long finish. Excellent. It's delicious with salmon.

Quality	🍷🍷🍷🍷🍷
Value	★★★
Grapes	chardonnay
Region	Adelaide Hills, SA
Cellar	🍾 3
Alc./Vol.	14.0%
RRP	$49.00 💰

Hardys Eileen Hardy Chardonnay

Hardys have really nailed great Burgundy-style chardonnay since they've been bringing grapes in from Tasmania and other really cool parts of the country. This has won five gold medals and three trophies at major shows, but we'd be surprised if it doesn't add to the tally before its time is up. Maker: Tom Newton.

CURRENT RELEASE 2002 A really exciting chardonnay! It's very complex and has a touch of the low-level sulphide character of many Burgundies, coupled with multi-faceted grapefruit, gooseberry and tropical-fruit aromas. The palate is powerful but also nervy and penetrating with thrilling acidity and fantastic length. It should keep well, too. It's a wine we'd never tire of sipping, especially with crayfish.

Quality	🍷🍷🍷🍷🍷
Value	★★★★★
Grapes	chardonnay
Region	43% Tasmania; 28% Yarra Valley, Vic.; 20% Tumbarumba, NSW; 8% Adelaide Hills, SA
Cellar	🍾 5+
Alc./Vol.	13.0%
RRP	$50.00 [$]

PENGUIN BEST WHITE WINE and BEST CHARDONNAY

Haselgrove HRS Reserve Chardonnay

HRS stands for Haselgrove Reserve Series. We were hoping it had something to do with paying tribute to one of the original members of a famous family – winemaker Ronald Haselgrove. Now that would be worth making a fuss about.

CURRENT RELEASE 2004 This is a good wine, nicely showcasing Adelaide Hills' finesse and subtlety. The colour is light and undeveloped; the aromas are of citrus, butter and bracken herbal notes, with a touch of nougat. Grapefruit is the main palate flavour, enhanced by a little sweetness. Tangy acid chimes in towards the finish. It's slightly disjointed as a youngster, so we suggest keeping it for about six months. Then serve with prawns in beurre blanc.

Quality	🍷🍷🍷🍷
Value	★★★★
Grapes	chardonnay
Region	Adelaide Hills, SA
Cellar	🍾 3+
Alc./Vol.	13.5%
RRP	$25.00 💰 (cellar door only)

Bargain Hunters' Tips

The price of wine, like every other commodity, tends to move steadily upwards. And there's more and more wine in the high-value, super-premium category constantly vying for our attention. But you can still buy decent wine cheaply if you know where to look. Here are a few tips:

• Take advantage of case discounts. Most retailers offer 10 per cent off for dozen buys, some do it on half-dozens, and some offer more than 10 per cent off. In theory, you can buy 11 bottles of Jacob's Creek and one of Dom Perignon, and get the case price for the Dom, which is a nice little saving.

• Scan the newspaper ads. Retailing is desperately competitive right now and there are some amazing discounts. The Saturday and Tuesday papers are big wine advertising days, particularly in Sydney and Melbourne: grab them and move fast to get the good prices. The same goes for retailer newsletters and email bulletins: get on their mailing lists and do some homework on prices so you'll recognise a bargain when you see it.

• Go to the auctions, especially the non-wine specialists such as Grays, Lawson Menzies and Fowles Overett, where you can find some surprisingly good prices – frequently on mature vintages, too. Even the premium wine specialists such as Langton's (Sydney/Melbourne) and Oddbins (Adelaide) can give remarkable value on cheaper wines. The specialist wine auctioneers are pretty good at quality control, but it's a good rule to physically check the condition of stock before you bid.

• Cleanskins are the biggest phenomenon in low-priced bottled wine, and these can be great value but we regard them as a lottery – from out-and-out rubbish to remarkably good stuff. Even if you find a good one, you've no way of identifying it, and when you return to buy more, the wine could be a completely different batch. Caveat emptor! Always hit the retailer for a taste.

• A new phenomenon is the wine clearance house, where you may find some good value as a result of distressed sales by wineries and wholesalers.

• Returnable bottles (often in one-litre, swing-top, polyagonal bottles) can also be good value. Again – try before you buy.

• Keep the retailers honest. If they bung on that 'We'll match anyone's price' bluster, take them at their word!

Houghton Museum Release Chardonnay

Quality	♀♀♀♀!
Value	★★★★★
Grapes	chardonnay
Region	Frankland River, WA
Cellar	▮1
Alc./Vol.	13.5%
RRP	$26.00 Ⓢ

Margaret River seems to command all the limelight in Western Australia, but the Great Southern is also a producer of tremendously good, often age-worthy, chardonnay – and this is an example. It's won five gold medals and has done well to make it to seven years old in this condition.
CURRENT RELEASE 1998   The colour is very deep yellow and the fully mature bouquet is rich and very complex. Smoky bacon, buttered toast and butterscotch aromas flow from the glass. It's not as rich in the mouth as the best Margaret River chardonnays, but has real finesse, length and style. It would go well with a runny aged brie.

Hungerford Hill Fish Cage Chardonnay Viognier

Quality	♀♀♀!
Value	★★★★
Grapes	chardonnay; viognier
Region	not stated
Cellar	▮2
Alc./Vol.	13.0%
RRP	$14.00 Ⓢ ⧖

Viognier is not commonly blended with chardonnay, but occasionally we've seen it used to add some extra richness to a wine. Chardonnay doesn't usually lack richness by itself, though.
CURRENT RELEASE 2004   No great finesse here, but it's a wine of generous fruity flavour and good value for money. The colour is light to medium yellow with green tints, and the aromas recall peach, nectarine, mango and other tropical fruits, with oak playing a very minor role. The palate is a touch thick and broad, but chill it well and it's bound to be a crowd-pleaser. Serve with chicken cacciatore.

Kirrihill Companions Chardonnay

Quality	♀♀♀!
Value	★★★★
Grapes	chardonnay
Region	not stated. SA
Cellar	▮1
Alc./Vol.	13.9%
RRP	$12.99 ⧖

What sort of chardonnay do you get for $12.99? Price isn't necessarily an indicator of quality, but low-priced chardonnays can be pretty ugly. This one ain't no oil painting, but it's better-looking than a lot of others.
CURRENT RELEASE 2003   A brightly coloured chardonnay with an old-fashioned personality due, perhaps, to it being stainless-steel fermented, then partially oak aged, rather than barrel-fermented. The nose has vanillin and bacony-oak aromas with a core of peachy fruit, and the palate is oaky as well, but it's clean-tasting and well made with a long finish. Try it with Malaysian chicken curry.

Kooyong Chardonnay

In common with many Mornington Peninsula estates, Kooyong makes a speciality of pinot noir, but in our opinion the estate's chardonnay is their top wine. Rather than change to screw-caps to address the problems posed by corks, Kooyong uses a new state-of-the-art type of particle cork that they claim is taint-free.

CURRENT RELEASE 2003   This has an attractive pale green–gold colour, and the nose has syrupy fig and peach aromas of true subtle complexity. Oak is perfectly integrated, and the palate has lovely seamless, creamy texture and a fine long finish. It's a modern style with plenty happening on nose and palate, but thankfully it's not as overworked as some new-wave chards. Enjoy it with roast free-range chicken.

Quality	♒♒♒♒♒
Value	✦✦✦
Grapes	chardonnay
Region	Mornington Peninsula, Vic.
Cellar	🍷 2
Alc./Vol.	13.0%
RRP	$38.00

Kooyong Clonale Chardonnay

Clonale is the white companion to Kooyong's Massale Pinot Noir. It's a chardonnay that takes its name from selection clonale, the practice of using a mix of different clones of vine in the vineyard. This wine is made from ten different clones of chardonnay.

CURRENT RELEASE 2004   A very good effort for a second label, this pale-straw-coloured wine smells subtle and fragrant with nectarine-like fruit, a nice barley sugarish touch, and an attractive thread of nutty lees and barrel character. The palate has a smooth feel with a dry finish and a long savoury aftertaste. Try it with scallop brochettes.

Quality	♒♒♒♒
Value	✦✦✦✦
Grapes	chardonnay
Region	Mornington Peninsula, Vic.
Cellar	🍷 2
Alc./Vol.	13.5%
RRP	$24.00

Lake's Folly Chardonnay

Because of drought, the yields were crucified and only a fraction of the usual quantity of chardonnay was harvested. The upside is that it made a superb wine with above-average concentration. Maker: Rodney Kempe.

CURRENT RELEASE 2003   This is a ripper of a Hunter chardonnay. It's bright, full yellow in colour and the nose is big on pineapple/tropical aromas, with well-harmonised oak leaving the fruit in the spotlight. The palate flavour is deep, rich and lingering, with a winning vibrancy. A year or two in the cellar will bring even more complexity, but it's a superb drink now, with grilled lobster.

Quality	♒♒♒♒♒
Value	✦✦✦✦
Grapes	chardonnay
Region	Hunter Valley, NSW
Cellar	🍷 4+
Alc./Vol.	13.7%
RRP	$50.00

Leeuwin Estate Art Series Chardonnay

Quality	♛♛♛♛♛
Value	★★★★﹨
Grapes	chardonnay
Region	Margaret River, WA
Cellar	▮6+
Alc./Vol.	14.5%
RRP	$80.00

A feature of the Art Series labels is their centrepiece of original paintings, which change with the vintage. This one is 'Body Paint' by Minnie Pwerle. The yields were cut by half in 2002 because of spring storms which damaged the young shoots. The result should be even more concentrated wine than usual.

CURRENT RELEASE 2002   And concentrated it is. The colour is medium-full yellow but lighter than most chardonnays of its age – a hallmark of Leeuwin. It's a great chardonnay: penetrating flavours of grapefruit and other citrus, honey and nougat, very powerful and long-lasting in the mouth. Lively acidity carries the flavour and cuts through the considerable weight and richness of the wine. Beautifully integrated and focused. Serve with lobster.

Leeuwin Estate Prelude Vineyards Chardonnay

Quality	♛♛♛♛
Value	★★★﹨
Grapes	chardonnay
Region	Margaret River, WA
Cellar	▮3+
Alc./Vol.	14.0%
RRP	$30.00

This is the junior Leeuwin Estate chardonnay, a prelude to the full symphony, no doubt, which is the Art Series bottling. While the Art Series always comes from Block 20, this is made from other estate vineyards. Chief winemaker: Bob Cartwright.

CURRENT RELEASE 2003   This is a very good example of the style, a warm-up act for the Art Series and significantly below it in concentration and complexity. It has good intensity length and balance. The oak level is on the high side, although good peachy varietal fruit shines through. It finishes clean and dry with good drinkability and style. It would suit BBQ chicken shish kebabs.

Lindemans Reserve Chardonnay

Quality	♛♛♛﹗
Value	★★★★
Grapes	chardonnay
Region	various, SA
Cellar	▮1
Alc./Vol.	13.5%
RRP	$14.50 Ⓢ

We reviewed this last year but the wine is still current. Does that mean Southcorp sales have slowed down? If so, it's Beringer Blass's problem now, as BB launched a successful takeover bid for Southcorp in early 2005.

CURRENT RELEASE 2003   The nose is shy but the taste is very good, specially considering the price. It's a fruit-driven style with fruit-salad aromas and a rounded, nicely balanced palate that smooths out to a lingering, dry, clean finish. Good mid-palate intensity and focus. Try it with chicken nuggets.

The Little Penguin Chardonnay

This brand was created especially for the US market, which had revealed a distinct liking for Yellow Tail (named after a wallaby) and other 'critter wines', as the Americans so aptly call them. Crocodile Rock is another. This is Southcorp's answering shot.

CURRENT RELEASE 2004 Our bottle was full yellow and very forward in development for an '04, while the nose showed very simplistic and rather herbaceous chardonnay aromas of parsley and sundry green herbs. The palate is distinctly sweet and broad, and somewhat disjointed, but it's okay at the price and certainly offers flavour and drinkability for very little outlay. Fish and chips would suit.

Quality	🍷🍷½
Value	★★★★
Grapes	chardonnay
Region	South Eastern Australia
Cellar	1
Alc./Vol.	13.0%
RRP	$11.00

Moss Wood Chardonnay

Australia and New Zealand lead the way when it comes to exploring alternatives to cork. Moss Wood is one of a handful of leading Margaret River wineries who have committed to screw-caps instead of corks. It means consistent, reliable wine, rather than the hit-and-miss quality of wines sealed with natural cork.

CURRENT RELEASE 2004 Straw-coloured and youthful-looking, this has a powerful nose and a complex one. It's scented with oatmeal, light cream toffee, green melon, peach, and nutty, biscuity characters. The palate has a lovely feel and it's very complex with lots of impact and power, good length and a tangy end. It's still unevolved, but it has real potential. Try it with salmon.

Quality	🍷🍷🍷🍷½
Value	★★★
Grapes	chardonnay
Region	Margaret River, WA
Cellar	1–5
Alc./Vol.	14.0%
RRP	$52.50

Mount Horrocks Chardonnay

Clare isn't generally considered the ideal spot to produce chardonnay, but Stephanie Toole does an admirable job at Mount Horrocks. She employs barrel fermentation and eight months' lees stirring to build a little bit extra into it.

CURRENT RELEASE 2004 Peaty, nutty, funky lees aromas are the first things we noticed with this wine, and combined with a little reductive character they add a slightly Frenchy pong to it. Hints of stone fruit dabbed with spicy oak complete the picture. In the mouth it's smooth with a plump mid-palate and a dry finish. One for those who like their chardonnays with a bit of country charm. Serve it with soft cheeses.

Quality	🍷🍷🍷🍷
Value	★★★
Grapes	chardonnay
Region	Clare Valley, SA
Cellar	2
Alc./Vol.	13.0%
RRP	$23.00

Nine Eleven Tasmanian Chardonnay

Quality 🍷🍷🍷½
Value ★★★★
Grapes chardonnay
Region various, Tas.
Cellar 🍾 2
Alc./Vol. 13.2%
RRP $15.99

The Nine-Eleven retail group in Hobart hope to break into the mainland market, selling high-quality Tassie wines made by well-known winemaker Julian Alcorso. We think they deserve to succeed, really good Tasmanian wine is rarely this inexpensive.
CURRENT RELEASE 2004 A straightforward chardonnay that relies on pristine fruit character rather than winemaking technique. It's relatively pale in colour and smells of citrus fruits, guava and melon. There's a whisper of nuttiness in the background, but oak isn't readily apparent. In the mouth there are hints of fig and citrus in its smoothly appealing flavour, and it finishes with a pleasant tang. Good with seafood stirfry.

Orlando Jacob's Creek Reserve Chardonnay

Quality 🍷🍷🍷🍷½
Value ★★★★★
Grapes chardonnay
Region various, SA
Cellar 🍾 2
Alc./Vol. 12.5%
RRP $17.00 [$]

When the first Jacob's Creek Reserve wines arrived a few years ago, they astonished us with their value for money. This latest chardonnay shows that it wasn't a flash in the pan. It also shows that Oz chardonnay doesn't have to have 14 per cent alcohol to have presence.
CURRENT RELEASE 2003 This has a remarkably fine nose of fig, peach and citrus aromas, touched by subtle nutty/mealy complexity. There's a whisper of high-toned oak too, but it doesn't intrude. The silky palate is long in flavour with a slightly minerally/savoury quality and a chalky dry finish. Oak comes through more in the mouth than on the nose, but the overall impression remains smooth and tasty. Serve it with fish cooked en papillote.

Orlando St Hilary Chardonnay

Quality 🍷🍷🍷🍷
Value ★★★½
Grapes chardonnay
Region Padthaway, SA
Cellar 🍾 2
Alc./Vol. 13.5%
RRP $20.00 [$]

This is one of a very good selection of under-$20 chardonnays from the Orlando stable. Thoughtful winemaking gives it a veneer of real style. Shop around for the best price, as it's often discounted. Makers: Phil Laffer and team.
CURRENT RELEASE 2003 A flavoursome chardonnay of surprising elegance. The nose has aromas of nectarine, grapefruit, gently dusty, mealy notes, the lightest touch of toffee and attractive spicy oak. The wood has a definite influence but it's in no danger of killing the wine, an object lesson in how to apply oak to commercial chardonnay. It has great mouthfeel and it finishes long and dry with an appetising citrus tang. Sip it with stir-fried prawns.

Padthaway Estate Unwooded Chardonnay

A lot of the cheaper chardonnays about today are unwooded or at least very lightly wooded, but not all of them say so up-front. This one does.
CURRENT RELEASE 2004   The colour is light to medium yellow and the aromas are simple, grapey and varietal, smelling of peach and grapefruit. It has good palate weight and texture considering it's an oak-less type, and there is a pleasing lack of bolstering residual sugar. A clean, well-made, basic chardonnay that will offend no one. It goes with steamed Chinese chicken dumplings.

Quality	♈ ♈ ♈ ♈
Value	★★★★
Grapes	chardonnay
Region	Padthaway, SA
Cellar	▮ 1
Alc./Vol.	13.0%
RRP	$15.00 (cellar door)

Penfolds Koonunga Hill Semillon Chardonnay

It's amazing how a jolt of semillon can add vitality and spine to a floppy, mid-priced chardonnay. The regular Koonunga Hill chardonnay is not a bad drink, but this is better.
CURRENT RELEASE 2003   The colour is bright, light to medium yellow and the aromas are fresh and youthful, depicting some herbal semillon fruit as well as peach/melon chardonnay, with oak taking a back seat. The palate is delicate but intense and tautly structured, fruit-driven and dry on the finish, which also carries some alcohol warmth. An affordable white of some backbone and length. It suits san choy bow.

Quality	♈ ♈ ♈ ♈
Value	★★★★♦
Grapes	semillon; chardonnay
Region	not stated
Cellar	▮ 2+
Alc./Vol.	13.5%
RRP	$16.00 Ⓢ ⤴

Penfolds Rawson's Retreat Chardonnay

We're not sure what the retreat is all about but Rawson was the second name of Dr Christopher Penfold, who started the whole thing back in 1844. He began by making medicinal wines for patients: who knows what he'd think of today's massive public company.
CURRENT RELEASE 2004   Simple, grapey, soft and open, this is a conventional commercial chardonnay made to a price, and offering good quality for the money. Aromas of peach/nectarine and parsley/herbs lead the way. It's soft, fruity and very subtly oaked if at all, with fairly low acid and a slight impression of sweetness. It goes with fried whitebait.

Quality	♈ ♈ ♈ ♈
Value	★★★★
Grapes	chardonnay
Region	various
Cellar	▮ 2
Alc./Vol.	13.0%
RRP	$10.00 Ⓢ

Penfolds Reserve Bin 03A Chardonnay

Quality	♟♟♟♟♟
Value	★★★
Grapes	chardonnay
Region	Adelaide Hills, SA
Cellar	▶ 4
Alc./Vol.	13.5%
RRP	$85.00 ⊜

This is the alter ego of Yattarna: made from slightly richer fruit, and produced with more wild-yeast, solidsy, buttery-malo complexities, it makes a big statement. Maker: Peter Gago & team.

CURRENT RELEASE 2003   A more funky, complex, layered and up-front wine than Yattarna, this has some buttery malo and bready sur-lie characters among its very complex mealy aromas. It's rich and mouth-filling with magnificent flavour and style, but less restraint than Yattarna. Great power and length of palate, too. Serve it with chicken and pistachio gallantine.

Penfolds Yattarna Chardonnay

Quality	♟♟♟♟♟
Value	★★♦
Grapes	chardonnay
Region	Adelaide Hills, SA; Tumbarumba, NSW & Drumborg, Vic.
Cellar	▶ 5+
Alc./Vol.	13.5%
RRP	$115.00

Penfolds winemakers source the grapes for Yattarna from the coolest sites they can find, and in the super-cool 2002 summer, the Adelaide Hills produced the right sort of fruit, so this year it's based on that area.

CURRENT RELEASE 2002   Pristine chardonnay! The colour is remarkably light for its age, and it's a super-fine wine of great finesse and restraint, built to age. Grapefruit, minerals, hints of passionfruit, oak barely noticeable it's so well integrated, and the palate is very long and finely structured. A stunner, to serve with lobster.

Pepperjack Barossa Chardonnay

Quality	♟♟♟♟
Value	★★★♦
Grapes	chardonnay
Region	Barossa Valley, SA
Cellar	▶ 2
Alc./Vol.	13.5%
RRP	$24.00 Ⓢ ⊜

The Beringer Blass organisation pushes out brands like there's no tomorrow. Some stick, some don't. Pepperjack is one of many sub-brands of Saltram. It's survived for two or three years so far. Winemaker is nominally Nigel Dolan.

CURRENT RELEASE 2004   While Barossa chardonnay seldom gets our pulses racing, this is a commendable effort. The aroma is a touch subdued, and the wine is rather straightforward, but it does carry some appealing richness and texture, with oatmealy flavours and decent length. The finish carries some phenolics and a little sweetness. It makes a pleasant drink with smoked chicken and salad.

Petaluma Chardonnay

The grapes came from seven separate vineyard sites in the Piccadilly Valley in the central Adelaide Hills, and all of the vines were at least 19 years old as of the 2003 harvest.
CURRENT RELEASE 2003   The first impression is of buttery, butterscotch malolactic characters, together with spicy oak and mealy, ground-nut and cedar aromas. It's quite a big style for Petaluma, and really fills the mouth. It is very flavoursome and soft, and relatively accessible as a newly released young wine. It can be served with Thai stuffed chicken wings.

Quality	♟ ♟ ♟ ♟ ♟
Value	★ ★ ★ ꜀
Grapes	chardonnay
Region	Adelaide Hills, SA
Cellar	🍾 3
Alc./Vol.	13.5%
RRP	$48.85

Petaluma Summertown Vineyard Chardonnay

Brian Croser says Summertown is one of seven distinguished sites Petaluma has in the Piccadilly Valley, and it's only the second one to be bottled separately, after the original, Tiers. The soil structure is quite different, Tiers being on 1800-million-year-old rock, while Summertown is on much more recent soils.
CURRENT RELEASE 2001   The wine is ageing well: it's medium to deep yellow and the bouquet is all about cashew-nutty and grapefruit aromas, of moderate complexity. The palate is rich and full, lively and lingering, albeit not as fine or tightly wound as Tiers. A very good effort from what was supposedly a hot year. Serve it with grilled flathead.

Quality	♟ ♟ ♟ ♟ ♟
Value	★ ★ ★ ꜀
Grapes	chardonnay
Region	Adelaide Hills, SA
Cellar	🍾 2
Alc./Vol.	13.5%
RRP	$52.00

Petaluma Tiers Chardonnay

We reviewed this last year but it's still current and certainly not fading. We do wonder at the price: you can buy good premier cru burgundy for $150 and get a more exciting wine. And you can get two bottles of Leeuwin or three of Eileen Hardy for the price of one Tiers. Makers: Con Moshos and Brian Croser.
CURRENT RELEASE 2001   A complex chardonnay that's ageing gracefully, showing macaroon, toasted-nut, marzipan and mealy characters. It's very refined, with richness and depth but also a seamless quality that we admire. An excellent chardonnay, but there's a curious lack of excitement or dynamic X factor about it. Crayfish would be the right accompaniment.

Quality	♟ ♟ ♟ ♟ ♟
Value	★ ★
Grapes	chardonnay
Region	Adelaide Hills, SA
Cellar	🍾 3
Alc./Vol.	13.5%
RRP	$150.00

Picardy Chardonnay

Quality 🍷🍷🍷🍷🍷
Value ★★★½
Grapes chardonnay
Region Pemberton, WA
Cellar 4
Alc./Vol. 13.5%
RRP $40.00

The Pannells of Picardy aim to make elaborately flavoured, richly textured wines that look more towards the Old World than the New. They succeed admirably.

CURRENT RELEASE 2004 This very subtle chardonnay shows that complex doesn't mean obvious. It grows in the glass, revealing citrus, apple, spice, marzipan and nutty aromas with restrained, almost Vegemitey lees character. There's a whisper of earthiness and the texture is seamless, leading through a long savoury finish. Full of interest. Serve it with soft, mild cheeses.

Pike & Joyce Chardonnay

Quality 🍷🍷🍷🍷½
Value ★★★★
Grapes chardonnay
Region Adelaide Hills, SA
Cellar 2
Alc./Vol. 14.0%
RRP $30.00

The Pike is Neil Pike from Clare; the Joyce is the vineyard owner – at Lenswood in the cool heights of the Adelaide Hills. Maker: Neil Pike.

CURRENT RELEASE 2003 A complex, fairly heavily worked wine, with some meaty reductive characters plus oak-derived complexities. It has full body and a lingering intensity that suggests smoked and roasted nuts. The primary fruit is somewhat buried in the melange of artefact flavours. It's a real mouthful and would go a treat with grilled spatchcock.

Port Phillip Estate Chardonnay

Quality 🍷🍷🍷🍷½
Value ★★★½
Grapes chardonnay
Region Mornington Peninsula, Vic.
Cellar 3
Alc./Vol. 14.0%
RRP $30.00

Winemaking at Port Phillip Estate has passed from Paringa's Lindsay McCall to Kooyong's Sandro Mosele. It will be interesting to see how the wines evolve under the new boy.

CURRENT RELEASE 2003 This has a bright-greenish straw colour that looks youthful and attractive. The nose is very complex with some 'wild' secondary characters lording it over chardonnay fruit. Barrel influence, peaty yeast lees and creamy-solids influence make it hard to ignore. Flavour is ripe, texture is fine and the finish is long and clean. A characterful mouthful of Mornington chardonnay, smooth and classy. Serve it with salmon.

Preece Chardonnay

Preece is Mitchelton's mid-priced, drink-now, value-for-money range – and fulfils its duties extremely well. Don Lewis heads the winemaking team along with Neville Rowe and Tony Barlow.
CURRENT RELEASE 2004 This is squeaky clean, crisp as newly ironed linen; a pristine chardonnay with negligible oak but lovely simple peachy, nectarine-like fruit leading the way. It's a basic but technically A1, beautifully made chardonnay that is a delight to drink with sautéed prawns.

Quality 🍷🍷🍷½
Value ★★★★½
Grapes chardonnay
Region not stated
Cellar 🍾 2
Alc./Vol. 13.5%
RRP $15.00 [$]

Riddoch Chardonnay

There are more Riddochs in Coonawarra than you can poke a stick at. John Riddoch cabernet at Wynns, this one, and Rymill used to have a Riddoch Run wine – there are probably others. The claim here is that the winery at Katnook Estate (which owns this brand) was the original woolshed of the 'father of Coonawarra', John Riddoch.
CURRENT RELEASE 2003 With an extra year of age over most of its competitors, this is a good-value uncomplicated style of chardonnay. The colour is bright, full yellow; the bouquet is clean, cashew-nutty and fairly conventional with a touch of marzipan and a little nettley green-herbiness. It's of only modest complexity but is mainly about fruit and a little bottle-development. Try it with chicken kebabs.

Quality 🍷🍷🍷🍷
Value ★★★★
Grapes chardonnay
Region Coonawarra, SA
Cellar 🍾 1
Alc./Vol. 13.5%
RRP $17.00 [$]

Rosemount Diamond Label Chardonnay

The full name of the wine is Rosemount Estate, but we're being ornery and leaving the estate word out, because there is no way this is an estate-grown wine. Estate-grown means the grapes were all grown on the proprietor's own vineyard(s). This big-production wine long ago outgrew the Rosemount (or Southcorp, for that matter) vineyards.
CURRENT RELEASE 2004 This is a simple, rather sweet chardonnay these days, a sort of soft drink for grown-ups. It is clean and fresh (thanks partly to the synthetic Nomacork that seals it) with peach/nectarine and cashew-nut flavours, fairly low acidity and good drinkability as long as you accept the sweetness. It could be served with san choy bow.

Quality 🍷🍷🍷
Value ★★★★
Grapes chardonnay
Region various
Cellar 🍾 1
Alc./Vol. 13.5%
RRP $15.00 [$]

Rosemount Orange Vineyard Chardonnay

Quality	♥♥♥♥♥
Value	★★★★᛫
Grapes	chardonnay
Region	Orange, NSW
Cellar	▮3
Alc./Vol.	13.5%
RRP	$28.00 Ⓢ

The Rosemount style sure has taken a turn towards the more refined in recent years, especially this Orange wine, which is the coolest site that's employed in Rosemount wines. The grapes come from Philip Shaw's own vineyard at Orange.

CURRENT RELEASE 2003   This is a restrained, refined, tautly structured, savoury style of chardonnay. It evidences plenty of toasty/cedary French oak, coupled with refined fruit and a touch of malolactic butterscotch and nougat. It's still tight and tidy on the palate with some refinement, as well as impressive balance. It's excellent value, and goes with smoked chicken salad.

Rosily Vineyard Chardonnay

Quality	♥♥♥♥
Value	★★★★
Grapes	chardonnay
Region	Margaret River, WA
Cellar	▮3+
Alc./Vol.	13.7%
RRP	$20.00 ⬳

This 13.5-hectare Wilyabrup vineyard is an alliance between the Scott and Allan families. Winemaker is Mike Lemmes. Rosily provides some of the best value for money in Margaret River.

CURRENT RELEASE 2004   The colour is bright mid-yellow and the bouquet is clean and fresh, exuding aromas of high-quality oak and peachy fruit, with a slight lift that may come from some wild-yeast fermentation. The oak is certainly on the generous side, while the finish carries a certain warmth from alcohol. It's a good wine, but our feeling is that more fruit power would have better balanced the oak and the alcohol. It suits kedgeree.

Scotchmans Hill Chardonnay

Quality	♥♥♥♥᛫
Value	★★★
Grapes	chardonnay
Region	Geelong, Vic.
Cellar	▮1
Alc./Vol.	14.0%
RRP	$27.00 ⬳

Scotchmans Hill is the pre-eminent wine producer on the Bellarine Peninsula, a lovely pastoral landscape near Geelong with some wonderful old seafront towns that are well worth exploring.

CURRENT RELEASE 2003   Scotchmans Hill Chardonnay continues in its pleasant middle-of-the-road manner with the '03 edition. Subtlety is the order of the day, and it gets better with each sip, building character and interest. It smells of melon and citrus with well-handled subtle oak. The palate is clean and elegant with an appealing touch of creamy lees character. It finishes long and tasty. Serve it with baked snapper.

Seppelt Jaluka Chardonnay

Made entirely from grapes grown at Seppelt Drumborg vineyard in Victoria's south-west, this excellent line in chardonnay has only emerged in recent years, but it already has an enviable record for quality and value. Maker: Arthur O'Connor.

CURRENT RELEASE 2004   Cool growing conditions show in this wine's elegance, which is miles away from the Aussie bottled-sunshine type of chardonnay, nor is it weighed down with alcohol. Instead there's a smoky, minerally nose with honey, nectarine and very subtle spicy oak in the background. In the mouth it's fine in texture and flavour, richly flavoured but with a lean-boned underlying structure that should augur well for a couple of years' bottle-age. Sip it with chilled Moreton Bay bug tails.

Quality	▼▼▼▼▼
Value	★★★⟩
Grapes	chardonnay
Region	Portland, Vic.
Cellar	▮ 4
Alc./Vol.	13.0%
RRP	$23.95 Ⓢ ⧽

Shadowfax Chardonnay

Although Shadowfax winemaker Matt Harrop is based at Werribee, on the way out of Melbourne towards Geelong, he isn't averse to obtaining grapes from much further afield for his very good range of wines.

CURRENT RELEASE 2003   Not a sweet-fruity type of chardonnay, this is a more subtle wine that gets better with every glass. It seems to show some solids/lees influence that adds savoury complexity to quite delicate citrus and nectarine fruit characters. Spicy oak is subtly folded into it, and the palate is smooth, soft and long. A chardonnay of some finesse to serve with skewered swordfish.

Quality	▼▼▼▼▼
Value	★★★
Grapes	chardonnay
Region	Geelong, Beechworth & Yarra Valley, Vic.; Adelaide Hills, SA
Cellar	▮ 2
Alc./Vol.	13.5%
RRP	$30.00 ⧽

Shaw and Smith M3 Chardonnay

M3 is a reference to the three Ms of the Shaw and Smith operation: brothers Michael and Matthew Hill Smith, and their cousin Martin Shaw. It's a quality-oriented enterprise.

CURRENT RELEASE 2003   This Adelaide Hills flagship chardonnay is a very refined style. Complex yet subtle, it isn't a Burgundy look-alike; instead it sums up the best qualities of the Australian chardonnay style. The nose has juicy stone fruit, barley sugar, almond syrup and beautifully integrated nutty oak in lovely harmony. The palate has pleasantly understated richness and slightly austere underlying structure, but there's enough 'give' for it to be an appetising drink glass after glass. Try it with barbecued bug tails.

Quality	▼▼▼▼▼
Value	★★★⟩
Grapes	chardonnay
Region	Adelaide Hills, SA
Cellar	▮ 3
Alc./Vol.	14.0%
RRP	$38.00

Simon Gilbert Chardonnay

Quality	▼▼▼▼
Value	★★★★⑁
Grapes	chardonnay
Region	Central Ranges, NSW
Cellar	◧ 2
Alc./Vol.	13.5%
RRP	$15.00 ⊗

This is a public company located in Mudgee. Management was taken over in mid-2004 by a group of ex-Southcorp bods, including Bruce Kemp, Paul Pacino and David Combe. Andrew Ewart (ex-Mountadam) is chief winemaker. CURRENT RELEASE 2003 Nice wine. It's a fairly straightforward, pure-fruited wine which tastes of melon and citrus and is very clean and correct, with little evidence of oak. The finish is crisp, fresh and long, and it's pleasingly vibrant on the tongue. Not a complex wine, but a good drink, especially with whole baked snapper.

Sirromet Seven Scenes Chardonnay

Quality	▼▼▼▼
Value	★★★
Grapes	chardonnay
Region	Granite Belt & South Burnett, Qld
Cellar	◧ 2
Alc./Vol.	13.5%
RRP	$26.00

Chardonnay grows just about everywhere in Australia, from cool Tasmania and the Alpine slopes of Victoria, through to the torrid Riverina and subtropical Queensland. And it can produce a passable drop in most places, something that can't be said for many other grape varieties. Sirromet is one of Queensland's best known. CURRENT RELEASE 2003 Smoky oak plays a notable role in this chardonnay, but it stops short of taking over completely. There are slightly feral hints too, and a core of stone-fruit and melony flavour. The palate is smooth and complex with a drying finish. Overall it's a pretty good effort, with plenty of flavour and good general appeal. Try it with sautéed chicken in white wine.

Stonier KBS Vineyard Chardonnay

Quality	▼▼▼▼⑁
Value	★★★
Grapes	chardonnay
Region	Mornington Peninsula, Vic.
Cellar	◧ 2
Alc./Vol.	14.0%
RRP	$55.00

The KBS Vineyard takes its name from (Kenneth) Brian Stonier, the man behind this very good Mornington Peninsula establishment. In common with many other wineries in the region, they put a lot of effort into pinot noir, but chardonnay is consistently their best wine. CURRENT RELEASE 2002 A more 'worked' type of Stonier Chardonnay, made as a flagship by former winemaker Tod Dexter before he handed over the reins to Geraldine McFaul. Complexity is the thing, with a very rich bouquet that has smoky aromas of cassata, butterscotch and candied fig, along with a wild feral note. In the mouth it's rich and full with smooth, complex, persistent flavour and fine acidity to keep it on track. A big chardonnay to serve with salmon.

Stonier Reserve Chardonnay

This is Stonier's signature wine, a lush type of chardonnay that sums up the best of the Mornington Peninsula. Longtime winemaker Tod Dexter left a couple of years ago, with his assistant Geraldine McFaul taking over as a very able successor.

CURRENT RELEASE 2003 Not as rich or buttery as the '02 wine, this heads in a more elegant direction. It smells of citrus, stewed apple, subtle spicy oak, and a hint of toffee. The palate is smooth and fine without quite the same measure of overt creaminess found in most Stonier Reserves. It has great texture, medium body and fine flavour that lasts long and fragrant. A classy wine that suits grilled lobster well.

Quality	🍷🍷🍷🍷🍷
Value	★★★½
Grapes	chardonnay
Region	Mornington Peninsula, Vic.
Cellar	🍾 3+
Alc./Vol.	14.0%
RRP	$39.00

Tatachilla Keystone Chardonnay

A keystone is the stone that sits at the top of a stone archway, and locks all the other stones securely in place. Nothing to do with bumbling cops in silent movies. Maker: Fanchon Ferrandi.

CURRENT RELEASE 2004 It's a light, straightforward and rather basic chardonnay with buttery, malt and butterscotch malo overtones dominating the bouquet. It's lean and fairly light on the palate, clean and dry at the finish and balanced to go with food. A subtle chardonnay that would go with cold smoked chicken.

Quality	🍷🍷🍷🍷
Value	★★★½
Grapes	chardonnay
Region	McLaren Vale, SA
Cellar	🍾 2
Alc./Vol.	14.0%
RRP	$18.00 [$] 🌀

Taylors Jaraman Chardonnay

Jaraman is the relatively new Taylors brand that plugs the price gap between the well-known regular Clare Valley wines and the top-end St Andrews bottlings. Some of the wines include fruit shipped in from other regions. Winemaker: Adam Eggins.

CURRENT RELEASE 2003 This is developing quickly: the colour is deep yellow already and the bouquet has acquired the marzipan and roasted-hazelnut characters of an aged chardonnay, tending towards a hint of rubber. There are suggestions of barrel-ferment and stirred-lees characters. The palate is rich and smooth, with excellent texture and finishes clean, dry and satisfying. It suits chicken satays.

Quality	🍷🍷🍷🍷
Value	★★★★
Grapes	chardonnay
Region	Clare Valley & Adelaide Hills, SA
Cellar	🍾 2
Alc./Vol.	13.5%
RRP	$23.00 [$] 🌀

Terra Felix Chardonnay

Quality	♥ ♥ ♥ ♥
Value	★ ★ ★ ★ ⅓
Grapes	chardonnay
Region	Goulburn Valley, Vic.
Cellar	↓ 3
Alc./Vol.	13.0%
RRP	$15.00 ⅊

The Terra Felix samples arrived with a press release (usual) and a music CD (unusual). The latter was a band called The Cat Empire, in which the front man is Felix Riebl, son of the winery's founder and owner Luis Riebl. It sort of makes sense . . .

CURRENT RELEASE 2004   This is a well-priced, affordable chardonnay with modest aspirations, but which over-delivers. It's a straightforward, possibly unwooded style that exudes nectarine and peach in a pristine fruit-driven, easy-drinking style. It's delicate, lean and uncomplicated. The finish is clean and dry with crispness and balance. It would go with nicoise salad. (The music's good, too!)

Tisdall Chardonnay

Quality	♥ ♥ ♥ ♥
Value	★ ★ ★ ★
Grapes	chardonnay
Region	Goulburn Valley, Vic.
Cellar	↓ 1
Alc./Vol.	13.0%
RRP	$15.50 Ⓢ ⅊

The vineyard that's behind this brand is Rosbercon, a large spread at Picola, near Echuca. It was first planted by Dr Peter Tisdall and in those days the winemakers were John Ellis, of Hanging Rock fame, and Jeff Clarke, now chief winemaker of Montana in New Zealand.

CURRENT RELEASE 2003   Showing some age-development already, this wine is full yellow in colour and has a resiny kind of toasty bouquet that could be due to stressed vines. The palate is quite big and heavy, a touch clumsy, with a little sweetness which puts it firmly in the commercial category. It's a decent chardonnay at a very fair price. Try it with chicken burgers.

Toolangi Reserve Chardonnay

Quality	♥ ♥ ♥ ♥ ♥
Value	★ ★ ★ ★
Grapes	chardonnay
Region	Yarra Valley, Vic.
Cellar	↓ 3+
Alc./Vol.	14.0%
RRP	$62.00

The grapes were grown on the Toolangi estate at Dixons Creek, supplemented by a Coldstream grower, and the wine made by Rick Kinzbrunner of Giaconda fame. The vineyard is owned by Gary and Julie Hounsell, whose vines are only young, but Toolangi is off to a flying start.

CURRENT RELEASE 2003   A very complex, burgundy-style wine with layers of barrel-ferment and stylish fruit flavours. It opens fairly shyly, with barley-sugar and brackeny notes, then unfolds nougat, citrus/grapefruit, vanilla and oatmeal characters, the oak nicely harmonised. The palate is lean and elegant and builds richness as the wine warms in the glass. The finish is clean, dry and more-ish. You'll find yourself drinking the whole bottle! Serve with roast chicken.

Toolangi Yarra Valley Chardonnay

This is the cheapest of three Toolangi chardonnays, the
Reserve being made by Rick Kinzbrunner, the other two by
Tom Carson of Yering Station. This is the second vintage
for Toolangi and adds to an enviable early reputation. The
grapes for this wine all came from a grower at Coldstream.
CURRENT RELEASE 2003   A lightly oaked, subtle youngster
with relatively straightforward fruit but also significant
charm. There's a hint of gaminess together with peach/
stone-fruit flavours, and a suggestion of sweetness at the
finish. It's well balanced and eminently drinkable. It would
suit Chinese eggs fu-yung.

Quality	♟♟♟♟
Value	★★★⚁
Grapes	chardonnay
Region	Yarra Valley, Vic.
Cellar	🍷 2
Alc./Vol.	13.5%
RRP	$20.00

Trentham Murphy's Lore Chardonnay

Murphy's Law is what comes into play when a less-than-
optimistic Australian accepts the dictum 'Whatever can
go wrong, will'. The Murphy family's winery is successful,
contrary to Murphy's Law.
CURRENT RELEASE 2004   The colour is medium yellow
indicating fairly forward development; the wine has
peachy/stone-fruit aromas and it's light, simple and fresh
to taste. It has a tickle of residual sugar but also lots of rich,
ripe flavour. A crowd-pleaser. Drink up soon, perhaps with
fish and chips.

Quality	♟♟♟♟
Value	★★★★
Grapes	chardonnay
Region	Riverland, Vic.
Cellar	🍷 1
Alc./Vol.	13.0%
RRP	$11.00 Ⓢ ⛉

Two Rivers Wild Fire Unwooded Chardonnay

Unwooded chardonnay can be okay but you need to have
it young. Most makers use lesser-quality grapes, and such
wines invariably reach their peak within a few months of
bottling and then start their gradual, inexorable decline.
CURRENT RELEASE 2004   This has some dusty, earthy
aromas as well as green-apple, and the appley flavours
are also found on the palate coupled with noticeable
sweetness. It has that purity and simplicity of flavour that
comes with the unwooded territory. It's a clean, well-made
wine, to have with a cold seafood platter.

Quality	♟♟♟
Value	★★★★
Grapes	chardonnay
Region	Hunter Valley, NSW
Cellar	🍷 1
Alc./Vol.	13.0%
RRP	$14.40 Ⓢ ⛉

Wirra Wirra Adelaide Hills Chardonnay

Quality	🍷🍷🍷🍷
Value	✶✶✶
Grapes	chardonnay
Region	Adelaide Hills, SA
Cellar	🍾 2
Alc./Vol.	13.0%
RRP	$28.00 ⊜

Wirra Wirra lost its founder, the irrepressible Greg Trott, recently. Back in 1969 the Trott cousins, Greg and Roger, restored the old winery and over subsequent years built it into one of McLaren Vale's best-known names.
CURRENT RELEASE 2004   A well-proportioned chardonnay, Wirra Wirra's brightly coloured '03 smells attractively of fig syrup, stone fruit, minerals and subtle, nutty, spicy oak. In the mouth it's smooth and round with excellent fruit/oak balance and good length of clean flavour. The finish is soft and creamy, yet it has a crisp tang. Try it with pan-fried fish.

Yabby Lake Vineyard Chardonnay

Quality	🍷🍷🍷🍷🍷
Value	✶✶✶✶
Grapes	chardonnay
Region	Mornington Peninsula, Vic.
Cellar	🍾 2
Alc./Vol.	14.5%
RRP	$38.50

This no-expense-spared vineyard project of Robert and Mem Kirby arrived spectacularly last year with a pair of superb wines. The Pinot Noir carried off the *Guide*'s Best Red Wine award, and the Chardonnay wasn't far behind. The '03 Chardonnay continues in the same tradition. Maker: Larry McKenna.
CURRENT RELEASE 2003   A complex flagship chardonnay for the Mornington Peninsula, this brightly coloured wine shows less development than the precocious '02 at the same stage, but it is already well out of the throes of youth. It's a delicious drink that looks to Burgundy for inspiration. Nose and palate have super-complex mealy, buttery and roasted-nut characters, and there's full body and lovely richness. The seamless nose and palate combined with its length and intensity make it a joy to sip. Perfect with lobster in a creamy sauce.

Yalumba Oxford Landing Chardonnay

Quality	🍷🍷🍷
Value	✶✶✶✶
Grapes	chardonnay
Region	Murray Valley, SA
Cellar	🍾 1
Alc./Vol.	13.5%
RRP	$10.80 Ⓢ

Oxford Landing is an actual place, unlike the fabricated quirky names borne by some modern Australian wines. It's a spot in the vast vineyard lands of the Murray River in South Australia.
CURRENT RELEASE 2004   This is exactly what one should expect in a $10 chardonnay. A sunshiny tropical-fruit nose, some melony varietal cues, a light lick of oak, all of it direct and uncomplicated. The ripe, soft palate has plenty of flavour at the price, and a crisp finish. A good party wine.

Yering Station Chardonnay

This is Yering Station's standard chardonnay. We've watched it step up a notch over recent years, evolving into a more complex, serious wine than before. The price makes it a great buy.
CURRENT RELEASE 2004   This has good colour for a young chardonnay, straw with a slight greenish touch. Thankfully it has none of the golden tones that ring warning bells for us when we see them in one-year-old Yarra Valley wine. The nose is smart too, with green-melon varietal notes, touches of cashew and minerals, a slight earthy, Frenchy pong, and a veneer of subtle dusty oak. In the mouth it has smooth ripe flavour that's succulent and long, middling body and a dry finish. Well-made Yarra chardonnay at a fair price. Try it with ocean trout risotto.

Quality	♀ ♀ ♀ ♀ ¦
Value	★ ★ ★ ★ ¦
Grapes	chardonnay
Region	Yarra Valley, Vic.
Cellar	▮ 3
Alc./Vol.	13.0%
RRP	$20.50 ⊜

Zilzie Unwooded Chardonnay

If the secret of successful wine marketing is a distinctive brand name, we reckon this should be a tearaway. Zilzie apparently has something to do with 'home turf' in Scotland, origin of the owning Forbes family. Bob Shields is chief winemaker.
CURRENT RELEASE 2004   The nose is typical of young, unoaked chardonnay: fresh cashew nuts and peaches galore. It's simple, grapey and not entirely dry, but the sweetness is countered by some sprightly acidity. There isn't much finesse in the wine but it is good value, especially as it's often discounted.

Quality	♀ ♀ ♀
Value	★ ★ ★ ★
Grapes	chardonnay
Region	Riverland, Vic.
Cellar	▮ 1
Alc./Vol.	12.5%
RRP	$16.00 Ⓢ ⊜

Pinot Gris and Pinot Grigio

There are two broad style groups with this grape: the rich, spicy, high-alcohol Alsace pinot gris style and the earlier-harvested, lower alcohol, more delicate Italian pinot grigio style. The Alsace style is often slightly sweet and balance becomes a debating point. The Italian style is often the more approachable, with better drinkability and food compatibility. We like both, when they're well done! Australia has embraced this grape with gusto and so have our export markets. While many examples tend towards weak and bland, some have real character and individuality. We consider a faint pink colouring acceptable, as long as it's not the result of oxidation but because of the grape's skin colour.

Bay of Fires Tigress Pinot Gris

Quality	🍷🍷🍷🍷½
Value	★★★★
Grapes	pinot gris
Region	various, Tas.
Cellar	🍾 2
Alc./Vol.	13.0%
RRP	$26.00 [$] 🌀

Aussie pinot gris/grigio is mostly pretty bland and simple, and more often than not, it's a sugar-coated pill, with obvious residual sugar. Tassie has the potential to make superior PG, and Fran Austin at Bay of Fires is doing a sterling job.

CURRENT RELEASE 2004 A worthy follow-up to the very good '03, this Tasmanian is one of the better PGs around. Bready/estery, lightly spiced, stone-fruit aromas lead into a palate that has more richness than most. It's fresh and juicy, finishing with excellent balance and drinkability. Best drunk young, it goes well with chicken pie.

Dal Zotto Pinot Grigio

Quality	🍷🍷🍷🍷
Value	★★★½
Grapes	pinot gris
Region	King Valley, Vic.
Cellar	🍾 2
Alc./Vol.	12.5%
RRP	$21.00 🌀

It's fascinating to observe the multitude of approaches to this grape variety across Australia. Some try to ape the Italian style (of Friuli and Trentino) while others shoot for the richer Alsace style. A certain amount of manipulation is often apparent in order to coax the grapes into the desired style. This one certainly fits the Italian model.

CURRENT RELEASE 2004 Grigio style is correct, here: the wine has a cured meadow-hay aroma, some hints of blond tobacco, and is quite oxidative in style – not unlike some Italian examples we've seen. It's light-bodied and a touch broad on the palate, finishing with some sweetness. A curious wine, not very delicate, but full of interest and could take a decent chill. Try it with antipasto.

Holly's Garden Whitlands Pinot Gris

Bruce Dowding previously owned Rochford in the Macedon Ranges. Holly's Garden is one of his new brands, based on a vineyard planted at Whitlands by Rachael Croucher. At 850 metres altitude, the pinot gris is harvested in May – at amazing numbers: 16 degrees Baumé of sugar, 3.2 pH and 9 grams per litre of acid. CURRENT RELEASE 2004   This is a challenging wine that resists pigeonholing. Confectionery-like aromas remind of bubblegum with a subtle complexing hint of oak from barrel-fermentation. It finishes with a touch of residual sugar and a certain hardness from the combination of high acidity and alcohol. Not a subtle wine, but generously proportioned, it jars a little on the palate. It will be interesting to watch the development of this style. Try it with white-mould cheeses.

Quality	♥ ♥ ♥ ♥
Value	★ ★ ★ ⁀
Grapes	pinot gris
Region	King Valley, Vic.
Cellar	🍾 2+
Alc./Vol.	15.5%
RRP	$25.00 ⑤

Miceli Iolanda Pinot Grigio

When is a gris more like a grigio, and vice versa? The grigio name suggests it's in the more delicate, lean, Italian style. Or is it just that the Micelis are of Italian extraction? CURRENT RELEASE 2003   This is a lovely PG, whatever you want the G to stand for. It has an exotic, honeyed side to its considerable personality, and what a technocrat might call 'solidsy' character. The palate is lively, zesty and juicy with a clean, lingering finish. It has a fair bit more depth and flavour interest than most PGs and goes well with spicy Szechuan Chinese food.

Quality	♥ ♥ ♥ ♥ ♥
Value	★ ★ ★ ★ ⁀
Grapes	pinot gris
Region	Mornington Peninsula, Vic.
Cellar	🍾 2+
Alc./Vol.	13.5%
RRP	$20.00 ⑤

Seppelt Coborra Pinot Gris

Seppelt's Drumborg vineyard, near Portland in southern Victoria, has been producing pinot gris since 1997. This first release is named after the Coborra State Forest, next door to the vineyard.
CURRENT RELEASE 2004   This is one of those white wines that grows on you, especially sipped over a leisurely meal. It has good varietal personality reminiscent of honey, flowers and marzipan with a minerally aspect. There's also a whiff of sulphur that might disturb some people, but those accustomed to European pinot gris won't worry too much. The palate is smooth, yet it has structure and a very dry, firm finish. Enjoy it with Thai fish cakes.

Quality	♥ ♥ ♥ ♥
Value	★ ★ ★
Grapes	pinot gris
Region	Drumborg, Vic.
Cellar	🍾 3
Alc./Vol.	13.0%
RRP	$25.00 ⑤

Stefano Lubiana Pinot Grigio

Quality	▼▼▼▼
Value	★★★
Grapes	pinot gris
Region	Derwent Valley, Tas.
Cellar	▯ 2
Alc./Vol.	13.0%
RRP	$27.00 ⬲

Steve Lubiana cut his winemaking teeth at his parents' Riverland winery. His move to the Hobart region of southern Tasmania was quite a radical step at the time. A more different kind of viticultural environment would be hard to imagine.

CURRENT RELEASE 2004 Definitely one of the better pinot gris/grigio styles we've seen lately. The wine is clean and fresh, smelling of talcum powder and bready/yeast esters, while the palate is lively and properly dry, with some persistence and good refreshing acidity. It's smooth and nicely textured. It has more intensity than most PGs doing the rounds. It would go well with oven-baked snapper.

Wellington Pinot Grigio

Quality	▼▼▼▼
Value	★★★⭐
Grapes	pinot gris
Region	northern Tas.
Cellar	▯ 2
Alc./Vol.	13.0%
RRP	$22.00 ⬲

Along with parts of southern Victoria, northern Tasmania is being mooted as a great place to grow pinot grigio. In both cases we've had a number of disappointments, but Andrew Hood does a good job with his Wellington version.

CURRENT RELEASE 2004 This food-friendly pinot grigio is much better than most of its peers. It has an appetising and quite complex nose that's reminiscent of pears, spices, honey and banana, with a flinty touch underneath. In the mouth it has a smooth, soft middle with a mouth-watering fruit/acid balance that makes it very appealing. The finish is very dry. Try it with onion quiche.

Riesling

Riesling was once *the* prestige Australian white wine grape, until chardonnay arrived in the 1970s and became a formidable adversary. At the same time riesling suffered an identity crisis – some became sweeter, which confused everybody, and the word 'riesling' was misused more than ever to denote just about any cheap dry-ish white wine. Riesling's popularity fell with the consumer-friendly result that it became just about the best buy around. And unlike most chardonnay, there's no hurry to drink it; riesling ages superbly. Price tags are starting to climb, but we reckon that many Australian rieslings remain seriously undervalued, a great thing for all of us.

Angoves Vineyard Select Clare Valley Riesling

Angoves' Vineyard Select range is based on classic regional styles of South Australia. Clare Valley Riesling naturally fits the bill.
CURRENT RELEASE 2004   This has quite deep colour for an '04, a pale yellow–green of some concentration. The rich nose has aromas of stewed apple, lime-juice cordial, fresh citrus and light spice. In the mouth it's dry and richly flavoured with quite a full and relatively viscous texture. Maybe it lacks a little finesse compared to the best Clare rieslings, but it has plenty of weight and flavour for the price. Serve it with Vietnamese lemon-grass chicken.

Quality	♟ ♟ ♟ ♟
Value	★ ★ ★ ★
Grapes	riesling
Region	Clare Valley, SA
Cellar	▮ 2
Alc./Vol.	12.5%
RRP	$17.00 Ⓢ 🍶

Annie's Lane Riesling

The Annie's Lane wines are based on the excellent Clare vineyards that once provided the fabled Quelltaler rieslings. They continue the tradition.
CURRENT RELEASE 2004   The classical interplay between ripe fruit and steely austerity gets a good showing here. Greenish in colour, it has a pure, intense aroma of apple, lime and dry spices. The palate is smooth with good depth, textural interest and flavour development. Deceptively harmonious and easy to drink now, it also has the structure to develop. Try it with mixed vegetable tempura.

Quality	♟ ♟ ♟ ♟ ♟
Value	★ ★ ★ ★
Grapes	riesling
Region	Clare Valley, SA
Cellar	▮ 5+
Alc./Vol.	11.5%
RRP	$17.75 🍶

Bay of Fires Tasmania Riesling

Quality 🍷🍷🍷🍷🍷
Value ★★★★
Grapes riesling
Region Tamar Valley, Tas.
Cellar 🍾 10
Alc./Vol. 12.0%
RRP $29.00 [$] 🔩

Bay of Fires is the Hardys winery in Tasmania, and the second label is Tigress. The 2004 wines point towards this being a high-acid year with some botrytis influence, a year that encouraged the leaving of a little judicious residual sugar in riesling.

CURRENT RELEASE 2004 The colour is pale and the aromas are a restrained mixture of mineral and nettley herbal nuances. The tart green fruit characters continue on the palate, where the wine is crisp and clean with some sweetness balancing the mouth-watering acidity. It's somewhere between Trocken and Kabinett on the German scale. A good wine to serve with Thai fish cakes.

Bellarmine Pemberton Dry Riesling

Quality 🍷🍷🍷🍷
Value ★★★★½
Grapes riesling
Region Pemberton, WA
Cellar 🍾 6+
Alc./Vol. 12.0%
RRP $15.00 🔩 (cellar door)

This is a promising new producer in the Pemberton–Manjimup region, with a commitment to very classic and age-worthy wine styles, if their first releases are any guide. Maker: Mike Bewsher.

CURRENT RELEASE 2004 The colour is very pale and almost colourless; the nose is minerally and herbal and has a twist of sulphur. The palate is very delicate, restrained and taut. It's a cellaring style of riesling, and not really 'commercial' or of broad appeal. And it's cheap! Serve with any seafood, especially oysters.

Bellarmine Pemberton Riesling

Quality 🍷🍷🍷🍷
Value ★★★★½
Grapes riesling
Region Pemberton, WA
Cellar 🍾 6+
Alc./Vol. 11.5%
RRP $15.00 🔩 (cellar door)

The Bellarmine labels are seriously different and interesting: each one carries a charcoal rubbing as its centrepiece, and each design is taken from ancient architectural features in the German wine regions.

CURRENT RELEASE 2004 This wine is very similar to the dry version except for its sweetness – which is very minor and more like a German Trocken than a Kabinett. It's a touch neutral, again sulphury and minerally, but has a little honey and floral flavour in the palate, which also carries a little residual sweetness. It could turn out very well with some bottle-age. It goes with Thai fish cakes.

Brown Brothers Victoria Riesling

It's surprising this wine doesn't have the King Valley designation. There is plenty of riesling grown in the district; but then, we're not privy to how much of this wine they make every year. Like many of Brown Brothers' activities, it could be a lot bigger than it seems!
CURRENT RELEASE 2004   There's a touch of reductive character at first, then some floral and straw aromas. The palate is soft and full-ish, and perhaps a touch broad, but it is a commercial style at a very affordable price. It's gentle, fruity, soft and accessible, with a pleasing touch of richness. Good easy-drinking riesling to partner with fish soup.

Quality	⬤⬤⬤⬤
Value	★★★★
Grapes	riesling
Region	various, Vic.
Cellar	3+
Alc./Vol.	12.0%
RRP	$14.40 (cellar door)

Chain of Ponds Purple Patch Riesling

This wine takes its name from the purple patch of *Echium plantagineum L.* that grows around the Chain of Ponds riesling vineyard. This purple flowered plant is damned by rural Australians as Paterson's curse, but it certainly adds colour to a rural landscape. Maker: Neville Falkenberg.
CURRENT RELEASE 2004   A minerally thread through this young riesling is emphasised by some slightly reductive aromas, but there are also intense lime and apple fruit aromas. The clean, dry palate has good intensity and persistence with a tight framework of lemony acidity. A good match for fried whitebait.

Quality	⬤⬤⬤⬤
Value	★★★
Grapes	riesling
Region	Adelaide Hills, SA
Cellar	4
Alc./Vol.	12.0%
RRP	$19.95

Cheviot Bridge Riesling

Victoria's Yea Valley isn't one of our best-known places for riesling. It's really still an emerging area, feeling its way with many grape varieties. The signs are, though, that riesling is a success already.
CURRENT RELEASE 2004   A pale young riesling with a delicate floral perfume, an appetising aroma of apple sauce, as well as more traditional lime and mineral varietal cues. In the mouth it has good intensity and richness with smooth easy texture. A whisper of mid-palate sweetness is balanced by firm acidity. An adventurous match with a rocket, pear and blue-cheese salad.

Quality	⬤⬤⬤⬤
Value	★★★
Grapes	riesling
Region	Yea Valley, Vic.
Cellar	4
Alc./Vol.	12.5%
RRP	$20.00 Ⓢ

Chrismont Riesling

Quality	♥♥♥♥♥
Value	★★★★★
Grapes	riesling
Region	King Valley, Vic.
Cellar	▮ 5
Alc./Vol.	12.5%
RRP	$15.00 ⬛

Arnie Pizzini planted his first plot of riesling vines in the King Valley in the 1980s. The wines he produces from them showcase the region's great suitability for the variety.
CURRENT RELEASE 2004   A pale, straw-coloured young riesling with a shy nose of lime and delicate blossom-like floral notes. A little touch of sulphur isn't too intrusive, and should disappear with time. The palate is clean and intense with long, dry varietal flavour and lemony acidity. It should develop in richness and interest with some age. A good style to match tempura.

Cookoothama Riesling

Quality	♥♥♥♥
Value	★★★⋆
Grapes	riesling
Region	King Valley, Vic.
Cellar	▮ 3
Alc./Vol.	12.5%
RRP	$14.95 ⬛

Although originally based in the Riverina, Cookoothama now sources fruit from its large vineyard in Victoria's King Valley. The King Valley is proving a good source of quality riesling, both under the Cookoothama label and others.
CURRENT RELEASE 2004   Brilliant straw-green colour is promising here, and the nose has straightforward varietal aroma suggesting lime juice, herbs and florals. There's also the whiff of sulphur you sometimes see in young rieslings like this, but it's no big problem. The palate is intense and lip-smacking with bracing acidity giving a sherbet-like tang. Try it with sushi.

Crawford River Riesling

Quality	♥♥♥♥♥
Value	★★★
Grapes	riesling
Region	Henty, Vic.
Cellar	▮ 7
Alc./Vol.	12.0%
RRP	$30.50 ⬛

This isolated patch of viticulture is at Condah in Victoria's south-west. The Thomson family (not to be confused with the Thomsons of Great Western) make excellent riesling in this sometimes chilly corner of the country.
CURRENT RELEASE 2004   This has an exotic perfume of flowers and cosmetics with stone-fruit and citrus aromas mixed in. The palate is delicately flavoured and fine, but rich in an understated sort of way with good length and a zesty, fruit-fragrant finish. Serve it with Thai duck salad.

Dal Zotto Riesling

We reckon winemaker and proprietor Otto Dal Zotto has a very marketable name. His son Michael has joined him lately as assistant winemaker. The family has 40 hectares of vines at Cheshunt and Whitfield, both at the upper end of the King Valley.

CURRENT RELEASE 2004 The colour is pale and the wine is nicely restrained overall. There are some slightly oddball pineapple, passionfruit and orange/citrus aromas, while the palate has some juiciness due to subtle sweetness which doesn't quite balance the slightly sour acidity. We're not sure where this style is headed, but it looks to have cellaring potential. It would suit crab salad with a citrus dressing.

Quality	🍷🍷🍷½
Value	★★★★
Grapes	riesling
Region	King Valley, Vic.
Cellar	🍾 4+
Alc./Vol.	12.0%
RRP	$17.00 🔩

De Bortoli Windy Peak Victoria Riesling

Windy Peak is a broad-catchment label that is made in the company's Yarra Valley winery, from grapes grown in several Victorian regions. Makers: Steve Webber and team.

CURRENT RELEASE 2004 This is an exaggerated style of riesling which has an almost lime-essence or cordial aroma, overlaid by a whiff of sulphur in its youth. There are sweaty and passionfruit aromas which come through on the palate as well. There's a twist of sweetness that makes it almost exotically juicy. It's tight and lean in the mouth and actually tastes pretty good. Serve with duck à l'orange.

Quality	🍷🍷🍷½
Value	★★★★
Grapes	riesling
Region	various, Vic.
Cellar	🍾 4
Alc./Vol.	12.0%
RRP	$14.00 [$] 🔩

Delatite Riesling

Delatite is a low-profile winery: it keeps on doing good things – especially riesling – without ever making a fuss. Vivienne Ritchie, mum of winemaker Rosie, who co-founded the vineyard with husband Robert Ritchie, retired during 2004.

CURRENT RELEASE 2004 This is an outstanding riesling in typical Delatite style. It has a very light colour and smells of slate and minerals without much floral perfume, while the palate is tight and dry and refined – almost austere. Without food, it is a touch forbidding. With fish, it's transformed, and is very fine, crisp and intense: a great food wine with great cellaring potential. Serve it with any white-fleshed fish.

Quality	🍷🍷🍷🍷🍷
Value	★★★★★
Grapes	riesling
Region	Mansfield, Vic.
Cellar	🍾 10+
Alc./Vol.	11.5%
RRP	$20.00 🔩

PENGUIN BEST RIESLING

Frankland Estate Isolation Ridge Riesling

Quality	♛♛♛♛♛
Value	★★★★★
Grapes	riesling
Region	Great Southern, WA
Cellar	▮ 10+
Alc./Vol.	13.0%
RRP	$23.00 🥂

Frankland Estate produces three individual vineyard rieslings, from different soil types; the others being Poison Hill and Cooladerra. We thought this was the best of the 2004 trio. It's from their own vineyard. Maker: Barrie Smith.

CURRENT RELEASE 2004   Delicate restrained riesling at its best. Slatey, minerally, dry-straw aromas lead the way in this restrained wine which promises to develop slowly and retain its finesse. The palate flavours are concentrated and long, and the texture is fine and seamless; all components are beautifully harmonised. It would go well with yabbie salad.

Garlands Riesling

Quality	♛♛♛♛♛
Value	★★★★★
Grapes	riesling
Region	Mount Barker, WA
Cellar	➡-1–5
Alc./Vol.	12.0%
RRP	$17.00

The Mount Barker–Frankland River end of Western Australia is excellent riesling country. Garland's effort is very good, and it has a price tag that makes it a bargain.

CURRENT RELEASE 2004   This has a greenish flash to its pale colour – a true high-quality riesling look. The aroma is clean and pristine with delicate, crisp notes of florals and lime juice. A touch of underlying steel backs it up. In the mouth it's clean-tasting and persistent, with a whisper of fruit sweetness in the middle adding a dimension of richness. Zippy acidity and a fragrant aftertaste complete the picture. It should improve with a few years in bottle. Try it with grilled fresh garfish.

Geoff Weaver Riesling

Quality	♛♛♛♛♛
Value	★★★★
Grapes	riesling
Region	Adelaide Hills, SA
Cellar	➡-1–10
Alc./Vol.	12.5%
RRP	$23.80 🥂

Geoff Weaver's Lenswood rieslings are outstanding examples of regional style. Not only does Geoff make wine, he also paints pictures. The lovely pastoral landscape that graces these elegant labels is one of his.

CURRENT RELEASE 2004   Geoff Weaver riesling at its zesty best. Lime juice, green apple, slate and steel mark the nose, giving a fresh spring-like impression. In the mouth it's clean and dry with great purity of varietal flavour, serious depth and length, and some minerally austerity on the finish. It's attractive now with great balance and intensity, but really it needs time to evolve and show its best. Serve it with Thai grilled chicken salad.

Gilberts Mount Barker Riesling

Gilberts is an understated, homey operation that seems to encapsulate the differences between the modest scale of things at Mount Barker, compared to the slick scene of Margaret River and other more hyped wine regions. It's a charming place, and riesling is a regional speciality.

CURRENT RELEASE 2003 In among the 2004 rieslings this '03 wine shows a little more development, but it's still a pup in the bigger scheme of things, and Mount Barker rieslings do age very well. The nose has delicate pear, apple, lime and steely aromas that are understated and refined. The palate is minerally, savoury and dry with a long clean finish. Serve it with sushi.

Quality	4½ glasses
Value	★★★★
Grapes	riesling
Region	Mount Barker, WA
Cellar	6+
Alc./Vol.	11.8%
RRP	$19.00

Goundrey Homestead Riesling

Goundrey's Homestead range are sharply priced young wines from the south-west of Western Australia. Quality can be miles better than the modest price tag might suggest.

CURRENT RELEASE 2004 For a modestly priced riesling, this is an interesting wine. The nose is quite powerful with a surprising hint of Germanic spice, a touch of sulphur, and some steely minerality. There are green-apple, herb and lime-like fruit aromas too. In the mouth it's not as dry as most Mount Barker rieslings. A whisper of residual sugar fills it out, finishing with tingling acidity. Good value, especially when it's discounted below the $15 full retail price. Serve it with chicken and mango salad.

Quality	3½ glasses
Value	★★★★
Grapes	riesling
Region	90% Mount Barker; 10% Porongurups, WA
Cellar	2
Alc./Vol.	12.5%
RRP	$15.00 ($)

Grant Burge Thorn Riesling

Grant Burge has great riesling 'cred' and the moderate pricing is a bonus. This Eden Valley wine shows classical regional qualities.

CURRENT RELEASE 2004 This has a brilliant greenish colour and a pure, fresh nose that's reminiscent of lime juice, spices and mint. In the mouth there are crisp lemon and lime-like flavours of good intensity and real depth, finishing dry and zesty. Try it with sushi.

Quality	4½ glasses
Value	★★★★½
Grapes	riesling
Region	Eden Valley, SA
Cellar	5
Alc./Vol.	11.5%
RRP	$16.50 ($)

Heggies Museum Reserve Riesling

Quality	🍷🍷🍷🍷🍷
Value	★★★★★
Grapes	riesling
Region	Eden Valley, SA
Cellar	🍾 4+
Alc./Vol.	13.0%
RRP	$27.00 🌀

For the first time, Yalumba has released a six-year-old reserve riesling from Heggies, as they've been doing for several years with Pewsey Vale. Great idea! Great wines! Let's hope it's ongoing. Maker: Louisa Rose.

CURRENT RELEASE 1999 The wine is glowing deep yellow, and has a very rich, mellow aged bouquet of buttered toast and a faint hint of kero. It's very fine on the palate, beautifully balanced and subtle, with long lingering flavour that's still quite fresh and refined, although there's no denying the classic aged characters. Taut structure, great length and finesse. Serve with something fishy.

Heggies Riesling

Quality	🍷🍷🍷🍷🍷
Value	★★★★½
Grapes	riesling
Region	Eden Valley, SA
Cellar	🍾 8+
Alc./Vol.	12.5%
RRP	$20.50 [$] 🌀

The 2004 South Australian summer had some very hot spells, and the Eden Valley seems to have weathered it better than Clare. Its rieslings are finer and less-forward, which reflects the slightly cooler Eden Valley climate.

CURRENT RELEASE 2004 This is a concentrated riesling which took some time to open up in the glass. It had a dusty aroma to begin and, as it warmed, it revealed lemon/citrus and herb/spice aromas, with a dab of honey: quite complex and inviting. There's a juicy quality to its palate, as well as a seamless fruitiness, good balance and persistence. Drink it with sautéed scallops and rocket salad.

Helm Premium Riesling

Quality	🍷🍷🍷🍷
Value	★★★
Grapes	riesling
Region	Canberra district, NSW
Cellar	🍾 6
Alc./Vol.	12.0%
RRP	$33.00 🌀

In 2004, Ken Helm decided to make a reserve riesling, although it's not called a reserve. His vineyard is at Murrumbateman, just outside the Australian Capital Territory – but then most of the Canberra region is outside the boundary. It's in New South Wales!

CURRENT RELEASE 2004 This is a cut above the regular Helm riesling, which is also a good wine. Clean, fresh, vibrant lemon-peel aromas with a green-edged limey aspect signal it's a cool-climate riesling. It's very intense in the mouth – lean, refined and crisply acidic, although it also manages to retain softness. Very cellarable, but you can drink it now with pan-fried fish.

Henschke Julius Riesling

Henschke is probably best known as a red wine company (Hill of Grace and Mount Edelstone tend to hog the limelight!) but its whites can also hit the heights – especially its rieslings (this and the Adelaide Hills wine, Green's Hill). Makers: Stephen Henschke and Michael Schreurs; viticulturist is Prue Henschke.

CURRENT RELEASE 2004   Pristine Eden Valley riesling! The colour is light yellow–green and the aroma is restrained, but expresses minerals, citrus and a touch of herb – as pure as the driven snow. The palate is very dry, lean and serious, bordering on the austere, with the finesse and structure to help it age while holding its tightness. It suits trout gravlax.

Quality	🍷🍷🍷🍷🍷
Value	★★★★★
Grapes	riesling
Region	Eden Valley, SA
Cellar	🍾 9+
Alc./Vol.	12.5%
RRP	$23.50

Houghton Museum Release Riesling

Houghton has done us a favour by cellaring some of its cool-grown southern Western Australian whites to maturity, giving them the time they so richly deserve. It's just a pity they didn't have screw-caps back then: there'd be fewer corked and oxidised bottles and they'd probably all be a bit fresher. The '95 has won three trophies and nine gold medals.

CURRENT RELEASE 1995   Deep golden yellow colour and a marvellous buttered-toasty bouquet show the maturity of this superb old riesling. The wine is concentrated and the fruit tastes ripe and healthy. It's slightly bigger than the '96, with a tickle of sweetness, rich toasty flavour of great length and harmony, and a clean dry finish. It deserves smoked salmon mousse.

Quality	🍷🍷🍷🍷🍷
Value	★★★★★
Grapes	riesling
Region	Frankland River, WA
Cellar	🍾 2
Alc./Vol.	13.0%
RRP	$26.00 $

CURRENT RELEASE 1996   With two golds to its credit, this is not quite as sublime as the '95 but is also delicious. It has a faint trace of paraffin together with buttered-toast complexity on the nose, and some lovely lime-citrus flavour, toasty maturity and excellent balance in the mouth. Thoroughly yummy. Try it with smoked trout pâté.

Quality	🍷🍷🍷🍷🍷
Value	★★★★★
Grapes	riesling
Region	Frankland River, WA
Cellar	🍾 2
Alc./Vol.	12.5%
RRP	$26.00 $

Howard Park Riesling

Quality	♛♛♛♛♛
Value	★★★★★
Grapes	riesling
Region	Great Southern, WA
Cellar	🍾 10
Alc./Vol.	12.5%
RRP	$25.00 ⚅

Mike Kerrigan is doing great things with Howard Park while maintaining the high standard of wines such as this riesling, which were already 'up there' before he arrived. The company has a winery in Margaret River as well as one at Denmark in the Great Southern. Luxury!
CURRENT RELEASE 2004   The colour is pale and the aromas recall passionfruit and other tropical aromas that take us straight to Western Australia when riesling is concerned. It's a restrained, young, tightly wound riesling that's tangy and long in the mouth, and promises much for the future. A pristine wine of great finesse – and it's not as forbiddingly tart as some vintages have been. Serve with snapper quenelles.

Jasper Hill Georgia's Paddock Riesling

Quality	♛♛♛♜
Value	★★★
Grapes	riesling
Region	Heathcote, Vic.
Cellar	🍾 2
Alc./Vol.	12.0%
RRP	$29.00

This vineyard's fame rests squarely on its shiraz-based reds, but the riesling can be excellent. In recent years the biodynamically managed, unirrigated vineyards have been especially vulnerable to the ongoing drought. Maker: Ron Laughton.
CURRENT RELEASE 2004   The colour is a little forward and the essency, lemon-juice aroma lacks a little vibrancy. The palate is rich, fruity, soft and a touch developed for its age; it's a trifle broad and lacks the traditional Jasper Hill finesse. Plenty of flavour, but it's probably not for keeping more than a couple more years. Try it with fish and chips.

Jim Barry The Lodge Hill Riesling

Quality	♛♛♛♛
Value	★★★★⌐
Grapes	riesling
Region	Clare Valley, SA
Cellar	🍾 8+
Alc./Vol.	13.0%
RRP	$20.00 Ⓢ ⚅

Jim Barry's Lodge Hill vineyard is on the northern side of Clare township, near Petaluma, Brian Barry and Knappstein's vineyards. Viticulturist is John Barry and winemaker is Mark Barry.
CURRENT RELEASE 2004   The colour is an encouraging very light yellow–green, while the aromas suggest minerals and earth with a struck-flint minerality and a slight hint of reduction. The palate is delicate, very dry and steely – the style of Lodge Hill– which the Barrys describe as their best-cellaring riesling. There are some bread-doughy esters, too. It has good depth of flavour and length, although it's a bit austere. We expect it to age well. As a youngster it would suit oysters.

Kirrihill Estates Riesling

Clare-based Kirrihill is one of the most ambitious new wineries in South Australia. Although less than 10 years old, it's already established a name for quality and reliability. Good vineyard sources – in the Adelaide Hills, and at Langhorne Creek as well as Clare – and the experienced hand of winemaker David Mavor combine well.

CURRENT RELEASE 2004 This is a fuller, richer type of Clare Valley riesling. It opens with lemonade, apple and lime-leaf aromas. The palate is smooth, and rich in texture and flavour with good substance and a long lemony finish. A substantial wine that drinks well in its youth. Try it with Thai chicken salad.

Quality 🍷🍷🍷🍷½
Value ★★★½
Grapes riesling
Region Clare Valley, SA
Cellar 4+
Alc./Vol. 12.8%
RRP $19.00

Knappstein Hand Picked Riesling

A few wineries, like Knappstein in the Clare Valley, make a big deal of 'hand picking' their grapes. The alternative of machine harvesting is supposed to give an inferior result. Maker: Paul Smith.

CURRENT RELEASE 2004 This is a bright-greenish straw colour, the typical appearance of good young riesling. On the nose there's a steely strength underneath, with lime and spicy hints in the mix, and there's a delicate floral overlay of real charm. In the mouth it's admirably concentrated and fuller than most rieslings, while retaining a clean tang. Try it with sashimi.

Quality 🍷🍷🍷🍷½
Value ★★★½
Grapes riesling
Region Clare Valley, SA
Cellar 6
Alc./Vol. 13.0%
RRP $20.00

Knappstein Single Vineyard Watervale Riesling

The grapes for this wine were grown on the Ackland Vineyard, which was planted at Watervale in 1969. Watervale has been the source of many of Australia's greatest rieslings.

CURRENT RELEASE 2004 This is a well-concentrated, pale greenish riesling with a nose of lime, spice, floral talc and dissolved minerals. It has essency varietal purity that leads to an intense mouthful with rich mid-palate flavours perfectly counterpointed by lemony/minerally acidity. Serve it with grilled garfish meuniere.

Quality 🍷🍷🍷🍷🍷
Value ★★★★
Grapes riesling
Region Clare Valley, SA
Cellar 6+
Alc./Vol. 13.0%
RRP $26.00

Leasingham Bin 7 Riesling

Quality	♥♥♥♥⁵
Value	★★★★★
Grapes	riesling
Region	Clare Valley, SA
Cellar	🍾 6+
Alc./Vol.	12.5%
RRP	$21.00 Ⓢ ⛾

This brand, which sits between the Leasingham Classic (released with about five years of bottle-age) and the Bastion, offers consistently great value for money. Leasingham has 314 hectares of vineyards in Clare. Winemakers are Kerri Thompson and Simon Cole. CURRENT RELEASE 2004 The colour is light, bright yellow and it has a delicious aroma of creamy citrus/lemon, herb and citron: squeaky clean and fresh. It's very lively in the mouth, with great refinement, delicacy and finesse. It drinks beautifully now but will repay cellaring, too. Serve it with salmon gravlax.

Leeuwin Estate Art Series Riesling

Quality	♥♥♥♥
Value	★★★⁺
Grapes	riesling
Region	Margaret River, WA
Cellar	🍾 4
Alc./Vol.	12.0%
RRP	$23.50 ⛾

Margaret River isn't a great riesling area; we tend to look towards the Great Southern for the WA benchmarks. But Leeuwin does a consistently good job with it. And we love the John Olsen frog label: it's worth buying just for that. CURRENT RELEASE 2004 The colour is just a little grey but the aroma is very floral, a touch slatey and mineral, while the palate is soft and slightly broad, lacking the tension and finesse of a great Aussie riesling. It does provide satisfying up-front flavour, while the acid sticks out a bit on the finish. It would go well with oily fish such as ocean trout.

Leo Buring Eden Valley Riesling

Quality	♥♥♥♥♥
Value	★★★★★
Grapes	riesling
Region	Eden Valley, SA
Cellar	🍾 6+
Alc./Vol.	13.0%
RRP	$18.00 Ⓢ ⛾

Leo Buring makes riesling from two regions: the Clare and Eden valleys. There are normally three releases, one from each area, plus a more expensive Leonay – the reserve label – that can be from either region, depending on which produced the best wines that year. Maker: Matt Pick. CURRENT RELEASE 2004 The Eden Valley is the finer, brighter and more vibrant of the two entry-level wines in '04. It has a fresh tangy mixed citrus peel aroma and is light but intense in the mouth. Flavours of lemon, lime and even grapefruit abound. It suits grilled Western Australian marron.

Mesh Riesling

Quality	🍷🍷🍷🍷🍷
Value	★★★★
Grapes	riesling
Region	Eden Valley, SA
Cellar	2–8
Alc./Vol.	13.0%
RRP	$27.00

Mesh is a collaboration between Robert Hill Smith of Yalumba and Jeffrey Grosset, two of Australia's leading riesling producers. The wine is made from Eden Valley riesling 50/50 in each winery, then blended.

CURRENT RELEASE 2004 An intense young riesling that was still all knees and elbows when we first tasted it. It really needs time to come together. That said, it looks promising in infancy. The nose has lime, lemon and guava aromas, with hints of spice and a slightly earthy reductive quality that we reckon will transform with age into a complex factor. The palate is rich with good fruit depth and a firm spine. Keep it for a few years, then serve it with sautéed scallops.

Mitchell Watervale Riesling

Quality	🍷🍷🍷🍷½
Value	★★★½
Grapes	riesling
Region	Clare Valley, SA
Cellar	1–8
Alc./Vol.	12.0%
RRP	$20.70

Mitchells were among the prime movers in getting most Clare Valley winemakers to switch from cork-sealed bottles to screw-caps. After some early hiccups, this now means that Clare riesling is one of Australia's most reliable white wines.

CURRENT RELEASE 2004 This has lime and apple-like varietal aromas that are nicely concentrated but not without delicacy. The last couple of vintages seem to have lost the sulphide, reductive problems that marked the transition to screw-cap a few years ago. The palate is full of rich fruit with excellent poise, and bracing acidity keeps it fresh and zippy. Still quite unevolved. A good partner for grilled South Australian whiting.

Mount Horrocks Watervale Riesling

Quality	🍷🍷🍷🍷½
Value	★★★½
Grapes	riesling
Region	Clare Valley, SA
Cellar	5+
Alc./Vol.	12.5%
RRP	$28.00

The Mount Horrocks cellar door is in a station on the long-abandoned railway formation that runs through the Clare Valley. The old line now forms the 'Riesling Trail' that provides a well-graded walking and cycling trail through this picturesque old wine region.

CURRENT RELEASE 2004 A brilliant-looking, pale wine, with a concentrated nose of apple, herbs, citrus and lemonade-like aromas. The palate has more 'give' than the '03 at a similar stage, with excellent levels of richness and good weight. Its concentration and its typically tangy and steely backbone give it the requisite structure to age well in the medium term. Try it with maki sushi.

Mount Langi Ghiran Riesling

Quality	♀♀♀♀
Value	★★★
Grapes	riesling
Region	Grampians & Henty, Vic.
Cellar	▮ 4
Alc./Vol.	13.4%
RRP	$20.00 ⬧

Langi riesling is usually a bigger wine than we expect from cool-climate riesling, with plenty of flavour and weight. Sometimes a bit too much so, but when it works it's a flavoursome alternative to more delicate wines.
CURRENT RELEASE 2004   Pale in colour, this looks quite delicate, but appearances can deceive. On the nose it has plenty of concentration, with lime, nectarine and cosmetic-like fruit aromas interwoven with a slatey touch. The palate is round and full with good depth and a rather firm, dry finish. A powerful riesling to enjoy with Vietnamese-style stir-fried pork with mint.

Murdock Coonawarra Riesling

Quality	♀♀♀♀♀
Value	★★★→
Grapes	riesling
Region	Coonawarra, SA
Cellar	⬤–1–6
Alc./Vol.	12.0%
RRP	$20.00 ⬧

Coonawarra has a long history with riesling, although these days it's the red varieties that hold sway in the minds of wine lovers. In fact as recently as 15 years ago there was almost as much riesling grown there as cabernet sauvignon.
CURRENT RELEASE 2004   A pale wine with an extraordinary perfumed nose of spring blossom, lime-juice cordial and steel. In the mouth it has great palate structure with excellent depth of citrus flavour and a lean spine of firm acidity. Still unevolved, this should grow into a beauty with bottle-age. Try it with fresh shellfish.

Neagles Rock Frisky Filly Reserve Riesling

Quality	♀♀♀♀♀
Value	★★★★→
Grapes	riesling
Region	Clare Valley, SA
Cellar	▮ 8+
Alc./Vol.	11.5%
RRP	$28.00 ⬧

Yet another new reserve bottling. Everyone's doing it, and not all of them justify the price or the name 'reserve'. This one does! Growers and makers: Steve Wiblin and Jane Willson.
CURRENT RELEASE 2004   This is a very fine, minerally riesling which has a steely core that should ensure it ages well. The colour is palish yellow and the aromas include boiled-lolly and lemon, while the palate is delicate, intense and tangy, with crisp mineral/citrus flavours and good length, finishing properly dry. It has softness of palate while retaining crisp, dry structure, without austerity or hardness. It suits baked snapper.

Orlando Jacob's Creek Reserve Riesling

The Orlando name has been linked with great riesling from the Barossa and Eden valleys for generations. Quality has always been good, even in the less expensive wines, and the best wines can age spectacularly.

CURRENT RELEASE 2004 A bright young thing with an aroma of raw lime juice and slate. It's a serious style, not a pretty floral thing, but it has true regional subtlety and backbone. The palate has more give than the nose would indicate with good depth and a dry, tangy, very long finish. A very classy traditional Eden Valley style that should develop well. Serve it with yum cha goodies.

Quality	🍷🍷🍷🍷🍷
Value	★★★★★
Grapes	riesling
Region	Eden Valley, SA
Cellar	🍾 1–10
Alc./Vol.	12.5%
RRP	$17.00 [$] ⚘

Pauletts Antonina Riesling

This is a new reserve bottling for Neil Paulett, who reckons it's the best riesling he's ever made – and he's made quite a few! Antonina was the daughter of Andreas Weiman, the first white inhabitant of the Paulett property. Only 100 cases were bottled.

CURRENT RELEASE 2004 It is an outstanding wine but it's very tart, shy and undeveloped, and needs cellaring. The colour is very light and the style is delicate and minerally. Restrained and refined but intense on the palate, it has seamless structure and very good length. If you have it with fish, the fierce acid level is counteracted and it actually drinks well already. But we suggest cellaring first.

Quality	🍷🍷🍷🍷🍷
Value	★★★★
Grapes	riesling
Region	Clare Valley, SA
Cellar	🍾 2–10+
Alc./Vol.	12.0%
RRP	$38.00 ⚘ (cellar door)

Penfolds Rawson's Retreat Riesling

This comes in a burgundy bottle, which is a bit of a shock for a riesling. It is bigger and more obvious than a classic riesling but has an extraordinary amount of flavour and appeal for your miserly tenner.

CURRENT RELEASE 2004 This is a lovely white wine, whether it tastes very much like riesling or not. There are gooseberry/spicy aromas and it has a different fruit spectrum to most rieslings. The palate is tight and remarkably refined for a cheapie, with excellent focus and length. The finish is clean and dry, too. It hasn't been sugared up. It just lacks the spine of acidity and varietal fruit we look for in top riesling, but those are minor quibbles beside its superb flavour. It goes with scallops and mussels.

Quality	🍷🍷🍷🍷½
Value	★★★★★
Grapes	riesling
Region	South Eastern Australia
Cellar	🍷 3
Alc./Vol.	12.5%
RRP	$10.00 [$] ⚘

Penfolds Reserve Bin Eden Valley Riesling

Quality 🍷🍷🍷🍷🍷
Value ★★★★★
Grapes riesling
Region Eden Valley, SA
Cellar 🍾 8
Alc./Vol. 12.5%
RRP $27.80 [$] 🔩

We always said Yattarna should have been a riesling, not a chardonnay. Southcorp has been producing riesling of this quality for many years, under the Leo Buring and Seppelt as well as the Penfolds names. This is a classic example. Maker: Oliver Crawford and team.

CURRENT RELEASE 2004 This is a breathtaking riesling that showcases the floral, dried-herb, dried-wildflower aromas of Eden Valley riesling in a pristine package. It's very concentrated, intense and long, and combines power with finesse. A structured riesling with excellent cellaring potential, although it's delicious now – with steamed scallops, ginger and shallots.

Peter Lehmann Eden Valley Riesling

Quality 🍷🍷🍷🍷🍷
Value ★★★★★
Grapes riesling
Region Eden Valley, SA
Cellar 🍾 7+
Alc./Vol. 12.0%
RRP $15.00 [$] 🔩

Lehmann make three rieslings: a cheaper Barossa version, this one, and the reserve, which is released at five or six years of age. This one is a re-birthing of the somewhat out-there Blue Eden, which had a blue bottle.

CURRENT RELEASE 2004 This is a seriously good-value riesling, a gold-medal-quality wine at an everyday price. The light yellow colour has green tinges, and it has a fresh lime-juicy aroma with a hint of quince paste. The taste is taut, fresh, refined and intense, with good balance and length. It's dry but avoids austerity. A delicious seamless drink. Team it with snapper quenelles.

Pewsey Vale The Contours Riesling

Quality 🍷🍷🍷🍷🍷
Value ★★★★★
Grapes riesling
Region Eden Valley, SA
Cellar 🍾 4+
Alc./Vol. 12.5%
RRP $28.00 🔩

Selected from the oldest contour-planted vines on the Pewsey Vale vineyard, which are now around 35 years old, bottled under screw-caps and cellared before release, this is Yalumba's gift to riesling lovers. Maker: Louisa Rose.

CURRENT RELEASE 1999 This utterly beautiful semi-mature riesling has built a gorgeous bouquet of mellow floral/lime-juice aromas, coupled with the hot-buttered-toast aroma of a gently aged riesling (with none of the kerosene character of lesser wines). It has great intensity and length of flavour, yet delicacy and refinement as well. Possibly the best yet of a marvellous succession of wines under this label. The price is an act of charity. Drink with baked snapper.

Pikes The Merle Reserve Riesling

Andrew and Neil Pike have built up a formidable range under the Pikes label, including some sensational Reserve bottlings. This wine, from the oldest vines on their own Polish Hill River vineyard, has been labelled Reserve in the past but this year they added their mother's name as a tribute. CURRENT RELEASE 2004   This is a classic age-worthy Polish-style riesling, i.e. it's very minerally, nervy and tight, with great delicacy and palate length. The colour is pale and it's very fine and vivacious, a great food wine now but undoubtedly built to age. Try it with pan-fried whiting.

Quality	🍷🍷🍷🍷🍷
Value	★★★★★
Grapes	riesling
Region	Clare Valley, SA
Cellar	🍾 8+
Alc./Vol.	12.0%
RRP	$32.00 🥂

Richmond Grove Watervale Riesling

Veteran winemaker John Vickery is still listed as the man to refer all queries to re Richmond Grove riesling, although he's basically retired. Now in his 70s, Vickery has done more for the cause of riesling in Australia than anyone. CURRENT RELEASE 2004   Marvellously intense, fragrant riesling with superb immediate drinkability and also cellaring potential. The colour is bright and youthful; the nose is rich and deep and the palate has fine balance and a clean, dry finish. It's a stylish wine, with lemon/lime flavours of real intensity, finishing with a candied-citron taste. The finish resonates long. Serve with pan-fried whiting.

Quality	🍷🍷🍷🍷🍷
Value	★★★★★
Grapes	riesling
Region	Clare Valley, SA
Cellar	🍾 7+
Alc./Vol.	12.0%
RRP	$16.00 ⑤ 🥂

Seppelt Drumborg Riesling

Seppelt's Drumborg vineyard, near Portland in southern Victoria, was planted in 1964 to supply high-quality, cool-climate fruit, mainly for sparkling wine. It was almost a failure, but Seppelt's perseverance has brought us this excellent line of age-worthy rieslings.
Previous outstanding vintages: '93, '98, '00, '03
CURRENT RELEASE 2004   Few rieslings are as austere and mean-spirited in youth as Seppelt Drumborg, and it's like an article of faith to buy them and put them away for the bottle-ageing that transforms the caterpillar into the butterfly. The 2004 has a little more give than the '03 at the same stage with spice and lemon varietal aromas touched by floral talc and flint. The steely palate still has quite high acidity. Despite its immaturity, we like it very much, even in youth, and predict a great future for it over a decade or so. When it's developed a bit, serve it with pan-fried fish.

Quality	🍷🍷🍷🍷🍷
Value	★★★�→
Grapes	riesling
Region	Henty, Vic.
Cellar	�'3–10+
Alc./Vol.	12.5%
RRP	$27.00 🥂

Shadowood Riesling

Quality 🍷🍷🍷🍷
Value ★★★
Grapes riesling
Region Eden Valley, SA
Cellar 🍾 5
Alc./Vol. 11.5%
RRP $17.35

The Eden Valley is one of South Australia's two greatest riesling districts. While the other one, the Clare Valley, is increasingly regarded in most circles as *numero uno*, we think that the Eden Valley is up there with the best.
CURRENT RELEASE 2004 Floral, musky and sweet lime aromas build with breathing, and the varietal character has a fresh, pristine feel to it that is typically Eden Valley. The lifted, intense nose is followed by a zesty palate with a fruity middle, and a clean, bone-dry finish. Try it with grilled South Australian whiting.

Southern Highland Winery Riesling

Quality 🍷🍷🍷🍷½
Value ★★★★
Grapes riesling
Region Southern Highlands, NSW
Cellar 🍾 3+
Alc./Vol. 11.0%
RRP $20.00 ≋ (cellar door)

The trend to name wineries and brands after the region continues. Unfortunately, it's usually the first, or one of the first, to set up shop that pinches the region's name, and the confusion is entrenched from the start.
CURRENT RELEASE 2004 This is a lovely wine in a style this region should probably specialise in. It's a natural. It's almost Alsatian. The aroma is very fragrant, spicy and lifted, suggesting a touch of botrytis. There's a little sweetness and the sherbetty acidity is what gives it its zing. The flavours are delicious. A very minerally, European style of riesling that would suit spicy Thai fishcakes.

St Hallett Riesling

Quality 🍷🍷🍷🍷½
Value ★★★½
Grapes riesling
Region Eden Valley, SA
Cellar 🍾 5+
Alc./Vol. 12.5%
RRP $19.85 [$] ≋

A couple of decades ago St Hallett was a rather obscure Barossa winery, but now it's successfully taken to the national and international stage with an excellent range of honest regional wines. This is due in large part to former boss Bob McLean.
CURRENT RELEASE 2004 Typically green-tinged young Eden Valley riesling appearance here. The nose is very tight and unevolved with lime and spice aromas, and an almost Vichy-water-like minerality. The palate is classical Eden Valley riesling with good depth and spicy richness, real length and palate interest, and clean lemony acidity to keep it all together. Excellent with Thai duck salad.

Stringy Brae Riesling

Stringy Brae is a slightly obscure, small operation in the high-quality Sevenhill part of the Clare Valley. Riesling is made into a reserved regional type of high quality. This won the National Riesling Challenge in Canberra in 2004. CURRENT RELEASE 2004 Correct greenish-straw colour here, and the nose is pristine and delicate with classical floral aromas, and tight threads of lime and spice. The palate is lemony, minerally and dry with relatively gentle acidity for young Clare riesling. The finish is long and fine. Serve it with tempura.

Quality	▼▼▼▼▼
Value	★★★�→
Grapes	riesling
Region	Clare Valley, SA
Cellar	▮ 6
Alc./Vol.	12.0%
RRP	$18.50 ⬚

Tamar Ridge Riesling

Tamar Ridge was established by mercurial Tassie businessman Joe Chromy and is owned these days by the biggest timber and forestry company in Tasmania, Gunns Ltd, which is regularly in the gun with the Greenies. Maker: Michael Fogarty.
CURRENT RELEASE 2004 The colour is very light and there's a whiff of reductive character on the quite complex bouquet. It also has lemon and lime aromas, while the taste is crisp and tangy with liberal acid and the merest hint of sweetness. It's beautifully balanced, crisp and nervy. Still a babe, it will age slow and long. As a youngster it suits Tassie Pacific oysters.

Quality	▼▼▼▼▼
Value	★★★★★
Grapes	riesling
Region	Tamar Valley, Tas.
Cellar	▮ 9+
Alc./Vol.	12.5%
RRP	$20.00 ⬚

Taylors Riesling

Taylors have always been specialists in riesling, and they manage to serve up this particular wine in large licks as well as good quality. It's usually one of the better buys in the region. Maker: Adam Eggins.
CURRENT RELEASE 2004 It's a very serviceable riesling that can be drunk now or kept a while. The colour is bright and light, the aromas are softly flowery and ripe, while the palate shows generous flavour of depth and strength. It's quite long and structured and would go well with food: try pan-fried flounder.

Quality	▼▼▼▼
Value	★★★★�→
Grapes	riesling
Region	Clare Valley, SA
Cellar	▮ 5+
Alc./Vol.	13.0%
RRP	$18.00 Ⓢ ⬚

Taylors St Andrews Bottle Aged Riesling

Quality 🍷🍷🍷🍷½
Value ★★★★
Grapes riesling
Region Clare Valley, SA
Cellar 🍾 2
Alc./Vol. 12.5%
RRP $33.00

This is one of the last of the Mohicans: since it went into bottle, Taylors have gone 100 per cent into screw-caps for the Australian market. They had some serious cork trouble with earlier vintages of this wine – white wines under cork can suffer big variation with bottle-age – but our bottle of 2000 was in good nick. Maker: Adam Eggins.

CURRENT RELEASE 2000 The colour is a lovely bright, deep yellow and the bouquet of hot buttered toast displays classic aged Clare riesling character. It's mellow, mature and complex – if a touch forward for a five-year-old. The palate is very dry, yet soft and smooth thanks to its age. It's full and rounded and there's no kerosene character! It's probably at its best now and should be drunk up, perhaps with smoked trout pâté.

Tower Estate Clare Valley Riesling

Quality 🍷🍷🍷🍷
Value ★★★½
Grapes riesling
Region Clare Valley, SA
Cellar 🍾 5+
Alc./Vol. 13.0%
RRP $26.00 (cellar door)

Tower Estate still uses cork to seal all of its wines. We suspect that while Len Evans breathes, there'll be no plastic or screw-lids allowed on the property. He is a confirmed cork devotee. Maker: Dan Dineen.

CURRENT RELEASE 2004 This is a good riesling, although we detect a faint greenness in it; a kind of fresh herb aroma allied with a hint of earthiness. The palate is excellent: it has a classy, restrained intensity. Finesse and length are encouraging signs for its cellaring future. It's delicate and has a clean, dry finish. It would suit pan-fried Murray cod.

Twofold Riesling

Quality 🍷🍷🍷🍷🍷
Value ★★★★½
Grapes riesling
Region Clare Valley, SA
Cellar 🍾 5+
Alc./Vol. 12.0%
RRP $25.00 [$]

The Stock brothers, Tim and Nick, are both former sommeliers of considerable experience who have branched out into other areas of the wine business. Tim runs a wholesale business in Sydney and Nick is involved in retail, writing and consultancy in Melbourne. This is their own brand, made by Neil Pike in the Clare Valley from a dry-grown vineyard at Sevenhill.

CURRENT RELEASE 2004 This is an excellent Clare riesling that can be either drunk now or cellared. Its lemon acid-drop aromas are enticing, and it's very vibrant and frisky in the mouth, with plenty of attack but also real finesse. The palate has very good length and a clean, emphatic finish. It would drink well now with pan-fried whiting.

Wellington FGR Riesling

FGR stands for Forty Grams Residual, a reference to the level of natural sweetness left in the finished wine. It could also mean Flaming Good Riesling or . . . well, what it means is up to you.

CURRENT RELEASE 2004 This is a Germanic type of riesling with low alcohol and notable sweetness, a type that's rare in Australia. It has a nose of sweet citrus, rock candy and a herby thread. In the mouth there's a succulent balance between sweetness and tingly acidity, and its delicacy and poise make it light and fresh on the palate. Not quite as delicate as the best Germans, but pretty good. Try it as an afternoon refresher with friends.

Quality 🍷🍷🍷🍷½
Value ★★★½
Grapes riesling
Region Coal River Valley, Tas.
Cellar 🍾 5
Alc./Vol. 8.0%
RRP $24.00

Wellington Riesling

Few Tasmanian winemakers have the breadth of experience of Andrew Hood. Not only does he make excellent regional wines under the Wellington label, he makes under contract for a large number of other Tassie growers. Riesling is one of his real specialities.

CURRENT RELEASE 2004 Bright-looking with an appetising green tinge, this has a scent that's hauntingly delicate, yet intense enough to make you sit up and take notice. Spiced-apple, blossom, lime and mineral aromas lead to a tight flavoury palate of medium depth and real persistence. The high acidity is a very Tassie thing that gives a bracing zip on the finish, and should ensure longevity. Try it with sushi.

Quality 🍷🍷🍷🍷½
Value ★★★★
Grapes riesling
Region Southern Tasmania
Cellar 🍾 1–8
Alc./Vol. 12.0%
RRP $20.00

Wirra Wirra Hand Picked Riesling

Wirra Wirra has made this wine for 35 consecutive vintages. Recent years have seen it moving away from its McLaren Vale roots, incorporating fruit from cooler and more classical riesling regions to lift the quality.

CURRENT RELEASE 2004 The nose of this young riesling shows a savoury spiciness that's very inviting. Lemon and lime-like fruit are also intense, and the palate has attractive depth combined with delicate flavour, underpinned by a zippy tang of acidity. Good with Indonesian-style fried chicken.

Quality 🍷🍷🍷🍷½
Value ★★★★½
Grapes riesling
Region Adelaide Hills, Fleurieu & Clare Valley, SA
Cellar 🍾 5
Alc./Vol. 12.5%
RRP $17.00 [$]

Wolf Blass Gold Label Riesling

Quality 🍷🍷🍷🍷½
Value ★★★½
Grapes riesling
Region Eden & Clare valleys, SA
Cellar 🍾 5+
Alc./Vol. 11.5%
RRP $22.00 [$]

Big-name wines like this are sometimes bagged by wine fashionistas in favour of anything made by a small maker, but we don't play favourites on that basis. This top Wolf Blass riesling has impressed us for quality and value over many editions of the *Guide*. It's also likely to be discounted below the $22 listed here, which makes it even better!
CURRENT RELEASE 2004 It's a bit steelier and more classically styled than some previous vintages, but this still delivers the goods: bright colour, a nose of wildflowers, green limes and minerals, and a refined palate of some delicacy that's attractively long and tangy. Worth cellaring medium-term, but right now it works well with stir-fried squid.

Wynns Coonawarra Riesling

Quality 🍷🍷🍷🍷½
Value ★★★★★
Grapes riesling
Region Coonawarra, SA
Cellar 🍾 5+
Alc./Vol. 12.5%
RRP $15.00 [$]

Wynns is the grand-daddy of Coonawarra rieslings, and it's outlasted many others that shared shelf space with it 20 or 30 years ago. Older examples have shown great ageing potential. Some wines of the 1980s tasted by the authors recently were in very good nick, so at this price it might be worth putting a few away for the future.
CURRENT RELEASE 2004 This looks to be a better effort than the 2003. It smells of green limes and apples, intense and with a minerally backbone. The palate is clean-tasting and tangy with a dry, flinty finish. It should do well with a few years in bottle. Serve it with Thai fish cakes.

Yalumba Y Series Riesling

Quality 🍷🍷🍷🍷
Value ★★★★★
Grapes riesling
Region not stated
Cellar 🍾 3+
Alc./Vol. 12.5%
RRP $12.95 [$]

Bargains abound among the ranks of Australian rieslings, and the big makers lead the way. This great-value wine from one of the country's most experienced riesling exponents is one of the best examples.
CURRENT RELEASE 2004 This is a very aromatic, lively young wine with real intensity of varietal character. The nose has spicy floral touches to clean lime-like fruit, and similar flavours mark the palate. It's intense, clean and dry-tasting with an appetising lemony acidity underneath. Try it with Thai crab cakes.

Sauvignon Blanc and Blends

In recent years Australia has played underdog to New Zealand with sauvignon blanc. But lately we are seeing more Australian sauvignons which, while they might not rival Marlborough's, are nevertheless excellent. This trend had a boost from the record cool 2002 season. The Adelaide Hills and southern areas of Western Australia seem to do best with this difficult grape. Margaret River's 'sem-sav' style, which can be either semillon- or sauvignon-dominant, has become a classic blend, highly popular with local and overseas drinkers. Sauvignon blanc can be wood-aged but is usually not. The good ones have distinctive varietal character that tends more to the tropical-fruit spectrum rather than the herbaceous aroma/flimsy palate style of the past.

Alkoomi Sauvignon Blanc

When it comes to sauvignon blanc, Alkoomi is one of the best in the West. The cool Frankland and nearby Mount Barker regions look well-suited to this variety.
CURRENT RELEASE 2004   Bright and pale in colour, this has exemplary varietal qualities on the nose that combines lively tropical fruit with some minerally, flinty aromas. The palate is light, clean and dry with good length and relatively subtle development of flavours, ending dry with lemony acidity. Try it with oyster fritters.

Quality	♀♀♀♀
Value	★★★↓
Grapes	sauvignon blanc
Region	Frankland River, WA
Cellar	▮ 1
Alc./Vol.	12.0%
RRP	$19.00 ⌇

Beelgara Estate Woorawa Sauvignon Blanc

Beelgara is the former Rossetto's Wines at Beelbangera, near Griffith. It's another of the many Riverland and Riverina wineries sourcing grapes from cooler climes for its finer dry whites.
CURRENT RELEASE 2004   This has a nicely restrained colour and smells appealingly of salad greens and garden herbs, plus a hint of gooseberry. It tingles the palate with sherbetty acid and zesty fruit, and the whole thing is softened off by a trace of sweetness. It would go well with Chinese steamed dim sims.

Quality	♀♀♀↓
Value	★★★★
Grapes	sauvignon blanc
Region	Coonawarra & Adelaide Hills, SA
Cellar	▮ 1
Alc./Vol.	11.5%
RRP	$12.00 Ⓢ ⌇

Beresford Highwood Sauvignon Blanc

Quality	♀♀♀
Value	★★★★
Grapes	sauvignon blanc
Region	not stated
Cellar	▮ 1
Alc./Vol.	12.5%
RRP	$15.00 ⓢ ⱬ

Beresford is one of the many brands of the omnipresent Rob Dundon, whose Step Rd Winery is in the Langhorne Creek region.

CURRENT RELEASE 2004   Pale, delicate and fragile to look at, this subtle, budget-priced savvy is good value and has flavour above its station. It's fragrant and not unlike a Kiwi sauvignon blanc in aroma, while the palate has nicely concentrated fruit and all things in good balance. Serve with mussels mariniere.

Bidgeebong Tumbarumba Sauvignon Blanc

Quality	♀♀♀♀
Value	★★★ⱦ
Grapes	sauvignon blanc
Region	Tumbarumba, NSW
Cellar	▮ 3+
Alc./Vol.	12.9%
RRP	$20.00 ⱬ

There are very few wineries but quite a lot of growers in the Tumbarumba region, so a lot of Tumbarumba bottlings are vinified by winemakers based outside the area, such as the highly competent Andrew Birks of Bidgeebong.

CURRENT RELEASE 2004   This took a while to open up and display its full charms. The bouquet unfolded a charismatic fragrance of gooseberry, grassiness and citrus, while the taste is fresh and lively but with softness and a degree of richness. It's good by itself, or you could try it with Chinese scallops with ginger and spring onions.

Brangayne of Orange Sauvignon Blanc

Quality	♀♀♀♀
Value	★★★ⱦ
Grapes	sauvignon blanc
Region	Orange, NSW
Cellar	▮ 1
Alc./Vol.	12.5%
RRP	$22.00 ⱬ
	(cellar door)

The Hoskins of Brangayne are great opera buffs, in particular they love Wagner, so you'll see names like Tristan and Isolde as well as Brangayne itself on their labels.

CURRENT RELEASE 2004   The colour has a youthful green tint and the nose is all about green salad, fruit salad and subtle spiciness. The palate is delicate and light on its feet, with good freshness and zing, and although it might lack a bit in strength it is attractive. It goes well with caesar salad.

Bridgewater Mill Sauvignon Blanc

Bridgewater Mill is Petaluma's second label, named after the old Bridgewater flour mill with its whopping waterwheel, in which Petaluma built its restaurant, cellar-door sales and bubbly-maturation cellars.

CURRENT RELEASE 2004 This is that rare thing, an Aussie sauvignon blanc with real intensity and strength of flavour. It's not wishy-washy or sweet. The colour is pale and the aromas recall passionfruit, green salad and bread-dough with a hint of apricot nectar. It tastes as if the grapes were ripe. It's fresh and youthful, delicate yet concentrated. It would go well with grilled prawns.

Quality 🍷🍷🍷🍷½
Value ★★★★½
Grapes sauvignon blanc
Region Adelaide Hills, Coonawarra & Clare, SA
Cellar 🍾 1
Alc./Vol. 13.0%
RRP $21.00 [$] 🔩

Cape Mentelle Sauvignon Semillon

Long a benchmark for this style in Margaret River, Cape Mentelle's Sauvignon Semillon (sometimes it's Semillon Sauvignon – varietal make-up can change with the vintage) is a well-made modern white, complete with a dab of oak to add dimension.

CURRENT RELEASE 2004 If our memories serve us correctly, this is a little more oaky in its youth than the '03, but the wood still plays only a supporting role to lively fruit, rather than dominating. Lemon, green-leaf and tropical-fruit aromas and flavours are the main game, and it has medium depth and good length of flavour, finishing dry and clean. Serve it with shellfish.

Quality 🍷🍷🍷🍷
Value ★★★
Grapes sauvignon blanc 53%; semillon 47%
Region Margaret River, WA
Cellar 🍾 2
Alc./Vol. 13.5%
RRP $24.00

Cape Mentelle Walcliffe

Quality	♟♟♟♟♟
Value	★★★
Grapes	sauvignon blanc 65%; semillon 35%
Region	Margaret River, WA
Cellar	🍾 2
Alc./Vol.	13.3%
RRP	$35.00

Walcliffe is Cape Mentelle's attempt at working more interest, richness and substance into a sauvignon blanc-semillon blend. This is achieved via wild yeast fermentation in barrel, yeast-lees influence, and sometimes malolactic fermentation. Both the '02 and '03 have succeeded admirably.

Previous outstanding vintages: '01

CURRENT RELEASE 2002   An outstanding vintage has helped make the '02 Walcliffe the best yet. It has excellent integration of citrus and lightly vegetal fruit character with nutty-oak and earthy-lees characters. The palate has excellent texture and flavour development. It's soft, rich and long with a gentle tang. Serious sauvignon-semillon. Enjoy it with scallops.

Quality	♟♟♟♟♟
Value	★★★
Grapes	sauvignon blanc 70%; semillon 30%
Region	Margaret River, WA
Cellar	🍾 3
Alc./Vol.	13.5%
RRP	$35.00

CURRENT RELEASE 2003   Another complex, stylish wine under this label, the '03 has more notable oak at the moment, but harmony should come with a little time in bottle. It smells of lemon grass, spice and slightly mulchy, grassy elements, with nutty-vanillin oak surrounding the fruit. The palate has great feel, smooth and long with a zesty finish, but it doesn't quite have the polish of the '02.

Centennial Vineyards Sauvignon Blanc

Quality	♟♟♟♟♟
Value	★★★★
Grapes	sauvignon blanc
Region	Southern Highlands, NSW
Cellar	🍾 1
Alc./Vol.	12.5%
RRP	$20.00 🍸

The Southern Highlands of New South Wales, not much more than an hour's drive from Sydney, is a cool-climate wine region that looks to be suitable for a broad range of grape varieties. Centennial Vineyards is one of the best producers, and most of their wines are good buys at cellar-door prices.

CURRENT RELEASE 2004   Although this is a cool-grown sauvignon, the expected green leafy, herbaceous traits are well under control. The ripely aromatic nose has nectarine, citrus and a hint of green salad to it, the palate is intense with great purity of ripe varietal flavour. It finishes long and fine. Drink it with quick-fried calamari and warm tomato coulis.

Coolangatta Estate Sauvignon Blanc Verdelho

Now there's a different idea for a blend! But, why not? If it works, why let hang-ups about varietal purity get in the way? This is a 50/50 blend, all estate-grown at the vineyard near Nowra, and vinified at Tyrrell's in the Hunter.
CURRENT RELEASE 2004   And it's a thoroughly delicious white wine. The aroma is more lemon-juice than anything, with a lacing of salad greens and fresh herbs. It's clean and vibrant, while a trace of sweetness enhances the pineapple/ tropical and citrus palate fruit. It's particularly good in the mouth. Try it with steamed coral trout with ginger and spring onions.

Quality	♟♟♟
Value	★★★★♩
Grapes	sauvignon blanc; verdelho
Region	Shoalhaven, NSW
Cellar	▮ 3
Alc./Vol.	12.5%
RRP	$16.00 ⊠ (cellar door)

Cullen Sauvignon Blanc Semillon

The varietal make-up of this blend changes from year to year depending on how the two varieties perform in the vineyard. Sometimes it's predominantly semillon, in other years sauvignon takes precedence. The '04 wine has an unusually high proportion of sauvignon blanc.
CURRENT RELEASE 2004   If you like your sauv blanc-sems to be simple fruity wines this won't be your bag. It's a bright, pale wine with a very complex nose of smooth yeast lees, subtle smoky-barrel ferment, and subdued citrus fruit. In the mouth it follows the same track: smoky and subtle with lovely succulent balance and integration of complex flavours. It's seamless and long, with a clean dry aftertaste. Serve it alongside shellfish stew with fennel.

Quality	♟♟♟♟♟
Value	★★★
Grapes	sauvignon blanc 77%; semillon 23%
Region	Margaret River, WA
Cellar	▮ 4
Alc./Vol.	14.0%
RRP	$35.00

Edwards Sauvignon Blanc

The little yellow Tiger Moth named Matilda that resides at Edwards' Margaret River vineyard has a real tale to tell, having flown all the way from England to Australia. Brian Edwards undertook the solo adventure to honour the memory of his father, a Lancaster bomber pilot lost over Germany in 1943, and to raise money for Legacy.
CURRENT RELEASE 2004   A pale wine with a nose that immediately shows the influence of barrel fermentation. It smells nutty and subtly complex with tropical fruit woven attractively through the wood. The palate is smooth and ripely flavoured with hints of gooseberry jam and spice, finishing dry and clean. Try it with goat's cheese and red pepper bruschetti.

Quality	♟♟♟♟
Value	★★★
Grapes	sauvignon blanc
Region	Margaret River, WA
Cellar	▮ 2
Alc./Vol.	12.5%
RRP	$19.00 ⊠

Fuse Semillon Sauvignon Blanc

Quality	♥ ♥ ♥ ⁊
Value	★ ★ ★ ★
Grapes	semillon; sauvignon blanc
Region	Adelaide Hills, SA
Cellar	▮ 1
Alc./Vol.	13.0%
RRP	$19.00 ⊜

The Fuse concept is all about blending sympathetic grape varieties. Hence there's a grenache shiraz mourvèdre, a cabernet merlot, and this sem-sav in the range. Maker: Neil Pike.

CURRENT RELEASE 2004   The bouquet is certainly clean and crisp, with dusty herbaceous aromas that could reflect marginal ripeness, while the palate has more appealing grapefruit and lemon citrusy flavours, softened and rounded off by a tickle of residual sweetness. The acid balance is soft, mild and easygoing. Drink it with salads and cold seafood.

Geoff Weaver Sauvignon Blanc

Quality	♥ ♥ ♥ ♥ ⁊
Value	★ ★ ★
Grapes	sauvignon blanc
Region	Adelaide Hills, SA
Cellar	▮ 2
Alc./Vol.	13.5%
RRP	$24.00 ⊜

The Adelaide Hills region has become Australia's best-known source of high-quality sauvignon blanc. Geoff Weaver's is one of the best, with a little more to it than most, not surprising given Weaver's quality credentials.

CURRENT RELEASE 2004   This typifies the Weaver sauvignon blanc style; it's not a simple tropical type of sauvignon, nor is it one those green, super-grassy examples. Instead there's a bit of complexity and interest. The nose has blackcurrant, herb and stone-fruit aromas, and the palate is smooth without any sharp edges. It finishes dry, minerally and somehow more substantial than most of its peers. Try it with whitebait fritters.

Hanging Rock The Jim Jim Sauvignon Blanc

Quality	♥ ♥ ♥ ♥ ⁊
Value	★ ★ ★ ⁊
Grapes	sauvignon blanc
Region	Macedon Ranges, Vic.
Cellar	▮ 3
Alc./Vol.	12.0%
RRP	$27.00 ⊜

The Jim Jim is the name of the Hanging Rock Winery property, with its original 8-hectare vineyard near the township of Newham. The company also has 8 hectares at Heathcote. Chief winemaker: John Ellis.

CURRENT RELEASE 2004   High acid is a hallmark of this estate-grown savvy from chilly Macedon. It's ripe-smelling, only lightly grassy and capsicum-like, but also slightly floral and musky. The palate is smooth, with good weight of fruit, and tapers towards a very crisp, tangy finish. A sprightly sauvignon to serve with goat's cheese and witlof salad.

Henschke Coralinga Lenswood Sauvignon Blanc

The vines from which this wine comes are on the slope directly opposite the Henschke family's own vineyard at Lenswood.

CURRENT RELEASE 2004 The light yellow colour has a green tint, which is a good sign. The aromas are unusual: there's a seabreezy, oyster-shell tang over the herbal varietal fruit. The palate is light and very delicate, and has a refreshing quality. Not complex, but a good quaffing white to go with cold seafood salad.

Quality	🍷🍷🍷🍷
Value	★★★
Grapes	sauvignon blanc
Region	Adelaide Hills, SA
Cellar	🍾 1
Alc./Vol.	14.0%
RRP	$22.00 [$] 🔩

Hesperos Sauvignon Blanc

Hesperos is the weekend job of Xanadu chief winemaker Jurg Muggli, which has grown into more than that. Hesperos opened its own cellar door last year, adjacent to a 30-hectare vineyard which was planted in 1999.

CURRENT RELEASE 2004 It's not pungent like some savvies, and not as immediately arresting, but it's all the better for that. The colour is pale yellow and the nose is shy and subdued, but clean and ripe, resembling straw-hay and dried herbs. The palate has delicacy and freshness, with length and intensity. A wine of real charm and the backbone to go with food – such as slow braised calamari with garlic and herbs.

Quality	🍷🍷🍷🍷½
Value	★★★★½
Grapes	sauvignon blanc
Region	Margaret River, WA
Cellar	🍾 1
Alc./Vol.	13.0%
RRP	$17.50 🔩

Hill Smith Estate Sauvignon Blanc

The Hill Smith family is the owner of Yalumba, one of the oldest family winemaking businesses in Australia. It was started by English migrant brewer Samuel Smith in 1849. One of their Eden Valley vineyards is called the Hill Smith Estate.

CURRENT RELEASE 2004 This is a sauvignon blanc on the edge! It has a decidedly green-tangy fruit character that reminds us of some Marlborough wines. The aromas are at once sweaty, tropical and cosmetic, with a hint of apricot. The palate is very tangy and high in acid, but we'd expect it to have softened and filled out a little by the time you read this. It would go well with oily fish, such as salmon.

Quality	🍷🍷🍷🍷
Value	★★★
Grapes	sauvignon blanc
Region	Eden Valley, SA
Cellar	🍾 2+
Alc./Vol.	11.0%
RRP	$20.00 🔩

Lark Hill The Fledgeling

Quality	▼▼▼▼
Value	★★★↓
Grapes	sauvignon blanc; chardonnay
Region	Canberra District, NSW
Cellar	▌3
Alc./Vol.	12.0%
RRP	$20.00 🥂 (cellar door)

Perhaps it's made from young vines. Whatever, we like the name: it's the baby lark that's just a beginner and still learning how to fly. Wine at Lark Hill is a family affair with Sue and David Carpenter now joined by their son Chris as assistant winemaker.

CURRENT RELEASE 2004 An unusual blend of sauvignon blanc and chardonnay that emphasises peach and melon aromas, is very fruity without being obviously sweet, and is sure to have broad commercial appeal. There are some confectionery nuances in the mouth, where it also shows pleasing balance and medium persistence.

Leeuwin Estate Siblings Sauvignon Blanc Semillon

Quality	▼▼▼▼
Value	★★★
Grapes	sauvignon blanc; semillon
Region	Margaret River, WA
Cellar	▌1
Alc./Vol.	12.5%
RRP	$22.50

Margaret River isn't one of Australia's coolest wine regions, but somehow it has proven itself outstanding for sauvignon blanc, especially when it's blended with semillon.

CURRENT RELEASE 2004 Capsicum, lantana and passionfruit are the aromas that flow from this decidedly green-edged wine, and there's more than an echo of New Zealand. The palate has a trace of acid hardness which is countered by some sweetness. The result is a tangy, fruity finish and an appealing wine. Try it with crab cakes.

Logan Sauvignon Blanc

Quality	▼▼▼▼⸔
Value	★★★★
Grapes	sauvignon blanc
Region	Orange, NSW
Cellar	▌2
Alc./Vol.	13.0%
RRP	$19.00 🥂

Logan Wines is based in Mudgee, and takes quite a bit of fruit from Orange for its better wines. Second label is Apple Tree Flat. The Logan family runs the business and winemaker is Peter Logan.

CURRENT RELEASE 2004 An excellent sauvignon blanc, which shows the classic gooseberry flavour of cool-climate sauvignon blanc. There are herbal and mint aromas as well, and it's very fresh and vibrant. Good intensity and delicacy. It's juicy on the palate and fruit – not sugar – sweet. It suits calamari braised with herbs.

The Long Flat Wine Company Adelaide Hills Sauvignon Blanc

This sort of thing must put the frighteners into the stalwarts of the Adelaide Hills: their signature wine, widely selling at just $11 or $12 a bottle! It's enough to make you hit the bottle.

CURRENT RELEASE 2004 The aromas are correct and inviting – herbal, slightly vegetal and brackeny as well as gooseberry scented. The palate emphasises the greener spectrum of sauvignon blanc flavour but has good intensity and vitality: it doesn't fall apart on the finish like some do. It's fruity but not sugared up, either. A great bargain. Serve with snapper poached with fennel root.

Quality	🍷🍷🍷🍷
Value	★★★★★
Grapes	sauvignon blanc
Region	Adelaide Hills, SA
Cellar	🍾 1
Alc./Vol.	12.8%
RRP	$14.00 [$] 🔩

Millbrook Sauvignon Blanc

The Perth Hills region doesn't attract the same attention as the more fashionable Western Australian wine regions, like Margaret River. Millbrook is one of the high-points and wine quality is very good.

CURRENT RELEASE 2004 A middle-of-the-road sauvignon blanc that combines ripe-fruit characters with more tangy herbaceous traits. On the nose there are attractive herbal, mineral and tropical-fruit aromas, with pleasantly ripe flavour and richness in the mouth. It finishes tangy and fresh. Try it alongside a prawn, mint and pink-grapefruit salad.

Quality	🍷🍷🍷🍷
Value	★★★
Grapes	sauvignon blanc
Region	Perth Hills, WA
Cellar	🍾 1
Alc./Vol.	13.0%
RRP	$20.00

Nepenthe Sauvignon Blanc

Businessman Ed Tweddell and his family established their vineyard and winery at Balhannah back in 1994. They have 100 hectares of vines in three locations now. Chief winemaker is Peter Leske.

CURRENT RELEASE 2004 This is a very minerally style of savvy, dusty and crisp with great freshness, which is preserved by its screw-cap. There are classic gooseberry and citrus flavours. The palate is lean, dry but fruity, and tangy in a restrained, undeveloped style that is just delicious to drink. It's a good mate for barbecued scampi.

Quality	🍷🍷🍷🍷½
Value	★★★★½
Grapes	sauvignon blanc
Region	Adelaide Hills, SA
Cellar	🍾 2
Alc./Vol.	12.5%
RRP	$21.00 🔩

Nugan Estate Frasca's Lane Sauvignon Blanc

Quality 🍷🍷🍷🍷
Value ★★★★
Grapes sauvignon blanc
Region King Valley, Vic.
Cellar 🍾 1
Alc./Vol. 13.5%
RRP $21.00 [$] 🔩

This spent a bit of time in French oak barrels, which is an unconventional approach to making Australian sauvignon blanc. It does add an extra dimension to what might otherwise be fairly simple fruit flavour. Maker: Daren Owers.

CURRENT RELEASE 2003 The colour is bright, light to medium yellow, and it's holding its freshness well at this age. There's a whisper of nutty oak, barely apparent in the bouquet, while the fruit style is ripe and non-pungent. The flavours are lemony. It's a flavoursome, fruity, well-made white wine with a whisper of sweetness and again the barest touch of oak on the palate. It would go with antipasto.

Pikes Sauvignon Blanc Semillon

Quality 🍷🍷🍷🍷
Value ★★★½
Grapes sauvignon blanc 73%; semillon 27%
Region Clare Valley, SA
Cellar 🍾 3
Alc./Vol. 12.5%
RRP $18.00 🔩

In Clare, sauvignon blanc is much less aromatic than in cooler climes, so having a blend with a high sauvignon blanc fraction tends to be less pungent than in some other places. Maker: Neil Pike.

CURRENT RELEASE 2004 The colour is a promisingly fresh, light yellow–green, and it has a vibrant aroma of lemon, subtly seasoned with fresh herbs. The palate is soft and rounded but certainly doesn't lack acidity. It's quite well-balanced and has riper than usual sauvignon blanc flavours. It would suit Chinese pork and coriander dumplings.

Preece Sauvignon Blanc

Quality 🍷🍷🍷½
Value ★★★★
Grapes sauvignon blanc
Region not stated
Cellar 🍾 1
Alc./Vol. 13.5%
RRP $15.00 [$] 🔩

Colin Preece was the consultant who helped the Shelmerdine family set up Mitchelton in the late 1960s. He had retired as chief winemaker and manager of Seppelt Great Western, where he made his mark as one of our country's greatest ever winemakers. Preece is a Mitchelton sub-brand.

CURRENT RELEASE 2004 Preece savvy usually punches above its weight. This one is typically pale-coloured and smells fragrantly of floral, herbaceous and lightly tropical-fruit aromas, quite strongly aromatic. The palate is light, lean and shy, a touch unforthcoming, but not tart or austere. It's a vibrant, simple but soft and nicely balanced, easy-drinking wine to serve with cold seafood.

The Rothbury Estate Orange Sauvignon Blanc

Rothbury is part of the vast Beringer Blass empire owned by Foster's these days. The Hunter isn't renowned for great sauvignon blanc, so it makes sense to bring the grapes in from the more suitable Orange region.
CURRENT RELEASE 2004   This is slightly offbeat but it is very cheap for an Orange-region wine. It has some sweaty aromas together with a whiff of Vitamin B and a suspicion of botrytis. There are stalky herbaceous flavours and a slightly sappy finish. Serve it with Lebanese stuffed vine leaves.

Quality	♟♟♟
Value	★★★★
Grapes	sauvignon blanc
Region	Orange, NSW
Cellar	▮ 1
Alc./Vol.	12.0%
RRP	$13.00 ⓢ ≋

Rymill Sauvignon Blanc

Peter Rymill's operation is a substantial one, with 170 hectares of vineyards and a showpiece winery at the northern end of the terra rossa strip. John Innes is chief winemaker.
CURRENT RELEASE 2004   A pale-coloured, shy sauvignon that has a lot of twiggy, stemmy, dusty, somewhat green varietal aromas. It's delicate and tautly structured, with high acid and a firm, dry, very tangy afterpalate. It needs food and goes well with salade nicoise.

Quality	♟♟♟♟
Value	★★★★
Grapes	sauvignon blanc
Region	Coonawarra, SA
Cellar	▮ 2
Alc./Vol.	12.0%
RRP	$16.00 ⓢ ≋

Sabotage Sauvignon Blanc

Peter Kopiec and David Baldet of Sabotage are inspired by the wines of France in their winemaking. Thus their sauvignon blanc has more of a French accent than an Australian or New Zealand one. Barrel ferment, wild yeast and lees contact add some mystery to the formula.
CURRENT RELEASE 2004   This pale wine is very interesting, although its out-there Frenchy style won't necessarily appeal to those who like their sauvignons forward, fresh and fruity. It has an unusual earthy, farmyardy thing to it, along with a minerally thread, a hint of mint, and gentle barrel aromas. In the mouth it's smooth with minerally flavours that are dry and lasting, finishing in chalky dryness. A Loire look-alike from Victoria. Try it with mature goat's cheese.

Quality	♟♟♟♟
Value	★★★
Grapes	sauvignon blanc
Region	Seymour & Mornington Peninsula, Vic.
Cellar	▮ 2
Alc./Vol.	12.5%
RRP	$20.00

Shaw and Smith Sauvignon Blanc

Quality	♥♥♥♥
Value	★★★
Grapes	sauvignon blanc
Region	Adelaide Hills, SA
Cellar	▯ 1
Alc./Vol.	13.0%
RRP	$24.80 ⊜

Martin Shaw and Michael Hill Smith's sauvignon blanc is the one to show those cocky Kiwis who think we can't make good sauv blanc in Oz. Since the initial 1989 vintage it's invariably been excellent.
CURRENT RELEASE 2004   Archetypal Shaw and Smith. It's pale in colour, with a combination of flinty, minerally aromas and sweet tropical varietal notes on the nose. The palate is light and fresh, yet it doesn't skimp on intensity of lively varietal flavour. A zippy, delicious accompaniment to good yum cha.

Smithbrook Sauvignon Blanc

Quality	♥♥♥♥
Value	★★★
Grapes	sauvignon blanc 94%; semillon 6%
Region	Pemberton, WA
Cellar	▯ 1
Alc./Vol.	13.0%
RRP	$19.00 ⊜

The Pemberton–Manjimup region of Western Australia is a rather isolated spot with some impressive forests of skyscraping karri trees. At Smithbrook, visitors drive through a picturesque stand of the trees to reach the vineyard. Sauvignon blanc is a speciality. Maker: Michael Symons.
CURRENT RELEASE 2004   Notwithstanding a small proportion of barrel fermented material in the mix, this remains at the piercing, take-no-prisoners end of the sauvignon spectrum. True aficionados wouldn't have it any other way. It has brilliant greenish colour and a super-penetrating aroma of spiky green leaves and tropical fruits. In the mouth it tastes blackcurrant and zesty, with good depth and a brisk tang at the end. Serve it with rocket leaves and goat's cheese croutons.

Smithbrook The Yilgarn Blanc

Quality	♥♥♥♥
Value	★★★⟩
Grapes	sauvignon blanc
Region	Pemberton, WA
Cellar	▯ 3
Alc./Vol.	13.5%
RRP	$28.00

Yilgarn is the granitic rock that underlies the vineyards of Western Australia's Pemberton region. This is the first white wine under Smithbrook's Yilgarn banner and it's made from sauvignon blanc rather than chardonnay. And 100 per cent barrel fermentation makes it a much more complex wine than most antipodean sauvignons.
CURRENT RELEASE 2004   There's no missing the new French oak influence here, but winemaker Michael Symons has stopped short of letting it dominate the fruit. As a result the gooseberry and green-lime fruit characters are smoothly interwoven with the nutty, spicy qualities of the oak. The result is a smooth palate of some complexity that still retains a varietal tang. Try it with tuna sashimi.

Southern Highland Winery Sauvignon Blanc

This grape should be one of the best-suited to the Southern Highlands, because of the cool, inland climate. One disadvantage, though, is that it's a high-vigour region with high rainfall and rich soils, and sauvignon blanc grows like a weed at the best of times! Winemaker is Eddy Rossi. CURRENT RELEASE 2004   This is a ripper of a sauvignon blanc: pale-coloured, it has a highly perfumed nose that suggests passionfruit and gooseberry. It's very classic. The same flavours appear in the mouth, where it's even more tropical/pineappley and has a lick of sweetness. It's fine, light and lively – a very good drink with seafood and salads.

Quality	🍷🍷🍷🍷🍷
Value	★★★★
Grapes	sauvignon blanc
Region	Southern Highlands, NSW
Cellar	🍾 2
Alc./Vol.	13.5%
RRP	$20.00 🍷 (cellar door)

Stefano Lubiana Sauvignon Blanc

Stefano Lubiana's winemaking roots go back to the family vineyard in the hot South Australian Riverland. When he struck out on his own he went to a dramatically different environment, the cool valleys of southern Tasmania. While it's a more marginal climate, the quality possibilities are much better and it shows in his range of excellent Tassie wines.
CURRENT RELEASE 2004   This zippy young wine is at the green-grassy end of the sauvignon spectrum, but that's not a bad thing. It smells and tastes a bit like fresh asparagus with a blackcurrant edge, and there's a whisper of lees character to add a little extra depth and interest. The zesty fruit is the main game though, and it tracks down the palate with a brisk tang that really gets the mouth watering. Try it with crispy steamed fresh asparagus and hollandaise.

Quality	🍷🍷🍷🍷
Value	★★★
Grapes	sauvignon blanc
Region	Southern Tasmania
Cellar	🍾 1
Alc./Vol.	12.0%
RRP	$26.50 🍷

Tamar Ridge Tasmania Sauvignon Blanc

This won a trophy at the '04 Perth Wine Show, no doubt beating a strong team of WA wines. Like Marlborough savvies, it will appeal to those who like definite, full-frontal sauvignon blanc personality. Maker: Michael Fogarty.
CURRENT RELEASE 2004   This is a very smart wine from a tricky Taswegian vintage. The aromas of crushed vine-leaf and lantana smell a touch underripe, and the palate is very acidic, but it has intense varietal fruit flavour that leaves a big impression on the palate. There is a suggestion of sweetness to balance that fierce acidity but the overall impression is good. And it goes well with natural oysters.

Quality	🍷🍷🍷🍷
Value	★★★★
Grapes	sauvignon blanc
Region	Tamar Valley, Tas.
Cellar	🍾 3
Alc./Vol.	12.5%
RRP	$20.00 🍷

TK Adelaide Hills Sauvignon Blanc

Quality	♥♥♥♥♥
Value	★★★★★
Grapes	sauvignon blanc 98%; semillon 2%
Region	Adelaide Hills, SA
Cellar	🍷 2+
Alc./Vol.	12.5%
RRP	$22.00 ⬛

In 2004, Tim Knappstein changed the branding of this wine from Lenswood Vineyards to TK, in recognition of the fact that to wear a regional or sub-regional name (like Lenswood), the wine must be at least 85 per cent from that area. But in 2004 the wine is only 79 per cent Lenswood, the rest being from Oakbank. It also contains 2 per cent semillon for good luck.

CURRENT RELEASE 2004   Again, the Tim Knappstein style is a subtle but beautifully made one that really grows on you as you drink it. The colour is pale but bright; the nose is shy and clean, with hints of fresh-picked herbs, garden salad and lemon, and the taste is clean and dry, soft and smooth, juicy and seamless with a great deal of finesse. It's great with Chinese pork dumplings.

PENGUIN BEST SAUVIGNON
BLANC AND BLENDS

Tobacco Road Sauvignon Blanc Semillon

Quality	♥♥♥◗
Value	★★★★◗
Grapes	sauvignon blanc; semillon
Region	Gundagai, NSW; King Valley, Vic.
Cellar	🍷 1
Alc./Vol.	12.0%
RRP	$11.00 Ⓢ ⬛

'Tobacco Ro-o-o-o-oad . . . and it's ho-o-o-ome.' Nice choice of names: it brings back musical memories for baby boomers. We couldn't stop humming the song after we tried the wine.

CURRENT RELEASE 2004   This gives you plenty of wine for your eleven bucks, and no doubt it's cheaper in the mega chain stores. It smells of snapped twigs and herby green stems, a touch of snow pea, and is soft and easygoing on the palate. There's plenty of up-front, gently rounded fruit and its soft finish carries a twist of sweetness. A very passable Rosemount imitation! It would suit Cornish vegetable pasties.

Water Wheel Sauvignon Blanc

Quality	♥♥♥♥
Value	★★★★
Grapes	sauvignon blanc
Region	Bendigo, Vic.
Cellar	🍷 1
Alc./Vol.	12.0%
RRP	$16.20 ⬛

The Bendigo region really is first and foremost red wine territory, but a smattering of smart whites show that the district can serve up a lot more. Water Wheel's sauvignon is one of them, and the reasonable price makes it even better.

CURRENT RELEASE 2004   Pale with a slightly green tinge, this has less in-your-face varietal qualities than some sexier sauvignon blancs. It smells of citrus and fruit salad, ripe and appealing, with freshness and vitality. The palate is pleasantly intense, with clean fruit flavour in the middle, and a crisp end. Try it with vegetable yaki soba.

Wedgetail Par 3 Sauvignon Blanc

The golfing name of Wedgetail's Par 3 comes from a small fairway and single hole at the bottom of this Yarra Valley vineyard. This sauvignon blanc blends Yarra Valley material with fruit from Australia's premier sauvignon blanc region, the Adelaide Hills.

CURRENT RELEASE 2004 An aromatic varietal nose reminds us of dry grass, citrus and tropical fruit. It's made with the currently fashionable inclusion of 10 per cent barrel-fermented wine, and it works well – not as a strong flavour influence, but more as a seasoning and structural component. The palate is clean, intense and appetising with a little whisper of oak on the aftertaste. Try it with a mixed shellfish platter.

Quality	♟♟♟♟
Value	★★★
Grapes	sauvignon blanc
Region	Yarra Valley, Vic.; Adelaide Hills, SA
Cellar	🍾 1
Alc./Vol.	12.5%
RRP	$22.00 ⧈

West Cape Howe Sauvignon Blanc

In less than ten years West Cape Howe has made a reputation for itself as an excellent source of well-made Great Southern varietal wines. An added bonus is that they offer very good value for money.

CURRENT RELEASE 2004 You'd be hard pressed to find a more pristine example of sauvignon blanc in Australia. It smells of gooseberries, cut grass and passionfruit. It's a thrilling introduction to a palate that boasts soft tropical fruit, combined with more savoury herbal and lemony notes, finishing with a piercing tang of acidity. Serve it alongside stir-fried fish with ginger and spring onion.

Quality	♟♟♟♟♟
Value	★★★★
Grapes	sauvignon blanc
Region	Mount Barker & Frankland River, WA
Cellar	🍾 2
Alc./Vol.	12.0%
RRP	$18.00 ⧈

Wirra Wirra Scrubby Rise Sauvignon Blanc Semillon Viognier

In the way of things at Wirra Wirra, the Scrubby Rise vineyard is flat and completely free of scrub! In a wine world that takes itself increasingly seriously, thank heavens for a little humour.

CURRENT RELEASE 2004 An unusual mix of varieties has produced a very attractive young white. The aroma is quite complex with citrus, floral and tropical-fruit characters of good intensity. A small proportion (10 per cent) of barrel-fermented material acts more as a textural adjunct than a flavouring element, and it finishes long and bone-dry. Try it with lemon chicken.

Quality	♟♟♟♟
Value	★★★★
Grapes	sauvignon blanc; semillon; viognier
Region	McLaren Vale, SA
Cellar	🍾 2
Alc./Vol.	12.5%
RRP	$17.00 Ⓢ ⧈

Wolf Blass Gold Label Sauvignon Blanc

Quality 🍷🍷🍷🍷
Value ★★★
Grapes sauvignon blanc
Region Mount Gambier, SA
Cellar 🍾 1
Alc./Vol. 11.0%
RRP $22.00 [$]

The comprehensive Gold Label range is part of a revamp of the Wolf Blass wines that's been taking place over the last few years. The style is more contemporary and they are very fair value for money.

CURRENT RELEASE 2004 Archetypal young sauvignon aromas are spot-on, combining a tangy, herbaceous touch with succulent guava and lime fruit. The palate has good balance of tropical-fruit flavour and herby notes, tasting tangy and clean, and finishing light and dry. It falls away a little in the mouth, but the up-front varietal fruit is what it's all about and it succeeds admirably in that respect. Serve it with lemony grilled prawn and rocket salad.

Zilzie Buloke Reserve Sauvignon Blanc

Quality 🍷🍷🍷½
Value ★★★★
Grapes sauvignon blanc
Region Murray Valley, Vic.
Cellar 🍾 1
Alc./Vol. 11.5%
RRP $10.00 [$]

Buloke Reserve is not a reserve wine per se: the name is a reference to the fenced-off area where native bulokes or casuarina trees grow on the property, which is owned by the Forbes family.

CURRENT RELEASE 2004 This is good value: a savvy that tastes like one from the hot irrigation area of the Murray Valley. It has some passionfruit and salad-herb aromas, a twist of sweetness and perhaps a smidgen of oak, while the finish is clean and dry. It's a good match with yabbies and salad.

Semillon and Blends

The classic Hunter Valley semillon dry white style has enjoyed a high profile over the years. Some of the fame has been deserved, but what's too often overlooked is the good semillon grown in many other parts of Australia. Some excellent wines are emerging from South Australia and Western Australia, and winemakers are honing techniques with semillon to offer another quality white wine alternative. The multiplicity of semillon-sauvignon blanc blends is more of a mixed bag: the best are thrilling, but too many fit a lean-and-mean profile that's far from lovable. As for Hunter semillon, at best it remains a true classic, and the ready availability of aged examples means it's easy to enjoy them at their mature best.

Brookland Valley Verse One Semillon Sauvignon Blanc

The name Verse One begs the question: what happened to the rest of the song? We learnt Verse One years ago when Jane Rutter played the flute in the vineyard, but where do we go from there? The Verse One wines have always served up steady reliable quality at a fair price.

CURRENT RELEASE 2004 The aromas are typical Margaret River: twiggy, smoky and cedary – which is the regional semillon style asserting itself. The palate has delicacy and balance, with pleasant flavour and a clean, dry, food-friendly finish. It suits Chinese wonton soup.

Quality	🍷🍷🍷½
Value	★★★½
Grapes	semillon; sauvignon blanc
Region	Margaret River, WA
Cellar	🍾 2
Alc./Vol.	13.0%
RRP	$20.00 [$]

Classic McLaren Semillon Sauvignon Blanc

Classic McLaren Wines is a substantial operation that was established as recently as 1996. It has 57 hectares of vines in McLaren Vale and Tony De Lisio is winemaker. We wonder if the name isn't a bit confusing by incorporating the region's name; the branding is not very clear.

CURRENT RELEASE 2003 With a little extra bottle-age over most of its competitors, this has a medium to full yellow colour and is developing lemon-pith semillon aromas with a hint of bottle-age. Its drinkability is enhanced by that little extra age. The palate is smooth and long, with a clean, dry, well-balanced finish. It's delicious with cold meats and salads.

Quality	🍷🍷🍷🍷½
Value	★★★★★
Grapes	semillon; sauvignon blanc
Region	McLaren Vale, SA
Cellar	🍾 2+
Alc./Vol.	13.0%
RRP	$14.00 💸

De Bortoli Black Creek Semillon

Quality 🍷🍷🍷🍷
Value ★★★★½
Grapes semillon
Region Hunter Valley, NSW
Cellar 5
Alc./Vol. 11.0%
RRP $14.00 ($)

Black Creek actually exists: it runs through the Lovedale locality of the lower Hunter Valley, where De Bortoli's winery is situated. The place was formerly known as Lesnik's Wilderness Estate. Maker: Scott Stephens.

CURRENT RELEASE 2004 A very attractive fresh style of unwooded, classic semillon; grapey and soft in the mouth with a trace of sweetness to round it out. The bracing aromas are of lemon zest, lemon butter and passionfruit. Plenty of flavour here, and it would go well with stuffed zucchini flowers.

De Bortoli Montage Semillon Sauvignon Blanc

Quality 🍷🍷🍷
Value ★★★★
Grapes semillon; sauvignon blanc
Region various, NSW
Cellar 1
Alc./Vol. 12.0%
RRP $9.00 ($)

A montage is a picture pieced together from diverse fragments, and the art is in the selection of the pieces. It's a bit like blending a wine, where the whole is greater than the sum of the individual parts.

CURRENT RELEASE 2004 The greener spectrum of semillon and sauvignon aromas are on display here. The aroma reminds of chopped parsley. It's drier than expected on the palate; usually this kind of white at this price level is a bit sweet these days. The flavour is light and fresh and very new-tasting, and it's a tiny bit austere. It would welcome a big Greek salad.

Eagle Vale Semillon Sauvignon Blanc

Quality 🍷🍷🍷🍷½
Value ★★★★
Grapes semillon 77%; sauvignon blanc 23%
Region Margaret River, WA
Cellar 3
Alc./Vol. 13.0%
RRP $19.70

Eagle Vale was established quite recently, in 1997, with a 12-hectare vineyard and winery on Caves Road, although the wine is made off-site. Guy Gallienne is in charge of production.

CURRENT RELEASE 2004 Lemon and lime fruit aromas with a twist of herbal greenery combine in the attractive perfume this classic Margaret River blend. It's intensely flavoured and tightly focused on the palate. The texture is fine and it lingers well on the aftertaste. It's a fine wine and a good partner for grilled garfish.

Fermoy Estate Reserve Semillon

The Margaret River semillon style is one that tends to polarise technical tasters. The lifted aromatics are captivating, but there can be a hard greenness that sometimes detracts from the palate. The real success story is with semillon-sauvignon blanc blends.
CURRENT RELEASE 2002   With a light yellow colour this is ageing slowly. Capsicum, snow-pea, green-herb aromas dominate, and the palate is delicate and lemony with soft clean acid and some richness derived from ripe fruit. It's an attractive easy-drinking wine, to serve with Chinese lemon chicken.

Quality	♈♈♈♈
Value	★★★
Grapes	semillon
Region	Margaret River, WA
Cellar	▮ 3+
Alc./Vol.	13.0%
RRP	$31.00

Fermoy Estate Semillon

We have for a long time found Fermoy's whites much better than its reds, which is curious considering its location, next to Moss Wood in Wilyabrup, the most distinguished terroir in Margaret River. Maker: Michael Kelly.
CURRENT RELEASE 2003   Subtle cedary aromas from French oak combine with snow-pea regional semillon characters and the beginnings of bottle-age, to give us a distinctive Margaret River style of semi. It has very good intensity and harmony in the mouth, with fine texture and softness, and a lingering finish. It's a clever style but does push oak to the limit. It would be perfect with smoked chicken and salad.

Quality	♈♈♈♈♈
Value	★★★★
Grapes	semillon
Region	Margaret River, WA
Cellar	▮ 3+
Alc./Vol.	13.5%
RRP	$21.70

Ferngrove Frankland Semillon Sauvignon Blanc

The 2004 vintage resulted in high yields and a lot of the sem-sav blends were a bit on the thin, hollow side. Not this one: it's one of our favourites from the vintage. Maker: Kim Horton.
CURRENT RELEASE 2004   Good concentration and a riper spectrum of flavours are the hallmarks of this wine. The usual green-salad and garden-herb aromas are there in abundance, with a trace of tropical fruits, while the palate has some power and depth. It has a good tangy acid zing and doesn't rely on sweetness. A lovely drink, to serve with sushi.

Quality	♈♈♈♈♈
Value	★★★★★
Grapes	semillon; sauvignon blanc
Region	Great Southern, WA
Cellar	▮ 2
Alc./Vol.	12.5%
RRP	$15.00 (S) 🍸

PENGUIN BEST SEMILLON AND BLENDS

Glenguin Estate The Old Broke Block Semillon

Quality 🍷🍷🍷🍷
Value ★★★
Grapes semillon
Region Hunter Valley, NSW
Cellar 🍾 5+
Alc./Vol. 11.0%
RRP $19.00 🔩

Robin and Andrew Tedder of Glenguin winery are the grandsons of Lord Tedder, Baron of Glenguin, who was General Eisenhower's deputy and the commander of allied air power during the liberation of Europe in World War II. Lord Tedder's title came from an entirely different type of 'wine', the malt whisky of Glenguin (now Glengoyne) Distillery where he was born.

CURRENT RELEASE 2004 This pale fresh Hunter semillon has a pure varietal nose of lemon blossom, herbs and lime. The palate is intensely flavoured and a bit more modern and forward in style than the classic Hunter type, showing more 'give' and softness. It has surprising concentration for a wine of 11 per cent alcohol and it finishes clean and crisp. Serve it with pan-fried trout with almonds.

Grant Burge Barossa Vines Semillon Sauvignon Blanc

Quality 🍷🍷🍷🍷
Value ★★★★½
Grapes semillon; sauvignon blanc
Region Barossa Valley, SA
Cellar 🍾 2
Alc./Vol. 11.5%
RRP $12.00 [$]

Semillon has a long history in the Barossa Valley, where it was once known as 'madeira' for reasons that are lost in the mists of time. It can perform well there, and Grant Burge's low-alcohol model is always a pretty smart wine at the price.

CURRENT RELEASE 2004 This has lemony and slightly sweaty aromas with semillon holding sway over sauvignon. The palate is plump and juicy with straightforward flavour that's clean-tasting and tangy, with a long lemony finish. Very good value. It would go well with grilled fish.

Grant Burge Zerk Semillon

Quality 🍷🍷🍷🍷
Value ★★★½
Grapes semillon
Region Barossa Valley, SA
Cellar 🍾 2+
Alc./Vol. 12.0%
RRP $16.50 [$] 🔩

This Barossa semillon takes its name from Robert and Janine Zerk's 75-year-old vineyard. It's always a good example of how a judicious touch of oak can make poor old Barossa sem into a worthy alternative to chardonnay.

CURRENT RELEASE 2004 The colour is bright and inviting, and the lemony semillon-varietal aroma is very attractive. It's made sweeter and more complex by a dab of oak, and the palate has good depth and smooth feel, finishing clean and dry. Good drinking with grilled chicken and lime pickle.

Grosset Semillon Sauvignon Blanc

Quality	🍷🍷🍷🍷½
Value	★★★
Grapes	semillon; sauvignon blanc
Region	Clare Valley, SA
Cellar	🍾 2
Alc./Vol.	13.0%
RRP	$29.80 🔩

Jeffrey Grosset's drive to make the most pure expressions of the Clare Valley fruit available to him has resulted in an enviable range of classic wines. For some reason this blend doesn't quite attract the accolades given to his other wines, but it sells out just as quickly, and like the others it can be hard to find.

CURRENT RELEASE 2004 This has typically Grosset essency fruit character: intense, pure and succulent. The nose is reminiscent of mixed citrus and tropical fruits, and there's an appealing 'Juicy Fruit' gum character that reminds us of our innocent youth. The palate is smooth and long in flavour with a dry finish. Enjoy it with chilled shellfish.

Lindemans Hunter Valley Semillon Bin 0455

Quality	🍷🍷🍷🍷
Value	★★★★
Grapes	semillon
Region	Hunter Valley, NSW
Cellar	🍾 5
Alc./Vol.	12.0%
RRP	$20.00 [$] 🔩

After five years in the wilderness, Lindemans is back making classic Hunter wines for general release. Although, with the takeover by Beringer Blass, we guess the whole question is back up in the air again. Maker: Matthew Johnson.

CURRENT RELEASE 2004 Delicate, restrained, crisp and fresh, this is a lovely traditional Hunter semillon with lemon-pudding and twiggy, cedary aromas. It's light-bodied and very sprightly, crisp on the tongue and tangy, fruity and yet soft at the finish. It's balanced well for current drinking and would take some age quite well. Try it with sushi.

McGuigan Bin 9000 Semillon

Quality	🍷🍷🍷🍷
Value	★★★★½
Grapes	semillon
Region	Hunter Valley, NSW
Cellar	🍾 4+
Alc./Vol.	11.5%
RRP	$15.00 [$] 🔩

Hunter River semillon rarely comes this cheap, and we're pleased to announce that it has the quality to equal a lot of more expensive wines. Made in true regional style with relatively low alcohol, no wood and no artefact, it's worth grabbing to drink straight away, but there's no hurry, it should also age well in the mid-term.

CURRENT RELEASE 2004 Very Hunter sem: pale, appetising, aromas of lemon and laundry soap, understated yet more-ish flavour, medium depth and a long savoury finish. What more could you want for your $15? The palate is smooth and dry with good vinosity. Try it with chicken grilled on the barbecue.

Merum Semillon

Quality	♥♥♥♥♥
Value	★★★↓
Grapes	semillon 90%; chardonnay 10%
Region	Pemberton, WA
Cellar	▮ 4+
Alc./Vol.	13.3%
RRP	$26.00 ⧖

Merum is the Latin term for pure undiluted wine. This semillon from Pemberton is a complex drop, with 10 per cent chardonnay and 30 per cent new French oak making a worthwhile contribution to it.

CURRENT RELEASE 2004 A pale, greenish-straw colour looks good, and the nose is vinous and minerally, with some well-handled solids and barrel influences giving it a smoky French accent. As well there's crisp fruit character reminiscent of herbs, lemon and pear. The smooth palate has lovely texture and good depth, with a savoury backbone and bone-dry finish completing things perfectly. Enjoy it with pan-fried fish.

Mistletoe Hunter Valley Reserve Semillon

Quality	♥♥♥♥♥
Value	★★★★
Grapes	semillon
Region	Hunter Valley, NSW
Cellar	▮ 10+
Alc./Vol.	10.5%
RRP	$20.00 ⧖ (cellar door)

Some of this reserve wine is released as a youngster, but most is put away for release as a mature wine. It's made from grapes grown at Belford, and won a gold medal in Rutherglen in 2004 at its first showing.

CURRENT RELEASE 2004 Pale, youthful, undeveloped, this classic-style Hunter semillon is a crisp and delicious seafood wine right now but shows the potential to age well if cellared. It's fragrantly lemony, minerally and has a tart, lean, angular palate which is low in alcohol, high in acid and promises to mature into a traditional bottle-aged classic. Cellar, or serve now with oysters and lemon juice.

Mistletoe Hunter Valley Semillon

Quality	♥♥♥♥
Value	★★★★
Grapes	semillon
Region	Hunter Valley, NSW
Cellar	▮ 5+
Alc./Vol.	10.5%
RRP	$16.50 ⧖ (cellar door)

This is blended from grapes grown at Belford and at the Mistletoe vineyard in Pokolbin. Winemaker is Ken Sloan.

CURRENT RELEASE 2004 This is the little brother of the same maker's reserve, and is a slightly softer, simpler wine as you might expect. Green-herb/parsley/basil and candied-lemon-peel aromas are discernible, and there's a suggestion of sweetness that could just be nice soft fruit and lower acid than its more austere brother. It still has good intensity and style. Try it with any white-fleshed fish.

Mount Horrocks Semillon

This is one of the best of the oak-aged Clare Valley semillons. It's an underrated wine type that deserves more recognition. Maker: Stephanie Toole.
CURRENT RELEASE 2004   Eight months on lees in French oak has given extra dimension to this excellent semillon, and not at the expense of fruit character or drinkability. It starts off with fine lemon and peachy aromas, and the nutty, yeasty influences season it perfectly, giving it a slightly European feel. The palate is rich and very lingering, with firm acidity helping bring out its harmonious flavours. Stephanie Toole seems to have divined semillon's true worth. Delicious with roast spatchcock.

Quality	🍷🍷🍷🍷🍷
Value	★★★⁺
Grapes	semillon
Region	Clare Valley, SA
Cellar	🍾 3
Alc./Vol.	13.0%
RRP	$27.50

Mount Pleasant Lovedale Semillon

The Lovedale vineyard traditionally makes the finest semillons in the Mount Pleasant folio, and they always incorporate one ingredient that makes Hunter sem into a classic: bottle-age. The current wine is always about five years old when released, and it's usually one of the best of the breed.
Previous outstanding vintages: '75, '79, '84, '86, '95, '96, '97, '98
CURRENT RELEASE 1999   Brilliant yellow–green in colour, this mature Hunter semillon has all the classic attributes. The nose has honey, toast, citrus and linseed aromas of delicious savoury richness. The palate seems rounder than usual, with long flavour, excellent balance and very fine mouth-feel. Serve it with grilled prawns.

Quality	🍷🍷🍷🍷🍷
Value	★★★★
Grapes	semillon
Region	Hunter Valley, NSW
Cellar	🍾 5
Alc./Vol.	11.5%
RRP	$44.00

O'Leary Walker Watervale Semillon

Clare Valley semillon has been made with oak treatment for many years. In fact both authors remember a few special wood-aged Clare semillons of many years ago as some of the first barrel-influenced Australian white wines they'd tasted.
CURRENT RELEASE 2004   Spicy oak plays a significant part in this young white. It doesn't obscure the fruit though, which is as it should be. Citrus-like aromas and flavours are very appealing and well-concentrated, standing up to nutty oak in fine style. The palate is smooth and dry with good vinosity. Drink it with chicken grilled on the barbecue.

Quality	🍷🍷🍷🍷
Value	★★★
Grapes	semillon
Region	Clare Valley, SA
Cellar	🍾 3
Alc./Vol.	11.5%
RRP	$19.85

Penfolds Rawson's Retreat Semillon Chardonnay

Quality 🍷🍷🍷
Value ★★★★
Grapes semillon; chardonnay
Region South Eastern Australia
Cellar 🍾 1
Alc./Vol. 13.0%
RRP $11.50 [$]

Exactly what Rawson was retreating from, we've never been informed. Perhaps he saw a vision of the Beringer Blass takeover posse riding over the hill brandishing their twin pearl-handled chequebooks. As we write, Beringer has just completed its takeover of Southcorp.

CURRENT RELEASE 2004 This is one of those innocuous wines that won't offend anyone; neither will it delight anyone. It's just a straightforward, well-made commercial quaffer with a trace of sweetness and some pleasant enough parsley/herbal, fruity aromas. Flavour with softness is the order of the day. It would suit most cold meat and salad meals.

Pepper Tree Wines Reserve Semillon

Quality 🍷🍷🍷🍷
Value ★★★★
Grapes semillon
Region Hunter Valley, NSW
Cellar 🍾 5+
Alc./Vol. 10.5%
RRP $25.00

John Davis, who bought this Hunter Valley winery from James Fairfax not long ago, owns a lot of vineyards: 40 hectares in Pokolbin, 12 hectares in Coonawarra, 15 hectares in Orange and a massive 100 hectares in Wrattonbully.

CURRENT RELEASE 1999 At six years old, this is incredibly restrained and still has a long life ahead of it. It must have been very austere as an infant. The colour is medium–light yellow; the bouquet shows flint, minerals and candle-wax, with suggestions of wet river rocks. True! The palate is lean and lemony, tartly acidic and is yet to really fill out much. It's still quite steely, and begs to be drunk with food – we suggest any kind of seafood.

Pepperton Estate Rascals Prayer Semillon Sauvignon Blanc

Quality 🍷🍷🍷
Value ★★★★
Grapes semillon; sauvignon blanc
Region South Eastern Australia
Cellar 🍾 1
Alc./Vol. 12.6%
RRP $10.00

This brand is produced by the Toohey Brothers, Peter and David, who used to own a small chain of liquor stores in Sydney before selling out to Woolworths. They now produce inexpensive wines for own-brands and on-premises sales in restaurants and bars.

CURRENT RELEASE 2004 Clean and fresh, this light, straightforward dry white is herbal and slightly sweet, but is a perfectly decent quaffer for the money. It tastes of these two grapes and won't break the bank. A well-put-together low-cost sem-sav. Try it with caesar salad.

Peter Lehmann Barossa Semillon

For a Barossa winery, Peter Lehmann makes an awful lot of semillon – which is probably how it can field a wine of this quality and style at such a measly low price. It has a lot to choose from. Winemakers are Andrew Wigan, Leonie Lange, Peter Scholz and Ian Hongell.

CURRENT RELEASE 2003 The colour is medium yellow and the bouquet suggests baked lemon pudding with a sprinkle of herbs. It smells and tastes fully ripe and up-front, perhaps even a little forward. The palate is soft and gentle. It's nicely balanced for early drinking. Serve it with spaghetti marinara.

Quality	🍷🍷🍷½
Value	★★★★
Grapes	semillon
Region	Barossa Valley, SA
Cellar	🍾 2
Alc./Vol.	12.0%
RRP	$12.00 [$]

Peter Lehmann Semillon Chardonnay

The cheaper Peter Lehmann wines often deliver jaw-dropping bargains, totally out of keeping with their humble prices. This is one of those. Makers: Andrew 'Wigs' Wigan and team.

CURRENT RELEASE 2004 The colour is a somewhat developed medium–full yellow and the bouquet reminds of lemon juice and fresh herbs, with a 'Sunlight soap' kind of lemony-ness that reminds us of traditional Hunter semillon. It's certainly very generously flavoured, with richness, weight and persistence on palate. The finish is clean and tangy with freshness and balance. It deserves poached fish drizzled with beurre blanc.

Quality	🍷🍷🍷🍷🍷
Value	★★★★★
Grapes	semillon; chardonnay
Region	Barossa Valley, SA
Cellar	🍾 2
Alc./Vol.	12.0%
RRP	$12.00 [$] 🌀

PENGUIN WINE OF THE YEAR and BEST-VALUE WHITE WINE

Plantagenet Semillon Sauvignon Blanc

Curiouser and curiouser: Plantagenet, a Great Southern winery based in Mount Barker, is now producing a Margaret River sem-sav. We guess that's an acknowledgement that this blend and that region are a winning combination. Maker: Richard Robson.

CURRENT RELEASE 2004 It's a bit innocuous, a touch bland, but that's the nature of these blends when very young. They do build a bit of character once they've been in the bottle a few months. This has a light colour and a shy, vaguely green-salady aroma, with touches of lemon juice and stalky, underbrush notes. It's a very decent drink and goes well with cold seafood and salad.

Quality	🍷🍷🍷🍷
Value	★★★
Grapes	semillon; sauvignon blanc
Region	Margaret River, WA
Cellar	🍾 2
Alc./Vol.	12.5%
RRP	$23.00 🌀

Rosemount Diamond Label Semillon

Quality 🍷🍷🍷🍷
Value ★★★★
Grapes semillon
Region mostly Hunter Valley, NSW
Cellar 🍾 1
Alc./Vol. 13.5%
RRP $16.00 [$]

The entire Rosemount Diamond Label single-varietal series, as well as the split-label blends, are sealed with synthetic Nomacorks. We wouldn't be confident of keeping them longer than two or three years from bottling date, especially the whites – and yet this is a style of wine that has a name for ageing well.

CURRENT RELEASE 2003 The colour is medium–full yellow, and in both colour and bouquet it shows some subtle, positive age-development. It's still fresh and herbal to sniff, while the taste is soft and rich, smooth and rounded in a style that invites immediate drinking. It's very appealing, and goes well with barbecued calamari.

Rosemount Semillon Chardonnay

Quality 🍷🍷🍷
Value ★★★★
Grapes semillon; chardonnay
Region not stated
Cellar 🍾 1
Alc./Vol. 12.5%
RRP $12.00 [$]

We're surprised more wineries don't field a semillon chardonnay: they're often better than either grape singly, combining the best features of both. The blend often has the structure and finesse of semillon plus the rich fruitiness of chardonnay.

CURRENT RELEASE 2004 Having said the above, this is hardly a great example. It's a rather bland, innocuous style, a wine with a personality bypass, whose palate is softened by a deft touch of sweetness. There are some twiggy, dried-herb aromas and the acidity seems low. It has no real fault and slips down well enough with a chicken sandwich.

Rosemount Semillon Sauvignon Blanc

Quality 🍷🍷🍷
Value ★★★★
Grapes semillon; sauvignon blanc
Region not stated
Cellar 🍾 1
Alc./Vol. 12.0%
RRP $12.00 [$]

We found it hard to distinguish between the sem-sav and the sem-chard from Rosemount. It's like they all came out of the same massive witch's cauldron.

CURRENT RELEASE 2004 Softly fruity, just off-dry, simple and mono-dimensional, but hard to really dislike – that's the style of the modern corporatised big global brand. It is probably quite acceptable to those who buy it regularly, but it tastes bland and soulless to picky folks like us. And there are a dozen other wines just like it in the Southcorp portfolio. Try it with cocktail frankfurts watching the footy.

Rosily Vineyard Semillon Sauvignon Blanc

Some small French oak was used in the making of this wine. The usual way is for a small percentage of the grapes – usually some of the semillon component – to be fermented in barrels, then possibly aged in the same barrels for a short period.

CURRENT RELEASE 2004 There's a minty, almost confectionery aspect to the aroma and the palate is fruit-sweet and has a touch of richness. There's a little alcohol warmth on the finish and the oak has been deftly handled, as it barely shows up. The wine has plenty of weight and lots of flavour, and the mouth-feel is soft. A good wine to serve with whole barbecued snapper.

Quality 🍷🍷🍷🍷
Value ★★★★
Grapes semillon; sauvignon blanc
Region Margaret River, WA
Cellar 🍾 2+
Alc./Vol. 13.5%
RRP $19.00

Rothvale Vat 8 Hunter Semillon

Rothvale is owned and operated by the Patton family, with Max and his son Luke sharing the winemaking duties. The vineyard is well sited in central Pokolbin, on Deasy's Road.

CURRENT RELEASE 2002 Three years in the bottle and this is starting to show some excellent bottle-aged development. The medium-yellow colour retains some green tints and the vibrant aromas are of lemon juice and green herbs, with sidenotes of cured straw-hay and subtle toastiness. The palate is enlivened by frisky acidity that is just a touch hard – but it carries food well and should continue to age gracefully for many years. Try it with roast chicken.

Quality 🍷🍷🍷🍷½
Value ★★★★½
Grapes semillon
Region Hunter Valley, NSW
Cellar 🍾 6+
Alc./Vol. 11.0%
RRP $20.00 [$]

Sirromet Queensland Semillon

The Sirromet winery and restaurant is at Mount Cotton, only 30 minutes drive south-east of Brisbane. It's an ideal place to snare the tourist market, but the Sirromet crowd also have an eye to wine quality, so they have their vineyards in the much cooler high-altitude Granite Belt further inland.

CURRENT RELEASE 2004 Pale and classical, there's more than a touch of the Hunter about this young semillon. It smells of citrus, straw and herbs with a very slight sulphury touch that blows off with air. The palate is lemony and austere with a bone-dry finish. A wine that should build in interest with a few years in bottle. Right now it goes well with Queensland spanner crab.

Quality 🍷🍷🍷🍷
Value ★★★
Grapes semillon
Region South Burnett & Granite Belt, Qld
Cellar 🍾 1–3+
Alc./Vol. 11.0%
RRP $18.50

Tatachilla Growers Semillon Sauvignon Blanc

Quality 🍷🍷🍷
Value ★★★★
Grapes semillon; sauvignon blanc
Region various, SA
Cellar 🍾 1
Alc./Vol. 12.5%
RRP $13.00 [$] 🌀

The Tatachilla labels have come in from the scrub and been for a visit to the style consultant. They now look very civilised, modern, even a touch stylish. We're not sure that putting a hand-on-heart quote from the winemaker on the front label is really kosher, though.

CURRENT RELEASE 2004 A whiff of passionfruit, a pale-ish colour, a plain and simple taste that won't offend, and what you have is a very easy-drinking quaffer at a more than fair price. The finish is clean and dry. It won't thrill, but neither will it disappoint. A good quaffer to serve with waldorf salad.

Thompson SSB Semillon Sauvignon Blanc

Quality 🍷🍷🍷🍷½
Value ★★★★
Grapes semillon 60%; sauvignon blanc 40%
Region Margaret River, WA
Cellar 🍾 3
Alc./Vol. 12.6%
RRP $20.00 🌀

This vineyard was established in 1994 on Harman's Road South, Wilyabrup. The vineyard area is 9.41 hectares, to be precise. The wines are made elsewhere by Mark Messenger (Juniper Estate), Michael Peterkin (Pierro) and Mark Lane (Flying Fish Cove). That's some lineup of helpers!

CURRENT RELEASE 2004 A very good, typical SSB, with a subtle trace of oak that is barely discernible, and lots of crunchy cucumber, sugar-snap pea aromas and flavours. The palate has good intensity and persistence, without sacrificing delicacy or balance. It's a superior version of this classic Margaret River style. Serve with blue eye cod.

Tulloch Semillon

Quality 🍷🍷🍷🍷
Value ★★★★
Grapes semillon
Region Hunter Valley, NSW
Cellar 🍾 4
Alc./Vol. 11.5%
RRP $15.00 [$] 🌀

The Tulloch family owns its own name once more, having bought back the ranch (or at least the name!) from Southcorp. This made the Top 40 Wines list at the New South Wales Wine Awards for 2004.

CURRENT RELEASE 2003 Traditional resiny, straw-like aromas of old-fashioned Hunter semillon are apparent here. The palate is delicate and dry, crisp and not-too-tart, subtle and unobtrusive, but with underlying flavour intensity – just the right style to go well with food, especially seafood.

Tyrrell's Lost Block Semillon

The Tyrrell family make more wines from semillon in any given year than any other, to our knowledge. Something like seven of them. This one is in the mid-range, and is a drink-or-cellar style. Maker: Andrew Spinaze.

CURRENT RELEASE 2004   Wow! This is racy. If high-acid dry whites that go with seafood are your bag, you'll love this. It really cuts a clean swathe across the palate. Fragrant herbal green-tinged aromas are very inviting, and not unripe. The acid is not hard, and anyway, it's mopped up nicely by food, especially shellfish.

Quality	♟ ♟ ♟ ♟
Value	★ ★ ★ ★ ★
Grapes	semillon
Region	Hunter Valley, NSW
Cellar	🍾 6+
Alc./Vol.	10.5%
RRP	$16.75 Ⓢ 🦪

The Willows Barossa Semillon

Peter Scholz, sometime winemaker at Peter Lehmann since many a year, runs this family-owned vineyard at Light Pass. His family have been in the Barossa for five generations, mostly as doctors. A portion of this wine was fermented in new French oak barrels.

CURRENT RELEASE 2002   This wine has a deep colour and looks very developed, but that's the way of three-year-old Barossa semillon – especially when it's been in oak. The bouquet is likewise developed and complex, showing toasty, smoky, straw- and hay-like aromas, very strong and obvious. It has big flavour in the mouth with good weight and also impeccable balance. The finish is clean and dry with a touch of firmness. Good with roast Barossa chook!

Quality	♟ ♟ ♟ ♟
Value	★ ★ ★ ★
Grapes	semillon
Region	Barossa Valley, SA
Cellar	🍾 2
Alc./Vol.	12.0%
RRP	$16.00

Viognier

This northern Rhône variety has become a very trendy white grape, with a wide range of Australian vineyard locations from cool Canberra to the torrid Murray. It's being made by all sorts of producers from great multinationals to hobby operations, but only a couple of growers have gone for it in a big way. Its potential is a bit of a mystery to us. It can be a rather confronting type of wine, with extraordinary aromatics, elevated alcohol, soft acidity, and all too often harsh phenolic extraction. In fact sometimes it's downright ugly. Yet the industry persists with it, and we have to say that some wines are brilliant. Its future will be interesting to watch.

Alan & Veitch Charleston Viognier

Quality	🍷🍷🍷🍷
Value	★★★⁴
Grapes	viognier
Region	Adelaide Hills, SA
Cellar	🍾 3
Alc./Vol.	13.5%
RRP	$28.00 🥂

Alan & Veitch is a second label of winemaker Robert Johnson, and also his parents' names. Johnson has a small 4.5-hectare vineyard in Eden Valley. Charleston is a sub-region of the Adelaide Hills.
CURRENT RELEASE 2004   The colour is a bright, light–medium yellow and the bouquet is floral, clean and attractive. The apricotty character common to this grape is not strident, as it can often be. The palate is very good: smooth, rich and slightly oily, with lots of varietal flavour, seemingly low acidity and a slight phenolic grip. It's not a complex wine, but very good – and tastes like the real thing. It would go with roast chicken.

Brokenwood Indigo Vineyard Beechworth Viognier

Quality	🍷🍷🍷🍷⁵
Value	★★★★
Grapes	viognier
Region	Beechworth, Vic.
Cellar	🍾 2+
Alc./Vol.	14.0%
RRP	$35.00 🥂

Brokenwood, with its manager/chief winemaker Iain Riggs and wine-savvy board of directors, is an adventurous company that's always seeking to make great wine. Its investment in Beechworth is one example of that creative urge at work.
CURRENT RELEASE 2004   This is a first-rate viognier, with typical apricot and ripe-peach touches combined with gentle hints of stirred-lees and barrel-ferment characters. It's full in the mouth, ripe-tasting and fresh: a wine of power and length. Try it with duck à l'orange.

By Farr Viognier

Viognier is generally not one of the subtlest white wines around: it tends to be big, brassy and showy – hence our rather wanton description of this wine. Maker: Gary Farr. CURRENT RELEASE 2003   A bodice-ripping viognier: big, voluptuous, exuberant! It has a full yellow hue and concentrated apricot and spice aromas that translate directly onto a powerful and very long palate. Happily, it doesn't finish with alcoholic hotness, as many viogniers do. It really satisfies, and drinks beautifully with snapper pie.

Quality	♟♟♟♟♟
Value	★★★★
Grapes	viognier
Region	Geelong, Vic.
Cellar	🍶 2+
Alc./Vol.	13.5%
RRP	$55.00

Clonakilla Viognier

From a modest plot of vines near Canberra, Tim Kirk of Clonakilla fashions two of Australia's greatest Rhône look-alikes. His shiraz-viognier is a benchmark, and in its own fragrant way this straight viognier is almost as outstanding. CURRENT RELEASE 2004   Archetypal viognier aromas meet the nose here. Musky floral, spice, apricot and slightly earthy reductive smells are very mysterious and seductive. The palate is smoothly textured and full of flavour, hinting appetisingly at apricots and spices. It finishes long and aromatic with a very light firmness underneath. A modern Australian classic. Serve it with pork chops and apple sauce.

Quality	♟♟♟♟♟
Value	★★★⭐
Grapes	viognier
Region	Canberra district, NSW
Cellar	🍶 2
Alc./Vol.	14.0%
RRP	$50.00 ⬛

D'Arenberg The Last Ditch Viognier

We reckon Chester Osborn is one of the most creative and energetic winemakers in the industry. He is constantly coming up with new wines and most of them are worth a detour. His able assistant winemaker is Phillip Dean. CURRENT RELEASE 2004   This one really grew on us as we sipped it. It was a bit quiet to begin with and opened up with aeration, to show hints of spice and honey on the nose, with a suspicion of oak, while the palate is soft and smooth and finely balanced. The finish is clean and dry and not too alcoholic – which can be a problem with this grape. Drink it with chicken cooked with apricots.

Quality	♟♟♟♟
Value	★★★★
Grapes	viognier
Region	McLaren Vale, SA
Cellar	🍶 3
Alc./Vol.	14.0%
RRP	$22.60 Ⓢ ⬛

Grant Burge Adelaide Hills Viognier

Quality 🍷🍷🍷🍷½
Value ★★★★
Grapes viognier
Region Adelaide Hills, SA
Cellar 🍾 2
Alc./Vol. 13.5%
RRP $19.90

Every so often Grant Burge Wines releases experimental wines, show wines and other curiosities that fall outside their standard range. They are invariably very interesting; this viognier is one of them.

CURRENT RELEASE 2004 An attractively green-tinged colour heralds an attractive viognier that's less pungent and confronting than some. The nose has floral, candied-cumquat, pink musk stick and dried-apricot aromas that are attractively outside the square. The palate is silky-smooth with aromatic musky fruit in the middle, ahead of a long tangy finish. Good with rosemary-studded roast pork.

Haselgrove HRS Reserve Viognier

Quality 🍷🍷🍷🍷
Value ★★★★
Grapes viognier
Region McLaren Vale, SA
Cellar 🍾 2
Alc./Vol. 12.5%
RRP $25.00 (cellar door)

The HRS range is a limited production line that's only available at the cellar door in McLaren Vale. Such a label gives the winemakers a chance to stretch out and be more creative. Chief winemaker Adrian Lockhart first rose to prominence at Briar Ridge in the Hunter Valley.

CURRENT RELEASE 2004 Classic viognier varietal signature here: apricotty, stone-fruit aromas burst from the glass, with some doughy yeast lees and a balsamic hint that may be due to wild-yeast fermentation. There's also a hint of the subtle oak character imparted by older barrels. There's a lot of fruit sweetness (as distinct from sugar) and the finish is clean. It's full of interest. Good with braised pork belly and an apple sauce.

Longview Beau Sea Viognier

Quality 🍷🍷🍷🍷½
Value ★★★★
Grapes viognier
Region Adelaide Hills, SA
Cellar 🍾 3
Alc./Vol. 13.5%
RRP $27.00

Longview is one of the most impressive new producers in the Adelaide Hills. It was started by Duncan MacGillivray, the creator of Two Dogs lemonade, with the cash he pocketed from selling Two Dogs to Pernod-Ricard.

CURRENT RELEASE 2004 The richness of viognier is here in all its glory, exuding stone-fruit/ripe apricot and peach aromas with good intensity and palate length. There's a bready, yeasty overtone as well. It has a trace of sweetness and is spotlessly clean, and full of character. Try it with crisply roasted snapper fillet on mash.

Millbrook Viognier

Is viognier the next big thing? We doubt it. Viognier wine can be rich and fat and we think public taste is running towards lighter, finer white wines.
CURRENT RELEASE 2004 Varietally very correct, this young wine sums up the characteristics that make viognier unique. The nose is a fusion of exotic floral aromas, spices and stone fruit, with a whisper of spicy oak in the background. In the mouth it's rich, full and slightly fruit-sweet with deep apricot-like flavour, and a long spicy finish that's also marked by some alcoholic heat. A potent viognier to try with pongy soft cheeses.

Quality	🍷🍷🍷🍷
Value	★★★
Grapes	viognier
Region	Perth Hills, WA
Cellar	🍾 1
Alc./Vol.	15.0%
RRP	$22.00 🥂

Pepperjack Viognier

This is a new release for Pepperjack, available only at the cellar door and on-premise (restaurants, pubs and bars). The reality with big-company wines (and this is a Beringer Blass brand) is if they don't have much quantity, they can't justify a national release to the entire trade.
CURRENT RELEASE 2004 Apricot is the signature of nice, ripe viognier and this wine has plenty. It's also spicy, honeyed and has a broad, oily palate structure and texture that distinguishes it. And in this case, a rather thick, hot aftertaste from phenolics and alcohol. It's a big, slightly fat viognier and not a bad introduction to the style. It would suit washed-rind cheeses such as Taleggio.

Quality	🍷🍷🍷🍷
Value	★★★
Grapes	viognier
Region	mainly Barossa Valley, SA
Cellar	🍾 2
Alc./Vol.	14.0%
RRP	$24.00 🥂 (cellar door)

Petaluma Viognier

The Petaluma viognier comes from the V & A Vineyard, which is planted on micaceous schist soils that are very similar to the soils of the Côte Rôtie in France's northern Rhône Valley, home of the world's greatest viognier and shiraz-viognier wines. Senior winemaker is Con Moshos, although Brian Croser is still involved as consultant and is listed as chief winemaker.
CURRENT RELEASE 2004 The Petaluma viognier is usually a touch more elegant than most. It has a light-yellow colour and smells subtly spicy and nicely fragrant – not outrageously apricotty, like some. The flavour is clean and elegant, rich, faintly sweet (probably not from sugar but fruit and glycerol) and very well balanced. A fine drink to pair with chicken stuffed with cheese and bacon.

Quality	🍷🍷🍷🍷🍷
Value	★★★★
Grapes	viognier
Region	Adelaide Hills, SA
Cellar	🍾 3
Alc./Vol.	14.0%
RRP	$38.00

PENGUIN BEST OTHER WHITES AND BLENDS

Pikes Gill's Farm Viognier

Quality 🍷🍷🍷🍷½
Value ★★★★½
Grapes viognier
Region Clare Valley, SA
Cellar 🍾 3
Alc./Vol. 13.0%
RRP $24.00 🔩

This was made from grapes grown on the Pike family's estate vineyard at Polish Hill River. The pike that adorns their labels is a notoriously aggressive fish – not at all like the placid Pike brothers, Andrew and Neil, who run this show.

CURRENT RELEASE 2004 A typical viognier, this has obvious ripe apricot aromas, fruit-driven and pungent with no apparent oak. The colour is an attractively bright medium yellow. The palate is rich and ripe-tasting – not exactly refined or subtle, but high-quality and typical of the grape. The alcohol is under control and it has a touch of the opulence that viognier lovers go for. Try it with chicken cooked with apricots.

Tallis Dookie Hills Viognier

Quality 🍷🍷🍷½
Value ★★★★
Grapes viognier
Region Dookie Hills, Vic.
Cellar 🍾 2
Alc./Vol. 13.5%
RRP $20.00 [$] 🔩

The Dookie Hills area is an up-and-coming region near Seymour in central Victoria. Brown Brothers buy some of their top red grapes from a vineyard there, and Dookie has one of Victoria's oldest agricultural colleges as well.

CURRENT RELEASE 2004 The typical richness and viscosity of viognier is here in spadefuls, but it avoids the oily heaviness of some viogniers. It opens with a little reduction, no doubt locked in by the screw-cap, which doesn't mar it. The palate is soft and rounded, and finishes clean and dry. Try it with coq au vin made with white wine.

Yarra Burn Viognier

Quality 🍷🍷🍷🍷
Value ★★★
Grapes viognier
Region Yarra Valley, Vic.
Cellar 🍾 2
Alc./Vol. 14.0%
RRP $28.00 🔩

Viognier is the grape responsible for Condrieu, one of France's most fascinating wines. Australia's winemakers, especially the Francophile fraternity, have embraced it enthusiastically as an alternative white variety. Results have been good.

CURRENT RELEASE 2004 This wine, sourced incidentally from the famous Yeringberg vineyard site, has a pungent nose that's very viognier with apricot flowers, a hint of pot-pourri, ginger and a touch of spicy oak on the nose. The unctuous palate has smooth, lush texture and flavour that falls a wee bit short, due to a dry touch of phenolic firmness on the finish. A good viognier to accompany crab cakes.

Other Whites and Blends

Experimentation with 'alternative' white grapes has grown apace in Australia over the past 15 years. This has sprung first from a curiosity on the part of winemakers, which has in turn affected and enthused wine drinkers. Variety is the spice of life, and the saying was never truer than for wine. Who wants a steady diet of chardonnay, sauvignon blanc and riesling? In the white Italian grape varieties alone, we now have people making interesting wine from cortese, arneis, picolit and verduzzo, as well as pinot grigio grapes. And on the French side we have petit manseng, viognier, the more established colombard, chenin blanc, gewürztraminer and more.

Angoves Butterfly Ridge Colombard Chardonnay

Down in the sub-$10 boondocks, a lot of white wine is comparable to ordinary wine-cask stuff, but there are still enough good 'uns to keep us interested. This is one of them.

CURRENT RELEASE 2004   Fair enough, it doesn't have great finesse, but there are far worse ways of spending seven bucks. It has a soft grapey nose with light touches of stone fruit and citrus. The gently fruity palate is quite dry, soft and appetising. For simple refreshment on a tight budget this is a winner. Try it with fish and chips.

Quality	♥♥♥⌣
Value	★★★★
Grapes	colombard; chardonnay
Region	Murray Valley, SA
Cellar	▮ 1
Alc./Vol.	12.5%
RRP	$7.00 ⓢ

Crittenden at Dromana Melon

We can't remember tasting an Australian melon before, except of course for the juicy ones that we buy at our local greengrocer. Melon is of course the grape behind one of France's most evocative white wines, muscadet. From the downstream end of the Loire Valley, it's a perfect seafood wine.

CURRENT RELEASE 2004   Pale straw in colour, this has a vinous nose that captures a little of Muscadet's character, but without quite the 'cut' of the original. The nose has herb and waxy aromas with a Frenchy whisper of mineral/earth character, and the palate is fresh and appetising with some of that particular drawing dryness that marks the French original. A good effort. Try it with the classical accompaniment, freshly shucked oysters.

Quality	♥♥♥♥
Value	★★★
Grapes	melon
Region	Mornington Peninsula, Vic.
Cellar	▮ 1
Alc./Vol.	13.0%
RRP	$25.00 ⓢ

Fox Creek Shadow's Run The White

Quality	🍷🍷🍷
Value	★★★★
Grapes	verdelho; chardonnay
Region	various, SA
Cellar	🍾 1
Alc./Vol.	13.5%
RRP	$12.00 [$] 🔩

Shadow is a black-and-white border collie who inhabits the Fox Creek vineyard. Apparently he has an endearing habit of racing up and down the rows chasing the zing of the wire, whenever a pruner's shears strike the trellis.

CURRENT RELEASE 2004 This is an appealing, simple, drink-now dry white that represents good value for money. There's a hint of coconut in the bouquet, together with some herbal and peachy notes. In the mouth it's a softer, richer, slightly broader style of wine with fairly low acid and some alcohol warmth to close. Not a fine wine, but a decent quaffer, especially with antipasto.

Giaconda Aeolia Roussanne

Quality	🍷🍷🍷🍷½
Value	★★★
Grapes	roussanne
Region	Beechworth, Vic.
Cellar	🍾 3
Alc./Vol.	13.8%
RRP	$85.00 🔩

Rick Kinzbrunner has been working with roussanne at Giaconda for a few years now, and the wine's stature increases with each new release. Although it shows the winemaker's influence, its exotic nature shows through with great clarity. PS: screw-caps are now an option on the Giaconda whites.

CURRENT RELEASE 2004 Another fascinating Aeolia. It's a bright green–yellow in colour, and the nose has aromas of flowering heather, honey and spices. The honeyed, lush palate has lovely depth and texture with harmoniously integrated subtle oak. It finishes fine, aromatic and dry. The finish is as hauntingly long as previous vintages. Try it with pork fillet.

Hardys Voyage Colombard Semillon Sauvignon Blanc

Quality	🍷🍷🍷
Value	★★★★
Grapes	colombard; semillon; sauvignon blanc
Region	not stated
Cellar	🍾 1
Alc./Vol.	12.5%
RRP	$6.00 [$]

Does the word Voyage add anything to the allure of this wine? Apart from cluttering the label and adding unnecessary words to its title? We wonder what voyage they are referring to – the voyage of discovery of Hardys' wines? With a $6 bottle? Hmmm.

CURRENT RELEASE 2004 Six bucks (undiscounted) isn't a lot to ask, and this is pretty fair value. It has flavour and decent drinkability. The nose has some powder-puff or cosmetic aromas which are typical of colombard, and some greener nuances from the other varieties. It's not too sweet and slips down quite nicely. It would suit sandwiches at a picnic.

Houghton Museum Release White Burgundy

It is remarkable how well the humble Houghton White Burgundies can age. They often carry off trophies against mature semillons, rieslings and chardonnays in Australian wine competitions. This one has five gold medals to its credit.
CURRENT RELEASE 1994   This is a delicious aged dry white. The colour is deep yellow with an amber tint; it smells straw-like, resiny and toasty rather like a mellow old Hunter Semillon. The palate has good depth of flavour reminiscent of orange peel and lemon drops. The finish is totally dry and very clean, although it has good length. It would be perfect with lemon chicken.

Quality	🍷🍷🍷🍷🍷
Value	★★★★
Grapes	chardonnay; chenin blanc; muscadelle, etc.
Region	various, WA
Cellar	🍾 1
Alc./Vol.	13.5%
RRP	$26.00 Ⓢ

Jimbour Station Queensland Verdelho

Verdelho is a grape that seems well suited to Queensland vineyards, the Robert Channon wines are winning successive gold medals at Queensland competitions and topping shows there. This one is made by Master of Wine, Peter Scudamore Smith.
CURRENT RELEASE 2005   Just weeks after it was bunches hanging on the vine, this was tasting terrific. Fresh pale-lemon coloured, it has vibrant aromas of musk, herbs, confectionery and honey, even a suggestion of peppermint Lifesavers. It's tangy and clean on the palate, crisp and zippy with no great depth or length but with a lovely immediate palate flavour and zing. Try it with salads and cold seafood.

Quality	🍷🍷🍷🍷
Value	★★★★
Grapes	verdelho
Region	Queensland
Cellar	🍾 2
Alc./Vol.	13.0%
RRP	$16.00 🥂

Lost Valley Cortese

We don't know of anybody else in Australia growing cortese grapes, and this unique example from the Victorian High Country is a laudable example of this obscure northern-Italian grape variety.
CURRENT RELEASE 2004   We think that this is the best Lost Valley Cortese yet. It's a ripe and fruity wine, yet it's less obviously so than most modern Aussie whites. Aromas of melon, passionfruit and herbs mark the nose, and the same clean and mellow fruit character makes the palate quite delectable. It's middling in body with typically soft acidity and is an altogether friendly companion. Try it with poached chicken and vegetables.

Quality	🍷🍷🍷🍷🍷
Value	★★★
Grapes	cortese
Region	upper Goulburn, Vic.
Cellar	🍾 2
Alc./Vol.	14.0%
RRP	$32.00 🥂

Something New to Try

ROUSSANNE (Colour: white. Origin: Rhône Valley, France)
While Australia has grown marsanne for many decades, we could be accused of neglecting its 'twin' sister, roussanne. Traditionally, the dry white wines of Hermitage, Crozes-Hermitage and St Joseph in the northern Rhône Valley were made from blends of these two grapes; these days, some producers such as Chapoutier use only the preferred roussanne.

There have been small plantings of roussanne in the Yarra Valley for a long time: Yeringberg has made an excellent marsanne-roussanne blend for 30 years and St Huberts has released a number of uncomplicated, fruit-driven straight roussannes. More recently, Giaconda has since 1999 been making a pure roussanne called Aeolia and a chardonnay-roussanne blend called Nantua Les Deux. Both are superb wines, even if they don't shed much light on the grape's varietal character. Yering Station has been selling a very interesting blend of the two in recent years, as has Seppelt. Elsewhere, McLaren Vale's D'Arenberg has a superb straight roussanne – if you can handle the high alcoholic strength – called The Money Spider, and others are starting to trial it. Being a proven good blender, roussanne is also likely to be seen in more blends in the future, along the lines of Mitchelton's Airstrip Block (marsanne, roussanne, viognier). Roussanne ripens late and therefore needs a warm climate; it has higher acidity than marsanne which helps it age better, and the grape has a russet-red appearance which probably accounts for its name.

McHenry Hohnen 3 Amigos Marsanne Chardonnay Viognier

Quality 🍷🍷🍷🍷
Value ★★★½
Grapes marsanne; chardonnay; viognier
Region Margaret River, WA
Cellar 🍾 2+
Alc./Vol. 15.0%
RRP $27.00

McHenry Hohnen Vintners is a new company started by Cape Mentelle founder David Hohnen and his brother-in-law, Murray McHenry, with help from Hohnen's daughter, Freya, a young qualified winemaker. They've released four wines, all made from grapes grown on their own vineyards in the southern half of the Margaret River region.

CURRENT RELEASE 2004 As you might expect from the alcohol reading, this is a big, hefty white wine with a lot of oily texture from alcohol and glycerol. It's quite a fat wine, with low apparent acidity, some alcohol heat and not a lot of delicacy. There's a trace of toasty oak character and some spice and stone-fruit aromas. It's very front-of-mouth in profile, while alcohol carries the finish. Not an easy wine to match with food: you could try a buttery chicken dish.

McWilliams Hanwood Verdelho

Quality 🍷🍷🍷½
Value ★★★★
Grapes verdelho
Region Riverina, NSW
Cellar 🍾 1
Alc./Vol. 13.0%
RRP $12.00 [$]

The most famous verdelho in the world is a fortified wine from the Portuguese island of Madeira. In modern Australia it's nearly always made into a soft dry white wine like this.

CURRENT RELEASE 2004 A palatable young white that smells of tropical fruit salad with a lemony edge. It has a smooth, direct palate that's fruity and easy to like. The dry finish has a whisper of slightly phenolic bitterness, but with food it works well. Try it with a Malaysian prawn curry.

Meerea Park Verdelho

Quality 🍷🍷🍷🍷
Value ★★★★½
Grapes verdelho
Region Hunter Valley, NSW
Cellar 🍾 2
Alc./Vol. 12.0%
RRP $12.95

Verdelho has a long history in the Hunter Valley where it makes a smooth type of white wine that's less reserved in its youth than its more famous white sibling semillon. Good examples like this one still retain a regional signature. Maker: Rhys Eather.

CURRENT RELEASE 2004 This bright young wine has an attractive nose that's not especially varietal in the accepted sense. Instead of juicy tropical fruit, it has lemon, straw and gentle pawpaw aromas that lean more towards regional character than typical verdelho. In the mouth it's smooth and succulent with clean flavours and a bone-dry finish. Serve it with fried prawns.

Oakvale Gold Rock Reserve Verdelho

Present owners, the Owens family, have smartened the place up a bit, but for some of us this will always be one of the historic properties of the Lower Hunter, and where the Elliott family made memorable wines in the early days.

CURRENT RELEASE 2004 Oakvale is a consistently good Hunter verdelho producer. This one has an appealing aroma of overripe banana, mango and an overtone of green herbs. In the mouth, it's green and herbal, with frisky acidity and a touch of sweetness. It's a bold wine that lacks a little finesse, but it's a crowd-pleaser. Try it with scallops, mango and rocket.

Quality	🍷🍷🍷🍷
Value	★★★½
Grapes	verdelho
Region	Hunter Valley, NSW
Cellar	🍾 2
Alc./Vol.	13.0%
RRP	$19.50

Pizzini Arneis

Arneis is one of the most prized white grapes in Italy's Piedmont region, together with cortese. Even in Italy there are many winemaking styles, so it's hard to get a handle on its varietal character.

CURRENT RELEASE 2004 The wine has plenty of personality and couldn't be accused of blandness. It has a sweetly spicy aroma that's grapey, subtle and clean. There's a whisper of sweetness and it's fuller on the palate than expected. Soft and fruity, it would make a good aperitif drink, or a partner for goat's cheese with witlof.

Quality	🍷🍷🍷🍷
Value	★★★★
Grapes	arneis
Region	King Valley, Vic.
Cellar	🍾 2
Alc./Vol.	13.2%
RRP	$24.00 [$]

Plunkett Gewürztraminer

Gewürztraminer is something of an orphan in Australia. Our wine producers don't seem to have it on their radar – unlike the Europeans, who love it. In Alsace, for example, it is usually the most pricey wine on the list, even above riesling.

CURRENT RELEASE 2004 This is very much down the delicate, restrained end of gewürztraminer's range. It's pale coloured and discreet to sniff, with the barest trace of spicy varietal fruit. The palate is delicate in the extreme, slightly angular and quite undeveloped, and has just enough lychee/jasmine flavour to raise our hopes that it will develop into a much more generous wine if given time. It would then suit richly sauced fish.

Quality	🍷🍷🍷🍷
Value	★★★½
Grapes	gewürztraminer
Region	Strathbogie Ranges, Vic.
Cellar	🍾 1–5+
Alc./Vol.	13.5%
RRP	$17.00

Seppelt Bellfield Marsanne Roussanne

Quality	♥♥♥♥
Value	★★★
Grapes	marsanne; roussanne
Region	Pyrenees, Vic.
Cellar	▮ 1
Alc./Vol.	12.0%
RRP	$23.95 ⧖

Seppelt's Glenlofty vineyard was planted in 1995 at the western end of Victoria's Pyrenees region. It's still early days but marsanne and roussanne appear to do well there.
CURRENT RELEASE 2004   The colour is a deep mid-yellow and the nose has an attractive vinous quality, rather like apples, spices and herbs in good harmony. In the mouth it seems to lack a little in depth and structure, but it's pleasant enough with a light, delicately dry flavour and a soft bone-dry finish. A whisper of barrel influence stays very much in the background. It needs food, so try it with a vegetable terrine.

Simon Gilbert Verdelho

Quality	♥♥♥♥
Value	★★★★
Grapes	verdelho
Region	Central Ranges, NSW
Cellar	▮ 2
Alc./Vol.	13.5%
RRP	$15.00 Ⓢ ⧖

The labels on this series of wines are taken from a set of antique playing cards that were owned by the Gilbert family, pioneers of winegrowing in the Eden Valley. The cards are now in the collection of the State Library of South Australia.
CURRENT RELEASE 2004   A streamlined verdelho that's crisp and clean and refreshing. The aromas are of lemon/ citrus, somewhat reminiscent of semillon, and the palate is lean and dry, with very sprightly acidity. Good flavour and drinkability. It suits a caesar salad.

Terra Felix Marsanne Roussanne

Quality	♥♥♥♥
Value	★★★★
Grapes	marsanne; roussanne
Region	various, Vic.
Cellar	▮ 3
Alc./Vol.	13.3%
RRP	$14.95 Ⓢ

Marsanne and roussanne are the two white varieties that go to make hermitage blanc in the northern Rhône Valley. Some producers favour one variety or the other: Chapoutier, for example, don't like marsanne and their wines are pure roussanne.
CURRENT RELEASE 2004   This is a rather shy, delicate dry white with a faintly spicy aroma and a little nuttiness, overlain by lanolin and sulphury characters. The palate is light and lean, a touch plain perhaps but it's a wine that has drinkability and good balance. It would suit Chinese dumplings.

Rosé Wines

There's been a revival of interest in this humble wine style over the past two or three years. Scores of wineries which never used to make rosé are having a go. They're making it in just about every region, from a number of different grape varieties, ranging from the logical low-coloured grenache and pinot noir through to shiraz, merlot, cabernet sauvignon and even chambourcin. Occasionally some white grapes are blended in, to further lighten the wine. Australians travelling to places like Spain, Portugal and southern France are enjoying the local habit of drinking rosé, and it stands to reason that rosé should be popular here, with our Mediterranean climate, long dry summers and outdoorsy eating habits.

Bay of Fires Tigress Rosé

Hardys have excelled themselves with the packaging of the Bay of Fires and Tigress wines. This rosé has the shadowy tigress surreptitiously holding a red rose in her teeth.
CURRENT RELEASE 2004 The colour is very pale pink – youthful and attractive, but just a bit on the watery side. It looks, smells and tastes like a white wine with red added for colouring. Floral, white-wine aromas tally with the colour and it's very delicate and simple in the mouth. The balance is good: it finishes without obvious sweetness and while it's very light, it's a good drink and a refreshing summer quaff. Try it with sashimi.

Quality	🍷🍷🍷🍷
Value	★★★
Grapes	not stated
Region	Tasmania
Cellar	🍾 1
Alc./Vol.	13.5%
RRP	$26.00 [$] 🔩

Castagna Allegro

Julian Castagna's Beechworth vineyard is operated on a biodynamic basis, and he is championing such viticultural and winemaking methods to a broader audience. His Shiraz and La Chiave Sangiovese are superb European styles of great distinction, and this pink Allegro is his homage to the dry rosés of France and Italy.
CURRENT RELEASE 2004 This is a palish rose pink with a slightly 'wild' nose reminiscent of earth, licorice and cherries. It also has a little countrified pong that will upset the technocrats and excite the hedonists. It comes into its own on the palate which is dry-tasting and earthy with long flavour and a soft finish. A tasty companion to a rustic terrine.

Quality	🍷🍷🍷🍷
Value	★★★
Grapes	shiraz
Region	Beechworth, Vic.
Cellar	🍾 1
Alc./Vol.	13.5%
RRP	$30.00

Garry Crittenden i Rosato

Quality	🍷🍷🍷🍷⦚
Value	★★★★
Grapes	sangiovese; barbera; nebbiolo; cabernet sauvignon; pinot noir
Region	various, Vic.
Cellar	🍶 1
Alc./Vol.	14.0%
RRP	$16.50 ⧉

Garry Crittenden has left his name on this range of i Italian varietals, although they're made by his son Rollo, winemaker at Dromana Estate. Dromana Estate has moved from its original site, and Garry has now established his new Crittenden at Dromana operation at the old Dromana Estate winery. Confused?

CURRENT RELEASE 2004   This has to be one of Australia's best pink wines, and it shows how well the savouriness of Italian grape varieties goes with this style. Salmon-pink in colour, it has an appetising, complex nose of raspberryish fruit, licorice and savoury/earthy, herby notes. The smooth palate has a fascinating interplay between dry, earthy Italianate flavours, the slightest whisper of fruit sweetness, and a dry clean finish. Very easy to drink cool on a warm afternoon with antipasto.

Hahndorf Hill Winery Rosé

Quality	🍷🍷🍷🍷
Value	★★★★
Grapes	trollinger 51%; lemberger 49%
Region	Adelaide Hills, SA
Cellar	🍶 2
Alc./Vol.	12.5%
RRP	$17.50 ⧉ (cellar door)

Larry Jacobs of Hahndorf Hill reckons his is the only vineyard in Australia growing trollinger and lemberger, the two German grapes used to make this rosé. The grapes were picked in May, which is late for cold-climate varieties!

CURRENT RELEASE 2004   The colour is light hot-pink and the wine has a touch of reductive smell riding above the attractive scent of sweet berries. The palate is light, soft, clean and fruity, without residual sugar – which is a refreshing change, as a lot of rosés are quite sweet. A charming, easy-quaffing wine to serve with bruschetta.

Hamilton's Ewell Stonegarden Rosé

Quality	🍷🍷🍷🍷
Value	★★★★
Grapes	cabernet sauvignon
Region	south-east SA
Cellar	🍶 2
Alc./Vol.	13.0%
RRP	$18.00 ⧉

The Hamiltons lay claim to planting the first vineyard in South Australia, back in the 1830s. The boss today is Adelaide lawyer Mark Hamilton. His father Robert is the patriarch, and still works in the business every day.

CURRENT RELEASE 2004   There's an interesting chocolate note in the aroma and taste of this rosé. The colour is a vibrant medium purple–pink, dark for a rosé, and there's a lot of dark-fruit aroma, especially cherry, with that whiff of chocolate. It's at the light-bodied dry red end of the spectrum: in other words, a fuller style of rosé. A clean, smooth, well-made wine without obvious sweetness, and a pleasure to drink with barbecued tuna steaks.

Kingston Sarantos Soft Press Scarlet Cabernet

These days wineries all over the country are having a go at a pink wine. This Murray Valley example joins Kingston Estate's early-drinking Sarantos range, named after the Moularadellis family's patriarch Sarantos.
CURRENT RELEASE 2004 Brilliant in colour, a bright rose pink, this has a nose of Ribena-ish blackcurrant aromas that's like a real caricature of cabernet varietal aroma. In the mouth is continues in the same fruity-fresh vein, with a hint of sweetness, soft mid-palate texture, and enough acidity to keep it tangy and refreshing. Serve it with a spring vegetable salad.

Quality	🍷🍷🍷½
Value	★★★½
Grapes	cabernet sauvignon
Region	Murray Valley, SA
Cellar	🍾 1
Alc./Vol.	12.5%
RRP	$15.50 [$] 🍴

Krinklewood Francesca Rosé

We've lost count of the wines that have been proudly named after a child or grandchild. In this case it's the first grand-daughter of Krinklewood proprietors Rod and Suzanne Windrim. They're in the Broke Fordwich sub-region of the Hunter.
CURRENT RELEASE 2004 The colour is correct – a light to medium hot pink–purple, and the bouquet has a touch of reductiveness overlying lolly-ish, cherry estery aromas. The wine is fresh and vibrantly fruity on the palate, with a well-judged touch of sweetness and a balanced finish. The acid is a touch hard but it's a good drink with pan-roasted salmon.

Quality	🍷🍷🍷🍷
Value	★★★★
Grapes	not stated
Region	Hunter Valley, NSW
Cellar	🍾 1
Alc./Vol.	12.3%
RRP	$18.00 🍴

Lark Hill Rosé

There are many wineries and vineyards in the Canberra region, but only six inside the Australian Capital Territory. Lark Hill is at Bungendore, about half an hour north-east of Canberra city. Maker: Sue Carpenter.
CURRENT RELEASE 2004 This is a sweeter style of rosé, but well-made and undoubtedly commercial. The colour is bright, light pink–purple and the aromas are sweet and confectionery-like. Sweetness and lively acidity lift the strawberry/cherry lollypop palate flavours. It's a good drink with spicy Szechuan food.

Quality	🍷🍷🍷🍷
Value	★★★½
Grapes	merlot; pinot noir; shiraz
Region	Canberra region, NSW
Cellar	🍾 1
Alc./Vol.	13.0%
RRP	$20.00 🍴 (cellar door)

Lindemans Bin 35 Rosé

Quality 🍷🍷🍷🍷½
Value ★★★★★
Grapes grenache
Region not stated
Cellar 🍾 1
Alc./Vol. 12.5%
RRP $10.00 [$]

The Lindemans Bin wines are sealed with synthetic 'corks', or stoppers, to give them a more accurate name. These are good for a year or two but we wouldn't be keeping the wines longer than that because they do admit some air which eventually damages the wine.

CURRENT RELEASE 2004 This is a revelation – a really excellent rosé at a bargain-basement price. The colour is a vibrant fresh medium–light pink–purple and it smells sweetly floral, estery and fresh, reflecting highly competent winemaking. It has decent weight in the mouth, with a certain textural richness from fruit plus well-judged phenolics and alcohol. And the finish is clean and near-dry, which is a pleasant surprise. Serve with antipasto.

Moondah Brook Cabernet Rosé

Quality 🍷🍷🍷½
Value ★★★★
Grapes cabernet sauvignon
Region various, WA
Cellar 🍾 1
Alc./Vol. 13.0%
RRP $14.00 [$] 🔩

Cabernet sauvignon makes good rosé. Its redcurrant/blackcurrant-like fruit aromas and flavours seem to suit the style very well; compared with traditional rosé grape grenache it has a lot more cut and tang to it.

CURRENT RELEASE 2004 Pink in colour with a slight purplish blush, Moondah Brook's rosé wine has succulent red-berry and redcurrant fruit aromas with a herbal edge. The palate has a whisper of residual sweetness, but it's not overdone, and a tangy clean finish gives it nice equilibrium. Sip it chilled with sushi.

Orlando Jacob's Creek Shiraz Rosé

Quality 🍷🍷🍷
Value ★★★★
Grapes shiraz
Region not stated
Cellar 🍾 1
Alc./Vol. 12.0%
RRP $9.95 [$] 🔩

The latest in the expansive Jacob's Creek range is this pale-pink wine designed to cash in on the 80 per cent increase in rosé consumption in Australia last year. The trend in Europe is the same, pink wine is on the move.

CURRENT RELEASE 2004 This has a blackcurranty aroma and flavour that's fruity and direct. In the mouth it's soft and appetising with a touch of sweetness to enhance the soft fruit character, and a very soft finish. A warm weather crowd-pleaser at a good price. Try it with ham off the bone in a baguette.

Pepperjack Grenache Rosé

Pepperjack is a modern label of Saltram's. In a reference to the dim dark past, the maker's name is given as W. Salter & Sons. William Salter was the chap who founded Saltram back in 1859.
CURRENT RELEASE 2004   This is a big-coloured, generously flavoured rosé in the currently fashionable Barossa style. The colour is full purple–pink, and it smells like sweet cherry essence: the ripe, confectionery-like grenache aromas are very appealing. It's full and soft in the mouth, with hints of vanilla and caramel. It's a bit big to be called a rosé, but we love it! Especially with bouillabaisse.

Quality	♟♟♟♟♟
Value	★★★★⁺
Grapes	grenache
Region	Barossa Valley, SA
Cellar	▮ 2+
Alc./Vol.	14.0%
RRP	$24.00 Ⓢ ⬤

Robert Stein Cabernet Rosé

Everyone's making rosé these days. The style seems to have finally caught on, and its popularity is reflected in the statistics collected by market researcher, A.C. Nielsen. This won a silver medal at the Mudgee Wine Show in 2004.
CURRENT RELEASE 2004   This is an attractive rosé in the slightly leafy-smelling cabernet style. There are smoky and mulberry aromas too, and the palate has unusual richness and texture for a rosé. There's quite a deal of sweetness, too, which broadens the finish. It would suit salt and pepper calamari with chilli sauce.

Quality	♟♟♟♟
Value	★★★★
Grapes	cabernet sauvignon
Region	Mudgee, NSW
Cellar	▮ 1
Alc./Vol.	13.5%
RRP	$15.50 ⬤

Tobacco Road King Valley Rosé

This wine is produced by the Victorian Alps Wine Co, which also makes the Gapsted and Tutu wines. Tobacco Road no doubt refers to the fact that a lot of tobacco is grown in the upper King Valley/Ovens Valley areas, the grape catchment area for this winery. Maker: Michael Cope-Williams.
CURRENT RELEASE 2004   The colour is an inviting medium–full pink with purple edges, and it smells enticingly of sweet strawberry with a bubblegum or confectionery accent. There's a trace of crushed leaf as well. It's clean and fruity in the mouth with noticeable sweetness, which is in balance, and the texture is soft, making it easy to quaff. Try it with tuna carpaccio.

Quality	♟♟♟♟
Value	★★★★★
Grapes	not stated
Region	King Valley, Vic.
Cellar	▮ 1
Alc./Vol.	13.0%
RRP	$11.00 Ⓢ ⬤

Willow Creek Pinot Saignée

Quality	♱ ♱ ♱ ♱ ♱
Value	★★★★
Grapes	pinot noir
Region	Mornington Peninsula, Vic.
Cellar	▮ 1
Alc./Vol.	13.0%
RRP	$20.00 ⬧

PENGUIN BEST ROSÉ WINE

It's amazing to think how much the fortunes of Australian pink wine have improved in recent years. All too often it was a repository for any old grapes hanging around a winery. Now it's enjoying a rebirth, partly based on fashion and lifestyle issues, and partly based on the fact that some of these wines are bloody good.

CURRENT RELEASE 2004   Made from a *saignée* of pinot noir, meaning free-run juice that's been bled from the main body of pinot juice to concentrate the remainder. A middling rosé pink in colour, it's a fragrant young wine with a vinous nose that suggests wild strawberries and spice. In the mouth it's smooth and attractive with more depth than some. It finishes soft and dry, perhaps marginally short but it's still great refreshment. Try it with cold cuts.

Yering Station ED Pinot Noir Rosé

Quality	♱ ♱ ♱ ♱
Value	★★★
Grapes	pinot noir
Region	Yarra Valley, Vic.
Cellar	▮ 1
Alc./Vol.	13.5%
RRP	$17.50 ⬧

Yering Station has carved a niche for itself with this excellent rosé. Fermented totally dry and given some oak-ageing, it's perceived as a more 'serious' wine than some of the competition. Maker: Tom Carson.

CURRENT RELEASE 2004   A more subtle shade of pink here, this is a wine that certainly asks to be taken seriously, but don't get too cerebral about it. The nose has aromas of red berries, cherries and spice, with a little dab of oak in the background, and it tastes dry and clean with a slightly firm structure underneath. Very much a food wine rather than something to sip alone, serve it with pâté or terrine and it's exactly right.

Red Wines
Cabernet Sauvignon and Blends

Cabernet runs second to shiraz in the red wine popularity stakes and the gap has widened. Shiraz-mania and the over-planting of cabernet has contributed to its over-supply. That's good news for punters: we can find good-value cabernet in the shops because prices have softened. Whereas top shiraz is grown in many regions, cabernet is more specific and the best sources are Coonawarra and Margaret River, followed by Langhorne Creek, the Yarra Valley, Great Southern and the Pyrenees. We like cabernet to taste like cabernet, with some blackcurrant character; and ripe, with fruit sweetness and elegance. We don't like it herbaceous, as much of it sadly is; and unripe cabernet has green tannins that can be quite bitter.

Angoves Vineyard Select Coonawarra Cabernet Sauvignon

There's been a distinct improvement in Angoves' table wines in recent years, and their value for money makes them worth looking at as an everyday drinking proposition. The Vineyard Select range slots into the higher end of the Angove scheme of things.
CURRENT RELEASE 2002   This has good concentration of syrupy blackcurrant character. It's a fruit-driven style with just a dab of dusty oak in the background. The palate has medium body and attractive texture. It falls just a whisker short in the mouth, but that's being super-critical, it's good value anyway. Serve it with lamb cutlets.

Quality	♟♟♟♟
Value	★★★★
Grapes	cabernet sauvignon
Region	Coonawarra, SA
Cellar	▬ 2
Alc./Vol.	13.5%
RRP	$18.00 ⓢ

Arlewood Reserve Cabernet Sauvignon

The Arlewood Reserve wines have been good for years, and steadily pushing the boundaries. The 15-hectare vineyard is in the blue-chip locality of Harman's South Road, Wilyabrup. Consulting winemaker is Janice McDonald.
CURRENT RELEASE 2001   A sensational cabernet, which adds more evidence that 2001 was an outstanding cabernet year in Margaret River. It's a wine of concentrated, essency black fruits, with overtones of meat stock and well-married cedary oak. The palate has density, flesh and richness, the tannins are supple and fully ripe. A blinder of a cabernet that suits aged Heidi gruyere cheese.

Quality	♟♟♟♟♟
Value	★★★★⸣
Grapes	cabernet sauvignon
Region	Margaret River, WA
Cellar	▬ 12+
Alc./Vol.	14.5%
RRP	$33.00 ▮

Balnaves Cabernet Merlot

Quality	♟ ♟ ♟ ♟ ♟
Value	★ ★ ★ ★ ★
Grapes	cabernet sauvignon; merlot
Region	Coonawarra, SA
Cellar	🍾 12+
Alc./Vol.	13.5%
RRP	$24.00 🍾
	(cellar door)

Balnaves is a family affair, with founder Doug Balnaves – a highly regarded Coonawarra viticulturist for many years before starting his own winery – running the show and his daughter Kirsty listed as production manager.

CURRENT RELEASE 2001   It's an excellent example of the lean, angular, cool-climate style of cabernet. The colour is deep and concentrated; the bouquet is fresh and shows perfectly ripened cabernet fruit: powerful dark berries and supportive high-quality oak. It has plenty of acid and the tannins are fine-grained and supple. It's a trifle stern in its extreme youth but will richly reward cellaring. Then serve it with a cheese platter.

Balnaves Cabernet Sauvignon

Quality	♟ ♟ ♟ ♟ ♟
Value	★ ★ ★ ★ ★
Grapes	cabernet sauvignon
Region	Coonawarra, SA
Cellar	🍾 15+
Alc./Vol.	14.0%
RRP	$31.00 🍾
	(cellar door)

PENGUIN BEST CABERNET
SAUVIGNON AND BLENDS

The Balnaves family have 52 hectares of mainly red grapes in their Coonawarra vineyards. They provide contract winemaking and viticultural consultancy services, as well as turning out an excellent range of their own wines. Maker: Pete Bissell.

CURRENT RELEASE 2001   This is a classy cabernet in classic Coonawarra style. It still shows some obvious showy oak in its youth, but is elegant and finely balanced in every other respect, with no excesses of alcohol, acid or tannin. The fruit flavours and tannins are perfectly ripe and the wine has concentration and fine balance. A great drink with roast lamb.

Balnaves The Tally Reserve Cabernet Sauvignon

Quality	♟ ♟ ♟ ♟ ♟
Value	★ ★ ★ ┥
Grapes	cabernet sauvignon
Region	Coonawarra, SA
Cellar	➡ 2–16+
Alc./Vol.	14.0%
RRP	$80.00 🍾
	(cellar door)

Today's Coonawarra winemakers have differing ideas of what a flagship regional wine should taste like. Some have gone all-out for ripeness, concentration and tannin in a 'no guts, no glory' style. Others express the terroir in a more age-worthy version of the region's natural style. This one's in the middle and certainly tastes like a Coonawarra.

CURRENT RELEASE 2001   The '01 is a puzzling wine, it needed a lot of breathing to come out of its shell and we feel it's still not showing its full potential. A reserved but deep, minty, coconutty, fairly oaky cabernet with a fleshy, chewy, tannic palate that's supple and ripe, but just a touch undeveloped. Cellar it, then serve with beef with mushrooms.

Banks Road Bendigo Cabernet

The Bendigo region is a bit of a conundrum: it has failed to fulfil its early promise while neighbouring Heathcote has attracted much more attention. This producer's business address is on the Bellarine Peninsula.
CURRENT RELEASE 2002   This is a smart young cabernet with very bright fruit, enlivened by acidity that some may find a trifle high – although drinking it with protein will soon solve that issue. The bouquet is ripe mulberry cabernet fruit with a fine lacework of toasty oak. The tannins are firm and a trifle furry, but the structure is robust and good. Plenty of intensity and length here. It would suit a complex aged cheese like reggiano.

Quality	🍷🍷🍷🍷
Value	★★★★
Grapes	cabernet sauvignon
Region	Bendigo, Vic.
Cellar	🍷 15
Alc./Vol.	14.0%
RRP	$26.00

Barons of Barossa HMS Cabernet Sauvignon

The initials stand for H.M. 'Bill' Seppelt. The Barons of Barossa are a club of distinguished Barossa people, who have small parcels of wine made for them by companies associated with members. They recently released some of them for general sale.
CURRENT RELEASE 2002   This is a whopper: a very big, robust red wine with a monster grip of firm tannin to close. Earthy, dusty, bacon-fat and mocha aromas, with sweet fruit in the mouth and a hint of new oak. A statuesque, solidly structured red for long-term cellaring, it demands high-quality hard cheese, such as aged English cheddar.

Quality	🍷🍷🍷🍷
Value	★★★
Grapes	cabernet sauvignon
Region	Barossa Valley, SA
Cellar	3–20+
Alc./Vol.	14.0%
RRP	$375 (4-pack)

Barons of Barossa WHS Cabernet Shiraz

This one's named after Wyndham Hill Smith, former head honcho of Yalumba and dad of the current MD, Robert Hill Smith. The wines were sold in four-packs of three reds and a riesling, all superb wines and all screw-capped. Collectors' items, for sure. West Gordon Fine Wines in Sydney may be able to track some down.
CURRENT RELEASE 2002   This is a ripper of a red, a great example of the top-rating '02 vintage. The colour is deep, the nose offers hi-fi charred barrel and rich ripe fruit aromas. It's a wine of great depth and structure, the berry fruit concentrated and vibrant on the palate. There's a lot of oak, but more than enough fruit to balance. It's worth cellaring long-term, especially under Stelvin. Great with rare roast beef.

Quality	🍷🍷🍷🍷🍷
Value	★★★
Grapes	cabernet sauvignon; shiraz
Region	Barossa Valley, SA
Cellar	🍷 20+
Alc./Vol.	14.0%
RRP	$375 (4-pack)

Barossa Valley Estate Ebenezer Cabernet Merlot

Quality 🍷🍷🍷🍷½
Value ★★★★
Grapes cabernet sauvignon; merlot
Region Barossa Valley, SA
Cellar 🍾 5
Alc./Vol. 13.0%
RRP $35.00 [$] 🍾

Ebenezer is a Barossa Valley sub-region. It's a dry, warm, northern area which produces some of the valley's most sought-after, super-ripe, concentrated red grapes.

CURRENT RELEASE 2001 This is a remarkably elegant wine for a hot year in Ebenezer. It has an attractive bouquet of crushed mulberry, laced with green-leafy merlot aromas and low-key oak. The tannins are fine-grained and the palate is smooth. The flavours are integrated and the overall impression is of elegance. It would go well with beef and onion kebabs.

Barossa Valley Estate Epiphany Cabernet Merlot

Quality 🍷🍷🍷½
Value ★★★★
Grapes cabernet sauvignon; merlot
Region Barossa Valley, SA
Cellar 🍾 4
Alc./Vol. 14.0%
RRP $15.00 [$]

An epiphany is defined as a manifestation of a super-human being, such as Christ. You've been over-indulging in Epiphany if you're seeing that kind of stuff, we reckon.

CURRENT RELEASE 2002 This is a light, straightforward kind of red as befits the entry-level price. It's a nice easy-drinking middleweight, smelling of blueberry and mint, with savoury flavours but also some primary fruit sweetness. It has some leanness that's typical of these grapes. It would go well with a meat pie from the Apex Bakery in Tanunda.

Bird in Hand Nest Egg Cabernet Sauvignon

Quality 🍷🍷🍷🍷
Value ★★★
Grapes cabernet sauvignon
Region Adelaide Hills, SA
Cellar 🍾 10
Alc./Vol. 13.5%
RRP $60.00

This is a fairly recent venture, established at Woodside in the Adelaide Hills by Andrew and Justin Nugent in 2001. They have 26 hectares of vines there – and another 7 hectares at Clare.

CURRENT RELEASE 2003 Elegant cool-area cabernet is the style here. It has some of the greener spectrum of cabernet flavours – crushed-leaf and herbs, as well as cassis and mulberry ripe notes. The palate has some attractive fruit sweetness and it has very good balance and style. Nice length, intensity and also subtlety. Try it with roast saddle of hare.

Blue Pyrenees Cabernet Sauvignon

The most recent Blue Pyrenees reds seem to have less of the eucalyptus character that we so often taste in reds from the Pyrenees region. That's a good thing, in our view. The winery got its name because the eucalypt-clothed hills of the area tend to have a blue-grey colouring when viewed from a distance.

CURRENT RELEASE 2002 This is a good, if slightly straightforward, cabernet with mulberry and blackcurrant aromas of good varietal signature. The palate has medium flavour and a touch of firmness in its tannins. Overall the balance is good, and so is the drinkability. It would suit veal cutlets.

Quality	🍷🍷🍷🍷
Value	★★★★
Grapes	cabernet sauvignon
Region	Pyrenees, Vic.
Cellar	🍾 5+
Alc./Vol.	14.0%
RRP	$19.00 [$]

Blue Pyrenees Estate Reserve Red

This is the blend on which Blue Pyrenees Estate hangs its hat. It's had a stream of winemakers have a bash at it: Christian Morlaes, Vincent Gere, Kim Hart, Greg Dedman, and now Andrew Koerner.

CURRENT RELEASE 2000 It's very much a Pyrenees regional style, with a strong eucalyptus presence. A strongly built, rather stolid wine with firm tannins and a touch of hollowness mid-palate. Like most eucalyptus-dominated wines, it's not really complex and we wonder if it ever will be. However, it has a lot of flavour and character and many will love it. Try it with minted roast lamb.

Quality	🍷🍷🍷🍷
Value	★★★½
Grapes	cabernet sauvignon 71%; shiraz 19%; merlot 9%; cabernet franc 1%
Region	Pyrenees, Vic.
Cellar	🍾 6+
Alc./Vol.	14.5%
RRP	$38.00 ⏳

Blue Pyrenees The Richardson Series Cabernet Sauvignon

Blue Pyrenees Estate started life as Chateau Remy, back in 1963, and was part of the French-owned Remy Cointreau group until fairly lately when it was sold to John Ellis. We've noticed a renewed vigour about the wines since then. The new winemaker is Andrew Koerner.

CURRENT RELEASE 2002 There was an odd medicinal/ sunscreen scent to our bottle of this red, which is probably just a random cork influence, because the wine tasted excellent in every other respect. It seems slightly closed at present but the structure is impressive, with masses of ripe tannin and some fairly high-class oak showing. It's a big, rich, savoury cabernet that shows every sign of good ageing potential. We'd serve it with aged hard cheese, such as tilsit.

Quality	🍷🍷🍷🍷½
Value	★★★
Grapes	cabernet sauvignon
Region	Pyrenees, Vic.
Cellar	🍾 1–15+
Alc./Vol.	14.5%
RRP	$52.00 ⏳

Bremerton Tamblyn Cabernet Shiraz Malbec Merlot

Quality 🍷🍷🍷🍷
Value ★★★★
Grapes cabernet sauvignon; shiraz; malbec; merlot
Region Langhorne Creek, SA
Cellar 🍾 5
Alc./Vol. 14.0%
RRP $17.50

Bremerton was the first of a small but important wave of new producers in Langhorne Creek in the last 15 years. Winemaker is Rebecca Willson and her sister Lucy is marketing manager.

CURRENT RELEASE 2002 This is in keeping with the typical Bremerton red-wine style: very savoury, with earth, animal-hide and meaty aromas coupled with sweet-berry cabernet fruit. The finish carries a drying, almost charcoal savoury grip, and it could take a few years of cellaring. It suits braised beef.

Brookland Valley Reserve Cabernet Sauvignon

Quality 🍷🍷🍷🍷
Value ★★★
Grapes cabernet sauvignon
Region Margaret River, WA
Cellar 🍾 12+
Alc./Vol. 14.4%
RRP $58.00 [$] 🍾

This wine has polarised tasters in a few venues where we've seen it pop its head up. Sometimes, such as at last year's WA Wine Show in Mount Barker, it comes away with trophies; at other times it's deemed a little too 'green'.

CURRENT RELEASE 2001 There's no doubting its cabernet varietal provenance, as it has a pronounced crushed-leaf aroma which is coupled with beef-stock, mocha and soy-sauce oak-derived complexities. There are hints of capsicum on one hand and licorice/anise on the other. The palate is rich and fruit-sweet with good fruit concentration and no green-tannin astringency. Try it with Greek moussaka.

Centennial Vineyards Reserve Cabernet Sauvignon

Quality 🍷🍷🍷🍷½
Value ★★★★
Grapes cabernet sauvignon
Region Orange, NSW
Cellar 🍾 5
Alc./Vol. 14.0%
RRP $25.00 (cellar door)

Centennial Vineyards are 3 kilometres west of Don Bradman's home town Bowral, a picturesque hamlet in the New South Wales Central Highlands. The first plantings were in 1998 and quality is already looking good. Maker: Tony Cosgriff.

CURRENT RELEASE 2003 This young wine has good balance of sweet blackcurranty fruit, briary notes, spicy oak and savoury, woodsy touches. In the mouth there's good concentration and textural interest, with fine cabernet flavour of elegant classical austerity. It finishes long and fine. A little more presence would see it rated even higher, but it's very good anyway. Serve it with roast veal.

Charles Melton Cabernet Sauvignon

The Charles Melton wines epitomise the best of the modern Barossa. They have no rough edges, they aren't fat and overblown, nor are they over-extracted or over-woody. All is harmony.

CURRENT RELEASE 2002 A deep, dense Barossa cabernet of real breeding, this has concentrated dark-berry, currant, spice, dark-chocolate and pleasantly jammy aromas. Perfectly ripe and complete. The palate has rich chocolatey fruit of lovely intensity, without excess. Oak is folded in seamlessly but that delicious Barossa cabernet character is what carries the wine. It finishes very long with soft, ripe tannins in support. Great. Try it with roast scotch fillet in the piece.

Quality 🍷🍷🍷🍷🍷
Value ★★★★
Grapes cabernet sauvignon
Region Barossa Valley, SA
Cellar 8+
Alc./Vol. 14.5%
RRP $40.00

Climbing Cabernet Sauvignon

This is one of the initial releases from Philip Shaw's Cumulus enterprise at Orange in New South Wales. The label depicts acrobats climbing ladders, an allusion to the altitude of the vineyards, and also perhaps to the wine climbing the quality ladder.

CURRENT RELEASE 2003 A medium-density cabernet with a rather merlot-like nose, that's very plummy and touched by spice, subtle oak and earthy notes. In the mouth it's ripe and succulent with medium body and easy soft tannins. A juicy young cabernet that drinks well in youth. Serve it with veal chops.

Quality 🍷🍷🍷🍷
Value ★★★½
Grapes cabernet sauvignon
Region Orange, NSW
Cellar 2
Alc./Vol. 13.5%
RRP $20.00

Coldstream Hills Cabernet Sauvignon

Although Coldstream Hills has sometimes released a straight varietal cabernet sauvignon under the Reserve label, this '03 is the first in the winery's standard range. Maker: Andrew Fleming.

CURRENT RELEASE 2003 This Yarra Valley cabernet is fairly complex, combining briar, blackcurrant and earthy, slightly feral notes in a way that evokes memories of Bordeaux. The palate is silky in texture with savoury flavour and good persistence. Tannins are soft and dry. It drinks well young, but will develop short- to mid-term. Try it with a leg of lamb.

Quality 🍷🍷🍷🍷
Value ★★★
Grapes cabernet sauvignon
Region Yarra Valley, Vic.
Cellar 4
Alc./Vol. 14.0%
RRP $25.95

Coldstream Hills Reserve Cabernet Sauvignon

Quality 🍷🍷🍷🍷🍷
Value ★★★½
Grapes cabernet sauvignon
Region Yarra Valley, Vic.
Cellar 8+
Alc./Vol. 14.0%
RRP $48.00

When the Coldstream Hills vineyard provides a parcel of outstanding cabernet, usually from the oldest part of the vineyard, the winemaking team makes a Reserve wine. It doesn't happen every year, but when it does it's worth looking for. Oak is always an emphatic addition to these wines, sometimes too much so for some people.

CURRENT RELEASE 2001 This has deep colour and the nose is very cabernet: violets, dark fruits, black olives, black chocolate, all very concentrated, but not without subtlety. Fragrant cedary oak contributes but as the wine breathes it doesn't overwhelm. The palate is long-flavoured and fine with balanced ripe tannins and tangy acidity to keep it in the frame. Really it still needs time in bottle. A high-class wine to enjoy with roast leg of lamb.

Crawford River Cabernet Merlot

Quality 🍷🍷🍷🍷½
Value ★★★½
Grapes cabernet sauvignon; merlot
Region Henty, Vic.
Cellar 5
Alc./Vol. 13.5%
RRP $30.50

The Henty region, near Portland in Victoria's south-west, is a pretty cool place to grow grapes. Weedy, green cabernet is what you might expect, but it ain't necessarily so. Crawford River's efforts with this grape variety are impressive.

CURRENT RELEASE 2002 A very stylish cool-climate cabernet blend. It has aromas of blackberry pastille, blackcurrant and cloves – succulent and appetising. A dusting of spicy oak adds dimension, and the palate is clean and tight with middling weight, good depth and impressive intensity. It finishes with a touch of cedar and a long, dry aftertaste. Serve it with Vietnamese mint-wrapped beef.

Cullen Diana Madeline Cabernet Sauvignon Merlot

Quality 🍷🍷🍷🍷🍷
Value ★★★
Grapes cabernet sauvignon 72%; merlot 20%; petit verdot 4%; malbec 4%
Region Margaret River, WA
Cellar 8+
Alc./Vol. 13.5%
RRP $90.00

The top Cullen cabernet is known as Diana Madeline, in honour of Cullen family matriarch Di Cullen, who passed away in 2003. She was a woman of great charm and generosity, and this great wine is a fitting memorial.

CURRENT RELEASE 2003 An almost gentle Cullen cabernet, without the power of the 2001, nor the austerity of the 2002. The nose has delicate aromas of flowering herbs, black fruits, mulberries, dry spices and cedar. The palate has a satin texture and fine flavour with a lingering, soft, fine finish and dry underlying tannins. An understated Margaret River red of real finesse. Try it with roast veal.

D'Arenberg The Coppermine Road Cabernet Sauvignon

D'Arenberg is one of the most interesting wineries around, always coming up with inventive new wines with quirky names. Winemaker Chester Osborn is a mine (coppermine?) of creativity. With his shock of curly hair he looks the part and could pass for an eccentric professor. CURRENT RELEASE 2002 This has an inky colour: density is the key word all round. It's very thick and soupy, and just a bit clumsy. The aromas remind of stewed fruits, prunes, tomato bush, dried herbs and oak. The palate is savoury, full of drying tannin, and not very varietal. We might have expected a more elegant cabernet from such a cool summer. The maker's style triumphs over the season! Try it with venison stewed in cherries.

Quality	♟♟♟♟♟
Value	★★★
Grapes	cabernet sauvignon
Region	McLaren Vale, SA
Cellar	➥2–10+
Alc./Vol.	14.5%
RRP	$60.00 ▮

Dorrien Estate Bin 7 Cabernet Sauvignon Shiraz

Dorrien Estate wines are made and retailed by Cellarmasters, the big direct-marketing wine selling business which is owned these days by Beringer Blass. The wines can be bought from www.cellarmasters.com.au CURRENT RELEASE 2003 The bouquet is so smoky it's almost bushfire in character, probably from charred oak barrels, while the palate also reveals some berry flavours and fruit sweetness, together with slightly jarring acid. It improves as it warms in the glass. An easy-drinking red to serve with savoury meatballs in tomato purée.

Quality	♟♟♟♟
Value	★★★★
Grapes	cabernet sauvignon; shiraz
Region	Barossa Valley, SA
Cellar	▮5
Alc./Vol.	14.0%
RRP	$15.99

Eagle Vale Cabernet Sauvignon Merlot Cabernet Franc

Eagle Vale was established as recently as 1997, with a cellar door on Caves Road, Margaret River, although the wines are made elsewhere – but it's already making its mark with some fine dry whites and reds. CURRENT RELEASE 2001 Typical regional dusty/herbal/ stalky aromas come off the glass first, then dark-berry and black-olive to olive-oil aromas, possibly from the merlot component. There's a generous input from oak and it's nicely entwined together with the fruit. The wine has serious structure, which augurs well for its ageing. It needs another year, then start opening bottles, perhaps with aged parmesan.

Quality	♟♟♟♟
Value	★★★⟩
Grapes	cabernet sauvignon; merlot; cabernet franc
Region	Margaret River, WA
Cellar	➥1–7+
Alc./Vol.	13.0%
RRP	$33.00 ▮

Edwards Cabernet Sauvignon

Quality	♥♥♥♥♥
Value	★★★➤
Grapes	cabernet sauvignon
Region	Margaret River, WA
Cellar	➥2–6+
Alc./Vol.	14.0%
RRP	$29.00

The Edwards vineyard is one of the newer Margaret River producers, being only 11 years old. Attention to detail and a commitment to quality have resulted in a good range of wines that won't break the bank.

CURRENT RELEASE 2003   This has cassis-like aromas that are tangy, almost tart; the penetrating varietal personality is lightly trimmed in cedary oak. The intensely focused blackcurrant fruit continues in the mouth, and the palate is long and silky with an austere underpinning of grainy, dry tannins. It needs bottle-age to be at its best, but the building blocks are there. Try it with baby lamb cutlets.

Elderton Ashmead Cabernet Sauvignon

Quality	♥♥♥♥♥
Value	★★
Grapes	cabernet sauvignon
Region	Barossa Valley, SA
Cellar	5
Alc./Vol.	14.5%
RRP	$82.75

Ashmead is Elderton's flagship cabernet, a sort of cabernet companion to Command Shiraz. Like Command it doesn't muck around when it comes to laying on the oak.

CURRENT RELEASE 2001   This is a very concentrated and powerful red with heaps of oak, contributing mocha, sweet vanilla and burnt-wood characters. It isn't all oak though, and that deep, jammy blackcurrant and blackberry fruit is very Barossa-sweet, especially coupled to all that timber. It has very smooth mouth-feel, ripe tannins underneath, and a long lip-smacking finish. A particular style of red that ought to please some American wine gurus. Serve it with chargrilled porterhouse.

Elderton Barossa Cabernet Sauvignon

Quality	♥♥♥♥♥
Value	★★★➤
Grapes	cabernet sauvignon
Region	Barossa Valley, SA
Cellar	10
Alc./Vol.	15.0%
RRP	$24.00

The Elderton style is oaky, ripe and full-on, and its many fans wouldn't have it any other way. The 2002 vintage was perhaps the best for Barossa cabernet in memory.

CURRENT RELEASE 2002   This is a densely coloured, glass-staining wine, with a big nose that combines aromas of toasty vanillin oak, blackberry and black plum. It's mouth-filling and rich with flavours of charry oak, black fruits, and dark chocolate that make for a ripe, full flavour. It's powerful and persistent, and well-balanced by furry dry tannins. Try it with a T-bone cooked to perfection on the barbecue.

Elmswood Estate Cabernet Merlot

If there were a prize for the greatest vineyard views in Australia, Elmswood would have to be a finalist. The vista across the Upper Yarra Valley is ultra-soothing to us city-slickers.
CURRENT RELEASE 2003   This is at the leaner end of the cabernet profile, but it's none the worse for that. There's a promisingly deep colour, and the nose is well-concentrated and savoury with smoky briary touches and a heart of blackcurrant cabernet fruit. In the mouth it's middling in body with silky blackcurrant-fruit character, clean, appetising acidity and good balance. Good with racks of lamb.

Quality	♟♟♟♟
Value	★★★
Grapes	cabernet sauvignon; merlot
Region	Yarra Valley, Vic.
Cellar	🍷 4
Alc./Vol.	14.0%
RRP	$26.00 (cellar door)

Epis and Williams Cabernet Sauvignon Merlot

This vineyard, originally planted in the 1970s by the late Laurie Williams, who pioneered viticulture in the beautiful Macedon region, is now owned by ex-footballer and all-round good bloke Alec Epis. In typical Epis fashion, he retains the Williams name on the label as a mark of respect for the original owner. Maker: Stuart Anderson.
CURRENT RELEASE 2003   From a region that isn't exactly cabernet heartland, this is a terrific effort. It retains cool-grown mint, herb and mulberry aromas with ripe elements of blackcurrant, touches of wood smoke and high-toned oak. It tastes elegant and fine-boned with a friendly softness mid-palate and admirably ripe, soft tannins. It's a very well-made cabernet that creeps up on you as it breathes and unfolds in the glass. An ideal partner for roast lamb.

Quality	♟♟♟♟♟
Value	★★★
Grapes	cabernet sauvignon; merlot
Region	Macedon Ranges, Vic.
Cellar	1–6
Alc./Vol.	12.9%
RRP	$35.00 (cellar door)

Flying Fish Cabernet Merlot

Flying Fish Cove is an important contract winemaking facility situated on Caves Road, Wilyabrup. The cheaper wines are just labelled Flying Fish, the dearer ones Flying Fish Cove. Makers: Janice McDonald and David Watson.
CURRENT RELEASE 2004   A very young, slightly raw wine, this needs a little more time to settle. Its cassis and herbal aromas are a touch unresolved, and it's a bit astringent in the mouth, with nice raspberry/cassis flavors and a touch of harshness at the end-palate. It could suit lamb cutlets with pesto.

Quality	♟♟♟♟
Value	★★★★
Grapes	cabernet sauvignon; merlot
Region	Margaret River, WA
Cellar	1–5+
Alc./Vol.	14.5%
RRP	$20.00 ($)

Flying Fish Cove Upstream Reserve Cabernet Sauvignon

Quality	▀▀▀▀▀
Value	★★★★﹢
Grapes	cabernet sauvignon
Region	Margaret River, WA
Cellar	➠1–10+
Alc./Vol.	15.0%
RRP	$35.00
	(cellar door)

Chief winemaker Janice McDonald, ex-Devils Lair and Little Creatures brewery, is having a major influence on wine quality and style in Margaret River via her numerous consultancies and the fact that Flying Fish is a major contract winemaker.

CURRENT RELEASE 2003   This is a very impressive cabernet, it's just a pity it's released so young. It has an excellent spectrum of flavours: rich, sweet, dark berry-ish cabernet varietal flavors allied with minty, herbal high notes. It's nicely concentrated: a wine of density, charm and good ageing potential. Serve it with roast venison.

Fox Creek Duet Cabernet Merlot

Quality	▀▀▀▀
Value	★★★★
Grapes	cabernet sauvignon;
	merlot
Region	McLaren Vale, SA
Cellar	▌5
Alc./Vol.	14.5%
RRP	$19.00

The Watts family's Fox Creek is known for robust reds, the epitome of McLaren Vale. Their Reserve Shiraz is their flagship wine. Makers: Tony Walker and Chris Dix.

CURRENT RELEASE 2002   From a record cool summer, this shows more of the herbal cabernet and merlot characters than usual for this winery. Tomato-bush, leafy, compost aromas are apparent, and there is a touch of green tannin in the palate, which lends a certain astringency. It does have lots of flavour, though, with riper berry, toast and earth characters as well. It needs food, drink it with Irish stew.

Fox Creek Reserve Cabernet Sauvignon

Quality	▀▀▀▀
Value	★★★﹢
Grapes	cabernet sauvignon
Region	McLaren Vale, SA
Cellar	▌6
Alc./Vol.	15.0%
RRP	$36.00

This winery and vineyard were set up by Dr Jim Watts and his family, and a syndicate of his fellow Adelaide medicos. It's most noted for heroic reds with hedonistic levels of alcohol. Our ambivalence about the style has never been hidden!

CURRENT RELEASE 2002   This will probably be a big crowd-pleaser, on account of its chocolatey, jammy, overripe fruit style and sweet-fruited, almost syrupy palate. It's big-structured, broad and gutsy, with lavish flavour but a hotness on the finish and fuminess on the nose that reflect high levels of alcohol that we find a touch out of balance. It needs hearty food, such as casseroled beef.

Giaconda Cabernet Sauvignon

In a time when one of the major problems worrying small vignerons is how to get their wines on retail shelves, Giaconda has successfully embraced the Internet as a sales vehicle. Buyers now dial up www.giaconda.com.au to find these sought-after wines.

CURRENT RELEASE 2003 An unusual Giaconda cabernet that reflects a hot, bushfire-affected vintage in Victoria's north-east. Winemaker Rick Kinzbrunner decided not to release his other '03 wines under the Giaconda label, due to them not measuring up to his very high standards. He was happy with this cabernet though. The nose and palate are big and full with smoky berry-like cabernet fruit. The palate has good weight and depth with very ripe fruit flavours, a touch of wood-smoke and a long tangy finish. A wine with real depth and palate interest, power and complexity, that improves greatly with breathing. Try it with barbecued butterflied leg of lamb.

Quality 🍷🍷🍷🍷½
Value ★★★
Grapes cabernet sauvignon
Region Beechworh, Vic.
Cellar 🍾 5+
Alc./Vol. 13.8%
RRP $65.00

Gramp's Cabernet Merlot

Johann Gramp was a pioneer of the Barossa Valley, planting vines at Jacob's Creek in 1847. His family went on to found the Orlando wine empire. He's remembered in this good range of reasonably priced table wines.

CURRENT RELEASE 2002 This is a generous cabernet blend with attractive intensity and varietal personality. The nose has plum, blackcurrant and a hint of briar to it, with a balanced dressing of smoky oak. There's good depth on the palate with pleasantly persistent fruit and moderate, ripe tannins. Try it with Lebanese-style marinated lamb kebabs.

Quality 🍷🍷🍷🍷
Value ★★★★
Grapes cabernet sauvignon; merlot
Region not stated
Cellar 🍾 3
Alc./Vol. 13.5%
RRP $18.45 [$]

Grant Burge Barossa Vines Cabernet Sauvignon Merlot

Old Barossa vines are at such premium these days that we suspect that the 'Barossa Vines' responsible for this wine are some of the younger plantings. This explains the reasonable price; old vines wines command a much higher tag.

CURRENT RELEASE 2002 This is an authentic regional cabernet blend that smells fragrantly of blackcurrants and briar. It has good intensity of clean, succulent flavour and medium body, with pleasantly understated oak and very soft tannins. An honest Barossa red to drink fairly young. Serve it with vegetable pasties.

Quality 🍷🍷🍷🍷
Value ★★★★½
Grapes cabernet sauvignon; merlot
Region Barossa Valley, SA
Cellar 🍾 3
Alc./Vol. 13.5%
RRP $14.90 [$]

Happs Cabernets

Quality 🍷🍷🍷🍷
Value ★★★½
Grapes cabernet sauvignon 53%; malbec 37%; cabernet franc 10%
Region Margaret River, WA
Cellar 🍾 5
Alc./Vol. 13.5%
RRP $20.00 (cellar door)

Erl Happ's winery is up the northern end of Margaret River, at Dunsborough. His top-end wines these days are sourced from his newer Karridale vineyard down south, and appear under the Three Hills label.

CURRENT RELEASE 2001 The style here is softer and lighter in an easygoing, current-drinking mould. It's clean, bright and driven by properly ripe fruit, with distinctly cabernet-like raspberry and cassis aromas, medium body and length. The texture is smooth with mild tannins and it's well balanced for ready drinkability. It suits duck risotto.

Heath Wines Southern Roo Cabernet Shiraz

Quality 🍷🍷🍷½
Value ★★★★
Grapes cabernet sauvignon; shiraz
Region various, SA
Cellar 🍾 2
Alc./Vol. 14.0%
RRP $15.00 [$] 💸

Come on fellas, haven't we had enough wildlife on wine labels for a while? Surely there is something else you could use to flog cheap booze overseas – what about a series on Australia's best loved politicians?

CURRENT RELEASE 2002 The bottle bears a sticker claiming this won a gold medal at the International Wine Challenge, which had us stumped. It's a decent quaffer but nothing like a gold-medal wine. It's got some edgy, tomato-bush/stemmy aromas together with a little raspberry, and the palate is lean and light and just a bit weak, finishing with a touch of residual sugar. It's soft, easygoing and makes an entertaining little quaffer. It might just suit chargrilled fillet of national symbol.

Henschke Cyril Henschke Cabernet Sauvignon

Quality 🍷🍷🍷🍷
Value ★★½
Grapes cabernet sauvignon; cabernet franc; merlot
Region Eden Valley, SA
Cellar 🍾 5
Alc./Vol. 14.0%
RRP $88.00 🍾

Cyril Henschke was the father of present winemaker Stephen Henschke, and died prematurely in the mid-'70s. He was a visionary who bottled his own wines instead of selling them in bulk, steered the company more towards table wines (instead of fortifieds) and created individual vineyard wines at a time when none of those things were the norm.

CURRENT RELEASE 2001 This is an improvement on the disappointing 2000, and although it is also a bit on the light side, it's a very attractive and nicely balanced drink. But it's not great value for money. Raspberry and vanilla aromas show, with a little of the jammy-blackcurrant style of the vintage, and the tannins are mild and soft. It's an easy-drinking red without the depth or length to age long-term. It would suit washed-rind cheeses.

Jamiesons Run Rothwell Cabernet Sauvignon

This is the top of the tree for the extensive Jamiesons Run portfolio. It sits above the Winemakers Reserve, the three single-vineyard reds, the Red Terra duo, and finally at the base of the pyramid, the regular Jamiesons Run range. Maker: Andrew Hales.

CURRENT RELEASE 2001   A very impressive red, although it's clearly been built up with liberal use of new oak. A concentrated wine with tremendous density of thoroughly ripe blackberry, mulberry-like fruit, it boasts a chewy, almost thick texture. The palate is loaded with smooth, supple tannins and it has mouth-filling richness and persistence. A solidly structured wine, it will take extended cellaring. Then enjoy it with aged hard cheeses.

Quality	♟ ♟ ♟ ♟ ♟
Value	★ ★ ★ ↓
Grapes	cabernet sauvignon
Region	Coonawarra, SA
Cellar	🍾 15+
Alc./Vol.	13.5%
RRP	$75.00 🍾

Jamiesons Run Winemakers Reserve Cabernet Shiraz

The Jamiesons Run reds have shot up in quality since Andrew Hales was made chief winemaker at the Beringer Blass Coonawarra winery. There's now an impressive range of wines with several labels at the super-premium end, of which this is one.

CURRENT RELEASE 2001   The colour is deep and dark; the bouquet reveals rich, ripe concentrated fruit with some chocolate but no sign of leafiness. The palate is almost opulent in its flavour and texture. It's a slightly pumped-up Coonawarra style but a lovely wine. A seductive red, to drink with boeuf en daube.

Quality	♟ ♟ ♟ ♟ ♟
Value	★ ★ ★ ★
Grapes	cabernet sauvignon; shiraz
Region	Coonawarra, SA
Cellar	🍾 15+
Alc./Vol.	13.5%
RRP	$57.00 🍾

John's Blend Cabernet Sauvignon No. 28

John Glaetzer is the fast-talking, chain-smoking, wise-cracking, mercurial Barossan who created the Wolf Blass red wine style: a dense, high-extract, chocolatey, minty, fruitcakey kind of soft-tannin style based on warmer regions such as Langhorne Creek, Barossa, Clare and McLaren Vale. The first John's Blend was the 1974.

CURRENT RELEASE 2001   The nose is dominated by sweet cassis, fruitcake and coconut oak and is not as eucalyptus-scented as some vintages. It's got density and flesh, plenty of weight and good balance. The finish is long and it has good ageing prospects. It's always going to be a fairly oaky style and there's a place for that. A top vintage for this label. It suits rack of lamb.

Quality	♟ ♟ ♟ ♟ ♟
Value	★ ★ ★ ★
Grapes	cabernet sauvignon
Region	Langhorne Creek, SA
Cellar	🍾 10
Alc./Vol.	14.5%
RRP	$45.00 🍾

Juniper Estate Cabernet Sauvignon

Quality	♗♗♗♗♗
Value	★★★★
Grapes	cabernet sauvignon
Region	Margaret River, WA
Cellar	▮ 12+
Alc./Vol.	14.5%
RRP	$33.00 ▮

Juniper Estate is based on the former Wright's vineyard, established on Harman's Road South near Vasse Felix way back in 1973. Winemaker is Mark Messenger, formerly of Cape Mentelle. The Estate label is for estate-grown wines; Juniper Crossing is the second label for fruit not necessarily grown on the estate.

CURRENT RELEASE 2001   We reviewed this last year but it's still around, and it's a very good cabernet. Concentrated, fleshy and tannic, it has a hint of funk but also lashings of sweet fruit plus charry smoky oak. The texture is rich, solid and yet silky. A ripper from a top cabernet vintage in the region. Serve with porterhouse steak.

Kirrihill Companions Cabernet Merlot

Quality	♗♗♗♗
Value	★★★★★
Grapes	cabernet sauvignon; merlot
Region	Clare Valley, Padthaway & Adelaide Hills, SA
Cellar	▮ 3
Alc./Vol.	14.0%
RRP	$13.00 ⊗

Kirrihill is a relatively new name on the list of notable Clare Valley producers. So far quality has been very good, first under the direction of ex-Leasingham winemaker Richard Rowe now David Mavor.

CURRENT RELEASE 2002   This has good depth of colour and a succulent nose of juicy black fruits, choc-mints, and a touch of bacony oak. The smooth, generous palate has medium body and intense flavour that treads an appetising line between ripe and savoury. Tangy acid and dry, slightly astringent tannins give it structure. It lacks a little persistence, but that's really carping, it remains fantastic value. Try it with barbecued meats.

Ladbroke Grove Killian Vineyard Cabernet Sauvignon

Quality	♗♗♗♗♗
Value	★★★★
Grapes	cabernet sauvignon
Region	Coonawarra, SA
Cellar	▮ 15+
Alc./Vol.	13.5%
RRP	$42.00

Ladbroke Grove has a history dating back to 1982 but was recently rejuvenated by John Cox and Marie Valenzuela. The label was re-launched and this cabernet immediately won several show awards, including trophies for best cabernet and best wine in the 2003 Boutique Wine Awards. They have 30 hectares of vines.

CURRENT RELEASE 2001   A lovely elegant cabernet, faithfully Coonawarra in style. It's quite youthful, which bodes well for its ageing potential. The nose and palate show excellent depth of fully ripe but definitely varietal cabernet fruit, dark berries predominating, suitably backed by subtle oak. Fruit sweetness is good and the tannins are supple. It suits venison.

Lake's Folly Hunter Valley

Lake's Folly has had a new lease of life since the Lake family sold it. Current owner is Perth businessman Peter Fogarty, who also owns Millbrook in the Perth Hills and recently added Margaret River's Deep Woods Estate to his portfolio. Maker: Rodney Kempe.
CURRENT RELEASE 2003   A curious wine that has polarised the critics. The colour is a vibrant deep purple–red and the aromas suggest smoky charred-oak, almost to the point of bushfire smoke, together with hints of leather and raw, somewhat undeveloped red-berry scents. It's also very grapey and fruity in the mouth and possibly just needs more time to come together. We'd like to see it again in a year or two. Roast venison here.

Quality	♟♟♟♟
Value	★★ꜜ
Grapes	cabernet sauvignon 63%; petit verdot 20%; shiraz 9%; merlot 8%
Region	Hunter Valley, NSW
Cellar	▬–2–10+
Alc./Vol.	12.5%
RRP	$50.00 🍶 (cellar door)

Leasingham Bastion Cabernet Sauvignon

Bastion is what the marketers like to call the entry-level range at Leasingham. It's quite inexpensive and subject to discounting, although like all Leasingham wines, the grapes are grown in the Clare Valley.
CURRENT RELEASE 2003   The colour is nice and dark, and the wine has plenty of density and grip. It's a gutsy wine without much finesse, and there's a whiff of hydrogen sulphide which is not objectionable. The tannins are a touch green on the finish. There's more than enough body and flavour to make it worthwhile. It suits osso buco.

Quality	♟♟♟
Value	★★★★
Grapes	cabernet sauvignon
Region	Clare Valley, SA
Cellar	🍶5+
Alc./Vol.	13.5%
RRP	$15.00 Ⓢ

Leconfield Cabernet Sauvignon

We've seen some disappointingly green, unripe cabernets appearing under this once-proud label. It's good to see the wheels back on the wagon in the 2002 vintage, at least. Let's hope the change is permanent. Ex-Rouge Homme winemaker Paul Gordon is in charge.
CURRENT RELEASE 2002   It starts out promisingly, with classic blackcurranty cabernet aromas, cedar cigarbox characters starting to develop. It's an elegant medium-bodied cab that's smooth, ripe and well structured with fine-grained tannins. A wine of finesse and balance that is a pleasure to drink. It suits veal scaloppine.

Quality	♟♟♟♟♟
Value	★★★★ꜜ
Grapes	cabernet sauvignon
Region	Coonawarra, SA
Cellar	🍶12+
Alc./Vol.	13.5%
RRP	$32.00 🍶

Lenton Brae Cabernet Merlot

Quality	♟ ♟ ♟ ♟
Value	★ ★ ★ ★
Grapes	cabernet sauvignon; merlot
Region	Margaret River, WA
Cellar	➡ 1–8
Alc./Vol.	13.5%
RRP	$23.00

Lenton Brae is one of several pretenders aspiring to join the first rank of cabernet producers in Margaret River. Winemaker Ed Tomlinson is very serious and is inching his way steadily up the ladder. This is his second-string wine: the top one is just called Margaret River.
CURRENT RELEASE 2002   Dusty earthy aromas and toasty oak are the first elements to greet the nose. Then a trace of mint and some dark-berry bass notes emerge. This is a lean, elegant, tautly structured, firm-finishing red that seems built to last. It needs a bit more time and should reward cellaring. Serve it with hard cheeses such as reggiano.

Lindemans Pyrus

Quality	♟ ♟ ♟ ♟ ♟
Value	★ ★ ★
Grapes	cabernet sauvignon; merlot; cabernet franc; malbec
Region	Coonawarra, SA
Cellar	▮ 5+
Alc./Vol.	13.5%
RRP	$55.00 $

Funny name, Pyrus. Its meaning seems lost in the mists of time but we have a vague memory that it was the name of a ship. Not to worry: just drink it and make up your own story.
CURRENT RELEASE 2000   This is one of the more successful 2000 vintage reds we've seen from South Australia. There's a lot of leafy and herbal aromas but it's not unripe – it's a lean, intense, tightly wound wine with plenty of structure and length in a medium- to full-bodied frame. An elegant wine, it's more about red berries than black. It should continue to age well. Try it with aged parmesan cheese.

Lindemans Reserve Cabernet Merlot

Quality	♟ ♟ ♟ ♟
Value	★ ★ ★ ★
Grapes	cabernet sauvignon; merlot
Region	various, SA
Cellar	▮ 2
Alc./Vol.	14.0%
RRP	$14.50 $

Lindemans was once a proud and distinguished company, one of the most distinguished in Australia. But over the last decade or so the name has been debased somewhat; it now stands for oceans of cheap and cheerful quaffing vino, and very little at the top level. Is Dr Lindeman still smiling up there?
CURRENT RELEASE 2002   This is good value for money: despite the aromas and flavours being more in the herbal and vegetal spectrum than red or black fruits, it is soft and smooth in the mouth, with decent weight, supple tannins, and respectable length and balance. Hard to knock that! Try it with veal cutlet stuffed with spinach and pancetta.

Lindemans St George Cabernet Sauvignon

The Lindemans Coonawarra trio don't get the kind of attention they used to, but in the more successful vintages they can be excellent. (We still find the Limestone Ridge a bit too oaky, however.) They're made at the Wynns winery these days but Greg Clayfield is still lurking in the background.

CURRENT RELEASE 2001 An extra year's bottle-age has lifted this up a little higher. It's a lovely drink, starting to show some maturity while retaining its cassis and blueberry-like fruit aromas. They've been joined by cedar and cigarbox complexities. Never a rich or opulent style, St George has a taut elegance in the riper years and this is a top vintage of it. It's classically streamlined, with power, elegance and terrific structure for ageing. Drink with roast leg of lamb.

Quality	🍷🍷🍷🍷🍷
Value	★★★½
Grapes	cabernet sauvignon
Region	Coonawarra, SA
Cellar	🍾 8+
Alc./Vol.	13.5%
RRP	$55.00 [$] 🍾

Long Flat Cabernet Merlot

Long Flat, created by Murray Tyrrell in the 1960s, was sold to the Cheviot Bridge group by Tyrrell's, and is now a much extended brand that offers surprising value for money across the board.

CURRENT RELEASE 2003 Hard to argue with the value here: the wine won't make the earth move but it's a decent quaffer at the often-discounted price. The colour is a touch light and the bouquet is a bit weak, but it does have drinkability, softness and balance, and wouldn't be out of place at a dinkum Aussie barbie.

Quality	🍷🍷½
Value	★★★★
Grapes	cabernet sauvignon; merlot
Region	not stated
Cellar	🍾 1
Alc./Vol.	13.5%
RRP	$10.00 [$]

Majella The Musician

The Musician is made in remembrance of budding guitarist Matthew Lynn, the son of Majella's co-owner Brian Lynn, who was the victim of a hit-run driver in January 2005. Matthew passed away two weeks later. He was only 20 years old. Our heartfelt sympathies go to the Lynn family.

CURRENT RELEASE 2004 This is a brilliant deep purple wine with the trademark purity of character that we've come to expect from Majella. It smells of blackcurrants, mint, spices and herbs, and it's intensely flavoured with excellent depth, attractive texture and balanced tannins. Flavours are ripe, yet tangy, and unlike the more expensive Majella reds there's very little perceptible oak. Try it with roast lamb Greek-style.

Quality	🍷🍷🍷🍷½
Value	★★★★★
Grapes	cabernet sauvignon 70% ; shiraz 30%
Region	Coonawarra, SA
Cellar	🍾 4
Alc./Vol.	13.5%
RRP	$18.00 🔩

Morgan Simpson Row 42 Cabernet Sauvignon

Quality	♥♥♥♥
Value	★★★★
Grapes	cabernet sauvignon
Region	McLaren Vale, SA
Cellar	▬ 3
Alc./Vol.	14.3%
RRP	$17.50

Morgan Simpson is a smaller McLaren Vale producer making wines of honest regional style from a 30-year-old vineyard. The elegant labelling belies the moderate asking price.
CURRENT RELEASE 2003   Not as concentrated as some better-known McLaren Vale reds, this still has plenty on offer. It smells invitingly of blackberries, spices and licorice, and in the mouth it's pleasantly understated with good intensity of flavour, real length and balanced tannins. Oak is barely apparent, helping make it an easy-drinking wine in its youth. Try it with veal chops.

Murdock Cabernet Sauvignon

Quality	♥♥♥♥♥
Value	★★★
Grapes	cabernet sauvignon
Region	Coonawarra, SA
Cellar	▬ 5+
Alc./Vol.	13.5%
RRP	$42.00

Murdock is one of our favourite new names. Their cabernet is one of the new stars of Coonawarra, thankfully made in true regional style. Maker is Pete Bissell at Balnaves.
CURRENT RELEASE 2000   The Murdocks release their wine slowly without any hard sell, so it has a chance to acquire a bit of age. At time of writing the 2000 was still current. It's a dense wine with aromas of cedar, blackcurrant and herbs. It has a mouth-watering tang on nose and palate, and that certain austerity which is a Coonawarra quality hallmark. This pristine regional/varietal character is typical of the Murdock wines; they have great *typicité* as the French would say. Enjoy it with roast nut of veal.

Murdock The Merger

Quality	♥♥♥♥
Value	★★★♪
Grapes	cabernet sauvignon 54%; shiraz 46%
Region	Coonawarra, SA
Cellar	▬ 4
Alc./Vol.	13.5%
RRP	$20.00 ⬚

Although the Murdock vineyard is a mature plot planted in 1973, wines under the family's name have only appeared in the last few years. The Cabernet Sauvignon is already one of the finest in the region. This new 'Merger' between cabernet and shiraz is a second-string red designed for earlier drinking. Maker: Peter Bissell.
CURRENT RELEASE 2003   Deep in colour, this looks the goods, and it delivers with an appetising aroma of blackcurrant syrup, cloves and plum all pulled together by smoky oak. The tangy palate has medium body and depth with tangy, fresh flavours and good balance. Serve it with a lamb and lentils casserole.

Orlando Jacaranda Ridge Cabernet Sauvignon

Big concentrated Coonawarra cabernet is what Jacaranda Ridge is all about. It's a regional flagship that's released after 22 months in French oak hogsheads and three and a half years in bottle. The age adds another aspect to a thoroughly impressive red wine, but it also has years ahead of it.

CURRENT RELEASE 1999 The colour doesn't really show the age here; it's still very dense and blackish. On the nose there are notes of cedar and lead-pencil-like oak that surrounds touches of blackberries, blackcurrants and black chocolate. In the mouth it's very concentrated with full body, smooth texture and a lush, mouth-coating feel. It finishes long with ripe firm tannins giving some grip. A substantial Coonawarra cabernet with a long future. Good with a fillet of beef.

Quality	🍷🍷🍷🍷🍷
Value	★★★
Grapes	cabernet sauvignon
Region	Coonawarra, SA
Cellar	🍾 6
Alc./Vol.	13.5%
RRP	$56.50 [$]

Orlando St Hugo Cabernet Sauvignon

Coonawarra has become one of Australia's prime places for cabernet sauvignon table wines. A far cry from 60-odd years ago when much of the harvest was distilled. St Hugo is a copybook example.

CURRENT RELEASE 2001 St Hugo is usually on the market a year or two older than its peers, which is a good thing. The '01 is still around, and it has an appetising nose of black fruits and cassis with floral and minty touches. Very cabernet sauvignon. The oak is smoothly handled if slightly resiny, and the long, tangy palate has intense blackcurrant and mint flavours that are supple and clean. Fine tannins give a balanced grip at the end. Try it with roast lamb.

Quality	🍷🍷🍷🍷½
Value	★★★
Grapes	cabernet sauvignon
Region	Coonawarra, SA
Cellar	🍾 8
Alc./Vol.	14.0%
RRP	$38.00

Orlando Trilogy

The trilogy in question is the Bordeaux trio of cabernet sauvignon, cabernet franc and merlot. By comparison with many inexpensive Bordeaux reds, this is a very clean, fresh style. Makers: Phillip Laffer and team.

CURRENT RELEASE 2002 Briary aromas of blackcurrant, berries and spearmint make an appetising introduction here, and while the palate is medium-bodied it has a lightness and freshness that gives it real charm. It has good intensity of cabernet/blackcurrant/leafy flavour, and there's real persistence of flavour, finishing with a lip-smacking tang. Good value. Serve it with grilled baby lamb cutlets.

Quality	🍷🍷🍷½
Value	★★★★
Grapes	cabernet sauvignon; cabernet franc; merlot
Region	various, SA
Cellar	🍾 2
Alc./Vol.	14.0%
RRP	$15.00 [$] 💰

Palandri Margaret River Cabernet Merlot

Quality 🍷🍷🍷🍷½
Value ★★★★½
Grapes cabernet sauvignon; merlot
Region Margaret River, WA
Cellar 🍾 10+
Alc./Vol. 14.0%
RRP $20.00 [$]

Palandri is a public company that made quite a stir when it set up shop in Margaret River, erecting a garish winery right beside the main drag. People loved to hate it. But we find the wines, especially under the lizard label, are often excellent.

CURRENT RELEASE 2003 This is a seriously good cabernet blend, especially at the price, with cabernet the dominant grape, displaying its trademark cassis, crushed-leaf, mint and raspberry aromas. It's a bright, vibrant wine that has real elegance in the mouth and some firmish tannins lending it good claret-like structure and additional length. Try it with braised lamb shanks.

Penfolds Bin 389 Cabernet Shiraz

Quality 🍷🍷🍷🍷½
Value ★★★★
Grapes cabernet sauvignon; shiraz
Region various, SA
Cellar ➖ 1–22+
Alc./Vol. 14.5%
RRP $40.00 [$] 🏺

Once known as The Poor Man's Grange, this is no longer within a bull's roar of Grange in price, and we no longer hear the Penfolds guys talking about it being matured in the used Grange barrels. It stands by itself, and is one of the most reliable and cellar-worthy of all the Pennies reds, year after year.

CURRENT RELEASE 2002 A tad more elegant than the usual 389, this is a classy model with clean, bright, blackberry ripe cabernet aromas predominating. There is plenty of oak, too, as you'd expect in a very young 389. The palate has excellent intensity and length, with again the cabernet shining at this stage of its life. Cellar, then serve with steak and chips.

Penfolds Bin 407 Cabernet Sauvignon

Quality 🍷🍷🍷🍷½
Value ★★★★½
Grapes cabernet sauvignon
Region various, SA
Cellar 🍾 15
Alc./Vol. 14.5%
RRP $30.00 [$] 🏺

Southcorp has been nurturing new vineyards in the south-east of South Australia over the last decade or so, in places like Bordertown, Wrattonbully and Robe on the Limestone Coast. Much of the fruit for this wine now comes from them. Makers: Peter Gago and team.

CURRENT RELEASE 2002 The aromas are pristine cabernet: blackcurrant and blackberry, lovely and clean and ripe. The palate has concentration and power, excellent ripeness of flavours and tannins, and it's a fruit-driven style with subtle oak – a different approach for Penfolds. Excellent value and will surely cellar well. Food: pink roast leg of lamb.

Penfolds Bin 707 Cabernet Sauvignon

Penfolds refrained from releasing a Bin 707 in both 1995 and 2000, as the wines were not up to par. This also reflects the fact that cabernet does not perform nearly as consistently as shiraz in the Barossa Valley, McLaren Vale, etc. *Previous outstanding vintages: '64, '66, '67, '76, '83, '84, '86, '88, '90, '91, '94, '96, '98, '01*
CURRENT RELEASE 2002   This is an outstanding Bin 707, from a vintage that really favoured cabernet in South Australia's warmer areas. In youth, it shows voluminous mocha, dark-chocolate and rich fruitcake aromas, with coconut and vanilla from American oak readily apparent and masses of smooth, ripe tannins providing formidable structure. It's destined to be a classic 707. Cellar, then serve with reggiano cheese.

Quality	♟ ♟ ♟ ♟ ♟
Value	★★★
Grapes	cabernet sauvignon
Region	Barossa Valley, McLaren Vale & Padthaway, SA
Cellar	➡2–25+
Alc./Vol.	14.5%
RRP	$155.00 ▮

Penfolds Koonunga Hill Cabernet Merlot

Some of the earlier Koonunga Hill shiraz cabernets were quite serious wines and aged well for many years. It's a while since we've seen one cast in that mould. The range has also grown: there are now two reds and three whites in the series.
CURRENT RELEASE 2003   The colour is fresh and deep-looking and it smells fresh and cabernet-like with cassis aromas and a hint of pea pod. The taste is lean and mild: raspberry fruit comes to the fore, and the finish is clean and dry with enough tannin to give it some structure. Try it with vitello tonnato.

Quality	♟ ♟ ♟ ♟
Value	★★★★
Grapes	cabernet sauvignon; merlot
Region	various, SA
Cellar	▮ 4
Alc./Vol.	14.0%
RRP	$16.00 Ⓢ ≋

Penfolds Rawson's Retreat Cabernet Sauvignon

What will the hierarchy be at Penfolds under the Beringer-Blass regime? Will Chris Hatcher become the Grange winemaker? We doubt it: even under Southcorp post the Rosemount merger, John Duval and then Peter Gago had charge of Pennies, and Philip Shaw was group chief winemaker.
CURRENT RELEASE 2004   This is a very decent quaffer for the price. It's clean and fresh and fruity: sweet-cherry/plum fruit aromas are joined by a touch of cassis in the mouth. Oak makes almost no statement at all. It's fairly light on the palate but well-balanced and smooth. It would go down well at a sausage sizzle.

Quality	♟ ♟ ♟
Value	★★★★
Grapes	cabernet sauvignon
Region	not stated
Cellar	▮ 2
Alc./Vol.	14.0%
RRP	$11.50 Ⓢ

Best Glassware for Fine Wine

The type of glassware you choose does have an impact on how wine smells and tastes. Not that long ago some of the grooviest cafes and restaurants began to serve wine in heavy little tumblers, which was a dreadful thing for those of us who actually cared about what we were drinking. Such glasses made great wine smell and taste like *vin ordinaire*, and the bowl-shaped 'Paris goblet' styles that traditionally graced restaurant and hotel tables weren't much better, but thankfully we've moved on, and glassware designed to bring the best out of your wine is now easier to find than ever before.

So what makes the ideal wine glass? In basic terms, anything that angles in towards the top of the glass is better than a flared shape. The narrowing towards the top helps capture the aromas that are such a part of experiencing good wine, and if the glass is of a good size, this narrowing shape allows you to slosh the wine around in the glass, freeing up the aromas without wearing the wine all over your clothes.

Within this general specification, not every glass suits every wine. Delicate wines don't benefit from a large glass, but big reds do. Sparkling wines are better in a narrower, longer glass; sherry's penetrating personality shows best in a small tulip shape. These considerations have led to the phenomenon of wine glasses specific to particular grape varieties and regional wine types.

The best-known exponent of this idea is the 250-year-old Austrian glass maker Riedel. About 45 years ago Riedel started producing wine glasses designed to bring out the best of particular wines via variations in glass form and size. Their design emphasised positive aspects of the wine's bouquet and directed a precise flow of wine to maximise its palate impact.

Inspired by the increasing sophistication of wine lovers and Riedel's success, other manufacturers now produce their own 'ideal' shapes for different wines. Brands like Zerrutti make glasses that flatter fine wines equally, and Luigi Bormioli produces the excellent, reasonably priced DOC range. Our favourite all-round wine glass is Riedel's elegant Chianti Classico, which suits a broad spread of wines quite superbly. On a budget, though, the Luigi Bormioli range is very hard to beat.

Penley Estate Phoenix Cabernet Sauvignon

Quality	🍷🍷🍷🍷
Value	★★★↓
Grapes	cabernet sauvignon
Region	Coonawarra, SA
Cellar	➡1–10+
Alc./Vol.	14.5%
RRP	$24.00

Phoenix is the name of Kym Tolley's second-string cabernet (Reserve is the top). It's named after a defunct Tolley family company from the dim, dark past.
CURRENT RELEASE 2003   This one has definite cool-climate overtones, with sharp-edged mulberry and crushed-leaf aromas, lean cabernet structure and some tight tannins to close. It verges on austere at the moment and could use some cellar time to soften and open up. It's a good example of varietal character, though. Serve it with pink lamb chops and mint sauce.

Penley Estate Reserve Cabernet Sauvignon

Quality	🍷🍷🍷🍷🍷
Value	★★★
Grapes	cabernet sauvignon
Region	Coonawarra, SA
Cellar	🍷15
Alc./Vol.	14.5%
RRP	$62.00

Penley Reserve is one of the outstanding cabernets of Coonawarra these days. Owner Kym Tolley worked for Penfolds for many years, so he knows a thing or two about red winemaking.
CURRENT RELEASE 2002   This is a 'cooler' tasting wine than some of the other recent Penley cabernets, an elegant medium-bodied wine with noticeable acidity and quite firm tannins. The aromas are of raspberry, blackcurrant cordial and crushed vine leaves with an overtone of gunpowder. It's lively and vibrant and should age well. Serve with lamb backstraps and pesto.

Petaluma Coonawarra

Quality	🍷🍷🍷🍷🍷
Value	★★★★
Grapes	cabernet sauvignon; merlot
Region	Coonawarra, SA
Cellar	➡2–15+
Alc./Vol.	13.5%
RRP	$60.00 🍾

Petaluma names its cabernet merlot blend simply Coonawarra, because it is the region rather than the grape varieties that they want to illuminate. The mix of cabernet and merlot varies according to the heat of the season (the hotter it is, the less merlot, and vice versa), so it's a moveable feast anyway.
Previous outstanding vintages: '86, '88, '90, '91, '92, '94, '98, '00, '01
CURRENT RELEASE 2002   A typically tight, reserved Petaluma Coonawarra, this is shy and undeveloped: anything but a showy, up-front fruit style. There are some discreet mulberry and cassis touches, but it's fairly closed and the nutty oak aromas are out-shining the fruit in its youth. The savoury palate has lots of drying tannin and really excellent structure for an age-worthy red. Cellar it, then serve with hard cheeses.

Preece Cabernet Sauvignon

The Mitchelton and Preece wines have taken a quality leap. It may be something to do with the fact they now pay their growers on quality rather than purely on tonnage. Winemaker is Tony Barlow, with Don Lewis mentoring.

CURRENT RELEASE 2003 Wow! This is an impressive wine for a very modest price! The colour is deep red–purple and it smells of deep, dark chocolate, dark berries, mocha and coffee, with a smooth fleshy palate that delivers far more flavour and concentration than we expected at the price. Oak has been used dexterously, helping to build up the wine without dominating. There's also a good solid tannin grip that helps it partner strong foods, and suggests it will keep well. Try it with fillet mignon.

Quality	🍷🍷🍷🍷½
Value	★★★★★
Grapes	cabernet sauvignon
Region	central and north-east Vic.
Cellar	🍾 5
Alc./Vol.	14.5%
RRP	$15.00 [$] 💰

PENGUIN BEST-VALUE RED WINE

Punt Road Cabernet Sauvignon

Anyone familiar with Melbourne knows Punt Road is one of the main arteries of that metropolis. Less well known nowadays is the fact that a century or so back, there were vineyards on Punt Road – forerunners of the modern Yarra Valley wine industry. Maker: Kate Goodman.

CURRENT RELEASE 2003 This has a distinctly smoky bouquet, almost bushfirey, perhaps due to some heavy-char oak barrels. The palate is light- to medium-bodied and smoothly balanced. It's been tailored for early drinking. Those hunting for a blockbuster should look elsewhere. It has a gentle finish of moderate length, and teams well with smoky barbecued lamb chops.

Quality	🍷🍷🍷🍷
Value	★★★
Grapes	cabernet sauvignon
Region	Yarra Valley, Vic.
Cellar	🍾 4
Alc./Vol.	13.0%
RRP	$25.00 [$]

Redbank The Fugitive Cabernet Sauvignon

Attractive packaging and evocative names are not the least of the attractions of the Redbank range of wines. There's this one, the Sunday Morning Pinot Gris and the Fighting Flat Shiraz. Maker: Natalie Fryar.

CURRENT RELEASE 2002 This is a remarkably good wine: it truly punches above its weight. The colour is deep and the bouquet is full of blackcurrant and blackberry, clean and properly ripe with nice background oak. The palate is tight, elegant and concentrated, with well-structured, lush fruit, and good 'line and length'. It has the grip to take some age, and would drink well with braised beef.

Quality	🍷🍷🍷🍷½
Value	★★★★★
Grapes	cabernet sauvignon
Region	King Valley & Ovens Valley, Vic.
Cellar	🍾 8+
Alc./Vol.	14.5%
RRP	$21.00 [$]

Redman Cabernet Sauvignon

Quality	▼ ▼ ▼ ▼
Value	★ ★ ★ ⬧
Grapes	cabernet sauvignon
Region	Coonawarra, SA
Cellar	🍾 15
Alc./Vol.	13.5%
RRP	$32.00 Ⓢ 🍾

Redman by name and nature. The Redman family have 32 hectares of vines in Coonawarra, all red – and to our knowledge, they have never produced a white wine. In other words, they focus on what the area does best. Maker: Bruce Redman.

CURRENT RELEASE 2001   Plenty of concentration here: the wine has a good spectrum of riper blackberry and blueberry aromas together with herbal, stalky high notes which foreshadow a touch of tannin astringency. It's a good wine, showing real palate depth and varietal character. It would suit roast saddle of hare.

Reynell Basket Pressed Cabernet Sauvignon

Quality	▼ ▼ ▼ ▼ ▼
Value	★ ★ ★ ★ ⬧
Grapes	cabernet sauvignon
Region	McLaren Vale, SA
Cellar	🍾 15+
Alc./Vol.	14.0%
RRP	$56.00 Ⓢ 🍾

This is one of the great show reds of recent years: it won six trophies, including the Tucker Seabrook (best show wine of the year) and Macquarie Bank (best wine at Sydney Royal Wine Show) trophies in 2004.

CURRENT RELEASE 1998   A very concentrated, powerfully built cabernet that has all the ripe, hot-year fruit sweetness without sacrificing varietal character or charm. Aromas of dark berries are augmented by toasty oak and some bottle-aged complexities starting up. On the palate it shows great depth, fleshiness and masses of tannin, which contribute to its impressive structure. Young for its seven years, it has a great future. An absolutely outstanding red. Serve with roast beef.

Robert Stein Reserve Cabernet Sauvignon

Quality	▼ ▼ ▼ ▼ ▼
Value	★ ★ ★ ★ ⬧
Grapes	cabernet sauvignon
Region	Mudgee, NSW
Cellar	⬤—2–17+
Alc./Vol.	13.5%
RRP	$27.50 🍾

This winery used to be called just Stein's Wines, but the founder's name has been promoted to centre-stage. This wine won a gold medal at the 2004 Mudgee Wine Show.

CURRENT RELEASE 2002   A typically robust Mudgee red wine, this. It has a bouquet of crushed leaves, blackcurrant and raspberry, and is grippingly tannic to taste. There is very good depth of flavour as well, that is slightly masked by the tannin at this stage. It will reward cellaring. Then serve it with a hearty meat dish such as beef Wellington.

Rosemount Cabernet Merlot

The cheapest Rosemount wines are sealed with plastic plugs. They couldn't switch to screw-caps even if they wanted to: the flange-lipped proprietary Rosemount bottle sees to that. We can't help wondering if they'll stick with that bottle indefinitely.

CURRENT RELEASE 2004 Do those who drink these wines regularly notice the sugar in them, and if so, does it make them more or less appealing? It offends the principles of winemaking to have sugar in reds, but wines like Yellow Tail and McGuigan prove its popularity with the public. This is a clean, well-made wine with good mulberry-like red-fruit aromas and okay personality, even if it is a bit short and sugar-reliant. Serve with footy franks.

Quality 🍷🍷🍷
Value ★★★★
Grapes cabernet sauvignon; merlot
Region not stated
Cellar 🍾 2
Alc./Vol. 13.5%
RRP $12.00 [$]

Rosemount Diamond Label Cabernet Sauvignon

The Southcorp ship has been rocked by instability for some years now but has managed to continue delivering decent wine at fair prices. But by the time you read this the Southcorp name may have disappeared altogether. Who knows what will happen under the Beringer-Blass aegis?

CURRENT RELEASE 2003 It's uncanny how similar the Southcorp reds around this price-level taste – under the Penfolds and Rosemount labels. They serve up decent flavour with a hint of varietal character in a smooth, balanced package that avoids greenness, grip or astringency. No faults, no complaints, no excitement. It's hard to complain because it's good value for money. Try this with veal scaloppine.

Quality 🍷🍷🍷½
Value ★★★★
Grapes cabernet sauvignon
Region not stated
Cellar 🍾 2
Alc./Vol. 13.5%
RRP $16.00 [$]

Rouge Homme Cabernet Sauvignon

This is riper and better than the cabernet merlot – same maker, same price. We often wonder, when the calibre of most Australian merlot is so poor, why so many wineries blend the stuff with their cabernet. We suspect it often lessens the blend.

CURRENT RELEASE 2003 The colour is good and the bouquet of sweetly ripe mulberry and cassis is both varietal and appealing. It's lightly herbal, with a hint of pea pods, but it's basically a clean, ripe-tasting, nicely balanced wine of some intensity and depth. There's a lick of firm tannin to close. Pair it with herbed rissoles.

Quality 🍷🍷🍷½
Value ★★★★
Grapes cabernet sauvignon
Region Limestone Coast, SA
Cellar 🍾 5
Alc./Vol. 13.5%
RRP $16.00 [$]

Saltram Mamre Brook Cabernet Sauvignon

Quality	🍷🍷🍷🍷½
Value	★★★½
Grapes	cabernet sauvignon
Region	Barossa Valley, SA
Cellar	2–8+
Alc./Vol.	14.5%
RRP	$25.50

Recent years have seen the Saltram wines leaning back towards their roots in the Barossa, after some years' flirtation with other regions. A good thing, given Saltram's history and influence in the district.

CURRENT RELEASE 2003 A densely coloured young Mamre Brook, and the nose has good varietal and regional intensity. The nose has boiled fruitcakey richness and concentration, with herby, earthy and smoky notes. In the mouth it has surprising weight with a firm backbone of grippy tannins. A solidly styled Barossa cabernet that needs time to soften and build complexity, but it's going to be pretty good if you can keep your hands off it. Try it with roast beef.

Sandalford Cabernet Sauvignon

Quality	🍷🍷🍷🍷½
Value	★★★½
Grapes	cabernet sauvignon
Region	Margaret River, WA
Cellar	1–6
Alc./Vol.	14.5%
RRP	$34.00

Sandalford's Margaret River cabernet isn't as sought after as regional benchmarks like Cullen and Moss Wood, but it's a lot cheaper and the quality is ever improving. Maker: Paul Boulden.

CURRENT RELEASE 2003 This smells very appetising with true varietal fruit in the blackcurrant vein leading the way, along with attractive minty, leafy cues and hints of cedar and spice from good oak. The palate has a tight linear structure, tangy flavour, fine-grained tannins and a long finish. An elegant style to open with baby lamb cutlets, grilled pink.

Seppelt Moyston Cabernet Sauvignon Merlot

Quality	🍷🍷🍷🍷
Value	★★★
Grapes	cabernet sauvignon; merlot
Region	73% Bendigo, 15% Grampians & 12% Pyrenees, Vic.
Cellar	4
Alc./Vol.	13.5%
RRP	$23.95

For many years Moyston was the companion wine to Seppelt Chalambar. The difference? Moyston was a claret, Chalambar was a burgundy, silly! Without getting into the whole story of the bad old days of generic labelling of Australian wines, we're much better off these days with varietal labels that say shiraz or cabernet.

CURRENT RELEASE 2003 A modern cabernet that combines berry, spice and licorice-like characters with some gum-leafy savoury traits and spicy oak in a medium-bodied, smoothly textured package. It doesn't quite have the quality of its Chalambar stablemate, but it's ripe and easy to drink. The palate is backed up by well-integrated drying tannins. Try it with goulash.

Seville Estate Reserve Cabernet Sauvignon

The sub-text on this label says 'Old Vines', a reference to the 1972-planted rows of cabernet that provided the fruit for it. Are 33-year-old vines really 'old?' In the Barossa they'd be youngsters, but for the Yarra Valley they're positively ancient.

CURRENT RELEASE 2003   This has a sweetly concentrated nose of violets, cassis, a hint of briar, and subtle spicy oak. The palate has plush velvety mouth-feel, and flavour that's rich and ripe. It's still a cool-grown style of cabernet, but the flavour is uncommonly rich and ripe with a floral fragrance in the mouth that's very seductive. Ripe tannins are in excellent harmony. A classy effort to enjoy with roast leg of lamb.

Quality	♥♥♥♥♥
Value	★★★⁴
Grapes	cabernet sauvignon
Region	Yarra Valley, Vic.
Cellar	➥2–8
Alc./Vol.	14.5%
RRP	$36.50 ⊠

Sirromet Mick Doohan Cabernet Sauvignon

There is a smattering of Queensland wines in each edition of the *Guide* and we're pleased to announce that they are improving all the time. This might just be the best red we've tasted yet. Maker: Adam Chapman.

CURRENT RELEASE 2002   A deeply coloured red, this full-bodied cabernet sauvignon boasts a very concentrated nose lush with blackberry and blackcurrant fruit aromas. This ripe fruit character is mated to subtle oak in a very appealing mod-Oz manner. In the mouth it's seamless in feel, deeply flavoured and persistent, with fine-grained tannins in excellent balance.

Quality	♥♥♥♥⁵
Value	★★★
Grapes	cabernet sauvignon 94%; merlot 6%
Region	Granite Belt, Qld
Cellar	▮5
Alc./Vol.	14.0%
RRP	$36.00

Stanton & Killeen Cabernet Merlot

The Rutherglen wineries work hard to promote their table wines, but still it's the fortifieds that are the belles of the ball, justifiably grabbing the headlines. Stanton & Killeen's red table wines are among the best of the wallflowers.

CURRENT RELEASE 2003   The nose is closed and restrained with a rather porty touch, due no doubt to a hot vintage. There are berry, plum, earth and spice aromas dressed in a little smoky oak. It smells more traditional than the usual S&K reds; they often tread a more elegant path than the old-fashioned Rutherglen styles. The palate is juicy and long with robust, slightly porty fruit flavours and some tannic grip. Try it with braised beef.

Quality	♥♥♥♥
Value	★★★
Grapes	cabernet sauvignon 56%; merlot 44%
Region	Rutherglen, Vic.
Cellar	▮5
Alc./Vol.	14.0%
RRP	$25.00

Summerfield Reserve Cabernet Shiraz

Quality 🍷🍷🍷🍷
Value ★★★
Grapes cabernet sauvignon 50%; shiraz 50%
Region Pyrenees, Vic.
Cellar 🍾 2–10+
Alc./Vol. 15.0%
RRP $50.00

The Summerfield wines are rather formidable as a result of the 2003 heatwave conditions, but the regional mintiness of the Pyrenees saves them from going too far over the top (but only just!). Be careful of the alcohol!

CURRENT RELEASE 2003 This blockbuster red has a strongly characterful nose that combines both overripe and possibly underripe components. It smells of plums, raisins, melted chocolate, cloves and smoky oak, with a herby thread. The powerful full-bodied palate has ripe, almost vintage port-like, dark fruit, with a minty touch. Big ripe tannins measure up to the butch proportions of the wine. Very macho. Try it with rare roast porterhouse.

Tahbilk Reserve Cabernet Sauvignon

Quality 🍷🍷🍷🍷🍷
Value ★★★½
Grapes cabernet sauvignon
Region Goulburn Valley, Vic.
Cellar 🍾 6+
Alc./Vol. 13.5%
RRP $70.00 🍾

Tahbilk claims to be Victoria's oldest winery and vineyard, celebrating its 145th anniversary in 2005. It's been owned for more than half its time by the Purbrick family, who took it over in 1925. Chief winemaker is Alister Purbrick.

CURRENT RELEASE 1999 This is a subtle, elegant, beautifully balanced cabernet that's showing the benefit of bottle-age. The Tahbilk style is all about displaying the fruit without the encumbrance of new oak. Aromas of mulberry and cassis are only lightly leafy and already it's showing considerable complexity. It's medium- to full-bodied and soft, with an underlying intensity that puts it in the top league and enables it to partner the strongest-flavoured foods. The tannins are very fine-grained. Drink it with aged hard cheeses, such as reggiano.

Taylors Jaraman Cabernet Sauvignon

Quality 🍷🍷🍷🍷
Value ★★★
Grapes cabernet sauvignon
Region Clare Valley & Coonawarra, SA
Cellar 🍾 1–10+
Alc./Vol. 14.5%
RRP $30.00 [$] 🔩

Taylors are big fans of the screw-cap: all of their wines are now being bottled with twisty tops, except the St Andrews wines still in the system (which are bottle-aged). The Jaraman range was new last year. Maker: Adam Eggins.

CURRENT RELEASE 2002 This is an oak-driven cabernet but not a bad effort. The cabernet character is a bit subdued but it's possible it needs more time, and the screw-cap may be slowing development a touch. It has good depth and structure, although there's a whisper of bitterness in the tannins. It responds well to breathing and needs to be paired with food: try a rolled beef roast.

Thompson Estate Cabernet Merlot

Dr Peter Thompson became involved in wine through his shareholdings in Pierro and Fire Gully. He planted his first vines in 1994 and has made an impressive start with his first couple of vintages. The chardonnay is made by Mike Peterkin of Pierro; this one is made by Mark Messenger of Juniper Estate.

CURRENT RELEASE 2002 Smoky, high-char oak is the first thing you smell, followed by blackberry, black-olive and other savoury complexities. There's plenty of tannin grip and the wine has the structure to go with hearty foods and to age well. There's generous rich fruit on the mid-palate: a good wine indeed. It suits spiced, marinated lamb fillets off the barbecue.

Quality	🍷🍷🍷🍷½
Value	★★★★½
Grapes	cabernet sauvignon; merlot
Region	Margaret River, WA
Cellar	🍾 8+
Alc./Vol.	14.0%
RRP	$23.00 🍶

Tisdall Cabernet Merlot

The grapes came from Tisdall's Rosbercon vineyard near Echuca, which is technically in the Goulburn Valley, although the growing conditions near Echuca are vastly different from the southern end of the region, around Seymour.

CURRENT RELEASE 2003 This modestly priced red has a pleasant bouquet of mulberry and cassis and is fruit driven and not especially complex. It's medium-bodied at best, with plenty of softly drying tannins on the finish. The leafy raspberry flavours have moderate persistence. It would go well with pork chops and mustard.

Quality	🍷🍷🍷½
Value	★★★★
Grapes	cabernet sauvignon; merlot
Region	Goulburn Valley, Vic.
Cellar	🍾 4
Alc./Vol.	13.5%
RRP	$15.50 [$]

Tobacco Road Cabernet Sauvignon

Not much tobacco road in this: by the look of the label and the taste of it, there's more South Australia than north-east Victorian tobacco-growing territory in the blend. Not to worry: it's a good drink and keen value.

CURRENT RELEASE 2002 The aromas are softly herbal and sweet mulberry-like, fruit-driven and not very complex, but easygoing and tailored for current quaffability. The tannins are light and gentle. It slips down rather nicely and would go well with shepherd's pie.

Quality	🍷🍷🍷½
Value	★★★★½
Grapes	cabernet sauvignon
Region	various, SA; Alpine & King valleys, Vic.
Cellar	🍾 3
Alc./Vol.	13.5%
RRP	$11.00 [$] 💸

Tollana Bin TR 222 Cabernet Sauvignon

Quality 🍷🍷🍷🍷
Value ★★★½
Grapes cabernet sauvignon
Region various, SA
Cellar 🍾 6
Alc./Vol. 13.5%
RRP $24.00 [$] 🌀

Tollana, which is part of the old Southcorp, used to be an Eden Valley brand, but these days it is a generic South Australian brand. The wines are still good, though. Bin TR 222 has a history that stretches back to the 1970s.

CURRENT RELEASE 2003 The clean mulberry and cassis flavours are fruit-driven and very likeable. It has good varietal character without being green, and the tannins are firm but measured. It has a depth of flavour that befits its price level, and is appropriately priced. It would suit slow-roasted duck.

Vasse Felix Heytesbury

Quality 🍷🍷🍷🍷½
Value ★★★½
Grapes cabernet sauvignon; shiraz; malbec; merlot
Region Margaret River & Mount Barker, WA
Cellar 🍾 1–12+
Alc./Vol. 14.0%
RRP $68.00 🏺

Heytesbury is the name of the Holmes à Court family's pastoral company, and is used as the name for their winery's flagship reds and whites. Chief winemaker is Clive Otto.

CURRENT RELEASE 2001 As usual, it's at the oakier end of the Margaret River style spectrum, and would be a better wine if they throttled back on the barrels, in our view. There's good fruit concentration, though, and plenty of grainy, smooth tannin, giving a pleasing texture. The flavours are savoury and run deep. It has a future, but will probably always be on the oaky side. It would suit chargrilled meats.

Voyager Estate Cabernet Sauvignon Merlot

Quality 🍷🍷🍷🍷🍷
Value ★★★★½
Grapes cabernet sauvignon; merlot
Region Margaret River, WA
Cellar 🍾 15+
Alc./Vol. 14.5%
RRP $40.00 🌀

Who said cabernet is out of style? Margaret River is still doing great cab, and this one is cheap at $40 when you compare it to the established quality leaders in the district. Maker: Cliff Royle.

CURRENT RELEASE 2001 Youthful for its age, this striking cabernet blend has a vibrant purple colour, mint and crushed-leaf varietal nuances plus a tidy, elegant yet concentrated, ripe red-berry flavour profile. Hints of violets, too. The palate is fine, long, balanced and it's been built to age, although it drinks well now, and is perfect with chargrilled lamb backstraps.

West Cape Howe Cabernet Sauvignon

West Cape Howe is less than 10 years old, but it's already made a mark with a consistently good range of wines. A bonus is their very competitive pricing, especially given the high price tags on some wines from Western Australia's south.

CURRENT RELEASE 2003 The colour is a clear ruby that appears a tad more developed than we would expect from an '03 cabernet, but the nose is as fresh and vital as can be. It has a nose of blackcurrant, briar, and smoky, savoury deli smells. The palate is intense and fine with good depth of flavour and a long, fine-grained finish. Try it with pink racks of lamb.

Quality 🍷🍷🍷🍷½
Value ★★★★½
Grapes cabernet sauvignon
Region Great Southern, WA
Cellar 6
Alc./Vol. 13.5%
RRP $24.00

Wirra Wirra The Angelus

The Angelus bell at Wirra Wirra came from the Jesuit Church at Norwood, South Australia. It weighs three-quarters of a tonne, and is rung to announce the commencement and finish of each vintage at Wirra Wirra.

CURRENT RELEASE 2002 This shows off a cooler vintage in its slightly Bordeaux-like herbaceous and cedary aromas. Blackcurranty fruit is intense and oak is a balanced veneer. The palate shows intensity and good texture, and lush blackcurrant fruit builds with breathing in the glass. There's some underlying power, but it's a more austere variation on the Angelus theme and really needs time to evolve. Give it a few years' age, then serve it with roasted racks of lamb.

Quality 🍷🍷🍷🍷½
Value ★★★
Grapes cabernet sauvignon
Region McLaren Vale & Coonawarra, SA
Cellar 3–8+
Alc./Vol. 14.5%
RRP $49.70

Wolf Blass Gold Label Cabernet Sauvignon

Gold Label is the Wolf Blass intermediate range of wine, encompassing a number of different varietal types, both red and white. The house style has generally been modernised to great effect, and quality has been very good from the outset.

CURRENT RELEASE 2003 The nose is very inviting with aromas of rich, earthy black fruit, sweet dark chocolate and a savoury touch of sage and onion stuffing. Oak is in balance and the palate has good concentration while remaining fresh and palatable. Tannins are fine and pleasantly grainy. Serve it with slow-braised lamb and onions.

Quality 🍷🍷🍷🍷½
Value ★★★½
Grapes cabernet sauvignon
Region Coonawarra, SA
Cellar 8
Alc./Vol. 14.0%
RRP $23.00 (\$)

Wolf Blass Gold Label Cabernet Sauvignon Cabernet Franc

Quality	❦❦❦❦❦
Value	★★★❧
Grapes	cabernet sauvignon; cabernet franc
Region	Adelaide Hills, SA
Cellar	▮ 6
Alc./Vol.	13.5%
RRP	$23.00 Ⓢ ⦾

Wolf Blass Gold Label wines cover a wide range of types and regional sources. The two cabernets come from different places, one Coonawarra, one Adelaide, but the family resemblance is strong.
CURRENT RELEASE 2003 A more forward wine than the Gold Label Cabernet Sauvignon, this has a sweet aroma that combines blueberry and blackberry fruit with a minty touch, against a background of sweet oak. In the mouth tangy black fruits flood the palate, which is trimmed in mouth-watering acidity and lightly firm tannins. Drink it with barbecued butterfly leg of lamb.

Wolf Blass Grey Label Cabernet Sauvignon

Quality	❦❦❦❦❦
Value	★★★
Grapes	cabernet sauvignon
Region	Langhorne Creek, SA
Cellar	▮ 8+
Alc./Vol.	14.5%
RRP	$41.50

The Grey Label has been a part of the Wolf Blass stable from the 1960s. It's evolved into a less oak-dominant wine lately but it's still generously proportioned, while the pale grey label of old has changed into the deep, designer grey of modern fashion.
CURRENT RELEASE 2003 This has a very dense appearance and the nose is powerful with blackcurrant, black-chocolate, mint and smoky barrel-ferment characters in good measure. In the mouth it's powerfully built with charry oak woven through dense, chocolatey black-fruit flavours. It's a big, well-made, forthright wine with long flavour and a firm backbone of ripe tannins. It drinks well now but should develop nicely in bottle. Try it with charry roasted rib of beef.

Wyndham Estate Bin 444 Cabernet Sauvignon

Quality	❦❦❦❦
Value	★★★❧
Grapes	cabernet sauvignon
Region	not stated
Cellar	▮ 1
Alc./Vol.	14.5%
RRP	$15.00 Ⓢ

Wyndham Estate had a lot to do with the trend towards residual sweetness in moderately priced Australian red wines. Sugar is a very seductive thing, especially in sweet-toothed export markets. It might have been toned down a bit lately.
CURRENT RELEASE 2002 This has aromas of earth, licorice, black plums and spice. The palate has friendly smoothness, good flavour and ripeness, and a soft finish. Not too sweet either. A crowd-pleaser when you have to cater for a big group. Great with pizza.

Wyndham Estate Show Reserve Cabernet Merlot

Wyndham Estate's Show Reserve label sometimes contains aged wines that are real crackers. This cabernet-merlot is a case in point. It's a very tasty drop.

CURRENT RELEASE 1998 The deep, dense colour is still relatively youthful, but the nose shows attractive maturity. It has harmoniously arranged smells of dark berries, raspberries, shiny leather and mild spices. The deep, velvety mature palate is long and complete, finishing in melting dry tannins. An aged red that's very 'together'. Serve it with roast beef.

Quality 🍷🍷🍷🍷🍷
Value ★★★★½
Grapes cabernet sauvignon; merlot
Region not stated
Cellar 🍾 2
Alc./Vol. 14.0%
RRP $24.00

Wynns Cabernet Shiraz Merlot

This is Wynns' middle-of-the-road Coonawarra red, originally designed as an earlier drinking style than the premium black-labelled Cabernet Sauvignon. It's often the least impressive of the range, but in good vintages it easily holds its own.

CURRENT RELEASE 2002 There's a herbal, briary, savoury thing going on here that's quite a regional quality. It's slightly mulchy, but not unpleasant. There are also riper cues like blackcurranty fruit and a certain earthiness. Oak is hardly perceptible. The dry middleweight palate is pleasantly flavoured with medium depth and a balanced foundation of dry tannins. Try it with minted lamb cutlets.

Quality 🍷🍷🍷🍷
Value ★★★
Grapes cabernet sauvignon; shiraz; merlot
Region Coonawarra, SA
Cellar 🍾 3
Alc./Vol. 13.0%
RRP $19.70 [$]

Wynns Harold Vineyard Cabernet Sauvignon

This is a special release of cabernet from a single block on Wynns Coonawarra Estate. Made to celebrate the fiftieth vintage produced by Wynns at Coonawarra, it's a rare beast, but one worth searching for.

CURRENT RELEASE 2001 This is a very concentrated cabernet with a lot more oomph than tradition would dictate. In style it's more of a modern take on Coonawarra. At the core is very concentrated blackcurrant liqueur-like fruit with hints of mint and earthy cabernet character. Cedary oak plays a positive role, and the palate is a bit like demi-glace, rich, full, beef-stock-like and velvety. A firm backbone of tannin supports everything and should help it hold together for many years. Perfect with beef fillet and a demiglaze sauce.

Quality 🍷🍷🍷🍷🍷
Value ★★★★
Grapes cabernet sauvignon
Region Coonawarra, SA
Cellar 🍾 2–15
Alc./Vol. 14.0%
RRP $40.00

Xanadu Lagan Reserve

Quality	🍷🍷🍷🍷
Value	★★★½
Grapes	cabernet sauvignon; merlot; cabernet franc
Region	Margaret River, WA
Cellar	🍾 10+
Alc./Vol.	14.0%
RRP	$50.00

Packaged in a massive, heavy bottle, which contrasts with the minimal label, this is winemaker Jurg Muggli's big-statement red. It is an emphatic style that not everyone takes to. Happily, he doesn't release it too young!

CURRENT RELEASE 1999 Starting to show some development in both colour and flavour, this heroic red wine has a complex bouquet of soy-sauce, Vegemite characters reflecting liberal use of oak plus some bottle-age. It is very big and tannic in the mouth, almost brutal, and you need to serve it with protein-rich food. Once you get used to the tannins, there is very good palate flavour lurking in there. Try it with rare steak and anchovy butter.

Yalumba Y Series Cabernet Sauvignon

Quality	🍷🍷🍷½
Value	★★★★
Grapes	cabernet sauvignon
Region	not stated
Cellar	🍾 3
Alc./Vol.	14.0%
RRP	$13.50 [$]

There was a time when cabernet sauvignon was a rare thing in Australia, and the wines available were usually 'top end' due to their scarcity and quality. Times have changed and today there are vast acreages of cab sauv made into everyday tipples like this one.

CURRENT RELEASE 2002 This has good varietal personality in a less austere mode for cabernet sauvignon. It smells of black fruits, earth and a light touch of oak, while the middleweight palate is relatively simple in flavour, but quite persistent. It finishes with a savoury measure of dry powdery tannins. Good value. Sip it with lamb stew and parsley dumplings.

Grenache and Blends

Not that long ago South Australians were being paid a bounty to pull it out, but after being a wallflower for many years, grenache is now the belle of the ball. Old-vine material is being bought at a premium, and the resulting wine, whether made as a straight varietal or blended with traditional companions like shiraz and mourvèdre, is attracting raves both locally and internationally. Grenache is mainly grown in the older wine regions of South Australia and styles vary from soupy and hot with alcohol, through smooth, generous, delicious middleweights, to spicy Rhône look-alikes. The cool 2002 vintage was especially kind to old-vine, dry-grown grenache. They are disappearing from the shelves fast, so grab some of these beauties while you can.

Charles Melton Nine Popes

Charlie Melton has helped put old-vine grenache back in its rightful place as one of Australia's great red wines. Nine Popes is made from a cocktail of grenache, shiraz and mourvèdre with the proportion varying with the vintage.

CURRENT RELEASE 2002 There have been few Nine Popes reds better than this one. Made only from grenache and shiraz, without the mourvèdre component, it sums up this generous style exactly. The nose has an essency quality; aromas of raspberries, plum pudding, leather, spices and vanilla are very concentrated, and the palate is velvety and warm. Rich earthy flavours are immensely satisfying, it has great depth, and fine-grained, ripe tannins are in harmonious balance. Serve it with a beef casserole.

Quality	🍷🍷🍷🍷🍷
Value	★★★★½
Grapes	grenache; shiraz
Region	Barossa Valley, SA
Cellar	10
Alc./Vol.	14.5%
RRP	$45.00

PENGUIN BEST OTHER REDS AND BLENDS

D'Arenberg The Cadenzia Grenache Shiraz Mourvèdre

This wine is sealed by a Zork, which is a soft-plastic stopper that has two parts: a plug that goes inside the bottle neck, and an outer casing that can be torn away to open the bottle. The McLaren Vale region is its major supporter.

CURRENT RELEASE 2003 This is a very good Rhône-style blend, as we've come to expect from d'Arenberg. It smells appealingly of sweet raspberries and jam, with a lick of spice – very classic ultra-ripe grenache aromas. It has excellent flavour and balance in the mouth, with nice fleshiness, light softly ripe tannins and an overall feel of harmony. Delish! Try it with steak and kidney pie.

Quality	🍷🍷🍷🍷½
Value	★★★★
Grapes	grenache; shiraz; mourvèdre
Region	McLaren Vale, SA
Cellar	5+
Alc./Vol.	14.5%
RRP	$25.00

D'Arenberg The Custodian Deep Sand Grenache

Quality	♥♥♥♥♥
Value	★★★★
Grapes	grenache
Region	McLaren Vale, SA
Cellar	▮ 7+
Alc./Vol.	15.0%
RRP	$60.00 (3-pack)

From the outstanding 2002 vintage, winemaker Chester Osborn produced not one but three Custodian grenaches off different soils, labelled Loam, Sand and Clay, and Deep Sand. They were initially marketed as a mixed three-pack, for $60. This one took a gold medal in Hobart and silver in Melbourne in 2003.

CURRENT RELEASE 2002   The colour is remarkably deep for a pure grenache, and the youthful aromas are delicious, redolent of sweet black cherry. It's medium-bodied, smooth and vibrant, with lashings of soft, ripe, well-balanced tannin. A high-quality grenache of real depth and style. Serve it with game pie.

D'Arenberg The Ironstone Pressings Grenache Shiraz Mourvèdre

Quality	♥♥♥♥♥
Value	★★★⁺
Grapes	grenache; shiraz; mourvèdre
Region	McLaren Vale, SA
Cellar	▮ 10+
Alc./Vol.	14.5%
RRP	$60.00 ▮

The 'pressings' or 'press-wine' is the fraction of the fermented wine that comes out of the wine press after pressure has been applied to the skins. It is highly prized, because it's especially deep in colour and rich in extract and tannin. Maker: Chester Osborn.

CURRENT RELEASE 2002   This is a luxurious Rhône-style blend from a top vintage. Gorgeously rich, ripe, sweet black-cherry, raspberry aromas have a subtle aniseed background with a hint of raisins, and the palate is big and voluptuous, with masses of ripe fruit and supple but assertive tannin. This is a biggie, and really needs food as a young wine. Try jugged hare.

Fuse Shiraz Grenache Mourvèdre

Quality	♥♥♥♥
Value	★★★⁺
Grapes	shiraz; grenache; mourvèdre
Region	Clare Valley, SA
Cellar	▮ 3+
Alc./Vol.	14.5%
RRP	$19.00 ⬧

Fuse is a new mid-market label produced by Pikes of Clare, sourced from various vineyards and regions. This one just happens to be made from Clare grapes, too. Maker: Neil Pike.

CURRENT RELEASE 2003   The sweet perfume reveals some overripe, jammy fruit together with some spices. It's a lighter-bodied red, smooth and nicely modulated for early drinking, without particular complexity. It has ample smooth tannins and the spice flavours permeate the palate, too. It would suit lamb's fry and bacon.

John Duval Plexus Shiraz Grenache Mourvèdre

John Duval is the former chief winemaker of Penfolds. He resigned from Southcorp in late 2003 after 30 years with Penfolds, a victim of the mayhem that followed the Rosemount merger. This is the first of the wines he was set to release during 2005.
CURRENT RELEASE 2003   An excellent red as we'd expect from Duval, and cast in a complex, savoury style without any excesses of oak or alcohol. The bouquet has dusty/toasty nutmeg and subtle mixed-spice aromas, together with raspberry and cranberry fruit characters. There are hints of prune and jam too. It has serious palate depth and smooth, ripe tannins. Lovely balance and ready drinkability. Try it with Barossa mettwurst.

Quality	♟ ♟ ♟ ♟ ♙
Value	★★★⟩
Grapes	shiraz; grenache; mourvèdre
Region	Barossa Valley, SA
Cellar	▮ 5+
Alc./Vol.	14.5%
RRP	$36.40 ▮

Penfolds Bin 138 Old Vine Grenache Shiraz Mourvèdre

Penfolds has established this as one of the benchmark GSM blends in the market. It is a more approachable style than many of its peers, as it is never porty, overripe or excessively oaky or alcoholic. Consequently, certain American critics probably wouldn't like it at all. All the more for us!
CURRENT RELEASE 2003   Mixed-spices, dried bay leaf, nutty and nutmeg aromas are present together with savoury mellow characters from ageing in older barrels. It's savoury throughout, with soft but gently drying tannins and modest persistence on the finish. A very good food-wine: serve it with herbed meatballs in tomato purée.

Quality	♟ ♟ ♟ ♟
Value	★★★★
Grapes	grenache; shiraz; mourvèdre
Region	Barossa Valley, SA
Cellar	▮ 4+
Alc./Vol.	14.5%
RRP	$26.00 Ⓢ

Reynell Basket Pressed Grenache

John Reynell established Chateau Reynella in 1838, and it's now in the middle of a southern Adelaide suburb called Reynella. The winery and its wines were once called Chateau Reynella; now the wines are simply Reynell.
CURRENT RELEASE 2002   This took time to open up and really rewarded decanting. It was transformed from a slightly closed and stolid wine into a sweetly floral, pepperminty, ripe-cherry tasting charmer with considerable depth and structure. It has those essency and floral characters that grenache gets when it's nice and ripe. Good balance and persistence: a serious grenache. Drink it with steak and kidney pie.

Quality	♟ ♟ ♟ ♟
Value	★★★⟩
Grapes	grenache
Region	McLaren Vale, SA
Cellar	▮ 5+
Alc./Vol.	14.0%
RRP	$32.00 Ⓢ ▮

Schild Estate GMS

- **Quality** 🍷🍷🍷🍷
- **Value** ★★★½
- **Grapes** grenache 50%; mourvèdre 30%; shiraz 20%
- **Region** Barossa Valley, SA
- **Cellar** 🍾5
- **Alc./Vol.** 15.0%
- **RRP** $19.00

We've had wine called MSG and GST, both of which can have less than pleasant connotations, as well as the more innocuous SMG and GMS. What does it all mean? G stands for grenache, M for mataro (aka mourvèdre), S for shiraz. And T, made famous in St Hallett's GST, means touriga.

CURRENT RELEASE 2004 This has real meaty old-vine Barossa grenache smells that remind us of stewed cherries, pepper, earth and spices. There's also a lifted, slightly spirity touch. It's a big nose and the palate follows true to type, big and warm with subtlety on hold. Tannins are balanced and ripe, and it finishes long and warm. Try it with spicy spare ribs.

Spinifex Esprit

- **Quality** 🍷🍷🍷🍷½
- **Value** ★★★
- **Grapes** grenache 40%; mourvèdre 34%; shiraz 21%; cinsault 5%
- **Region** Barossa Valley, SA
- **Cellar** 🍾4
- **Alc./Vol.** 15.0%
- **RRP** $30.00

Peter Schell and Magali Gely are a husband and wife team who came to Australia in the early 1990s from New Zealand to study oenology and wine marketing respectively. They've had a lot of experience in both Australia and France, and now they've launched their Spinifex range, employing old Barossa vineyards and non-interventionist winemaking to produce some excellent regional reds.

CURRENT RELEASE 2003 This Barossa blend has an attractively perfumed nose, reminiscent of mixed berries with a meaty touch underneath and some regional grenache earthiness and spice. The plump palate is smooth and seamless with good depth and persistence, finishing with soft tannins. It's all very harmonious, and a high level of alcohol doesn't intrude too much. It matches a hearty braised meat dish well.

St Hallett Gamekeeper's Reserve

- **Quality** 🍷🍷🍷🍷
- **Value** ★★★★½
- **Grapes** shiraz; grenache; touriga
- **Region** Barossa Valley, SA
- **Cellar** 🍾2
- **Alc./Vol.** 14.5%
- **RRP** $13.95 [$]

For many years now Gamekeeper's Reserve has been St Hallett's everyday red, always great value with real no-fuss drinkability and food-friendliness. The Portuguese touriga grape is an unorthodox addition to the blend.

CURRENT RELEASE 2004 This smells enticingly of spiced raspberries, plums, caramel and earth. Its uncomplicated personality has homely appeal, with a slightly European palate structure that finishes appetising and dry. It isn't a wine for cerebral appreciation, you just glug it down. Try it with lamb's fry and bacon.

Wirra Wirra Grenache

McLaren Vale and grenache go together like . . . grenache
and McLaren Vale. The region's long history with this grape
variety didn't mean a thing in the 1970s, when grenache's
future was under threat. Fortunately it survived.
CURRENT RELEASE 2003   A straightforward, honest
grenache that isn't stewed or overblown. It has great
varietal purity in its aromas of red berries, confectionery
and spice, and the palate is ripely fruity with excellent
ripeness and depth of flavour. Tannins are typically soft and
it finishes long and tasty. An excellent example. Serve it
with a Catalan-style stew of pork, chorizo and beans.

Quality	♀♀♀♀♀
Value	★★★
Grapes	grenache
Region	McLaren Vale, SA
Cellar	🍾 2
Alc./Vol.	14.5%
RRP	$30.00

Yalumba Bush Vine Grenache

The resurrection of Barossa grenache has meant an exciting
new wave of back-to-the-future reds employing fruit
from old almost-forgotten Barossa vineyards. Yalumba's
variations on the theme are right in regional style, and this
Bush Vine wine is very well-priced to boot.
CURRENT RELEASE 2003   This Barossa blend has the
up-front generosity that Barossa grenache is well-known
for. Quite old-worldy in style, it smells warm and spicy
with meaty, earthy touches to red-berry fruit. The palate is
smooth and ripe-tasting with good texture and a balanced
dry structure underneath. It's a sociable taste of tradition at
a fair price. Serve it with roast winter vegetable risotto.

Quality	♀♀♀♀
Value	★★★
Grapes	grenache
Region	Barossa Valley, SA
Cellar	🍾 3
Alc./Vol.	14.5%
RRP	$18.75 Ⓢ

Yangarra Estate Cadenzia

In keeping with the American ownership of Yangarra
Estate, this wine is made in the sweet, alcoholic style so
beloved of some influential US wine commentators.
CURRENT RELEASE 2003   With an alcoholic strength
higher than fino sherry, you'd expect this to be a little
more like a fortified wine than a light table wine, and in
a way you'd be right. The nose is smoky with some odd
earthy smells, a touch of oxidation, stewed-fruit character
and even a hint of sherry-like aroma. In the mouth it
tastes much better, with meaty, cherry-confectionery and
chocolatey flavours of richness and power. It's a strange
wine, but it grows on you and could be a good partner
for an after-dinner cheese platter.

Quality	♀♀♀♀
Value	★★★
Grapes	grenache; shiraz; mourvèdre
Region	McLaren Vale, SA
Cellar	🍾 4
Alc./Vol.	15.8%
RRP	$29.00

Merlot and Blends

Merlot is one of the fastest-growing varietal categories not only in Australia but around the world. This puzzles your authors because they are finding the good ones few and far between. What is it that appeals to wine drinkers about merlot? Perhaps it's the idea of merlot, which all the back labels will tell you is supposed to be soft, rounded, low in tannin and easy on the gums. Good merlot *is* like that, with a soft, plum or raspberry-like, sometimes olive-like fruit character. In reality much of it is underripe and green-tasting, often with harsh, astringent tannin or residual sugar 'papering over' its hardness. This section encompasses wines that are majority merlot: most will be between 51 per cent and 100 per cent merlot.

Bidgeebong Tumbarumba Merlot

Quality 🍷🍷🍷🍷
Value ★★★½
Grapes merlot
Region Tumbarumba, NSW
Cellar 🍾 3
Alc./Vol. 14.0%
RRP $24.00 🍾

Bidgeebong is a made-up name that combines elements of a couple of true-blue Aussie words. The 'Bidgee' (Murrumbidgee) is a major river that flows through some of the regions in which the company is based, such as Tumbarumba and Wagga. And a billabong is a quiet backwater of a river.

CURRENT RELEASE 2003 There is a sweetish vegetal character in the bouquet, coupled with garden mint and a touch of smokiness. The palate has some aggressive tannin and a hint of bitterness, but pair it with a meal and you find the astringency vanishes and there is plenty of attractive, plummy merlot flavour. Try it with roast lamb and mint sauce.

Blue Pyrenees Merlot

Quality 🍷🍷🍷🍷½
Value ★★★★★
Grapes merlot
Region Pyrenees, Vic.
Cellar 🍾 5+
Alc./Vol. 14.2%
RRP $19.00 [$]

This wine, which won a gold medal at the Royal Melbourne Wine Show (in 2004), was made from two blocks of 22-year-old vines on the Blue Pyrenees Estate near Avoca. The vines are low yielding and unirrigated.

CURRENT RELEASE 2002 Gosh, if only all merlots were this good, never mind the fact that it costs a mere $19, less on special. The colour is a bright, medium–deep red–purple and the aromas recall raspberry and mint, with oak well in the background. The palate is really excellent: plenty of body and a degree of muscularity seldom seen in mid-market Aussie merlot. There's a tickle of acid showing but the structure is exemplary. Try it with pink roast lamb.

Capel Vale Howecroft Merlot

Those who think of merlot as a forgettable soft no-excitement red wine should try this. It's a powerful drop with plenty going on. Serious red wine.
CURRENT RELEASE 2002   This has a dense colour and a very complex ripe nose and palate of syrupy plum, prune, earth and spicy oak. There are also touches of aniseed and bitter chocolate to it. The palate has great texture, ripe long flavour, and a firm foundation of grainy tannins. A substantial merlot with everything in the right place, this should work well with braised duck and winter vegetables.

Quality	♀♀♀♀♀
Value	★★★┤
Grapes	merlot
Region	Geographe, WA
Cellar	▮ 6+
Alc./Vol.	14.0%
RRP	$50.00

Capel Vale Merlot

Merlot has gained a solid foothold in Australia in recent years, but it's nowhere near as popular as it is in the USA where it's almost synonymous with 'red wine' in some circles.
CURRENT RELEASE 2002   This is quite a different thing to Capel Vale's Howecroft Merlot, gentler, less potent, more of an everyday drink. It has an attractive bouquet of red cherries, gentle spice and savoury earthiness. The palate is on the light side of medium-bodied, with middling intensity, good length and a slight astringency that dries out the finish and shortens it a little. Drink it with herbed veal cutlets.

Quality	♀♀♀♀
Value	★★★
Grapes	merlot
Region	Geographe, WA
Cellar	▮ 1
Alc./Vol.	13.5%
RRP	$23.00

Coldstream Hills Reserve Merlot

Coldstream Hills has built an enviable reputation for good merlot in a fairly short time. It comes in two octane ratings, a standard wine and this reserve version. The current vintage of Reserve at time of publication is the 2000, and it shows how a bit of bottle-age benefits this wine.
CURRENT RELEASE 2000   This is a complete, harmonious wine with a delicious sweet nose of plum, berries, earthy spices and mellow oak. The added veneer of bottle-age ties it all together well, and it tastes round, smooth and ripe. Mature, soft tannins give it excellent balance. An easy-going, maturing merlot to sip with a braised lamb dish.

Quality	♀♀♀♀⑂
Value	★★★┤
Grapes	merlot
Region	Yarra Valley, Vic.
Cellar	▮ 3
Alc./Vol.	14.0%
RRP	$48.95

Ferngrove Frankland River Merlot

- **Quality** 🍷🍷🍷½
- **Value** ★★★★
- **Grapes** merlot
- **Region** Great Southern, WA
- **Cellar** 🍾 4
- **Alc./Vol.** 13.5%
- **RRP** $18.00 [$]

Frankland River is one of the sub-regions of the Great Southern region in far south-west Western Australia. The other sub-regions are Mount Barker, Porongurup, Albany and Denmark. Winemaker at Ferngrove is Kim Horton.

CURRENT RELEASE 2003 Vibrant, fresh cherry, vanilla and cough-medicine-like aromas are the feature of this lively young merlot. It's not very vinous: a light-bodied, simple, grapey red with mulberry flavours on the palate, some tight tannins and a bit more depth than most merlots in its range. It would suit veal scaloppine.

Grant Burge Hillcot Merlot

- **Quality** 🍷🍷🍷🍷
- **Value** ★★★½
- **Grapes** merlot
- **Region** Barossa Valley, SA
- **Cellar** 🍾 4
- **Alc./Vol.** 13.5%
- **RRP** $18.50 [$]

Barossa merlot like this is a generous type of red wine, full flavoured and without aggressive tendencies. It makes a friendly alternative to big-tannin reds made from cabernet or shiraz.

CURRENT RELEASE 2002 This smells sweet and soft with jammy blueberry and forest-fruit aromas, dabs of mint and earth, and subtle oak. Very appealing, and very Barossa merlot. The palate is smooth and medium-bodied with good length. Fresh acidity and soft tannins keep it lively and easy to drink. It goes well with mild lamb biryani.

Howard Park Best Barrels WA Merlot

- **Quality** 🍷🍷🍷🍷½
- **Value** ★★★
- **Grapes** merlot
- **Region** various, WA
- **Cellar** 2–10
- **Alc./Vol.** 14.0%
- **RRP** $75.00

That's straightforward branding for you! No bulldust – just the truth. It was selected from their best barrels of merlot. It's a limited release, as there were only 200 dozen bottled. It's the debut of this label. Maker: Michael Kerrigan and team.

CURRENT RELEASE 2003 Remarkable depth of colour and concentrated flavour are the highlights of this rare merlot. The aromas are clean and vibrant, albeit a touch subdued in its extreme youth. There's some classy oak in support of rich, properly ripe fruit. There's a lot of smooth, supple tannin on the palate and a slight metallic note that raised our left eyebrow. If there is a trace of volatility, it doesn't worry the wine. This could be cellared. Serve it with a hearty veal roast.

Lindemans Reserve Merlot

The Lindemans brand used to stand for some of the best wines in Australia, but these days it's been debased and is now all about cheap and not always terribly cheerful stuff. The Reserve wines have an advantage over Southcorp's similarly priced Rosemount and Rawson's Retreat in that they're on sale a year older.

CURRENT RELEASE 2003 It starts off well, with good depth of colour and some appealing raspberry, blueberry and mulberry aromas, together with some earthy development. It's drinking well now, with that forward development contributing to softness in the mouth. It's nothing profound or complex, but a good easy-drinking glass of merlot for the price. It would suit lasagne.

Quality	🍷🍷🍷½
Value	★★★★
Grapes	merlot
Region	not stated
Cellar	🍾 3
Alc./Vol.	13.5%
RRP	$14.50 [$]

Lost Valley Hazy Mountain Merlot

The hazy mountain landscape around Lost Valley is a romantic place to grow vines. It's a labour of love for proprietor Dr Robert Ipasso. Merlot suits the site well.

CURRENT RELEASE 2003 A dense young wine with a smooth nose of plummy fruitcake, spice and dark chocolate, with a touch of undergrowth. The seamless palate is richly concentrated with a velvety feel on the tongue. The mid-palate smoothness runs on through ripe fine-grained tannins to a long finish. Great with veal and white bean casserole.

Quality	🍷🍷🍷🍷½
Value	★★★
Grapes	merlot
Region	Upper Goulburn, Vic.
Cellar	🍾 4
Alc./Vol.	14.0%
RRP	$34.00

Murdock Merlot

The Murdock vineyard hit the track running with its first couple of releases of straight cabernet sauvignon. Quality has been excellent and a good riesling and this merlot followed. The reds are usually a year or two older than most current release Coonawarras, which is a bonus.

CURRENT RELEASE 2001 A merlot of dense construction with a deliciously rich nose of berry jam, siena cake, cedar and spice. In the mouth it has medium body and concentrated flavour with silky smooth texture and a long finish. A classy straight merlot that lives up to the Murdock reputation for excellent regional wines. Try it with beef fillet and demiglaze.

Quality	🍷🍷🍷🍷🍷
Value	★★★★
Grapes	merlot
Region	Coonawarra, SA
Cellar	🍾 6
Alc./Vol.	13.5%
RRP	$28.00 [$]

Peter Lehmann Merlot

Quality 🍷🍷🍷🍷
Value ★★★★★
Grapes merlot
Region Barossa Valley, SA
Cellar 🍾 5
Alc./Vol. 14.5%
RRP $15.00 [$]

The Peter Lehmann mob reckon this is a voluptuous, velvety wine and they chose an appropriate Edwina White picture of a shapely female to adorn the label. Maker: Andrew Wigan and team.

CURRENT RELEASE 2003 Yet again, the team at Lehmann's have come up with a very smart wine for the price, which beats much of its opposition into a cocked hat. It has olivaceous, linseed-oil aromas typical of the grape, joined by dark-chocolate flavours in the mouth. There's good concentration and smooth, rounded fleshiness. The tannins are chewy and it has more gravitas than most $20 merlots. It would go with Wiener schnitzel.

Plunkett Strathbogie Ranges Merlot

Quality 🍷🍷🍷🍷
Value ★★★½
Grapes merlot
Region Strathbogie Ranges, Vic.
Cellar 🍾 3+
Alc./Vol. 13.5%
RRP $20.00

The Plunkett family are graziers turned grapegrowers in the Avenel area of the Strathbogie Ranges. They sell a fair quantity of their fruit, and Sam Plunkett makes wine in their own winery.

CURRENT RELEASE 2002 There are plenty of vegetal aromas here – mint, compost and humus – plus a more classic black- olive merlot character. It's a somewhat wild and woolly character that may polarise tasters. The palate shows slightly elevated acidity but also good flavour and character. It's quite complex, and would suit a lamb and vegetable stew.

Rosemount Orange Vineyard Merlot

Quality 🍷🍷🍷🍷
Value ★★★½
Grapes merlot
Region Orange, NSW
Cellar 🍾 5+
Alc./Vol. 13.5%
RRP $28.00 [$]

Former Rosemount chief winemaker Philip Shaw, whose vines probably produced most of this wine, swears that Orange has the best potential for merlot of anywhere in Australia. Time will tell, but there are already some runs on the scoreboard.

CURRENT RELEASE 2001 Some attractive green-olive and machine-oil aromas signal the merlot grape variety combined with some small-oak character, while the palate has good intensity, backbone and length. It's an elegant style but it's also a step up in intensity, weight and structure from most Australian merlots that cross our paths. It suits braised lamb shanks.

Stefano Lubiana Merlot

Stefano Lubiana's elegant label is worn by some of
Tasmania's best wines. In the hands of such a winemaker,
merlot looks to suit Tasmania very well.
CURRENT RELEASE 2003   This has a dense appearance
and a quite European bouquet that's complex with smoky,
earthy and vegimitey touches to concentrated raspberry
and plum fruit. The velvety palate is rich and long with
quite firm structure but the balance is good. It's not a
squeaky-clean merlot; it does have soul. In fact it's quite
majestic. Try it with venison or kangaroo.

Quality	▼▼▼▼▼
Value	★★★⁴
Grapes	merlot
Region	Southern Tasmania
Cellar	🍷 5+
Alc./Vol.	13.5%
RRP	$27.00

Summit Estate Merlot Cabernet Shiraz

Even Toowoomba has its own wine show these days. This
wine claims to have won a gold medal and the Grand
Champion prize at Toowoomba in 2003, and a silver at
Stanthorpe (Australian Small Winemakers Show) in 2003.
CURRENT RELEASE 2002   There is a pungent smoky,
peppery bouquet leading the way here, while the palate
is smooth and easygoing, with a light- to medium-body.
The pepper no doubt comes from the shiraz component.
It has good depth of flavour and softness although there
is a hint of sulphide that manifests itself in the bouquet
and the graphite-like finish. We liked it for its softness and
drinkability. It suits a lamb and barley casserole.

Quality	▼▼▼▼
Value	★★★⁴
Grapes	merlot; cabernet sauvignon; shiraz
Region	Granite Belt, Qld
Cellar	🍷 3
Alc./Vol.	13.0%
RRP	$22.00 (cellar door)

Yalumba Y Series Merlot

Merlot arrived in Australian vineyards when everybody
worshipped at the Bordeaux altar. Australians had
traditionally softened (and stretched) their cabernet with
shiraz, but the bordelais employed merlot to mellow
their cab. Soon cab-merlot was the thing, and then the
Americans fell in love with straight merlots, sparking a
worldwide trend for inexpensive straightforward wines like
this.
CURRENT RELEASE 2002   There's good varietal character
in this young merlot. Made in a modern international style,
it leads off with loganberry, plum and green-leaf aromas
that are forward and fruity. The palate has attractive
freshness and it's built smooth and easy. A drink-now
red wine to serve with Lebanese sausages.

Quality	▼▼▼⁴
Value	★★★★
Grapes	merlot
Region	not stated
Cellar	🍷 2
Alc./Vol.	14.0%
RRP	$13.50 Ⓢ

Petit Verdot and Blends

Petit verdot became known in Australia when winemakers started messing with tradition in the 1960s and '70s. A new generation saw potential in trying new things and their infatuation with Bordeaux led them away from familiar red grapes, like shiraz, grenache and cabernet sauvignon, towards a new world involving merlot, cabernet franc and petit verdot. Petit verdot is the most obscure of the trio, playing a bit part in multi-varietal Bordeaux red blends. In Australia the small quantities planted were almost always blended in like fashion, but recently it's appeared straight, especially in hot inland regions. In France it's prized for colour, acidity and tannin, rather than individual personality. Australia's warm climate suits its late-ripening tendencies and it can produce satisfying, solid reds of strength and character.

Angoves Stonegate Limited Release Petit Verdot

Quality	♓♓♓♔
Value	★★★★
Grapes	petit verdot
Region	Murray Valley, SA
Cellar	🍶 2
Alc./Vol.	13.5%
RRP	$8.99 ⓢ

Petit verdot, a late-ripening minor red grape from Bordeaux, is a relative newcomer to Australia's hot hinterland wine regions, but it shows great promise. Wineries everywhere are trying it out and Angoves is one of the latest to come to our attention.

CURRENT RELEASE 2003   This really is a pleasant drop of hooch, and the price is a welcome surprise. It's a lighter type, but it doesn't lose much intensity because of it. The nose has sweet cherry and berry aromas that are fresh enough, and there's good balance and softness in the mouth. Try it with spaghetti bolognese.

Kingston Estate Empiric Selection Petit Verdot

Quality	♓♓♓♓
Value	★★★
Grapes	petit verdot
Region	Murray Valley, SA
Cellar	🍶 3
Alc./Vol.	14.0%
RRP	$18.50 ⓢ

Kingston Estate's Bill Moularadellis has been championing petit verdot as an excellent grape variety for the South Australian Riverland for a while now.

CURRENT RELEASE 2003   A deeply coloured version of Kingston's petit verdot, Empiric is more concentrated and liqueurish, and more oaky than the standard wine. It has dusty oak, aniseed, spice and black fruits on the nose that are spicy, rich and ripe. The flavours are slightly vintage-porty with good depth of flavour, warmth and richness, finishing with soft tannins. Enjoy it with homemade lasagne.

Kingston Estate Petit Verdot

Petit verdot is a minor red grape of Bordeaux, where it's employed to give structure to cabernet and merlot. It's a late ripener which counts against it in Bordeaux's changeable climate, but in the sunny warmth of the Murray Valley it ripens perfectly. Winemakers in these hot hinterland Aussie vineyards are saying that petit verdot could have found its true home there.

CURRENT RELEASE 2002 This smells of spiced plums with a slight fruitcakey thing and some earthiness that makes it rather merlot-like. In the mouth it's smooth with good texture, a hint of licorice, plenty of flavour and personality. Slightly sinewy, but not intrusive tannins complete the picture. Serve it with pizza napolitana.

Quality	🍷🍷🍷½
Value	★★★½
Grapes	petit verdot
Region	Murray Valley, SA
Cellar	🍾 2
Alc./Vol.	14.5%
RRP	$12.90 [$]

Sexton Harry's Monster

From Phil and Allison Sexton's perfectly located Yarra Valley vineyard Giant Steps, this 'monster' is really quite a civilised critter. The latest edition reflects the Sextons' enthusiasm for petit verdot.

CURRENT RELEASE 2003 An interesting young red made from a variation on the 'Bordeaux blend' that reverses the usual order, making petit verdot and merlot the key players rather than cabernet sauvignon. It smells of redcurrants and blackcurrants with subtle oak and hints of bitter chocolate, briar and gravelly dirt. In the mouth it's a seamless progression of flavours with good depth and length, supported by some firm tannic astringency. A savoury, full-flavoured wine to enjoy with steak and kidney pie.

Quality	🍷🍷🍷🍷
Value	★★★
Grapes	petit verdot; merlot; cabernet sauvignon; cabernet franc
Region	Yarra Valley, Vic.
Cellar	🍾 5
Alc./Vol.	13.9%
RRP	$45.00 💰

Pinot Noir

The holy grail? Maybe. Pinot noir certainly excites the interest of our more quixotic winemakers, and frustrates them too. We've watched pinot's trials and tribulations in Australia over many years and we're pleased to report that the news gets better all the time. Increasing vine age, levels of experience and improving technique mean that wine quality has been moving ahead, and now pinot noir's mysterious, sensuous delights aren't as rare as they once were. It's still best to follow good advice to find the best wines, and if in doubt exercise caution, but in good years places like Tasmania, southern Victoria, the Adelaide Hills and Western Australia's far south are really coming of age with pinot. One welcome development in recent times has been the democratisation of pinot via a new crop of sub-$20 wines – some are surprisingly good.

Bannockburn Stuart Pinot Noir

Quality	▼▼▼▼▼
Value	★★★★
Grapes	pinot noir
Region	Geelong, Vic.
Cellar	▮ 4
Alc./Vol.	13.5%
RRP	$65.00

Bannockburn makes three pinot noirs when the season is suitable: the regular wine, this one and the Serré. Stuart is named after the founder of Bannockburn Vineyards, the late Stuart Hooper. The 2002 vintage was a very low-yielding year, but an excellent one.
CURRENT RELEASE 2002   Wonderful stuff! It is a beautiful harmony of undergrowth, sap, earth, stalky and dark-cherry flavours, with weight and concentration in the mouth. Softness and fleshy charm abound, and the fruit is sweet on the middle palate. It's a succulent, textural, lingering pinot of great charm and style. Drink it with veal sweetbreads.

Brokenwood Beechworth Pinot Noir

Quality	▼▼▼▼
Value	★★★┤
Grapes	pinot noir
Region	Beechworth, Vic.
Cellar	▮ 3
Alc./Vol.	13.5%
RRP	$24.00 ⅏

Brokenwood has never felt constrained by the boundaries of its Hunter Valley home base. It sources grapes from various regions that suit the varietal, in an effort to make the best wine possible. Makers: Iain Riggs and P.J. Charteris.
CURRENT RELEASE 2004   A lighter style of pinot than the previous Indigo Vineyard release, this has an estery, raspberry/bubblegum aroma which is clean, herbal and fairly simple. It's again quite light and straightforward in the mouth, with some tannin firmness and acidity showing. It resembles a beaujolais rather than a burgundy. A nice drink with beef carpaccio and shaved parmesan.

Castle Rock Estate Pinot Noir

Castle Rock is best known for its riesling, the Porongurup Ranges being one of the premier sources of fine riesling in Western Australia. Owners are the Diletti family; winemaker is Robert Diletti, son of the founders.
CURRENT RELEASE 2003   A typically light-bodied Castle Rock pinot, with medium-light red–purple colour and some boiled-lolly, cherry confection aromas of good ripeness and varietal charm. It has some attractive fleshiness and fruit sweetness on palate, but lacks a little intensity. With the right kind of food, such as salmon, it works a treat.

Quality	♟ ♟ ♟ ♟
Value	★ ★ ★ ★
Grapes	pinot noir
Region	Great Southern, WA
Cellar	🍾 3+
Alc./Vol.	13.5%
RRP	$25.00 🏷

Clos Saint Pierre Pinot Noir

Regular readers of this book will know how excited the authors are when they discover an under-$15 pinot noir that *actually* smells and tastes like the real thing. This one is a collaboration between French wine man Pierre Naigeon and the De Bortolis. It appears to be exclusive to the Dan Murphy chain of stores in Victoria and New South Wales.
CURRENT RELEASE 2004   This has appetising pinot scents that suggest the influence of some carbonic maceration, a method used in the French beaujolais region to produce fresh, low-tannin reds for early consumption. It has a nose of cherries, plums and almonds, with a light but pleasantly intense palate of succulent softness. It finishes clean and tasty. Ideal with a light chill and some grilled spiced chicken.

Quality	♟ ♟ ♟ ♟
Value	★ ★ ★ ★
Grapes	pinot noir
Region	Yarra Valley, Vic.
Cellar	🍾 2
Alc./Vol.	13.5%
RRP	$14.99

The Cups Estate Pinot Noir

The grapes for this wine were grown in a part of the Mornington Peninsula known as 'The Cups Country' due to the cup-like depressions between the rolling hills. Maker: Dr Richard McIntyre.
CURRENT RELEASE 2003   An attractive young pinot that is a fresher, cleaner wine than the Raimondo Reserve from the same producer. It smells of plums, prunes, tea leaves and earth; succulent and appealing, with a long-flavoured, medium-weight, plummy palate of good richness and balance. Serve it with porcini mushroom risotto.

Quality	♟ ♟ ♟ ♟
Value	★ ★ ★
Grapes	pinot noir
Region	Mornington Peninsula, Vic.
Cellar	🍾 3
Alc./Vol.	13.5%
RRP	$24.95

Foxeys Hangout Pinot Noir

Quality	♥ ♥ ♥ ♥
Value	★ ★ ★ ★
Grapes	pinot noir
Region	Mornington Peninsula, Vic.
Cellar	🍾 3+
Alc./Vol.	13.5%
RRP	$30.00

The name is right out of left-field. Seems that in the distant past hunters used to shoot foxes and hang their carcasses on a big tree in a paddock on what was known as Foxeys Corner. Fine line between macabre and quirky! The labels are excellent.

CURRENT RELEASE 2003   It opens with a fair quota of toasty-vanilla oak, and the palate seems rather oaky and even a touch stodgy. With time it opens up into a much more attractive pinot, nicely aromatic with black-cherry and meat-stock aromas, and a clean, juicy palate with real elegance, fruit sweetness and good length. It would suit barbecued marinated quails.

Freycinet Pinot Noir

Quality	♥ ♥ ♥ ♥
Value	★ ★ ★
Grapes	pinot noir
Region	East Coast, Tas.
Cellar	🍾 5
Alc./Vol.	13.5%
RRP	$55.00 🍾

Freycinet has long been regarded as one of the leading pinot makers in the country. It has a blessed site near Bicheno and the Freycinet Peninsula: a sun-trap bowl that gets the grapes nice and ripe, pretty well every year. Maker: Claudio Radenti.

CURRENT RELEASE 2003   This is a perplexing wine that takes a while to open up and reveal its true colours. The bouquet was very shy at first, and the palate muscular but a bit dried-out. It 'breathed up', to show attractive dark-cherry aromas and flavours, and good depth of palate fruit although it is at the firmer, more structured end of Freycinet – and Tasmanian – style. It suits pink lamb chops.

Giant Steps Pinot Noir

Quality	♥ ♥ ♥ ♥
Value	★ ★ ★
Grapes	pinot noir
Region	Yarra Valley, Vic.
Cellar	🍾 3
Alc./Vol.	14.0%
RRP	$29.95 🍾

Attack of the clones. No, not the *Star Wars* movie, the clones we're talking about are the different strains of pinot noir that cutting-edge pinot producers are populating their vineyards with these days. At Giant Steps there are no fewer than seven different pinot noir clones.

CURRENT RELEASE 2003   A ruby-coloured, clean, modern-smelling pinot with good varietal clues on the nose. There are sappy, plummy aromas with touches of spice, and a reasonable measure of oak. The intensely flavoured palate has ripe, fairly oaky flavour and good texture, finishing in relatively firm, drawing tannins that happily fall short of bitterness. Try it with grilled calf's liver.

Hochkirch Maximus Pinot Noir

We first reviewed Hochkirch Pinot Noir in the *Guide* a few years ago, when we thought it a promising newcomer. The site in Victoria's cool south-west is cultivated along burgundian lines and biodymanic principles.
CURRENT RELEASE 2003   A very interesting young pinot with some of the European-style richness and complexity that many Australian pinot-noir makers strive for, but few achieve. The nose has fragrant smoky, plummy aromas, along with some undergrowthy and gamey touches. In the mouth it's rich and rather wild-tasting with velvety fruit mid-palate and a slight stemmy firmness underneath. It's a first-class effort with a hint of France to it. Enjoy it with lyonnaise sausages braised with lentils.

Quality	𝟎 𝟎 𝟎 𝟎 ¡
Value	★ ★ ★
Grapes	pinot noir
Region	Henty, Vic.
Cellar	▮ 4
Alc./Vol.	13.0%
RRP	$30.00 Ⓥ

Kooyong Massale Pinot Noir

Massale is the lowest of Kooyong's three tiers of pinot noir. The name comes from the term *selection massale*, 'mass selection', a reference to the practice of planting a mixture of vine cuttings in a vineyard, rather than going for a single clone. A part of Kooyong's pinot noir vineyard is propagated accordingly.
CURRENT RELEASE 2003   This is an attractive young pinot that smells seductively of herbs, strawberries and cream, and other red fruits. The palate is on the light side of medium-body, and there's reasonable intensity ahead of a gently dry finish. It's what some would call an ideal 'restaurant wine': pleasant, undemanding drinking. Serve it with grilled chicken.

Quality	𝟎 𝟎 𝟎 𝟎
Value	★ ★ ★
Grapes	pinot noir
Region	Mornington Peninsula, Vic.
Cellar	▮ 2
Alc./Vol.	13.0%
RRP	$25.00

CURRENT RELEASE 2004   This is a bright young pinot with a sappy, red-cherry-scented nose of medium intensity. The palate is light and fresh with pleasantly aromatic fruit flavour, and a light structure of tannins that gives a drying finish. It thankfully avoids the stemmy qualities we've found in a lot of young Mornington pinots. Drink it fairly young with Chinese cold cuts and soy chicken.

Quality	𝟎 𝟎 𝟎 𝟎
Value	★ ★ ★
Grapes	pinot noir
Region	Mornington Peninsula, Vic.
Cellar	▮ 2
Alc./Vol.	13.5%
RRP	$26.00

Kooyong Pinot Noir

Quality	♥ ♥ ♥ ♥ ♥
Value	★ ★ ★
Grapes	pinot noir
Region	Mornington Peninsula, Vic.
Cellar	🍷 5
Alc./Vol.	13.0%
RRP	$43.00

We've had mixed feelings about the Kooyong Pinot Noirs in the past. Some have had the slightly bitter edge that we've seen in a few other young Mornington Peninsula pinots, but the 2003 wine looks to have it well under control.

CURRENT RELEASE 2003 In our opinion this is the best Kooyong pinot so far, a deep-coloured, spicy-rich wine with potential. The densely packed nose has plum, cherry and foresty notes that are ripe and sexy. In the mouth it has ripe flavour and a smooth profile, finishing with balanced ripe tannins. All it needs is a year or two in bottle to build in richness and flavour. Perfect with duck.

Lucinda Estate Reserve Pinot Noir

Quality	♥ ♥ ♥ ♥ ♥
Value	★ ★ ★ ★
Grapes	pinot noir
Region	South Gippsland, Vic.
Cellar	🍷 3+
Alc./Vol.	13.5%
RRP	$30.00

The blurb tells us this pinot was produced from 12-year-old vines cropped very low at 1 tonne per acre (2.5 tonne per hectare), on red volcanic soil at Leongatha, planted at a density of 6300 vines per hectare. You really needed to know that.

CURRENT RELEASE 2003 The colour shows some early development and it smells complex: lovely fragrant cherry and strawberry fruit scents allied with some stemmy, whole-bunch characters and a whiff of vanilla. A wine of character and fruit sweetness, it has ample soft tannins and a rounded, easygoing palate structure. The 'yum' factor is high! It goes well with a minute steak.

Main Ridge Half Acre Pinot Noir

Quality	♥ ♥ ♥ ♥ ♥
Value	★ ★ ★
Grapes	pinot noir
Region	Mornington Peninsula, Vic.
Cellar	🍷 3+
Alc./Vol.	13.5%
RRP	$48.00

Main Ridge pioneered the present Mornington Peninsula *vignoble* and continues as one of the district's most consistent producers. Nat and Rosalie White persevere in a difficult region with unfailing good humour.

CURRENT RELEASE 2003 Main Ridge's pinot is a delicate wine that faithfully reflects a cooler corner of the Mornington Peninsula in fine style. It always seems to avoid the stemmy greenness of some MP pinots. The clear, ruby-coloured '03 has subtle, harmonious aromas of plums, cherry confectionery, rhubarb and wild herbs. The palate has silky texture and gentle, delicate flavour with a long ethereal fragrance at the end. Try it with seared tuna.

Merricks Creek Nick Farr Pinot Noir

Peter and Georgina Parker's Merricks Creek vineyard produces three pinot noirs, Close Planted, Merricks and this one, which takes its name from consulting winemaker Nick Farr, son of noted Bannockburn winemaker and pinot specialist Gary Farr.

CURRENT RELEASE 2003   This is the pick of the '03s: a charming pinot of sweet cherry to raspberry scented varietal fruit with some tobacco, forest-floor savoury notes that add complexity. It has plenty of the mysterious earthy undercurrents we associate with good pinot. The texture is soft and velvety. It's a deep, quite sumptuous pinot that really captivates. It would suit barbecued pork ribs.

Quality	▯▯▯▯▯
Value	★★★⁺
Grapes	pinot noir
Region	Mornington Peninsula, Vic.
Cellar	▯ 4+
Alc./Vol.	13.5%
RRP	$45.00

Nine Eleven Pinot Noir

In the last *Guide* we were very impressed by the reasonably priced Tassie pinot from Hobart liquor store Nine Eleven. We're pleased to announce that it was no flash in the pan, this year's release of 2004 pinot is just as impressive. Maker: Julian Alcorso.

CURRENT RELEASE 2004   It's crept up a dollar in price since last year, but it's still a great-value pinot. The '04 opens with a sappy nose of cherry, earth and foresty notes. The palate is soft and fruity with a light framework of ripe tannins to keep it together. Juicy and fresh, it is an ideal partner for grilled quail.

Quality	▯▯▯▯
Value	★★★★⁺
Grapes	pinot noir
Region	various, Tas.
Cellar	▯ 2
Alc./Vol.	13.0%
RRP	$15.99 ⬧

Penfolds Cellar Reserve Pinot Noir

Peter Gago, Penfolds' chief winemaker, makes this wine himself at the ancestral home of Penfolds, the Magill Estate, using the old concrete open fermenters, 15 per cent stalk inclusion, one-week's cold soak, wild yeasts, heading-down boards, basket press and no filtration. This year, he cobbled together the output of 15 vineyards to make 1200 cases. *Previous outstanding vintages '99, '02*

CURRENT RELEASE 2004   It's a very complex wine with a lot of the earthy, undergrowth characters that Gago's pinots have always shown, possibly due to the whole-bunches and stalks. There's also good depth of sweet fruit on the palate, with ample strawberry and cherry flavours, some fresh acidity to close and medium concentration. It would work well with game risotto.

Quality	▯▯▯▯▯
Value	★★★⁺
Grapes	pinot noir
Region	Adelaide Hills & Eden Valley, SA
Cellar	▯ 5+
Alc./Vol.	14.0%
RRP	$45.00

Picardy Tête de Cuvée Pinot Noir

Quality 🍷🍷🍷🍷🍷
Value ★★★½
Grapes pinot noir
Region Pemberton, WA
Cellar 🍾 4+
Alc./Vol. 14.0%
RRP $45.00

Pinot noir enjoys a special place in the affections of Picardy's Bill Pannell. He loves French burgundy and it is his inspiration when he makes pinot. The results can be superb. Makers: Dan and Bill Pannell.

CURRENT RELEASE 2002 This has 'correct' pinot colour, a little paler and less dense than most other reds. It has a lovely nose of foresty scents, earth, wild strawberry, musk and malt. It's fascinating and harmonious, with a deliciously silky palate to follow. The flavour is very rich and long, wild and silky-textured with gentle but definite structure. It gets better with every sip. Try it with tagliatelle and sautéed chicken livers.

Pirie Estate Pinot Noir

Quality 🍷🍷🍷🍷½
Value ★★★½
Grapes pinot noir
Region Northern Tasmania
Cellar 🍾 1–5+
Alc./Vol. 14.2%
RRP $35.00 [$]

Yet to be released at time of writing, this pinot is a big brother to the Pirie South wine and as you might expect, has more depth and stuffing. The grapes were picked from selected blocks on the Glenwood vineyard at Relbia, just south of Launceston.

CURRENT RELEASE 2004 Plenty of toasty oak asserts itself on the nose, and this wine has far more body and dimension than the Pirie South pinot. It has good depth of colour and is rich and fairly high in tannin, with a solid, almost full-bodied palate that has richness and flesh. An impressive youngster that is certain to improve, given time. Then serve with roast guinea fowl.

Pirie South Pinot Noir

Quality 🍷🍷🍷🍷
Value ★★★½
Grapes pinot noir
Region Tasmania
Cellar 🍾 4
Alc./Vol. 13.5%
RRP $24.00 [$]

Andrew Pirie released his first wines in late 2004. Called the Pirie South Unwooded Series, they included chardonnay, riesling and pinot noir. They were somewhat like the Ninth Island range he created at Pipers Brook – early-release, uncomplicated cash-flow wines.

CURRENT RELEASE 2004 A very attractive early-drinking, fruit-driven pinot from a difficult first vintage. It has good depth of colour, a clean cherry aroma that isn't very complex but certainly ripe, clean and varietal. The palate has some richness and good black-cherry flavour, and should reward a year or two of further cellaring. It would suit lasagne.

Port Phillip Estate Pinot Noir

Port Phillip is one of the leading pinot noirs on the Mornington Peninsula, often exhibiting greater depth and finesse than most of its regional peers. The Blue Peter on the label is a reference to the maritime aspect of the beautiful vineyard.

CURRENT RELEASE 2003   There's a good measure of that elusive pinot mystery in this wine. It has concentrated black-cherry fruit on the nose, along with savoury/undergrowthy complexity, and a hint of gamey wildness. Cedary oak is very restrained. In the mouth it has a velvety feel and lovely integration of flavours that finish long and soft. An ideal match for pot-roasted pigeons.

Quality	♟ ♟ ♟ ♟ ♟
Value	★ ★ ★ ★
Grapes	pinot noir
Region	Mornington Peninsula, Vic.
Cellar	▮ 5
Alc./Vol.	14.0%
RRP	$35.00

Rees Miller Estate Wilhelmina Pinot Noir

The picturesque high country around Yea, beyond the Yarra Valley, is becoming a significant wine region. These vineyards on the way to the snowfields are distinctly cool – good conditions for pinot noir.

CURRENT RELEASE 2002   A straightforward type of pinot noir that doesn't have extraordinary complexity, but it does have varietal personality. There's a good measure of plummy fruit of good concentration, and the palate has silky texture and a soft, friendly finish. Try it with char siew-style roasted quail.

Quality	♟ ♟ ♟ ♟
Value	★ ★ ★ ⅃
Grapes	pinot noir
Region	Yea, Vic.
Cellar	▮ 2
Alc./Vol.	13.5%
RRP	$19.50

Scorpo Pinot Noir

The Scorpo vineyard is another new Mornington Peninsula name to conjure with, as if there weren't enough already. What's different here is that the wines have been full of personality since day one, and pinot noir, made by Paul Scorpo and Sandro Mosele at Kooyong winery, is already a speciality.

CURRENT RELEASE 2003   This young pinot pulls all the right strings with its dried-plum, spice, forest-floor and red-berry aromas. A whisper of volatility isn't a worry, and although the palate doesn't seem to have quite the richness or depth of the 2002 edition, it's pretty good. It tastes dry with some savoury charm, and it finishes with a slightly astringent note. Try it with Chinese BBQ pork.

Quality	♟ ♟ ♟ ♟ ♟
Value	★ ★ ★
Grapes	pinot noir
Region	Mornington Peninsula, Vic.
Cellar	▬ 1–5
Alc./Vol.	13.5%
RRP	$37.00

Scotchmans Hill Pinot Noir

Quality 🍷🍷🍷🍷
Value ★★★
Grapes pinot noir
Region Geelong, Vic.
Cellar 🍾 2
Alc./Vol. 13.5%
RRP $29.00 ≋

Scotchmans Hill Pinot Noir has long been a darling of restaurant customers in Melbourne and Sydney. Its recipe for success is that it drinks well young, while having enough interest and complexity to keep 'em sipping. Maker: Robin Brockett .

CURRENT RELEASE 2003 A middle-of–the-road pinot that faithfully follows the Scotchmans Hill pattern: plum, strawberry and rhubarb fruit on the nose, a smooth palate of no great power but ready drinkability, medium body and a light framework of tannins to hold it all together. Great with a mushroom and cheese risotto.

Seppelt Victoria Pinot Noir

Quality 🍷🍷🍷🍷
Value ★★★★½
Grapes pinot noir
Region Drumborg, Vic.
Cellar 🍾 2
Alc./Vol. 13.0%
RRP $16.95 [$] ≋

In recent years we've been excited by the growing number of pinot noirs that show real varietal personality at a budget price. The best pinot is always going to be expensive, but now we have wines with more modest aspirations that still offer character. This Seppelt offering is another that's attracted our attention.

CURRENT RELEASE 2004 This has a pale ruby colour and a fruity nose of cherries and spice. The palate is on the light side of medium-bodied, yet it doesn't lack intensity or length. The finish is savoury and dry with soft tannins. A food-friendly casual type of red that works well with Moroccan-spiced grilled chicken.

Seville Estate Reserve Pinot Noir

Quality 🍷🍷🍷🍷🍷
Value ★★★½
Grapes pinot noir
Region Yarra Valley, Vic.
Cellar 🍾 4
Alc./Vol. 14.5%
RRP $45.00

Seville Estate enjoyed cult following under the stewardship of Dr Peter McMahon. It was one of the modern pioneers of the Yarra Valley. Subsequent ownership changes have made the brand more mainstream, but quality remains very high.

CURRENT RELEASE 2003 This pinot has a middling colour, and a harmonious nose that thankfully doesn't have the edginess we often find in young cool-climate pinots. It smells of dark cherries with notes of spice, forest, wood smoke and game. It's subtle but the intensity grows in the glass. In the mouth it's complex, silky with good fleshy texture and a dry finish. In style it's quite European, not super fruity like some modern Aussie pinots. Try it with a terrine.

Sticks Pinot Noir

'Sticks' is the nickname of amiable winemaker Rob Dolan.
He once played footy as a ruckman for Port Adelaide where
his lanky frame came in handy.
CURRENT RELEASE 2003   A straightforward pinot that
boasts good varietal character at a price point where many
don't. It has rhubarb and plum aromas, a light vanilla-bean
oak influence, and a touch of earthy interest. It shows some
fruit sweetness that probably comes from the clever use of
whole berries. The smooth, tasty palate has a wee bit of
hardness, but with food it's not a problem. Better in a year
or so when you should try it with prune stuffed roast pork.

Quality	♟♟♟♟
Value	★★★ᵻ
Grapes	pinot noir
Region	Yarra Valley, Vic.
Cellar	▮3
Alc./Vol.	13.0%
RRP	$16.00

Stonier Reserve Pinot Noir

Stonier Reserve Pinot Noir has been up and down over
recent years, but it's back to form with this wine. It's one
of the best '03 Mornington pinots we've tasted.
**CURRENT RELEASE 2003   There's real finesse in
this Mornington Peninsula pinot, and a touch
of European-accented mystery. The nose has
plum and spice characters with some seductive
undergrowthy/earthy aspects and a hint of game.
Oak is sensitively handled throughout. In the
mouth it has satin and velvet smoothness with
lovely, intense fruit character in the middle. It
finishes with fine, ripe tannins in excellent balance.
Serve it with Peking duck.**

Quality	♟♟♟♟♟
Value	★★★★
Grapes	pinot noir
Region	Mornington Peninsula, Vic.
Cellar	▮4
Alc./Vol.	13.5%
RRP	$39.00

PENGUIN BEST PINOT NOIR

Stonier Windmill Vineyard Pinot Noir

These black-labelled Stonier pinot noirs have emerged in
recent years as 'specials' to highlight a particular batch of
fruit or an individual vineyard site.
CURRENT RELEASE 2003   This has a rather powerful,
slightly extractive nose of kernelly black cherry and plum.
It smells very ripe and concentrated and less 'burgundian'
than Stonier's Reserve wine of the same year, despite this
wine showing considerable whole-bunch influence. In fact
its concentration is such that you'd think it came from a
warmer climate than the Mornington Peninsula. The palate
is smooth and full with a plump middle and lush ripe fruit.
There's some foresty mystery and savouriness on the finish
which features attractively fine-grained soft tannins. Very
flavoursome pinot to drink with beef fillet.

Quality	♟♟♟♟ᵻ
Value	★★★
Grapes	pinot noir
Region	Mornington Peninsula, Vic.
Cellar	▮4
Alc./Vol.	13.0%
RRP	$55.00

Symphony Hill Reserve Pinot Noir

Quality	♥♥♥♥
Value	★★⁴
Grapes	pinot noir
Region	Granite Belt, Qld
Cellar	➦1–4+
Alc./Vol.	14.5%
RRP	$65.00 ▮⬤

Symphony Hill is at Ballandean in the high-altitude Granite Belt region. Its wines are price-leaders in the region but they're also generally very good. Blair Duncan, formerly of Southcorp, makes the wines.

CURRENT RELEASE 2003 The deep red–purple colour is notably dark for pinot, and the wine is good, although unequivocally oak-dominated. Smoky/charry new-barrel aromas pervade the bouquet, and although it has very good concentration and weight, softness and persistence, it's always going to be a fairly oaky style of pinot. No doubt that will be enjoyed by some as there's a lot of flavour in the bottle. Try it with roast pork belly.

T'Gallant Juliet Pinot Noir

Quality	♥♥♥♥
Value	★★★★⁴
Grapes	pinot noir
Region	Mornington Peninsula, Vic.
Cellar	▮3
Alc./Vol.	13.5%
RRP	$16.00 Ⓢ⬤

Yet another new label from the prolific T'Gallant team. They are nothing if not creative. T'Gallant is now owned by Beringer Blass, although founders Kathleen Quealy and Kevin McCarthy still run the show.

CURRENT RELEASE 2004 Cherry Ripe and strawberry aromas are uppermost in this lighter-framed, lightly coloured pinot. It's a sweetly toned, confectionery-like style which would go well with the right kind of food. The palate has a nice slippery texture that makes it a good drink-now bet. It would go well with roast turkey.

Ursa Major Pinot Noir

Quality	♥♥♥♥
Value	★★★
Grapes	pinot noir
Region	Mornington Peninsula, Vic.
Cellar	▮3
Alc./Vol.	13.9%
RRP	$28.00

A project of wine-loving Melbourne lawyer Steve Stern, Ursa Major is the wine label for the oddly named Yrsa vineyard on the Mornington Peninsula. To detail the origin of the name requires more space than we have here.

CURRENT RELEASE 2004 This has a fruity and at the same time savoury nose, reminiscent of cherries and undergrowth with a slight gamey touch and a whisper of mint leaf. The medium-weight palate boasts succulent ripe fruit character and a long, savoury, slightly peppery finish. It's a very drinkable style and a good effort from a new producer. Serve it with veal escalopes.

Willow Creek WCV Pinot Noir

The problematic climate of the Mornington Peninsula in 2002 meant a difficult time for local *vignerons*, but the best makers produced good wines, albeit in small quantities. Maker: Phil Kerney.

CURRENT RELEASE 2002 This smells savoury with the sort of subtle interplay of complex characters that makes pinot noir such a fascinating thing. There are strawberry, caramel cream and wilder earthy scents, along with a slightly feral touch, leading to a juicy palate of fine texture and good length. It's a lighter style of good flavour with a slightly wild touch and a tangy finish. Great with quick-fried salmon with sweet soy.

Quality	🍷🍷🍷🍷
Value	★★★
Grapes	pinot noir
Region	Mornington Peninsula, Vic.
Cellar	3
Alc./Vol.	14.0%
RRP	$25.00

Yabby Lake Pinot Noir

Last year the initial Yabby Lake Pinot Noir knocked the authors' socks off, winning Best Red Wine and Best Pinot Noir in the *Guide* for the excellent 2002 vintage. The '03 is a different wine, still good, but without the thrilling varietal purity of its predecessor.

CURRENT RELEASE 2003 This is a complex wine, but we think that it somehow misses the boat, lacking the exquisite silky lushness of the '02. Instead it's a bit 'dry reddish' with a minty, eucalyptus thread to its plum and cherry fruit. There's a lick of dusty oak too, and the smooth palate has good length, but again it doesn't quite capture that luxurious essence of pinot noir. Try it with fillet steak.

Quality	🍷🍷🍷🍷
Value	★★★
Grapes	pinot noir
Region	Mornington Peninsula, Vic.
Cellar	4
Alc./Vol.	14.0%
RRP	$55.00

Yarra Burn Pinot Noir

Just about every Yarra Valley vineyard has a pinot noir in their range. The region has made a speciality of it for longer than most and standards are generally good.

CURRENT RELEASE 2002 There are plenty of sweet varietal aromas here: red cherries and berries, earthy interest and smoky oak, all in the right places. The rich, ripe palate is smooth and satisfying, while a slightly stemmy edge doesn't intrude too much and gives it some structure. Good drinking with a mild duck curry.

Quality	🍷🍷🍷🍷
Value	★★★½
Grapes	pinot noir
Region	Yarra Valley, Vic.
Cellar	3
Alc./Vol.	13.0%
RRP	$25.00

Yering Station Pinot Noir

Quality	♥♥♥♥
Value	★★★★
Grapes	pinot noir
Region	Yarra Valley, Vic.
Cellar	▮ 3
Alc./Vol.	14.0%
RRP	$23.00 ⬢

Yering Station proudly boasts that it was Victoria's first vineyard, originally established in 1838. In the heady days of Queen Victoria's monarchy and the Victorian colony's nineteenth-century boom time, wines from this vineyard won international awards and titillated the palates of the colonial gentry.

CURRENT RELEASE 2003   At the moment we prefer this wine to the grander Yering Station Reserve. It has a lifted youthful varietal nose that suggests raspberries, herbs, sap and forest air. It's outdoorsy, fresh and aromatic. The palate is light and lively with middle-intensity varietal flavours, zippy acid and a long finish. Excellent with grilled chicken.

Sangiovese and Blends

With so many Aussies claiming Italian ancestry, and Italian culture and cooking so popular, it's surprising that only in the last decade have we begun to take Italian wine really seriously. Perhaps the improving quality of wine from Italy has shown us what's possible with varieties like sangiovese, or maybe it's our thirst for innovation, but plantings are increasing in many corners of the country. Victoria's King Valley leads the way via growers of Italian heritage, and the home-grown sangiovese is starting to achieve typically savoury dry fruitiness and attractive structural interest. The best sangioveses are excellent with a variety of foods, and it's also excellent as blending material, sometimes to give a savoury, appetising edge to cabernet or merlot.

Bimbadgen Art Series Sangiovese

Bimbadgen's art series features reproductions of pictures by contemporary Australian artists such as Howard Arkley. A percentage of sales goes to the Museum of Contemporary Art in Sydney.
CURRENT RELEASE 2004   This is a light-bodied, fairly simple sangiovese that has good balance and drinkability, but don't expect a Chianti Classico! The colour is medium red–purple and it opens with chocolate, mint and raspberry aromas, with underlying herbal and mint characters which point to less than fully ripe grapes. It would go with a steak sandwich.

Quality	❸❸❸❹
Value	★★★★
Grapes	sangiovese 85%; shiraz 15%
Region	Orange & Mudgee, NSW
Cellar	🍾 2
Alc./Vol.	14.5%
RRP	$20.00 🍷

Cardinham Sangiovese

Sangiovese is popping up all over. It's one of the most exciting new grape varieties around. This version comes from the Clare Valley.
CURRENT RELEASE 2004   This has typical sangiovese style. It's winey rather than raw-fruity, and it shares the variety's wonderful food-friendliness. The nose has cherry, licorice and earthy aromas that are savoury and inviting. There's a slightly rustic pong to it, and succulent berry fruit as well. The palate is light- to medium-bodied, dry and tasty. Try it with little veal sausages.

Quality	❸❸❸❸
Value	★★★
Grapes	sangiovese
Region	Clare Valley, SA
Cellar	🍾 2
Alc./Vol.	14.0%
RRP	$18.00 🍷

Chrismont La Zona Sangiovese

Quality	♟♟♟♟
Value	★★★
Grapes	sangiovese
Region	King Valley, Vic.
Cellar	▮ 3
Alc./Vol.	14.0%
RRP	$23.00

The King Valley's affair with Italian grape varieties has been an exciting thing for Australian wine consumers, presenting them with some interesting alternatives to a conventional diet of Australian shiraz, chardonnay et al. Sangiovese is one of the most successful of these Aussie-Italians.
CURRENT RELEASE 2003   This sums it all up really. If you like sweet-fruited Oz reds look elsewehere, if you like the savoury mystery of Italy, read on. This has a nose and palate that variously suggests dry herbs, cherries, leather and almonds. Its texture is grainy and interesting, and it finishes with a more-ish half-bitter Italian signature. Try it with veal chops.

Coriole Sangiovese

Quality	♟♟♟♟♟
Value	★★★┤
Grapes	sangiovese
Region	McLaren Vale, SA
Cellar	▮ 3
Alc./Vol.	14.0%
RRP	$19.50

Coriole first planted sangiovese many years before the variety became trendy, giving many of us our first taste of this excellent Italian red grape. These days, despite a plethora of competitors, Coriole's quality makes it one of the best.
CURRENT RELEASE 2003   This has a very Italian accent with some of those savoury Italian-deli smells that captivate us so much in sangiovese. Cherry-like fruit is at the core, and while it has good depth, it's fresh and easy to drink. Tannins are very fine-grained, providing a gently dry foundation. Excellent sangiovese to sip with a platter of mixed meat antipasti.

Penfolds Cellar Reserve Sangiovese

Quality	♟♟♟♟♟
Value	★★★┤
Grapes	sangiovese
Region	100% Barossa Valley, SA
Cellar	▮ 6+
Alc./Vol.	14.5%
RRP	$35.00 ▮

The Penfolds Cellar Reserve wines are made at the historic Magill Estate winery under the watchful eye of chief winemaker Peter Gago. They are made from relatively small parcels of fruit and for this reason are regarded as experimental, and a bit to the left of the Penfolds main game.
Previous outstanding vintages: '01 '02
CURRENT RELEASE 2003   Another very decent effort at this quirky Italian variety, with a medium-full red–purple hue and a pronounced dark-chocolate nose. It's full-bodied, with lots of flesh and density, plus abundant chewy tannins. A serious sangiovese that will reward cellaring. Then serve with hard cheeses like pecorino.

Pinocchio Sangiovese

Garry Crittenden's obsession with Italian wine led him to seek out pockets of these grapes; he encouraged others to establish them in their vineyards, and he became a local authority. Along the way he's made some excellent 'Australian-Italian' wines. No longer at Dromana Estate, where his son Rollo makes the wine, Garry has now launched these new Pinocchio wines from his Crittenden at Dromana enterprise.

CURRENT RELEASE 2003 This is a 'wild' and savoury sangiovese, full of personality. It smells of roasted fruits, prunes and cherries with touches of leather, earth and dried herbs. Rich mid-palate flavour is savoury, mouth-filling and more-ish, and it finishes very dry with a light tannic grip and brisk acidity. Try it with veal chops and sage.

Quality 🍷🍷🍷🍷½
Value ★★★½
Grapes sangiovese
Region King Valley, Vic.
Cellar 🍾 3
Alc./Vol. 14.5%
RRP $22.00 🔩

Rosemount Diamond Label Sangiovese

This is a repeat of last year's release, but it's still available and we think an extra year's bottle-age has been advantageous. Maker: Briony Hoare.

CURRENT RELEASE 2003 The medium red–purple colour has some black tints, and the bouquet is all about black cherry and smoky, almost bushfirey, charred-wood aromas. It's not a complex wine but has good depth of ripe fruit in the cherry to raspberry range. There are light but firm tannins in good balance. It goes with spicy Italian sausages.

Quality 🍷🍷🍷🍷
Value ★★★★
Grapes sangiovese
Region south-east Australia
Cellar 🍾 2
Alc./Vol. 13.5%
RRP $15.00 [$]

Stella Bella Sangiovese Cabernet Sauvignon

Sangiovese is the red grape of Tuscany, responsible for Chianti. It's also blended with cabernet to make some of the Super-Tuscans that have excited the wine world over the last couple of decades. This is an Australian version of the successful blend.

CURRENT RELEASE 2003 A very Italianate nose introduces this palatable blend. Cherry, aniseed, earth and dried-herb aromas combine in subtle harmony, with sangiovese leading the way over cabernet. The savoury/cherry and herb-flavoured palate is lightish, yet intensely flavoured, with appetising texture and balance. It finishes with light firmness and a long savoury aftertaste.

Quality 🍷🍷🍷🍷
Value ★★★
Grapes sangiovese; cabernet sauvignon
Region Margaret River, WA
Cellar 🍾 3
Alc./Vol. 13.5%
RRP $27.00

Stonehaven Winemaker's Release Sangiovese

Quality	♟♟♟♟
Value	★★★
Grapes	sangiovese
Region	Padthaway, SA
Cellar	▮ 3
Alc./Vol.	14.0%
RRP	$21.00

Your first taste of sangiovese can be a challenge. To palates attuned to big ripe (and sweet) Aussie shiraz, it's a paradigm shift. Persevere and it rewards you generously. The authors have no doubt that it's one of the world's great red grape varieties.

CURRENT RELEASE 2003   This young sangiovese has a distinctly 'foreign' nose of cherries, almonds, prunes and spice. It sums up sangiovese's Italian-deli smells well. In the mouth it's dry and firmly structured with an intriguing savoury flavour. Try it with Italian pork sausages.

Shiraz and Blends

Shiraz is Australia's signature grape, our most popular red wine both locally and overseas. In 2005, shiraz grapes made up about one-quarter of the total wine harvest: 454 000 tonnes. The real gob-smacker, though, is comparing that with 20 years ago: 56 500 tonnes! An eight-fold increase in two decades – largely export driven. The great thing about Aussie shiraz is its diversity: we can drink elegant, spicy styles from cooler climates; rich, chocolatey ones from the hotter regions; and many other permutations. There's a new fashion for viognier blends (just four or five per cent can make a big difference) and a trend towards using more French oak and less American. We like many styles of shiraz but, as in everything, balance is the key: wines that are too oaky, tannic or alcoholic or have 'dead fruit' character aren't rated highly.

Angoves Butterfly Ridge Shiraz Cabernet

Angoves Butterfly Ridge Shiraz Cabernet is one of a dying breed: a flavourful, easy-drinking, fault-free red for well under $10. Long live Angoves!

CURRENT RELEASE 2003 A brightly coloured young red with plenty of ripe berries on the nose. The smooth palate is straightforward and very gluggable with ripe flavour, soft tannins and some persistence. You could easily do worse at twice the price. Serve it with a pizza.

Quality	🍷🍷🍷
Value	★★★★
Grapes	shiraz; cabernet sauvignon
Region	Murray Valley, SA
Cellar	🍾 2
Alc./Vol.	14.0%
RRP	$7.75 [$]

Arakoon Doyen Shiraz

When do you drink a full-bodied red that tips the scales at 16.5 per cent alcohol? That's just a little off the strength of liqueur muscat and tawny port, and stronger than fino sherry. Perhaps in small glasses with cheese at the end of a meal? Or maybe *instead* of a meal.

CURRENT RELEASE 2003 This has impenetrable colour and a strong nose of jammy mixed berries, sweet spices, and an earthy/nutty character almost like the rancio you find in fortifieds. Despite an absurd level of alcohol for a table wine, it's not as hot or soupy on the nose as some such monsters, and the palate is velvety with an almost sweet flavour, great depth and length, and a hot-to-trot spirity aftertaste. It really needs a warning label though. Yes, why not serve it with mature cheddar after dinner.

Quality	🍷🍷🍷🍷
Value	★★½
Grapes	shiraz
Region	McLaren Vale, SA
Cellar	🍾 10
Alc./Vol.	16.5%
RRP	$50.00 🌀

Bannockburn Shiraz

Quality	♥♥♥♥
Value	★★⟩
Grapes	shiraz
Region	Geelong, Vic.
Cellar	▮ 3
Alc./Vol.	14.5%
RRP	$49.00

The Hoopers of Bannockburn are on their own now, having lost the services of long-time winemaker Gary Farr at the end of 2004. They had Rick Kinzbrunner as consultant for the '05 vintage but the permanent winemaking berth was vacant at time of writing.

CURRENT RELEASE 2002 The '02 season was a cool one, perhaps a bit too cool for shiraz in such a southerly region. The wine is quite mulchy and vegetal, and there are some undergrowth/foresty characters that are typical of Farr's whole-bunch ferment approach – which includes stalks. The palate is very drying and savoury, with a surfeit of tannin on the finish. It's all about secondary complexities rather than primary fruit, and will have its fans. Serve it with a lamb and vegetable casserole.

Battle of Bosworth Shiraz

Quality	♥♥♥♥
Value	★★★⟩
Grapes	shiraz
Region	McLaren Vale, SA
Cellar	▮ 4+
Alc./Vol.	14.5%
RRP	$24.00 ▮ ✿

The grapes for Battle of Bosworth wines are organically grown. The labels are suitably organic and recycled-looking: the paper resembles the plain brown wrapping paper that department stores used to use. Winemaker is the omnipresent Ben Riggs.

CURRENT RELEASE 2002 A fairly advanced style of shiraz, savoury rather than fruity, and smelling of smoke, leather and charcoal. It has good weight and concentration in the mouth, with a rich, soft texture and a drying tannin finish. An earthy red that would suit spaghetti bolognese.

Best's Great Western Bin 0 Shiraz

Quality	♥♥♥♥⟩
Value	★★★⟩
Grapes	shiraz
Region	Grampians, Vic.
Cellar	▮ 15+
Alc./Vol.	13.5%
RRP	$43.00 ▮

Shiraz has always been the mainstay of Great Western reds. These days cabernet, merlot and pinot noir are also grown, but shiraz was always the workhorse and continues to be. The vineyard was first planted by Henry Best in 1866.

CURRENT RELEASE 2001 This is a classic Best's shiraz: elegant and tautly structured with a whiff of mint among the spices, cherries and crushed leaf on the nose. There's a waft of gunsmoke and nicely balanced oak. It's a slow-ageing style that needs time to build complexity and soften, although it is smooth and enjoyable to drink already. It suits pink roasted leg of lamb.

The Black Chook Shiraz Viognier

McLaren Vale winemaker Ben Riggs has his fingers in so many pies we've lost count. The remarkable thing is that he manages to juggle so many skittles and turn out such a raft of excellent wines.
CURRENT RELEASE 2004   It's a bit young to be leaving its mother, but gee, it's a nice wine! The colour is vivid purple and the nose and palate exude great richness of very ripe black fruits. There are sweet floral overtones as well, which could be sheeted home to the viognier fraction. It's a forceful, concentrated wine in the mouth, with lashings of sweet fruit, toasty charred-barrel accents and medium length. It should go with a hearty beef casserole.

Quality	▮▮▮▮
Value	★★★★★
Grapes	shiraz; viognier
Region	various, SA
Cellar	▮ 6+
Alc./Vol.	15.0%
RRP	$19.50 🍷

Blue Pyrenees The Richardson Series Shiraz

The Richardson Series is named after the late Colin Richardson, one of the great gentlemen of the Victorian wine industry, a larger-than-life character who was a great communicator, an entertaining public speaker, and spent many years marketing and promoting Blue Pyrenees Estate. Maker is former Rosemount man Andrew Koerner.
CURRENT RELEASE 2002   Sweet, rich melted club chocolate is the dominant aroma here. The palate is lavishly endowed with both vanillan oak and rich, decadent fruit. Almost syrupy in its sweet fruit and glycerol, it has depth, density and flesh, but how much of it could you drink? Impressive stuff to serve with duck and sausage cassoulet.

Quality	▮▮▮▮▮
Value	★★★⅜
Grapes	shiraz
Region	Pyrenees, Vic.
Cellar	▮ 15+
Alc./Vol.	14.0%
RRP	$52.00 ▮

Bremerton Selkirk Shiraz

Visit Bremerton's cellar door sales and you'll see a levee bank around the old stone homestead and gardens. It's to save them from the Bremer River when it runs a torrent and inundates the vineyards and pastures of Langhorne Creek. Maker: Rebecca Willson.
CURRENT RELEASE 2002   This is a very good, easy-drinking red with richness, softness and some medium-term ageing potential. The bouquet has elements of mint, coconut and toastiness from oak, while the palate has flesh and weight, but also softness and nicely ripe chocolate/mocha flavours and tannins. A top vintage for this wine. It would suit braised beef.

Quality	▮▮▮▮▮
Value	★★★★★
Grapes	shiraz
Region	Langhorne Creek, SA
Cellar	▮ 10+
Alc./Vol.	14.0%
RRP	$22.00 Ⓢ

Cape Barren Wild Goose Shiraz

Quality	♀♀♀♀
Value	★★★♦
Grapes	shiraz
Region	McLaren Vale, SA
Cellar	▐ 4
Alc./Vol.	14.2%
RRP	$21.00

There are two Cape Barren wines, a more expensive single-vineyard Old Vine Shiraz and this softer, more approachable Wild Goose regional blend.
CURRENT RELEASE 2003 This has the earthy traits that are typical of McLaren Vale shiraz, mixed with blackberry aromas and a touch of licorice to make an appealing, soft regional nose. Subtle dusty oak keeps well in the background and it has a smooth, generous palate that's ripe and long, finishing with agreeably soft tannins. Try it with good homemade burgers.

Cape Mentelle Marmaduke

Quality	♀♀♀♀
Value	★★★★
Grapes	shiraz; grenache; mourvèdre
Region	Margaret River, WA
Cellar	▐ 3
Alc./Vol.	14.5%
RRP	$17.75 ✇

Marmaduke, Cape Mentelle's entry-level red, is named after Marmaduke Terry, one of the earliest European settlers in the Margaret River region. Unusually for Margaret River it's a blend of shiraz with grenache and mataro (mourvèdre).
CURRENT RELEASE 2003 A medium-depth young red that smells of red berries, dry spices and a touch of oak. The palate is medium-bodied with pleasant, straightforward flavour and easy texture. It all adds up to a red that's very pleasant to drink in the flush of youth. Try it with cannelloni.

Cape Mentelle Shiraz

Quality	♀♀♀♀♀
Value	★★★★
Grapes	shiraz 96%; grenache 4%
Region	Margaret River, WA
Cellar	▐ 10+
Alc./Vol.	14.9%
RRP	$36.00

Cape Mentelle Shiraz has thrown off the slightly grotty characteristics it had a few years ago and re-emerged as one of the West's best shirazes. Its complex personality is helped by a mix of winery techniques including 20 per cent whole bunch fermentation.
CURRENT RELEASE 2003 A delicious Cape Mentelle shiraz with deep colour and a captivating nose of dark plum, black cherry, mixed spices, mocha and skilfully handled charry oak. In the mouth it has great depth and a fleshy, seamless feel with complex flavour and ripe, fine tannins in true harmony. Serve it with a roasted fillet of beef.

Capel Vale CV Shiraz

Capel Vale's budget brand is CV, which stands for . . . um . . . is it Capel Vale? These wines sometimes have surprising character, and the almost 'Rhône-ish' shiraz falls well outside the run of the commercial mill. CURRENT RELEASE 2002   A rather meaty shiraz made in a fairly rustic style. As well as the meaty smells, there are aromas of plums, spice and subtle oak. In the mouth it has a succulent, fruit-dominant flavour, finishing with moderate tannins. A drink-now type of middleweight shiraz with more interest than many in this price range. Serve it with sautéed kidneys.

Quality	▆ ▆ ▆ ▆
Value	★ ★ ★ ⟩
Grapes	shiraz
Region	Pemberton & Geographe, WA
Cellar	▯ 1
Alc./Vol.	13.5%
RRP	$16.00

Capel Vale Kinnaird Shiraz

Kinnaird is Capel Vale's flagship shiraz. It was one of the first Australian wines to be packed in a toe-breaking super-heavy bottle. It's a substantial wine in a substantial vessel. Don't drop it on your foot! CURRENT RELEASE 2002   Capel Vale's Kinnaird has always been more of a warts-and-all red than the surgically clean prestige cuvées of many other vineyards. The '02 is typical, with an earthy, smoked-meat sort of touch to a nose of very ripe, spicy, raisiny fruit. Real character! It improves a lot with breathing. It's very powerful in the mouth with full body, and a big rich flavour that's smooth and long. Tannins are soft and friendly. Enjoy it with a dish of lip-smacking chicken cacciatore.

Quality	▆ ▆ ▆ ▆ ▆
Value	★ ★ ★ ⟩
Grapes	shiraz
Region	Geographe, WA
Cellar	▯ 5
Alc./Vol.	14.5%
RRP	$51.00

Charles Melton Shiraz

Charles Melton can claim a lot of responsibility for the new-found glamour and desirability enjoyed by the Barossa's oldest vineyards. Where once they were being pulled out at a rate of knots, now they are very desirable property, indeed. Charlie's reds are among the best of the crop. CURRENT RELEASE 2002   In keeping with Charlie Melton's traditional style, this is a generously built shiraz that's well made and friendly in disposition. The nose has black-cherry, spice, spearmint, herb and earthy aromas that lead smoothly to a velvety palate of generous proportions. Fleshy fruit floods the middle, and it lasts long and satisfying on the palate, with very soft tannins in support. An easy-drinking companion to herbed roast beef.

Quality	▆ ▆ ▆ ▆ ▆
Value	★ ★ ★ ⟩
Grapes	shiraz
Region	Barossa Valley, SA
Cellar	▯ 6+
Alc./Vol.	14.5%
RRP	$46.00

Chateau Tanunda Limited Release Grand Barossa Shiraz

Quality	♟♟♟♟
Value	★★★
Grapes	shiraz
Region	Barossa Valley, SA
Cellar	➡1–6
Alc./Vol.	14.5%
RRP	$38.00

Chateau Tanunda is one of the landmark buildings of the Barossa Valley, an impressive edifice that was for many years the home of Chateau Tanunda Brandy, one of Australia's bestsellers until the decline of local brandy production. Now it's a winery again, a very commercial tourist-oriented place worth seeing.

CURRENT RELEASE 2002   A densely coloured, blackish wine, this has almost boiled-down, syrupy, dark-berry fruit on the nose with hints of oriental spice and some meaty notes. In the mouth it's a solid drop with concentrated black-fruit and mocha flavours, followed by ripe tannins and a spicy aftertaste. It's a flavoury Barossa style of good balance. Try it with braised beef ribs Korean style.

Cheviot Bridge Yea Valley Shiraz

Quality	♟♟♟♟
Value	★★★★
Grapes	shiraz
Region	Yea, Vic.
Cellar	❶2
Alc./Vol.	14.0%
RRP	$19.00 ⊜

Bill Gurry's Larnoo Vineyard and the original Yea Valley vineyard provide the grapes for this rather European-accented shiraz (or should that be syrah?). Like all the Cheviot Bridge wines, pricing is very competitive.

CURRENT RELEASE 2003   This has a slightly meaty, funky earthiness on the nose as well as plums, blueberries and hints of spice and pepper. The tight palate is on the light side of medium-bodied with juicy berry flavour. It has some Côtes-du-Rhône-ish elements in aroma, weight and texture with soft tannins underneath. A wine to drink, not keep. Enjoy it with a rustic terrine.

Climbing Shiraz

Quality	♟♟♟♟
Value	★★★✦
Grapes	shiraz
Region	Orange, NSW
Cellar	❶3
Alc./Vol.	14.0%
RRP	$20.00 ⊜

Climbing wines come from the Orange–Central Ranges regions of New South Wales. At Orange the altitude of the vineyards climbs beyond 1000 metres, making it a very cool spot. Maker: Philip Shaw.

CURRENT RELEASE 2003   This is an aromatic red wine with an elegance that reflects its cool-climate origins. The nose has slightly floral, red-berry and spice aromas with a pronounced earthiness that's savoury and appealing. The middleweight palate has fine, earthy/berry flavours and a soft finish. A good first effort that's easy to like, and the sensible screw-cap makes it a reliable buy. Great with veal scallopine.

Clonakilla Hilltops Shiraz

First released a few years ago as an understudy to
Clonakilla's great shiraz viognier, this Hilltops Shiraz is
always a raw, unevolved wine when released, but we
reckon it has real potential. Maker: Tim Kirk.
CURRENT RELEASE 2004   As you'd expect from such a raw
youngster, this is still all knees and elbows, but the building
blocks of a pretty good drop are all there. Juicy black and
red-berry aromas and peppery spice meet the nose, and
the palate is rich and intense with a hint of ferment pong.
It should be put away to gain a bit of development, but we
think it will be very drinkable a couple of years down the
track: then try it with a lamb tagine and couscous.

Quality	▼▼▼▼
Value	★★★
Grapes	shiraz
Region	Hilltops, NSW
Cellar	➥2–6
Alc./Vol.	13.5%
RRP	$29.00

Craiglee Shiraz

Pat Carmody's distinctive shiraz are a must on any list of
Australia's great shirazes. Unfortunately wines like this rarely
receive plaudits from foreign commentators who think
Australian reds should be monolithically big and porty.
CURRENT RELEASE 2003   This typifies the fine Craiglee
style very well. The nose has plenty of spice and pepper-
trimmed ripe cherry fruit, and oak is a subtle seasoning.
The silky palate is intense, long and fragrant with spicy
flavour, good depth and lovely balance. It's not one of
the biggest Craiglees and it's still closed up and totally
immature, but it has that understated complexity of the
best. A wine with tons of character, but there's a real gentle
touch to it as well. Try it with pink double lamb cutlets.

Quality	▼▼▼▼▼
Value	★★★★
Grapes	shiraz
Region	Sunbury, Vic.
Cellar	➥2–10
Alc./Vol.	14.5%
RRP	$45.00

Dominique Portet Heathcote Shiraz

Dominique Portet is one of an increasing legion of older
winemakers who are now having a 'second coming'. He
helped set up Taltarni and ran the place for something like
25 years; now he has a new winery in the Yarra Valley and
a new lease of life.
CURRENT RELEASE 2003   This is a very good, very natural-
tasting shiraz. It has an excellent, dark colour and a sweetly
ripe, blood-plum aroma laced with vanilla from oak. The
palate is smooth and fleshy, with raspberry and plum
flavours, remaining admirably fruit-driven throughout. It
also has ample tannin which contributes to structure and
ageing potential. Very promising. It would go well with
braised lamb shanks.

Quality	▼▼▼▼⯪
Value	★★★⯪
Grapes	shiraz
Region	Heathcote, Vic.
Cellar	➥1–12+
Alc./Vol.	14.0%
RRP	$42.50

Edwards Shiraz

Quality	♥♥♥♥♥
Value	★★★★⅃
Grapes	shiraz
Region	Margaret River, WA
Cellar	▯ 5
Alc./Vol.	14.5%
RRP	$26.00 ⊗

When the pioneer vintners of Margaret River were planting their vineyards, cabernet sauvignon always seemed to take precedence as the red-grape variety of choice. Shiraz was secondary in the scheme of things, yet it can perform superbly in the region.

CURRENT RELEASE 2003   These Edwards wines get better with each vintage. This young shiraz has a copybook varietal nose, but in the modern cooler-climate vein, not the big sunshiny style. The smoothly inviting nose has sweet-berry fruit, spices, floral and some slightly gamey notes, with oak as a subtle seasoning. Silky, ripe and spicy, it tastes as good as it smells. It has medium body and soft tannins. Try it with roast duck.

Elderton Barossa Shiraz

Quality	♥♥♥♥
Value	★★★
Grapes	shiraz
Region	Barossa Valley, SA
Cellar	▯ 5
Alc./Vol.	14.5%
RRP	$26.50

This is the understudy to Elderton's premium Command Shiraz, without the sledgehammer oak influence. The result is a friendlier red, but still one with plenty of presence.

CURRENT RELEASE 2003   There's a fair dose of smoky barrel-ferment character here, both on the nose and in the mouth, but it doesn't overwhelm the senses. There's also good intensity of ripe-berry fruit of smoothly ripe flavour and mouth-coating texture. There's a hint of caramel there. The palate finishes long and ripe, and tannins aren't too assertive. Serve it with chargrilled lamb rump.

Eppalock Ridge Shiraz

Quality	♥♥♥♥❙
Value	★★★
Grapes	shiraz
Region	Heathcote, Vic.
Cellar	▯ 8+
Alc./Vol.	15.0%
RRP	$33.00

Heathcote shirazes keep coming, and the general quality of red wines from this new(ish) region is admirable. The Hourigans' Eppalock Ridge, established in the late '70s, is one of the oldest winemaking names in the district.

CURRENT RELEASE 2003   A wine of unusual power and concentration from Eppalock Ridge, this smells of stewed berries, mint, mocha, earth and ink. The palate continues the theme with great depth of flavour, smooth texture, warmth and concentration, finishing with grippy tannins. Great with roast beef and all the old-fashioned trimmings.

Ferngrove Frankland River Shiraz

This is Ferngrove's second-ranked shiraz. The first is called Dragon – Ferngrove names all its top wines after native wildflowers of the south-west of WA and pictures them on the labels. Maker: Kim Horton.

CURRENT RELEASE 2003 It's a medium-bodied, fruit-driven shiraz with a lot of spice – slightly green-edged spice – to it. The raspberry aromas are a touch tutti-frutti and a little bit sweaty. It's an attractive, elegantly framed shiraz, made for easy current drinking, but you need to like the extreme cool-grown spicy style. Enjoy it with Peking duck.

Quality	🍷🍷🍷🍷
Value	★★★★
Grapes	shiraz
Region	Great Southern, WA
Cellar	🍾 5+
Alc./Vol.	14.0%
RRP	$18.00 [$]

Fox Gordon Hannah's Swing Shiraz

Here we go again: another new brand, established in 2001. The owners have a vineyard at Williamstown in the southern end of the Barossa Valley. The wines are contract-made by the accomplished Natasha Mooney.

CURRENT RELEASE 2003 It's a whopper price for a wine with an unknown brand, but at least it's very good! The colour is deep and the aromas are dominated by chocolate, ripe-plum and vanilla, while the palate style is, in a word, sumptuous. Deep, dense, rich and fruit-sweet, it's smoothly textured and fluent – you might even say voluptuous. All the parts are skilfully melded together. Drink it with beef casserole.

Quality	🍷🍷🍷🍷½
Value	★★★
Grapes	shiraz
Region	Barossa Valley, SA
Cellar	🍾 8+
Alc./Vol.	14.5%
RRP	$49.00

Garlands Shiraz

'At Garlands the emphasis is on elegance and balance.' So says the Garlands label and it's a true reflection of the wine in the bottle; these aren't blockbusters, instead the emphasis is on finesse.

CURRENT RELEASE 2002 This is a spicy style with black-pepper and earthy notes on the nose, floral scents and aromas of raspberry and plum. It's medium in body and its supple palate has gently spicy flavour and a soft finish. A civilised shiraz to try with pâté en croûte.

Quality	🍷🍷🍷🍷½
Value	★★★★
Grapes	shiraz
Region	Mount Barker, WA
Cellar	🍾 3
Alc./Vol.	13.5%
RRP	$22.00

Gartelmann Diedrich Shiraz

Quality	▼▼▼▼⁵
Value	★★★★
Grapes	shiraz
Region	Hunter Valley, NSW
Cellar	🍾 5+
Alc./Vol.	14.0%
RRP	$32.00 ⬮ 🍾

There are few Australian wines that exhibit such 'spirit of place' as Hunter shiraz. When it's well done, like this one, it has both regionality and good-quality wine character. Sometimes, Hunter reds are recognisable for their 'sweaty saddle' or leathery smells of questionable origin!
CURRENT RELEASE 2002   This is a delicious Hunter shiraz that smells of walnut, leather, savoury/meat-stock complexities and a hint of jammy fruit. The palate is seductively smooth and fruit-sweet, with ample tannins, which are savoury but smooth and fine-grained. It finishes with balance and style. It would suit rabbit casserole.

The Gate McLaren Vale Shiraz

Quality	▼▼▼▼⁵
Value	★★★⁴
Grapes	shiraz
Region	McLaren Vale, SA
Cellar	🍾 5+
Alc./Vol.	14.5%
RRP	$45.00

Another new brand, appropriately packaged in a tall, heavy, elegant bottle. John and Kym Davey are best known for the more modestly priced Shingleback wines. Their vineyard is in the Willunga Basin at the southern end of McLaren Vale.
CURRENT RELEASE 2002   The Daveys describe this wine as a fruit-driven blockbuster, and we agree. The aromas recall rum-and-raisin chocolate, with a touch of prune, and the oak has been well harmonised. Its structure is fleshy and opulent, with lashings of soft, rich, ultra-ripe fruit. It's beautifully fleshy, but we're not sure it has the length or tightness to age as long as its makers hope. Not that anyone really cares. Drink with beef goulash.

Gibson Barossa Vale Shiraz

Quality	▼▼▼▼⁵
Value	★★★★
Grapes	shiraz
Region	Barossa Valley, SA
Cellar	🍾 5+
Alc./Vol.	14.5%
RRP	$33.50

Rob Gibson's wines are right in the best Barossa tradition, ripe and full, but thankfully without the excesses of some. A name to watch.
CURRENT RELEASE 2002   This has a deliciously warm, generous nose with touches of mint and milk chocolate on a core of spiced-blackberry fruit. Subtle charry background oak is perfectly poised, and the palate has smooth texture, and great intensity of dark-chocolatey flavour. It finishes with a persistent aftertaste, carried by balanced dry tannins. Serve it with braised lamb and kidney pie.

Grant Burge Barossa Vines Shiraz

Grant Burge's Barossa Vines wines usually sell for less than $15, which makes them a great buy. They do offer a bit of true Barossa personality on a budget, and can cellar well in the short term.

CURRENT RELEASE 2003 A well-made young Barossa shiraz that introduces itself with syrupy raspberry and blackberry aromas and an attractive earthy touch. A thread of vanillin oak adds dimension, and it tastes smooth and ripe with spicy-berry flavour, good length and soft tannins. Great with homemade meat pie.

Quality	🍷🍷🍷🍷
Value	★★★★
Grapes	shiraz
Region	Barossa Valley, SA
Cellar	🍾 3
Alc./Vol.	14.5%
RRP	$15.00 [$]

Grant Burge Filsell Shiraz

The Filsell vineyard is one of those plots of old-Barossa vines that form the foundation of the region's great reputation for hearty shiraz.

CURRENT RELEASE 2003 This has a deep, almost impenetrable appearance and a typically regional/varietal nose of ripe blackberries, chocolate, mint and well-handled vanillin oak. The palate has all the requisite richness and ripe flavour with good body and a firm backbone of fairly butch tannins. It should have a long life ahead of it. Good with braised beef.

Quality	🍷🍷🍷🍷🍷½
Value	★★★
Grapes	shiraz
Region	Barossa Valley, SA
Cellar	🍾 2–8+
Alc./Vol.	14.5%
RRP	$30.00

Grant Burge Miamba Shiraz

Miamba was a nineteenth-century vineyard that was once a household word as the source of Orlando's Miamba Claret. Amazingly the vines were pulled out as recently as 1980. Grant Burge replanted the site in 1987.

CURRENT RELEASE 2003 A generous mid-range shiraz of an ever-popular type, this has an inviting nose of syrupy black fruits and spices. It's medium-bodied with restrained oak influence; a straightforward, ripe, complete flavour; and a friendly backbone of moderate tannins. The essence of easygoing Barossa shiraz, and it won't break the bank. Serve it with Cantonese beef dishes.

Quality	🍷🍷🍷🍷
Value	★★★½
Grapes	shiraz
Region	Barossa Valley, SA
Cellar	🍾 5
Alc./Vol.	14.5%
RRP	$19.90 [$]

Green Point Victoria Shiraz

Quality	♥♥♥♥
Value	★★★
Grapes	shiraz; viognier
Region	various, Vic.
Cellar	▮ 3
Alc./Vol.	14.0%
RRP	$30.00 ⬥

The Rhône white grape viognier is creeping into more and more Australian reds, adding complexity, sometimes leavening their gruff characters, and sometimes overwhelming them. This Green Point Shiraz has only a small proportion in the mix but it has a positive influence. CURRENT RELEASE 2003 The nose is spicy with savoury, peppery and earthy notes, along with some softer florals, and the fruit aromas are cherry and plum. In the mouth it's fresh tasting and on the lighter side of medium body, with good length and spicy impact. There's a rather sinewy dry backbone and a fragrant floral aftertaste. Works well with steamed Chinese sausage with vegetables and rice.

Hamilton's Ewell Vineyards Stonegarden Shiraz Cabernet

Quality	♥♥♥♥
Value	★★★★
Grapes	shiraz; cabernet sauvignon
Region	Barossa Valley, SA
Cellar	▮ 3
Alc./Vol.	14.5%
RRP	$18.00 Ⓢ ⬥

The Hamilton's Ewell style is unashamedly full-on and often pushes ripeness to extremes. Industry veteran Robert Hamilton reckons today's ripeness is natural Barossa ripeness, whereas when he was in his prime the grapes were picked too early. CURRENT RELEASE 2001 While we doff our lids to Mr Hamilton Senior, we find this wine a bit porty, with desiccated or 'dead fruit' character. It certainly has plenty of body weight and flavour, but it is a sweet raisiny kind of flavour, with assertive drying tannins riding in on the finish. It really cries out for food, and we suspect parmesan cheese would work.

Hanging Rock Cambrian Rise Heathcote Shiraz

Quality	♥♥♥♥
Value	★★★ⅰ
Grapes	shiraz
Region	Heathcote, Vic.
Cellar	▮ 7
Alc./Vol.	13.5%
RRP	$27.00 ▮

As far as we're aware, this is a new label for Hanging Rock, their second Heathcote shiraz label. We find it less rich and concentrated than their flagship yellow-label bottling. But it is a fair bit cheaper. Maker: John Ellis. CURRENT RELEASE 2002 Signature Heathcote dried spices are evident in the bouquet of this youngster. There are meaty aromas to go with the cardamom and mace, and the palate adds mint and raspberry. It has the lively, somewhat intrusive acidity that we find in many Hanging Rock reds. Grainy tannins chime in towards the finish. It has good length, and would suit grilled lamb loin chops.

Hanging Rock Heathcote Shiraz

Hanging Rock is a famous natural feature in the hills of the Macedon Ranges near this winery. It featured in a film called *Picnic at Hanging Rock*, which tells the story of a party of girls on a school picnic. Maker: John Ellis.
CURRENT RELEASE 2002   Big, solid, weighty Heathcote shiraz here, with a slightly tough, grippy tannin palate. The colour is deep and dark; the bouquet has bacon-fat, dark-chocolate aromas, and the palate is rich, with ample ripe tannins that just lack suppleness. Not a wine of elegance or charm, but bags of flavour and cellaring potential. It would suit aged cheddar.

Quality	♟♟♟♟
Value	★★★
Grapes	shiraz
Region	Heathcote, Vic.
Cellar	🍷 10
Alc./Vol.	14.0%
RRP	$55.00 🍷

Hardys Eileen Hardy Shiraz

It's curious how the larger South Australian makers like Hardys make a big thing about using less American oak and more French, when the wines still taste pretty oaky to us. The oak is of a higher grade, and is less aggressive, but it's oak just the same.
CURRENT RELEASE 2001   There's no doubt about its concentration, structure and density of flavour – it just lacks charm and drinkability. In keeping with its antecedents, it's an oak-driven wine with some sweaty, meaty and metallic accents, coupled with smoky charred oak. The palate has hints of spice, blackberry and mocha, while the finish is dominated by oaky tannins and a little acidity. More bottle-age is likely to benefit. Then serve it with aged hard cheeses, like parmesan.

Quality	♟♟♟♟
Value	★★♦
Grapes	shiraz
Region	88% McLaren Vale, SA & 12% Frankland, WA
Cellar	🍷 15+
Alc./Vol.	14.0%
RRP	$100.00 Ⓢ 🍷

Heathcote Estate Shiraz

Heathcote Estate is a fairly new operation, owned by the Kirbys from Village Roadshow who also have Yabby Lake on the Mornington Peninsula. It is quite a different entity from the long-established Heathcote Winery. Maker: Tod Dexter.
Previous outstanding vintages: '02
CURRENT RELEASE 2003   Another sumptuous shiraz, with decadently sweet ripe fruit and tasting of blackberry, plum, chocolate, vanilla and herbs. There's a suggestion of smoky barrel-ferment as well. Quite big and deep, but also smooth and finely balanced, it is remarkably drinkable for such a youngster, thanks to ripe, fine-grained tannins and lovely balance. Drink with a rare, bloody steak.

Quality	♟♟♟♟♟
Value	★★★★
Grapes	shiraz
Region	Heathcote, Vic.
Cellar	🍷 15+
Alc./Vol.	14.5%
RRP	$45.00

Heathcote Winery Cravens Place Shiraz

Quality	ᵀ ᵀ ᵀ ᶴ
Value	★★★★
Grapes	shiraz
Region	Heathcote, Vic.
Cellar	▮ 5
Alc./Vol.	14.5%
RRP	$18.00 ⊜

Heathcote Winery was established by the Tudhope family in the main street of Heathcote in 1978. It has 25 hectares of vines and was one of the first Australian wineries to make a shiraz-viognier blend. Cravens Place is a new, lower-priced brand.

CURRENT RELEASE 2004   This is a touch porty, but certainly offers lots of body and flavour at a price that's modest by Heathcote standards. The colour is a lovely deep red–purple and the nose is all ripe plums and dark chocolate. It tastes less intense than it smells, and has a certain leanness of profile. The finish carries a whack of oak and alcohol. Take it to a barbie.

Henschke Henry's Seven Shiraz Grenache Viognier

Quality	ᵀ ᵀ ᵀ ᵀ ᶴ
Value	★★★★⁀
Grapes	shiraz; grenache; viognier
Region	Barossa Valley, SA
Cellar	▮ 4+
Alc./Vol.	15.0%
RRP	$27.30 ⊜

The brand is named after Henry Evans, whose Evandale vineyard was one of the first in the Eden Valley area. After he died, it was pulled out by his wife: she was a member of the temperance society! Makers: Stephen Henschke and Michael Schreurs.

CURRENT RELEASE 2003   This unusual mixture of grapes turns out to be a big success: it's a hedonistic little number, with lavish alcohol and sweet, jammy, overripe fruit characters that suit this style of wine well. Plum and plum-jam, vanilla and spicy aromas with a hint of extra aromatics from the white grapes; then in the mouth, it's rich and fruit-sweet with plushy texture and soft tannins. Try it with a gourmet hamburger with all the trimmings.

Henschke Mount Edelstone Shiraz

Quality	ᵀ ᵀ ᵀ ᵀ ᵀ
Value	★★★★
Grapes	shiraz
Region	Eden Valley, SA
Cellar	▮ 20
Alc./Vol.	15.0%
RRP	$76.00 ▮ ⊜

The first Mount Edelstone was the 1952 (making this the fifty-first vintage). The vines by then had already qualified for the epithet 'Old Vines', as the vineyard was planted way back in 1912 – by Ronald Angas, a member of the family that gave its name to Angaston. Maker: Stephen Henschke.

CURRENT RELEASE 2002   This is one of the best-ever Edelstones. It has great deep purple–red colour and lovely fruit aromas of perfectly ripened grapes, in the dark-berry to blood-plum range, with wafts of mint, oak and pepper/spice. It's already fascinatingly complex! The palate is clean, vibrant and seamless, with plenty of unobtrusive fine-grained tannin, and the alcohol doesn't show. It's perfect with roast guinea fowl.

Hesperos Shiraz

The grapes for this wine came not from the very young vines on the Hesperos property, but Rosapark, a mature vineyard 12 kilometres inland from the town of Margaret River. Maker: Jurg Muggli; 850 cases made.
CURRENT RELEASE 2002   It's a pretty, medium-bodied style that could easily be overlooked in the rush for the big bruisers. The shy nose has leafy, herbal, minty characters and the palate has medium depth and intensity. It finishes with firm tannins that go better with food than without: veal cutlets would be ideal.

Quality	▾ ▾ ▾ ▾
Value	★ ★ ★ ◆
Grapes	shiraz
Region	Margaret River, WA
Cellar	▮ 4
Alc./Vol.	14.0%
RRP	$24.00

Hewitson The Mad Hatter Shiraz

Who is the Mad Hatter? Surely not mild-mannered Dean Hewitson, he of the big round eyes and smiling countenance? Whatever, it is a catchy name for a wine brand. Output was 550 dozen.
CURRENT RELEASE 2002   Dried spices, nutmeg and mace in particular, dominate this wine, with its earthy, developing, savoury characters. It is vibrant and shows well-ripened fruit. The palate is gutsy and deep, with some earthy, meat-stock and minty flavours, drying tannins and alcohol warmth. Not an elegant wine, but generously flavoured. It would suit parmesan cheese.

Quality	▾ ▾ ▾ ▾ ▾
Value	★ ★ ★ ◆
Grapes	shiraz
Region	McLaren Vale, SA
Cellar	▮ 5
Alc./Vol.	15.0%
RRP	$49.00 ≋

Hungerford Hill Fish Cage Shiraz Viognier

Fish Cage is the cheapest Hungerford Hill range, and utilises one of the many quirky labels that were devised by the marketing bods at Southcorp, when Hungerford Hill was a Southcorp brand. Makers: Philip John and team.
CURRENT RELEASE 2004   This cashes in on the marketing trendiness of shiraz-viognier blends. It's a spicy, slightly vegetal, light-bodied red with some jammy and essency flavours that is a decent ready-drinker. It's a bit simple and not terribly intense, but is clean and well made and drinks agreeably now, thanks to its softness and balance. Try it with Lebanese yeeros.

Quality	▾ ▾ ▾ ▾
Value	★ ★ ★ ★
Grapes	shiraz; viognier
Region	not stated
Cellar	▮ 4
Alc./Vol.	14.0%
RRP	$14.00 Ⓢ ≋

Jeanneret Clare Valley Shiraz

Quality	♥♥♥♥
Value	★★★↓
Grapes	shiraz
Region	Clare Valley, SA
Cellar	➡2–12+
Alc./Vol.	14.5%
RRP	$22.00 ⬢

We're curious that the regular Jeanneret shiraz has a screw-cap while the more expensive one, the Denis, has a cork. Why are so many winemakers willing to risk their top wines while protecting their cheaper ones? The back label tells us the source vineyard suffered a 30 per cent crop reduction – probably due to drought.
CURRENT RELEASE 2003   This *tastes* like the product of a drought-year: it's thick and black-looking in the glass and it's heavy and chewy in the mouth. Concentrated, yes, but elegant, no! It's very grippy and has a long finish, but unless you can afford to cellar it, we'd only recommend it for lovers of hand-to-hand-combat wines! As for food, it needs protein, so try seared kangaroo fillet.

Jeanneret Denis Shiraz

Quality	♥♥♥♥♥
Value	★★★★
Grapes	shiraz
Region	Clare Valley, SA
Cellar	▮20
Alc./Vol.	15.0%
RRP	$55.00 ▮

Denis was the name of winemaker Ben Jeanneret's late father, who founded the winery. The wine is not produced every year and this is only the third one made. The grapes came from 138-year-old, low-yielding, dry-grown vines, and the wine saw French oak for 20 months.
CURRENT RELEASE 2002   From the record cool summer of '02, this is not a blockbuster, but a powerful and very elegant, beautifully proportioned shiraz. The colour is dense; the nose is rich and chocolatey, with lots of ripe-fruit aromas – plum, mocha and meat-stock – while the palate is saturated with mouth-flooding tannins. It's a very savoury, serious yet fruit-sweet red that is structured to age and to go well with protein-laden foods. Try rare roast beef.

Jim Barry The Lodge Hill Shiraz

Quality	♥♥♥♥
Value	★★★★
Grapes	shiraz
Region	Clare Valley, SA
Cellar	➡1–6+
Alc./Vol.	15.5%
RRP	$20.00 Ⓢ ▮

The previous vintage of this won a major trophy – for the best shiraz – at the International Wine Challenge in England. Quite a feat when you consider the best of the Rhône could have been in the field. Were the judges fooled by alcohol and mint?
CURRENT RELEASE 2003   A very good follow-up to the '02 and a similar style, bursting with gumleaf-mint, vanillan oak and chocolate/mulberry ultra-ripe fruit flavours. It's a pumped-up wine that builds essence-like raspberry jam flavours as it warms in the glass. A little bit goes a long way! Serve with kangaroo and pepperberries.

John's Blend Margarete's Shiraz No. 8

Margarete is Mrs John Glaetzer. This is the eighth vintage of this wine, although the original John's Blend, which is a pure cabernet sauvignon, has been produced every year since 1974.
CURRENT RELEASE 2002   Minty, chocolate aromas together with toasty barrel scents are reminiscent of the Wolf Blass style that John Glaetzer knows so well and helped create. There's plenty of evidence of smoky, toasty, coconutty oak. The palate is broad and chewy in texture, not really refined but it does deliver a lot of crowd-pleasing flavour and plenty of stuffing. Try it with roast beef and horseradish sauce.

Quality	▼▼▼▼
Value	★★★
Grapes	shiraz
Region	76% Langhorne Creek & 24% McLaren Vale, SA
Cellar	▮ 10+
Alc./Vol.	14.5%
RRP	$45.50 ▮

Kabminye Barossa Shiraz

Kabminye is another of the growing number of new Barossa Valley names, dedicated to making wines of true regional character. Their prices can be a lot more reasonable than some of their neighbours. By the way, Kabminye is an Aboriginal term meaning 'morning star'.
CURRENT RELEASE 2002   A densely coloured wine with an honest, meaty, regional nose that's reminiscent of gravelly soil, juicy black fruits and spice. The palate traces the aromas well, with sweet fruit in the middle, a lick of vanillin oak and soft tannins. A satisfying shiraz to enjoy with pasta and creamy mushroom sauce.

Quality	▼▼▼▼
Value	★★★
Grapes	shiraz
Region	Barossa Valley, SA
Cellar	▮ 5
Alc./Vol.	14.5%
RRP	$24.00

Kalleske Greenock Shiraz

Kalleske is the type of small Barossa estate that occasional American wine scribes seek out when they visit Australia. They see these sherry-strength wines as archetypically Australian, while ignoring regions that make delicate, fine wines designed to easily accompany food. We think there's room for them all.
CURRENT RELEASE 2003   This deeply coloured, dense wine is a formidable critter. The nose has stewed-blackberry fruit, jammy levels of extract, a hint of cinnamon spice, and touches of vanilla and chocolate. In the mouth it's dense and warmly alcoholic with powerful berry flavours, but there's more to it than a simple 'fruit-bomb.' The finish is long and aromatic. Try it with mature cheddar.

Quality	▼▼▼▼▼
Value	★★★
Grapes	shiraz
Region	Barossa Valley, SA
Cellar	▮ 10
Alc./Vol.	15.5%
RRP	$40.00

Kalleske 'K' Shiraz Viognier

Quality 🍷🍷🍷🍷½
Value ★★★★
Grapes shiraz; viognier
Region Barossa Valley, SA
Cellar 6+
Alc./Vol. 15.0%
RRP $33.00

Yet another shiraz with some trendy viognier blended in. We don't mind that when the wine is as good as this one. Kalleske is an up-and-coming Barossa maker; this wine was produced specially for Cellarmaster wine clubs. Order from www.cellarmasterwines.com

CURRENT RELEASE 2003 This is a slightly forward-developed red with lovely fragrant floral, spicy, plummy aromas and a distinct lacing of apricotty viognier. It's medium-bodied, intense and elegant. The palate has loads of flavour and ripe-fruit sweetness: it's a charmer. Stylish stuff to serve with roast pork and apple sauce.

Kirrihill Companions Shiraz

Quality 🍷🍷🍷½
Value ★★★★
Grapes shiraz
Region Langhorne Creek & Clare Valley, SA
Cellar 2
Alc./Vol. 14.7%
RRP $13.00 (S)

Companions is Kirrihill's budget brand and some of the wines, especially the whites, are excellent value. The reds aren't quite as impressive but they do offer honest flavour and a good price tag.

CURRENT RELEASE 2002 This is a deeply coloured young red with a rich nose of blackberries and sweet and savoury spices. The palate is smooth with balanced ripe flavour and agreeably soft tannins. As we said, honest and well priced. Try it with a mixed grill.

Kirrihill Estates Langhorne Creek Shiraz

Quality 🍷🍷🍷🍷
Value ★★★
Grapes shiraz
Region Langhorne Creek, SA
Cellar 5
Alc./Vol. 14.0%
RRP $21.50

Langhorne Creek is a little off the beaten track, which is possibly why it's never attained the fame of McLaren Vale et al. But make no mistake, the average quality of red wines from this South Australian region is the equal of those other better-known spots.

CURRENT RELEASE 2002 Juicy boysenberry aromas mark this fruit-forward type of red initially, and there's also a hint of earthy regionality with a light veneer of dusty oak. The palate is clean, smooth and flavoursome with medium body and good persistence, finishing soft and fine. An elegant, well-made reflection of the excellent 2002 vintage. Great with lamb kebabs.

Knappstein Shiraz

The Knappstein wines fill a middle-of-the-road spot in the Clare Valley scheme of things. The wines don't have the brilliance of some of the regional flagships, but they're consistent and good value.
CURRENT RELEASE 2002   A modern Clare red made in a crowd-pleasing style. It has deep colour and it smells of sweet berries, spices and cola (really). The palate has good intensity and medium body with smooth dark-berry flavours, a little subtle sweet oak woven in and fine, friendly tannins to finish. Good with cheese cannelloni.

Quality	♟♟♟♟
Value	★★★
Grapes	shiraz
Region	Clare Valley, SA
Cellar	▮ 4
Alc./Vol.	14.0%
RRP	$20.00 ⬆

Knots Sheepshank Shiraz

One time Balgownie winemaker Lindsay Ross is responsible for the Knots wines, which are based on material from the Bendigo and Heathcote regions. It's great shiraz country.
CURRENT RELEASE 2002   This has a dense, concentrated nose that hints at eucalypt, blackberries and green peppercorn trees. It's a very evocative regional aroma. The palate has medium body and good length of flavour, without the big structure of the fuller central Victorian shirazes. It's soft, savoury and tasty with attractive freshness. Enjoy it with roast lamb.

Quality	♟♟♟♟
Value	★★★
Grapes	shiraz
Region	Bendigo, Vic.
Cellar	▮ 3
Alc./Vol.	14.0%
RRP	$25.00

Lindemans Reserve Shiraz

Reserve is a much abused term. If this is Lindemans' reserve level, what does that make their Coonawarra Trio? And, can $14 wines really be reserve level? Perhaps they're using it like a football term – where reserve means second-rank.
CURRENT RELEASE 2003   A fairly forward-developed wine, this has vanilla and chocolate aromas and is a bit dried out on the palate, where there's a suggestion of boot leather. The tannic finish really puckers the mouth and it tastes a touch unbalanced, i.e. it needs more fruit. That said, it is quite a decent drink at the (oft-discounted) price. And we have seen fresher bottles than this – is the synthetic cork letting the wine down? Serve with savoury meatballs.

Quality	♟♟♟▵
Value	★★★★
Grapes	shiraz
Region	various, SA
Cellar	▮ 1
Alc./Vol.	14.0%
RRP	$14.00 Ⓢ

BYO Restaurants

Not that long ago, if you were passionate about wine, and weren't cashed up to the max, you went BYO, the peculiarly Australian phenomenon of the Bring Your Own restaurant.

Now things have changed, and general liberalisation of most Australian liquor laws has seen an explosion in the numbers of licensed restaurants at the expense of BYOs. It's not all bad news, though: wine prices in licensed restaurants have come down and service standards have often improved (though not always). However, this doesn't necessarily mean that the need for BYOs has decreased among wine lovers.

Some newly licensed restaurants choose wines based on obscurity rather than quality, avoiding reliable big-maker wines like the plague, in case of embarrassing (and unfair) price comparisons with discount stores by customers. Add licensed restaurants that entrust their wine lists to elements in the wine trade who unashamedly use the privilege as a marketing tool for their own products, and it adds up to make choosing a good bottle harder, even for the wine-savvy. In theory this is where the skills of a knowledgeable *sommelier* (aka wine waiter) come in.

Thankfully large numbers of unfussy, local, often ethnic, restaurants remain everywhere maintaining the BYO creed. And the best of both worlds is offered by the large number of licensed restaurants *also* allowing customers to BYO. Because of overheads these establishments often charge corkage, a quite justifiable thing. If you're unsure of a restaurant's wine policy, or you want to try a specific bottle you have at home, checking before booking makes good sense.

Here's a listing of a broad range of very good BYO-friendly restaurants in Melbourne and Sydney you might like to try. Check with them before you BYO, as some have restrictions of one type or another:

Melbourne: Abla's; Asiana; Bar Santo; Celadon; France-Soir; Harveys; La Luna; Lazars; Maris; Matteo's; Mrs Jones; Pacific Seafood BBQ House; Richmond Hill Cafe & Larder; Shira Nui; Supper Inn; Wabi Sabi.

Sydney: Billy Kwong; Claude's; Grappa; Il Baretto; La Goulue; L'Unico; Marque; Perama; Restaurant Balzac; Ristorante Riva; Sean's Panorama; Tables; Tetsuya's; Tran's; Zenith.

Longview Yakka Single Vineyard Shiraz Viognier

Quality	▼▼▼▼
Value	★★★★
Grapes	shiraz; viognier
Region	Adelaide Hills, SA
Cellar	▯ 5+
Alc./Vol.	14.5%
RRP	$27.00

Shiraz viognier blends are all the rage in Australia now. A little bit of viognier goes a long way and it's easy to overdo it. We prefer our shiraz to taste of red grapes rather than apricot jam!
CURRENT RELEASE 2003 There is a smidge of apricot discernible here, along with the more predictable spicy/peppery and leafy cooler-grown shiraz aromas. It's a delicious and very elegant red. There's a lot of very ripe, sweet fruit on the palate and it finishes with some quite firm tannin. It could reward from a little more time in the cellar. Then serve with grilled pork chops.

Longwood Old Vineyard Reserve Shiraz

Quality	▼▼▼▼▼
Value	★★★★★
Grapes	shiraz
Region	Strathbogie Ranges, Vic.
Cellar	▯ 15+
Alc./Vol.	14.0%
RRP	$20.00 (cellar door)

This wine comes from the original vines planted in 1969 by Andrew and Elly Cameron on The Falls vineyard in the Strathbogie Ranges. Sam Plunkett made the wine.
CURRENT RELEASE 2003 An elegant but powerful shiraz with profound flavour and structure. It has real old-vine concentration and fleshy extract: essency and underdeveloped. Plum and spice fruit; toasty, nutty oak; and smooth but persuasive tannins complete the picture. It's a wine that improves with airing: smooth and lush with plenty of bite and persistence. It goes well with roast duck in muscat and raisin sauce.

McWilliams Rosehill Shiraz

Quality	▼▼▼▼▼
Value	★★★★★
Grapes	shiraz
Region	Hunter Valley, NSW
Cellar	▯ 10
Alc./Vol.	14.5%
RRP	$32.00 ▯

Rosehill was added to the Mount Pleasant stable of Hunter Valley vineyards by Maurice O'Shea in 1945. Present winemaker Phil Ryan claims that the 2000 Rosehill is the best since 1959. We agree, it really is a memorable vintage.
CURRENT RELEASE 2000 This maturing wine was reviewed in last year's *Guide*, but it's still around if you search for it. To enjoy it at its best it needs decanting and plenty of air, after which it epitomises the unique qualities that make Hunter shiraz memorable. It doesn't overwhelm the drinker, quietly getting more interesting with every sip. Spice, raspberry, leather and odd, but not unpleasant, medicinal characters mark the nose and palate, and its satin texture and long flavour are supported by some sinewy tannins that soften as acquaintance develops. It suits Greek-style herb-marinated lamb.

Meerea Park Terracotta Shiraz

Meerea Park's Terracotta is often at odds with the more traditional, lighter reds of the Hunter Valley, but it does retain good regional character. Maker: Rhys Eather.
CURRENT RELEASE 2003   There's some of the leather, farmyard and spice of the Hunter tradition on the nose here, as well as more modern mixed-berry and sweet-oak aromas. In the mouth it's medium in body, smooth and pleasantly poised, but its immaturity shows in its slightly firm tannins. It's regionality comes through, despite a very un-traditional dose of viognier in the mix, and we think it should develop along classical lines over the mid-term. Try it with Florentine-style steaks.

Quality	♟♟♟♟♙
Value	★★★
Grapes	shiraz 92%; viognier 8%
Region	Hunter Valley, NSW
Cellar	➛2–8
Alc./Vol.	14.5%
RRP	$50.00 ⧖

Milvine Estate Shiraz

Milvine Estate at Heathcote had sold its shiraz grapes to regional wineries for eight years before fulfilling the ambition of producing an estate wine. This, the first, augurs well for the future.
CURRENT RELEASE 2003   A great first effort with an impenetrable colour and an intense nose and palate of dark plums, plum eau-de-vie, mellow spice, mineral and leathery notes. Dusty oak trims the fruit well and it tastes smooth with mouth-flooding flavour, dry tannins and a spicy finish. A label to watch. Serve it with braised lamb shanks

Quality	♟♟♟♟♙
Value	★★★
Grapes	shiraz
Region	Heathcote, Vic.
Cellar	▮5
Alc./Vol.	15.0%
RRP	$29.50

Mitchelton Crescent Shiraz Mourvèdre Grenache

Mitchelton's credentials with the so-called Rhône varieties are excellent, starting with marsanne and shiraz many years ago and more recently with other red and white grapes like mourvèdre, roussanne and others.
CURRENT RELEASE 2003   An honest, robust red wine of good character. The nose has quite exotic spice aromas, earthy touches and scents of raspberry, blackberry and aniseed. Subtle sweet/savoury oak takes a back seat. The palate is medium-bodied with firm structure and good flavour development. An unfussy red to sip with a thick-crusted family-style pizza.

Quality	♟♟♟♟
Value	★★★
Grapes	shiraz; mourvèdre; grenache
Region	various, Central Vic.
Cellar	▮4
Alc./Vol.	14.5%
RRP	$27.00

Mitchelton Heathcote Shiraz

Quality	▼▼▼▼▼
Value	★★★
Grapes	shiraz
Region	Heathcote, Vic.
Cellar	🍾 5+
Alc./Vol.	14.0%
RRP	$35.00

Heathcote is the buzzword in Australian shiraz these days. The ancient soils in this part of Victoria are producing so many impressive wines that it's hard to believe that only 30 years ago no wine was produced there at all. Mitchelton's new Heathcote effort is in the best regional style.
CURRENT RELEASE 2003   This has a meaty nose with smells of ironstone, juicy boysenberries, subtle spice and wood smoke. It's intense and subtly oaked with good texture, medium-body, ripe, fine tannins, and a long finish. Very Heathcote in its combination of robust flavour and finesse. Try it with braised lamb and onions.

Mitchelton Print Shiraz

Quality	▼▼▼▼▼
Value	★★★
Grapes	shiraz
Region	Goulburn Valley, Vic.
Cellar	➡ 2–10
Alc./Vol.	15.7%
RRP	$49.00

Mitchelton Print Label Shiraz is now packed in a very heavy bottle, which is entirely appropriate given the hefty construction of the wine within. The '02 vintage takes the line's traditional power and impact to a new level.
CURRENT RELEASE 2002   This really is a power-packed drop with heaps going on. The aroma is ripe, meaty and potent with a slightly rustic pong to super-concentrated dark fruit and spicy shiraz smells. A layer of sweet/smoky barrel ferment adds to the macho image, and the palate is densely packed with ripe, persistent flavour. It's still young and undeveloped but it has beautifully integrated grainy tannins. One of the better Print Shirazes, but at the high-alcohol end of the spectrum. Keep it, then serve it with oxtail.

Mitchelton Shiraz

Quality	▼▼▼▼
Value	★★★
Grapes	shiraz
Region	Nagambie Lakes, Vic.
Cellar	🍾 5
Alc./Vol.	14.5%
RRP	$20.00 ⬎

Mitchelton's headquarters is near Nagambie in one of the most historic pockets of Victorian viticulture. The neighbouring Tahbilk vineyard is one of the must-see destinations for any Australian vineyard traveller, and so, in its own way, is Mitchelton.
CURRENT RELEASE 2003   A modern, rather loose-knit style, with plenty of raspberry and blackberry fruit, spice and herb characters, and not much apparent oak. The palate has smooth fruit and easy texture with a balanced foundation of tannins. Sip it with lamb shanks.

Mount Horrocks Shiraz

Stephanie Toole's Mount Horrocks wines are a true reflection of their Clare Valley origins. Like many Clare winemakers, she favours screw-caps to retain freshness and reliability in her wines.

CURRENT RELEASE 2002   A more savoury shiraz type with a slight peppercorn edge to a nose of mixed berries, plum and earth. There's little apparent oak in the mix, and it's medium-bodied with spicy flavour and a long supple palate of good depth. Soft tannins make a harmonious foundation. Great with lamb's fry.

Quality	♉ ♉ ♉ ♉ ♉
Value	✷ ✷ ✷
Grapes	shiraz
Region	Clare Valley, SA
Cellar	🍷 5
Alc./Vol.	14.0%
RRP	$34.95

Mount Ida Shiraz

Despite an excellent site and maturing vineyard, the style of Mount Ida shiraz has meandered over the years, largely through various changes of ownership. Delicious in the early days, then ordinary, then super-oaky, and so on. Signs are good though and the current Beringer-Blass ownership is showing appropriate respect.

CURRENT RELEASE 2002   This wine shows how a little air can sometimes improve a young red. It opened a bit fusty, despite its screw-cap, but a bit of breathing helped it immensely. There's a good measure of high-toned oak on the nose here, with spicy, cherry eau-de-vie-like fruit underneath. The palate is silky and fine in feel, with good length and ripeness, finishing in fine ripe tannins. It's a different kind of Heathcote shiraz, oaky but less of a bruiser than some of its regional neighbours. Try it with steaks cut from a leg of lamb.

Quality	♉ ♉ ♉ ♉
Value	✷ ✷ ✷
Grapes	shiraz
Region	Heathcote, Vic.
Cellar	🍷 5
Alc./Vol.	14.0%
RRP	$46.30

Mount Langi Ghiran Cliff Edge Shiraz

The Cliff Edge vineyard really is near a cliff edge in a cool exposed location that makes viticulture bloody hard. As a result the Cliff Edge grapes are sometimes supplemented by other local growers.

CURRENT RELEASE 2002   Typical cool-climate shiraz cues on the nose here. Peppery spice, red berries, blackberries, herbs – all very savoury. The palate has silky texture and tangy flavours of black fruit, herbs and pepper. A lean-boned, austere cool-climate type of shiraz, but one that's nicely ripe and not too green or edgy. An appetising wine to have with duck.

Quality	♉ ♉ ♉ ♉
Value	✷ ✷ ✷
Grapes	shiraz
Region	Grampians, Vic.
Cellar	🍷 4
Alc./Vol.	14.0%
RRP	$25.00

Mount Langi Ghiran Langi Shiraz

Quality	♥♥♥♥♥
Value	★★★⁴
Grapes	shiraz
Region	Grampians, Vic.
Cellar	▮ 8+
Alc./Vol.	14.0%
RRP	$56.30

Langi Shiraz is rightly numbered among Australia's top shirazes. It follows a great shiraz tradition in the Grampians region of Victoria, and the best vintages are superb. CURRENT RELEASE 2000 An essay in harmony, this Mount Langi shiraz has a complex nose of plum, pepper and assorted spices, earthy notes and meatiness. It's been in bottle for a while, and is evolving some elaborate bottle-aged characters as well as primary fruit. Beautifully measured oak sits well in the mix. It finishes long, earthy and complete. A good wine to sip with braised duck, prunes and apples.

Mount Majura Shiraz

Quality	♥♥♥♥
Value	★★★
Grapes	shiraz
Region	Canberra, ACT
Cellar	⬤—1–6+
Alc./Vol.	13.1%
RRP	$25.00 ⅀

Most of the Canberra region's vineyards are outside the Canberra boundary – that is, they're in New South Wales. But Mount Majura is a true Canberra vineyard. This shiraz is estate-grown. Maker: Frank van de Loo. CURRENT RELEASE 2003 An unusual shiraz, this is a rather extracted, dense wine with grippy tannins and a chewy texture. There's a hint of volatility too, which doesn't get in the way, and it has plenty of weight and flavour with some herbal fruit notes. It has surprising weight for such a cool climate. Serve it with meatballs in tomato.

Mr Riggs Shiraz Viognier

Quality	♥♥♥♥⁵
Value	★★★★★⁴
Grapes	shiraz; viognier
Region	60% Langhorne Creek & 40% McLaren Vale, SA
Cellar	▮ 5
Alc./Vol.	14.5%
RRP	$26.50 ⅀

Mister Ben Riggs makes a shiraz-viognier blend that's in the more floral viognier-influenced part of the genre. It's a very aromatic, almost pretty wine, yet it has some stuffing too. CURRENT RELEASE 2003 This has a truly complex, heady nose. An attempt to describe it would have us writing about blackberries, apricots, liquorice, spice, flowers, aromatic black pepper and earth. This fascinating bouquet leads to a rich palate that's full of interest with supple stone-fruit and spice flavours, good length and a quite firm finish. Enjoy it with Italian-style pork sausages and lentils.

Murray Street Vineyards Shiraz

This is the label of Andrew Seppelt – yes, another Seppelt! Andrew is a younger-generation member of the famous clan, and he's based in Greenock, with vineyards in the Gomersal and Greenock districts. Murray Street Vineyards was set up in 2001.

CURRENT RELEASE 2002   A nicely balanced, elegant style of Barossa shiraz, with no excesses of alcohol, oak or any portiness. It's a really good drink, and doesn't fight its way down the throat. The aromas are of fragrant berry scents, fruit driven and clean; the palate is medium-bodied and it will come as welcome relief for a lot of people who can no longer drink Barossa shiraz. Try it with pan-fried veal.

Quality	♀ ♀ ♀ ♀
Value	★★★★
Grapes	shiraz
Region	Barossa Valley, SA
Cellar	🍾 5
Alc./Vol.	13.7%
RRP	$23.50

O'Leary Walker Shiraz

David O'Leary and Nick Walker only established their own brand in 2001, but both have lots of experience in the South Australian wine scene. They really know what they're about, a fact that's confirmed by the impeccable quality of their wines.

CURRENT RELEASE 2003   A very dense shiraz that treads an attractive middle line between the new wave and the traditional. The nose has raspberry jam and blackberry fruit with gentle sweet spice and just a little dusting of oak. It gives a pure, clean impression, but that doesn't mean it lacks character. The palate is velvet smooth, ripe and juicy with perfectly poised ripe, soft tannins behind it. A friendly shiraz. Enjoy it with braised beef.

Quality	♀ ♀ ♀ ♀ ♀
Value	★★★ ♪
Grapes	shiraz
Region	Clare Valley & McLaren Vale, SA
Cellar	🍾 5
Alc./Vol.	14.5%
RRP	$21.00

Orlando Jacob's Creek Reserve Shiraz

This step up the Jacob's Creek ladder is usually well worth the premium over the standard version, and it's often discounted. It has more of everything.

CURRENT RELEASE 2002   This is a more obvious Jacob's Creek Reserve than previous vintages. It has a jammy blackberry nose trimmed in vanillin oak. In the mouth it's chocolatey, ripe and full, with a slightly stewed-fruit character touched by sweet vanillin oak. In 2002 it has more power than previously, but not quite the same finesse. Still pretty good though. Try it with roasted vegetable lasagne.

Quality	♀ ♀ ♀ ♀
Value	★★★★
Grapes	shiraz
Region	various, SA
Cellar	🍾 3
Alc./Vol.	15.0%
RRP	$17.00 Ⓢ

Orlando Jacob's Creek Shiraz

Quality 🍷🍷🍷🍷
Value ★★★★½
Grapes shiraz
Region not stated
Cellar 🍾 2
Alc./Vol. 14.0%
RRP $10.00 [$]

Jacob's Creek is just about everywhere these days, so much so that it suffers a bit from the old 'familiarity breeds contempt' syndrome. If it's that popular it can't be any good, says this smartypants attitude. But look at the wine in the bottle and you'll see that this is astonishing value at under $10 a bottle. The perfect everyday red.

CURRENT RELEASE 2002 A good style at a great price. Sweet spice, earth, and red and black-fruit aromas that are surprisingly juicy and inviting, lead to a smooth palate of attractive richness. There's a bit of liqueur cherry to it and it has good persistence of flavour. The finish is soft and agreeable. Try it with spaghetti bolognese.

Outback Chase Shiraz

Quality 🍷🍷🍷½
Value ★★★★
Grapes shiraz
Region Coonawarra, SA
Cellar 🍾 2
Alc./Vol. 13.5%
RRP $9.50 [$]

Outback Chase is a Kingston Estate label that brings Coonawarra wine to the market at extraordinarily low prices. Quality is good. Maker Bill Moularadellis reckons it's a $15 wine for under $10 and he's not far wrong.

CURRENT RELEASE 2003 What does a $9 Coonawarra shiraz taste like? Pretty good, especially when it's in the market alongside a number of red wines that rely on sweetness for their success. While this has ripe, juicy berry aroma and flavour, it's drier and it has a touch of regional spice that takes it out of such company. The palate is smooth and easy, again with a hint of peppery spice to it. The palate finishes very soft, and maybe a tad short, but it's great value. Try it with moussaka.

Pauletts Polish Hill River Shiraz

Quality 🍷🍷🍷🍷½
Value ★★★★★
Grapes shiraz
Region Clare Valley, SA
Cellar 🍾 10
Alc./Vol. 14.5%
RRP $22.00 🌀

We are increasingly impressed with the Paulett wines, and that's not just because they've released two stunning reserve bottlings recently (Andreas shiraz and Antonina riesling). It's as though Neil Paulett has shifted into a higher gear. Great vintages like 2002 help, of course.

CURRENT RELEASE 2002 This is a lovely smooth, fleshy, easy-to-drink shiraz with superior depth and style for its mid-range price. Lightly spicy aromas are of aniseed, plum and jam, fruit-driven and not oaky; the palate is appealingly smooth and harmonious. It's very ripe but not porty. A fine partner for duck confit.

Penfolds Bin 28 Kalimna Shiraz

Bin 28 is one of the most reliable of all the Penfolds reds, and they are notable for their reliability. It is no longer a pure Kalimna wine – Kalimna is Penfolds' flagship Barossa vineyard, and the wine outgrew it long ago.

CURRENT RELEASE 2002 The '02 is a very good Bin 28: it shows the usual blackberry fruit with hints of fruitcake and jam, despite the very cool summer. It has a plump, full-bodied, rich palate with plenty of fruit sweetness followed by soft tannins and a drying savoury finish. A typical Pennies style and a good partner for civet of hare.

Quality	🍷🍷🍷🍷
Value	★★★★
Grapes	shiraz
Region	mainly Barossa Valley, SA
Cellar	🍾 7+
Alc./Vol.	14.5%
RRP	$26.00 [$] 🍾

Penfolds Bin 128 Coonawarra Shiraz

Bin 128 is one of the very few Penfolds wines sourced from a single region. Usually they are blends of vineyards, regions and grape varieties. The aim is to achieve a consistent quality and style from year to year. Maker: Peter Gago and team.

CURRENT RELEASE 2002 We opened three bottles and the third was the best. Peppery, gamey, spicy cool-year shiraz aromatics open out into a classic Coonawarra with elegant structure and medium body. It has soft fine-grained tannins and attractive fruit sweetness. The balance and drinkability are impeccable. Great with pink roast lamb.

Quality	🍷🍷🍷🍷
Value	★★★★
Grapes	shiraz
Region	Coonawarra, SA
Cellar	🍾 6+
Alc./Vol.	14.0%
RRP	$26.00 [$] 🍾

Penfolds Grange

Despite being the least impressive Grange since the '93, the price has hit a new record – probably because of the very small output (3000 cases). This in turn is due to the very ordinary quality of 2000 for South Australian red wine. Perhaps no Grange at all should have been released. The set-collectors and investors snapped it up faster than you could say 'rip-off'.

Previous outstanding vintages: '52, '53, '55, '62, '66, '71, '76, '83, '86, '90, '91, '94, '96, '98, '99

CURRENT RELEASE 2000 This vintage, sourced solely from the Barossa Valley, while a perfectly decent drink, is not a very good Grange at all: it lacks power and traditional Grange character, and is quite vegetal, with peppercorn, smoke, undergrowth and compost characters. The coconutty oak also sticks out somewhat. Best leave this one to the label-drinkers and collectors.

Quality	🍷🍷🍷🍷
Value	★½
Grapes	shiraz 100%
Region	Barossa Valley, SA
Cellar	🍾 10
Alc./Vol.	14.0%
RRP	$500–$550 🍾

Penfolds Magill Estate Shiraz

Quality	♟♟♟♟♟
Value	★★★
Grapes	shiraz
Region	Adelaide, SA
Cellar	🍷 15+
Alc./Vol.	14.0%
RRP	$90.00 🍾

Peter Gago makes this wine at the historic Magill Estate cellars. It's fermented in old open concrete vats with heading-down boards, basket pressed, matured in two-thirds French oak, and bottled without fining or filtration. *Previous outstanding vintages: '83, '88, '91, '96, '98, '99, '01* CURRENT RELEASE 2002 This is a lovely, savoury, old-fashioned style of red. Lashings of soft fruit, dried-herb, smoke and spice aromas; medium- to full-bodied, with soft tannins and beautifully integrated oak. A very good Magill Estate. It suits aged cheeses, such as Heidi gruyere.

Penfolds RWT Barossa Shiraz

Quality	♟♟♟♟♟
Value	★★★
Grapes	shiraz
Region	Barossa Valley, SA
Cellar	🍷 20+
Alc./Vol.	14.5%
RRP	$150.00 🍾

The Red Winemaking Trials that resulted in this new wine began in 1995 and the first vintage was 1997. It's an alter ego for Grange, entirely Barossa shiraz and selected for its up-front bright fruit, aged only in French oak and released earlier to capitalise on that terrific fruit. Makers: Peter Gago and team.
Previous outstanding vintages: '98, '99, '01
CURRENT RELEASE 2002 This is a ripper! Loads of sweet, ripe berry fruit and smoky, meaty barrel-ferment oak, hints of aniseed and rich but refined flavour. A wine that combines understated power with supreme elegance. A top wine, albeit not as big as the great '98. Serve it with venison.

Penfolds St Henri Shiraz

Quality	♟♟♟♟♟
Value	★★★★
Grapes	shiraz
Region	50% Barossa Valley, 31% McLaren Vale, 19% Padthaway, SA
Cellar	🍷 20+
Alc./Vol.	14.5%
RRP	$70.00 🍾

Max Schubert's friend and rival John Davoren created this wine at Auldana in the mid-1950s as a reaction to Grange, which he said was too big and oaky. It's aged only in large, old oak vats – never small barrels. The St Henri name and script dates back a lot further, to the start of the twentieth century when Auldana winemaker Edmond Mazure named a wine after his son Henri.
Previous outstanding vintages: '62, '63, '65, '66, '70, '71, '72, '73, '76, '83, '84, '85, '86, '90, '91, '94, '96, '98, '99
CURRENT RELEASE 2001 This is a St Henri of great colour and depth. It has meaty, spicy, leather and humus complexities, already developing mellowness, plus touches of the prune and anise characters of the '01 Penfolds vintage. Multi-layered flavours, developing nicely but very vibrant in the mouth. A very smart St Henri that deserves the best aged cheeses.

Penfolds Thomas Hyland Shiraz

Thomas Hyland married Georgina Penfold, daughter of the founder (Dr Christopher Rawson Penfold) and kick-started an era of phenomenal success and rapid growth for the fledgling Penfolds wine company. Makers: Peter Gago and team.

CURRENT RELEASE 2003 There are some fruitcakey, licorice and prune/raisin aromas here that remind us the 2003 summer in South Australia had quite a bit of heat. There are dusty, earthy, plum-pudding and aniseed flavours and the palate has richness and depth. The texture is quite chewy. It's more of an aerobically made than a fruity style. It could cellar well. Drink with beef olives.

Quality	🍷🍷🍷🍷
Value	★★★★½
Grapes	shiraz
Region	various, SA
Cellar	🍾 5
Alc./Vol.	14.0%
RRP	$20.00 [$]

Penley Estate Shiraz Cabernet

Kym Tolley's back labels were New Age before New Age was even thought of. They state: 'Experience was earnt, tradition was given, but my wines reflect what I feel'. What more can we say?

CURRENT RELEASE 2002 This is a well-put-together wine, showing a bouquet of high-toast oak and nicely ripened blackberry fruit, together with some earthiness. The palate is medium- to full-bodied and quite tannic, but the tannin grip is well balanced by deep fruit flavour that lingers long on the finish. It suits rare roast beef.

Quality	🍷🍷🍷🍷½
Value	★★★★
Grapes	shiraz 54%; cabernet sauvignon 36%; cabernet franc 10%
Region	various, SA
Cellar	🍾 10
Alc./Vol.	14.5%
RRP	$29.70 ⚱

Pepper Tree Grand Reserve Shiraz

Pepper Tree's owner has a very large vineyard at Wrattonbully – 100 hectares in fact. With all that fruit to select from it's little wonder the winery's Grand Reserve bottlings – chardonnay as well as shiraz – come from that area.

CURRENT RELEASE 2003 The wine is quite concentrated in colour, aroma and flavour, but lacks a little richness and flesh on the bones. It has a pungent gumleaf/mint aroma, with a trace of camphor. The palate is taut and lean, with good intensity of flavour, firm tannins and a long finish. It needs food: we'd recommend a rare porterhouse steak.

Quality	🍷🍷🍷🍷
Value	★★★
Grapes	shiraz
Region	Wrattonbully, SA
Cellar	🍾 2–10+
Alc./Vol.	14.9%
RRP	$55.00 ⚱

Pepperjack Shiraz

Quality	♈♈♈
Value	★★★⁴
Grapes	shiraz
Region	Barossa Valley, SA
Cellar	▮ 4
Alc./Vol.	14.5%
RRP	$24.00 Ⓢ

Where do the marketing brains trusts come up with these names? We suspect they sit around doing a few lines, brainstorm a list of names, then test them on a focus group of bored housewives to see which one they like best. Just like naming a new brand of motor car or cleaning product. CURRENT RELEASE 2003   This has some guts and should be a crowd-pleaser, especially at the discounted price. There are earthy, dusty developed savoury aromas and richer, jammy fruit scents, while the palate has a lot of tannin grip and savoury flavours. The texture is quite chewy and oak seems to have been used lavishly. It would go with savoury meatballs.

Petaluma Shiraz

Quality	♈♈♈♈
Value	★★★★
Grapes	shiraz; viognier
Region	Adelaide Hills, SA
Cellar	▮ 10+
Alc./Vol.	15.0%
RRP	$48.00 ▮

The grapes for this spectacular new wine come from a vineyard specially planted at Mount Barker, in the south-western part of the Adelaide Hills, with an extraordinary soil type called micaceous schist. The sun reflecting on the rock strewn around the vineyard gives it an amazing silvery sheen. Maker: Con Moshos.
Previous outstanding vintages: '02
CURRENT RELEASE 2003   Another superb shiraz from Petaluma, with cool-grown black pepper and spice varietal aromas, a touch of mint and a little floral/herbal aroma that may be due to the small viognier component. The palate is wonderfully flavoured and textured: it's highly concentrated and rich, but smooth and natural tasting, with great length and harmony. There's a hint of dark chocolate, too. Terrific focus and balance, it deserves the best T-bone steak.

Peter Lehmann The Futures Shiraz

Quality	♈♈♈♈
Value	★★★★
Grapes	shiraz
Region	Barossa Valley, SA
Cellar	▮ 5+
Alc./Vol.	14.5%
RRP	$30.00 Ⓢ ▮

This used to be a cellar-door-only release, but now it's more widely available. It spent 18 months in French and American oak hogsheads.
CURRENT RELEASE 2002   Already starting to show some development, this wine is crammed full of the earthy, chocolate and vanilla flavours of regional Barossa shiraz. The palate's smooth, fleshy texture and supple ripe tannins are highlights. It has plenty of richness and is smooth as plush. A lovely drink with braised lamb shanks.

Pikes The EWP Reserve Shiraz

The initials stand for Edgar Walter Pike, patriarch of the family. The back label says 2 per cent viognier was blended into the shiraz, but the wine is identified simply as shiraz on the front label. So it would be hard to accuse the Pikes of exploiting a marketing gimmick.
CURRENT RELEASE 2002   The sweet, smooth, fleshy texture of this wine is what sets it apart, and begs the question: how much of that does it owe to the viognier component? Whatever, it's a delicious red wine. Mocha, smoke and coffee-like aromas intertwine with pepper and other spices, and there's some heat and sweetness from high alcohol strength on the tongue. There's a hint of barrel-ferment and good fleshy extract. Drink it with a pork and vegie stirfry.

Quality	♥♥♥♥♥
Value	★★★
Grapes	shiraz 98%; viognier 2%
Region	Clare Valley, SA
Cellar	🍷 7+
Alc./Vol.	14.5%
RRP	$60.00

Plantagenet Hazard Hill Shiraz

This contains a 'small percentage of grenache' but obviously less than 15 per cent, as it would have to be listed then. Previous vintages have been labelled shiraz grenache. Chief winemaker these days is Richard Robson.
CURRENT RELEASE 2003   This is a slightly forward wine, showing some development, and is light- to medium-bodied with a lick of tannin astringency to close. The dominant flavours are of vanilla and chocolate, coupled with a hint of sweet, jammy black fruits. It is quite sweet and grapey on the palate and there's a hint of sulphide. A rustic cheapie to quaff around a smoky barbecue.

Quality	♥♥♥
Value	★★★★
Grapes	shiraz; grenache
Region	various, WA
Cellar	🍷 2+
Alc./Vol.	14.5%
RRP	$13.00 Ⓢ

Redbank Fighting Flat Shiraz

The Redbank brand was bought by Samuel Smith & Son (Yalumba) from the founders, the Robb family of Redbank Winery in the Pyrenees (the Robbs still own the winery). The wines are made in the Barossa, where the winemaker in charge of Redbank is Natalie Fryar.
CURRENT RELEASE 2002   It's curious this tastes like a Pyrenees wine, because it's not! The aromas are in the peppermint/garden-mint spectrum with some smoky, earthy nuances. The taste is quite intense and long, with good fleshiness and tannin, and although it's not especially elegant, it has loads of flavour and outstanding length. It suits barbecued kangaroo backstraps.

Quality	♥♥♥♥
Value	★★★★
Grapes	shiraz
Region	King Valley, Vic.
Cellar	🍷 5+
Alc./Vol.	14.5%
RRP	$21.00 Ⓢ

Robert Johnson Vineyard Shiraz Viognier

Quality	♥♥♥♥♥
Value	★★★★
Grapes	shiraz; viognier
Region	Eden Valley, SA
Cellar	🍾 13+
Alc./Vol.	14.5%
RRP	$41.00

Another new name already producing sensational wine! Established in 1997, Johnson has a 4.5-hectare vineyard in the Eden Valley, and also produces wine under the slightly cheaper Alan & Veitch label.

CURRENT RELEASE 2003   This is a real find! A superb young shiraz viognier that encapsulates the best advantages of these two grapes. It has a youthful colour and a complex pepper and clove spicy nose with some apricot viognier scents, while the palate is rich, deep and fleshy, with layered spicy flavours of great elegance and texture. The tannins are finely structured and it tastes ripe and lingering. Perfect with pepper steak.

Rockbare McLaren Vale Shiraz

Quality	♥♥♥♥
Value	★★★★
Grapes	shiraz
Region	McLaren Vale, SA
Cellar	🍾 5+
Alc./Vol.	14.5%
RRP	$20.00

Rockbare is a small, young company that uses other people's facilities, yet manages to market some remarkably good-value wines. It was set up by Tim Burvill, one of the young winemakers who was 'let go' by Southcorp following the fateful Rosemount merger.

CURRENT RELEASE 2003   This is a very appealing, chocolatey, easy-drinking shiraz with plenty of soft tannin and a lovely velvety texture. It's sweet-fruited, rich and ripe, in a familiar style that this region does so well. The finish lingers well; it would suit venison cutlets.

Rosemount Balmoral Syrah

Quality	♥♥♥♥♥
Value	★★★⟩
Grapes	shiraz
Region	McLaren Vale, SA
Cellar	🍾 5+
Alc./Vol.	14.0%
RRP	$70.00 🍾

We've always wondered why Rosemount called this a syrah, when it is as dinky-di as Aussie shiraz can be! We don't see much relationship to the famous shirazes of the French Rhône Valley, where the grape is called syrah. Maker: Charles Whish and team.

Previous outstanding vintages: '91, '94, '96, '98, '99

CURRENT RELEASE 2000   A triumph for the relatively ordinary season, this has a typical nose of melted club chocolate, mocha and espresso coffee. Blackberry fruit is buried in there somewhere, too, and some charred oak inflexions. The palate is flowing and seamless and beautifully textured. It's what some Americans label 'decadent' – an almost naughty drink for its sheer hedonism. Drinking superbly now, with venison braised in cherries.

Rosemount Diamond Label Shiraz

Quality	🍷🍷🍷🍷
Value	★★★★★
Grapes	shiraz
Region	various
Cellar	🍾 5
Alc./Vol.	14.0%
RRP	$15.00 [$]

This won a couple of trophies at the '04 Cowra Wine Show – including best shiraz and best red of show! We think it was pretty lucky, but at least the wine is good – very good when you consider the price and the volume that's made. It comes with a synthetic 'cork' called a Nomacork, which does a very good job. Just don't cellar 'em.

CURRENT RELEASE 2003 This is a good ready-drinking red with a bit more structure than you'd expect at the price. Dusty, herbal and lightly spiced traditional red-wine aromas lead into a smooth, sweet-fruited palate, which tastes of berries, jam and aniseed. The tannins are smooth and give just the right degree of firmness and dryness to the finish. Cleverly made. Enjoy it with roast pork.

Rosemount Hill of Gold Shiraz

Quality	🍷🍷🍷🍷
Value	★★★★
Grapes	shiraz
Region	Mudgee, NSW
Cellar	🍾 8+
Alc./Vol.	13.5%
RRP	$21.00 [$]

The locals are often heard to observe that Mudgee is a better region for shiraz than cabernet. The same observation could be made about most Australian wine regions. With Hill of Gold, we certainly preferred the shiraz to the cab this year.

CURRENT RELEASE 2003 Nutty and dried-spice aromas here show the savoury style of Mudgee shiraz, with some walnut and oak aspects. The palate is rich and soft, with a drying tannin finish that stays in balance, and has a degree of style. Because of its tannin, it's best drunk with protein-rich food, such as a rare steak.

Rosemount Mountain Blue Shiraz Cabernet

Quality	🍷🍷🍷🍷½
Value	★★★½
Grapes	shiraz; cabernet sauvignon
Region	Mudgee, NSW
Cellar	🍾 7+
Alc./Vol.	14.0%
RRP	$53.50 🍾

We reviewed this last year but it's still current at time of writing. The 2000 is a remarkably good wine considering the dodgy vintage. It was one of the wettest and least inspiring vintages in recent times at Mudgee. But this wine has won at least five gold medals.

Previous outstanding vintages: '96, '97, '98

CURRENT RELEASE 2000 Ginger/spice is a trait of good Mudgee reds, and this wine has a touch of that. It's also got plenty of eucalyptus/mint aroma, and the beginnings of bottle-aged character are starting to add another layer of complexity. The palate is rich and fleshy, with admirable concentration, lovely texture and mouth-feel. A rewarding big red to serve with aged cheeses, such as cheddar.

Rosemount Orange Vineyard Shiraz

Quality	🍷🍷🍷🍷
Value	★★★★
Grapes	shiraz
Region	Orange, NSW
Cellar	5+
Alc./Vol.	14.0%
RRP	$28.00 ⓢ

The Rosemount Orange wines are sourced from Philip Shaw's own extensive vineyard, so we wonder how they're divvying the fruit up, now that he no longer works for the company. Indeed, he's making his own wines from that vineyard now.

CURRENT RELEASE 2001   The cool Orange climate is evident in the peppery aromas. It's very spicy without being green or underripe, and has a medium body with raspberry and cherry flavours strongly evident in the mouth. The texture is fine and it's nicely balanced – without the usual density and guts of the regular warm-area Rosemount reds. It would go well with pink lamb chops.

Rosemount Shiraz Cabernet

Quality	🍷🍷🍷
Value	★★★★
Grapes	shiraz; cabernet sauvignon
Region	not stated
Cellar	2
Alc./Vol.	13.5%
RRP	$12.00 ⓢ

It's ironic to see the last of the wines made during the Oatley family's time of involvement still have back labels signed by the 'founder, Robert Oatley'! Since Oatley sold his shares to Beringer Blass, precipitating the takeover, he could be said to have thrown Southcorp to the wolves.

CURRENT RELEASE 2004   Despite the residual sweetness that's long been part of the style, this is a remarkably decent wine and excellent value. The colour is good and it smells appealingly of sweet, ripe plums. It's very simple and fruit-driven, finishing with just enough acid and tannin to firm and dry the aftertaste, disguising that softening sweetness. It suits hamburgers.

Rosemount Show Reserve Shiraz

Quality	🍷🍷🍷🍷
Value	★★★★
Grapes	shiraz
Region	McLaren Vale, Langhorne Creek & Currency Creek, SA
Cellar	8+
Alc./Vol.	14.5%
RRP	$27.00 ⓢ

This is still made at the McLaren Vale winery, but nowadays can include wine from other regions as well. Blending is all in the name of making the best wine possible at the price-point. It's won eight gold medals. Maker: Charles Whish.
Previous outstanding vintages: '91, '94, '95, '98, '99
CURRENT RELEASE 2001   The colour is deep cherry red and it smells of dark chocolate and vanilla. Ripe plum is the dominant flavour in the mouth. It's dense, fleshy and quite strongly tannic, finishing with a firm handshake that suggests it will age a lot longer. It's best drunk with proteinaceous food, such as chermoula-rubbed barbecued lamb fillet.

Saltram Mamre Brook Shiraz

Mamre Brook is an old Saltram name that was reserved for the winery's prestige reds in the 1960s. Lots of water has passed under the bridge since then, and now it's a more democratically priced brand of the Beringer-Blass empire. It still relies on the same Barossa vineyards.

CURRENT RELEASE 2002 Reflecting the outstanding '02 vintage, this is the best Mamre Brook for years. It's a deceptively friendly red, easy to drink and very smooth, but it has great flavour development, richness and balance. The nose has essency sweet berry aromas along with spices and balanced smoky-sweet oak. In the mouth it has lush fruit and a velvety, round texture. Flavour is ripe and generous, tannins are in laudable balance, and it lasts very long and aromatic in the mouth. Try it with beef fillet.

Quality 🍷🍷🍷🍷½
Value ★★★★
Grapes shiraz
Region Barossa Valley, SA
Cellar 🍾 10
Alc./Vol. 14.0%
RRP $24.00 [$]

CURRENT RELEASE 2003 Another generously proportioned Mamre Brook. From the very hot 2003 vintage, this is a more obvious, warm red than the excellent '02, offering earthy black-plum, glace-cherry and dark-mocha aromas of some power. Aromas of spice and clove, from oak, season it well. The palate has mouth-filling fruit that's densely constructed with a firm backbone of tannins. Its 15 per cent alcohol tends to make it a bit fumy, but lovers of big Oz reds won't mind. Enjoy it with rump steak.

Quality 🍷🍷🍷🍷
Value ★★★
Grapes shiraz
Region Barossa Valley, SA
Cellar 🍾 8
Alc./Vol. 15.0%
RRP $24.00 [$]

Saltram Metala Shiraz Cabernet

Back in the days when this was Stonyfell Metala it came in a numbered bottle. Now we notice that it does again. Our '02 was number 134 045 out of 396 000. A real collector's item!

CURRENT RELEASE 2002 An appetising, fruit-driven Langhorne Creek red of good concentration, this has aromas of mint, eucalypt, dark berries and plums. The palate is medium in body with good flavour intensity and a long aftertaste. Ripe tannins and fresh acidity keep it alive and tasty. Good with steak, chips and salad (*steak frites* for the Francophiles).

Quality 🍷🍷🍷🍷
Value ★★★½
Grapes shiraz 64%; cabernet sauvignon 36%
Region Langhorne Creek, SA
Cellar 🍾 5
Alc./Vol. 13.5%
RRP $21.00 [$]

Saltram Next Chapter Shiraz

Quality 🍷🍷🍷½
Value ★★★½
Grapes shiraz
Region Barossa Valley, SA
Cellar 🍾 3
Alc./Vol. 14.0%
RRP $16.00 [$]

Each new vintage brings a new chapter in a winery's story – 2005 brings the 146th chapter in the Saltram book.
CURRENT RELEASE 2002 A no-nonsense Barossa-based shiraz that perpetuates the Saltram tradition of bringing us reds of good character without a prohibitive price tag. It has red berries, plum and licorice aromas with a savoury hint of oak, and there's good depth of ripe flavour backed up by slightly sinewy tannins. A middle-of-the-road style that should please most people.

Saltram No.1 Barossa Shiraz

Quality 🍷🍷🍷🍷🍷
Value ★★★½
Grapes shiraz
Region Barossa Valley & Eden Valley, SA
Cellar 🍾 10+
Alc./Vol. 14.5%
RRP $66.00

The first wine produced by Saltram founder William Salter in 1862 was 1800 gallons of 'No.1 Shiraz'. Today the name is borne by this Barossa/Eden Valley classic. Maker: Nigel Dolan.
CURRENT RELEASE 2001 A very concentrated Barossa shiraz that captures syrupy blackberry fruit almost as an essence, but it stops short of being jammy or raisiny. There's sweet spice in there too, and well-handled oak adds vanillin and coconutty touches. In the mouth it's dark chocolatey-rich, full-bodied, lush and long-tasting, with ripe tannins seamlessly integrated into the fruit. Saltram's tour de force. Serve it with red wine braised oxtail.

Saltram The Eighth Maker Shiraz

Quality 🍷🍷🍷🍷🍷
Value ★★½
Grapes shiraz
Region Barossa Valley, SA
Cellar 🍾 10
Alc./Vol. 14.0%
RRP $1500 per eight bottles!

Present Saltram winemaker Nigel Dolan is the eighth winemaker at Saltram since the winery was founded in 1859. This prestigious wine, made from Saltram's choicest shiraz, celebrates them all in fine style. Ridiculously, it's intended to be sold in a numbered case of eight bottles for $1500.
CURRENT RELEASE 2001 The Eighth Maker bouquet has sweet raspberry, blackberry and plum fruit at the core, along with spicy, smoky, demiglaze, ironstone and herby elements. Twenty-four months in oak doesn't show as overt woodiness, rather it integrates everything into a silky, seamless progression across the palate. It's long in flavour and super-fine in texture, finishing with soft ripe tannins. Those who think that high-end Barossa shiraz should be all about high-octane power will be surprised by this wine; it is complex, fine and elegant. Enjoy it with roast veal.

Saracen Estates Shiraz

A new name from Margaret River but the address made us sit up and take notice. Caves Road, Wilyabrup is at the heart of one of the region's best vineyard localities.
CURRENT RELEASE 2001   This is a fruity young shiraz with jammy blackberry on the nose that's juicy and sweet, almost like fruit jubes. There's little apparent oak and the ripe palate has succulent berry fruit, good persistence and moderately grippy, ripe tannins. Try it with cotechino.

Quality	♟♟♟♟
Value	★★★
Grapes	shiraz
Region	Margaret River, WA
Cellar	▮ 3
Alc./Vol.	13.5%
RRP	$22.00

Schild Estate Barossa Shiraz

The Barossa's origins as a wine region are interwoven with the fortunes of the German immigrants who arrived in the mid-1800s. Present generations are Australian through and through, but the link remains in the surnames of so many Barossa winemaking families. Schild sounds as though it belongs perfectly, but in fact the family only arrived in the Barossa in the early 1950s.
CURRENT RELEASE 2003   A generous, well-balanced Barossa shiraz made in satisfying regional style. The nose has liqueurish dark-berry aromas with touches of vanilla and chocolate, and the palate is typically lush-textured and ripe with succulent fruit character of good depth and length. Fine, soft tannins make it a friendly proposition to drink now, but it should develop well in bottle. It would go well with roast beef.

Quality	♟♟♟♟♟
Value	★★★➔
Grapes	shiraz
Region	Barossa Valley, SA
Cellar	▮ 8
Alc./Vol.	14.5%
RRP	$24.00

Schild Estate Ben Schild Reserve Shiraz

Made to honour the memory of Johannes Hugo Bernhard (Ben) Schild who bought this Barossa estate in 1952. Although he'd spent most of his previous life farming in the Mallee, his name didn't look out of place among the old Germanic Barossa family names.
CURRENT RELEASE 2003   This is one of those tour de force Barossa reds, and like some others we actually prefer the more lowly 'standard' version of the estate shiraz. The nose is meaty, jammy and rather porty. This overripe fruit character translates into a fat, almost sweet palate that's big, powerful and warm. It finishes with soft ripe tannins and a bit of alcoholic heat.

Quality	♟♟♟♟
Value	★★★
Grapes	shiraz
Region	Barossa Valley, SA
Cellar	▮ 5+
Alc./Vol.	15.0%
RRP	$45.00

Seppelt Benno Shiraz

Quality 🍷🍷🍷🍷½
Value ★★★
Grapes shiraz
Region Bendigo, Vic.
Cellar 🍾 6
Alc./Vol. 13.5%
RRP $45.00

Benno Seppelt was the man who expanded the Seppelt enterprise well beyond its Barossa roots in the late ninetheenth and early twentieth centuries. He purchased the Seppelt Great Western vineyard from Hans Irvine in 1918.

CURRENT RELEASE 2003 The Seppelt name floundered under various Southcorp managements, but it's been rescued in recent years. Any red wine bearing the name is likely to be truly excellent and this new release of Bendigo shiraz is a worthy member of the family. It has fragrant cherry and boysenberry fruit aromas that are ripe and sweet. There are threads of spice and herbs through the nose, and a subtle touch of oak. In the mouth it's fine in flavour and texture with middling body, good acidity and grainy, slightly astringent tannins. Serve it with racks of lamb.

Seppelt Chalambar Shiraz

Quality 🍷🍷🍷🍷🍷
Value ★★★★
Grapes shiraz
Region Bendigo & Grampians, Vic.
Cellar 🍾 6
Alc./Vol. 14.0%
RRP $23.95 [$]

Chalambar had its fiftieth anniversary vintage in 2002. Over that time it's had its ups and downs, but we think the wines of today are superb value. There is never enough of it and each vintage sells out with indecent haste, so it may take a bit of searching to find. It's always worth the trouble.

CURRENT RELEASE 2003 The proportion of Bendigo fruit in this Chalambar was over 50 per cent for the first time, and it shows in a more spicy, aromatic wine than the '02. There's spicy pepper on the nose, and aromas of plums, berry fruits and a hint of eucalypt are in evidence. The palate is smooth and long in flavour with good concentration. Oak is subtle and tannins are fine. It continues to be one of the great values in Australian wine, a little behind the superb 2002, but still a bargain. Try it with venison.

Seppelt St Peters Shiraz

This Great Western shiraz is one of Australia's most illustrious red wines. It's fair value too, when you consider what people are prepared to pay for massive, nigh-on-undrinkable shirazes these days. Do yourself a favour and try it.

CURRENT RELEASE 2001   There's a gentle timelessness about this wine, and the 2001 is a welcome return to form after a slightly disappointing 2000 edition. The '01 has a subtle nose of spices, raspberries, plums and old leather. In the mouth it has lovely harmony with a velvety feel and subtly evolving, intense flavours. It's very long and fine with ripe tannins in perfect balance. Drink it with braised veal shanks.

Quality	♟♟♟♟♟
Value	★★★★
Grapes	shiraz
Region	Grampians, Vic.
Cellar	▮ 10
Alc./Vol.	14.0%
RRP	$52.00

CURRENT RELEASE 2002   A fairly traditional Great Western shiraz, this has earthy, tarry and leathery notes combining with plummy, spicy fruit on the nose. Oak is underplayed, and the palate is subtly flavoured and dry. It would be easy to overlook in a line-up of the biggest Aussie reds. Where it excels is in its lovely savoury length of flavour, supported by ripe, dry, integrated tannins. Try it with crispy roast pork.

Quality	♟♟♟♟♟
Value	★★★
Grapes	shiraz
Region	Grampians, Vic.
Cellar	▮ 12
Alc./Vol.	14.0%
RRP	$55.00

CURRENT RELEASE 2003   A more elegant Great Western shiraz than the 2002 St Peters, and quite superb. It has gently spicy, earthy, berry, plum and leather aromas that are subtle and refined. Spicy oak is woven subtly through the fruit, and the palate follows in the same vein, all restraint. It has that combination of subtlety and refinement that has always been a typical Great Western shiraz trait. Screw-capped for freshness, it's a deliciously understated wine that gets better with each sip. Cellar it for a while, then open it with osso buco.

Quality	♟♟♟♟♟
Value	★★★
Grapes	shiraz
Region	Grampians, Vic.
Cellar	▮ 10
Alc./Vol.	13.5%
RRP	$55.00 ⧤

Seppelt Victorian Shiraz

Quality	🍷🍷🍷🍷🍷
Value	★★★★★
Grapes	shiraz
Region	various, Vic.
Cellar	🍷 4
Alc./Vol.	14.0%
RRP	$17.50 Ⓢ 🥂

It seems that Seppelt can do no wrong these days, and it's strange to think that it was a brand that floundered in the Southcorp wilderness for many years. Now, the well-priced, high-quality Seppelt reds sell out with indecent haste. Be quick with this one.

CURRENT RELEASE 2003   This multi-regional Victorian blend has an immediately attractive nose that combines blackberry, plum, spice and earthy elements with some dark-chocolatey richness. It's right in the modern Seppelt mode, with stylish fruit leading the way, and oak in the back seat. The palate has lovely intensity and generous flavour with easy-drinking texture, finishing soft and right in sync. Serve it alongside Cantonese roast duck.

Serafino Shiraz

Quality	🍷🍷🍷🍷
Value	★★★
Grapes	shiraz
Region	McLaren Vale, SA
Cellar	🍷 6
Alc./Vol.	14.5%
RRP	$27.50

McLaren Vale shiraz is a mixed bag with various incarnations from the rustic/farmyardy wines tradition demands, to the clean, modern styles that capture the wider audience. Serafino fits into the latter category.

CURRENT RELEASE 2002   This is a generous type of McLaren Vale shiraz that boasts plenty of sweet fruit trimmed in a goodly measure of oak. The result is a complete wine with ripe and concentrated berry-shiraz characters, and a definite contribution from oak that gives aromas of pencil shavings and some woody flavours. The palate has excellent texture and good structure with well-integrated ripe tannins. Serve it with steak and onion pie.

Shaw and Smith Shiraz

Quality	🍷🍷🍷🍷🍷
Value	★★★★
Grapes	shiraz
Region	Adelaide Hills, SA
Cellar	1–10+
Alc./Vol.	14.0%
RRP	$38.00

PENGUIN BEST RED WINE and
BEST SHIRAZ

The second shiraz from Shaw and Smith further consolidates this new line as one of the best of the Adelaide Hills shirazes. It comes from a dry, warmish vineyard at Macclesfield that looks ideal for this variety.

CURRENT RELEASE 2003   A very fine follow-up to the excellent 2002, this has a deep, dense colour and an essency nose of blackberries, blackcurrant, aniseed, pepper and ink. Oak treatment is nicely restrained. The same intensity follows through the palate, which has ripe, piercing flavour that's long, tangy and complete. It finishes with ripe, fine-grained tannins and a soft, fragrant aftertaste. Try it with a rich duck and wild mushroom tart.

Sheep's Back Old Vine Shiraz

This wine is the result of a collaboration between Italian-based, New Zealand-born wine merchant Neil Empson and South Australian winemaker Dean Hewitson to produce a Barossa shiraz, primarily for export to the USA. Made from a 75-year-old plot of vines, it shows a lot more refinement than most reds produced for the cashed-up US market. CURRENT RELEASE 2002 Twenty-two months in French oak doesn't show here. Instead it relies on all those familiar, deliciously sumptuous Barossa shiraz elements, without entering that overblown, everything-gotta-taste-the-same territory that's the province of certain American wine gurus. The nose and palate are meaty-rich with sweetly spicy, stewed-blackberry and loamy characters on a rich, full, long-flavoured palate. The essence of what the Barossa should be, honest and rewarding. Serve it with steak and kidney pie.

Quality	♟ ♟ ♟ ♟ ♟
Value	★ ★ ★ ⸢
Grapes	shiraz
Region	Barossa Valley, SA
Cellar	▮ 8
Alc./Vol.	14.0%
RRP	$39.75

Shingleback Shiraz

Shingleback vineyard takes its name from the shingleback lizards found in the vineyard. They are known in other parts of the country as stumpy tails. Maker: John Davey. CURRENT RELEASE 2002 This seductive shiraz smells sweet and ripe, but not at all overblown or jammy. The nose has aromas of berries, spices, citrus peel and mocha – mellow and complex. It tastes finer than most McLaren Vale reds with long spicy flavour, good depth and soft tannins combining to make it very agreeable indeed. Serve it with minute steak.

Quality	♟ ♟ ♟ ♟
Value	★ ★ ★
Grapes	shiraz
Region	McLaren Vale, SA
Cellar	▮ 4+
Alc./Vol.	14.5%
RRP	$27.50

Shottesbrooke Shiraz

The Shottesbrooke wines of Nick Holmes are an altogether quieter type of McLaren Vale red, made to be drunk rather than marvelled at and put away. CURRENT RELEASE 2003 This young shiraz has a hint of peppery spice on the nose, and aromas of blackberries and raspberry sherbet add succulent appeal. There's also a touch of licorice and very controlled, subtle oak input. In the mouth it's medium-bodied and rather loose-knit in structure, finishing with very soft tannins. A friendly drink-now style to sip with friends while eating in the great outdoors.

Quality	♟ ♟ ♟ ♟
Value	★ ★ ★ ⸢
Grapes	shiraz
Region	McLaren Vale, SA
Cellar	▮ 4
Alc./Vol.	14.0%
RRP	$18.85

Simon Gilbert Central Ranges Shiraz

Quality 🍷🍷🍷🍷
Value ★★★★½
Grapes shiraz
Region Central Ranges, NSW
Cellar 🍾 3+
Alc./Vol. 14.0%
RRP $15.00 [$]

Central Ranges indicates the grapes came from Cowra, Mudgee or Orange – or a combination of those regions. Simon Gilbert is a public company that had a shake-up in mid-2004: three highly experienced former Southcorp men (Bruce Kemp, David Combe and Paul Pacino) were put into key positions. The new crop of wines are excellent value quaffers.

CURRENT RELEASE 2003 This is a plummy, lightly spiced, soft, nicely balanced red with a degree of elegance and excellent drinkability. It's light- to medium-bodied and the finish carries light, fine tannins so it slips down easily. It's well suited to bangers and mash.

Spinifex Indigene

Quality 🍷🍷🍷🍷🍷
Value ★★★½
Grapes shiraz 55%; mourvèdre 45%
Region Barossa Valley, SA
Cellar 🍾 1–6
Alc./Vol. 15.0%
RRP $44.00

The maker of the Spinifex wines, Peter Schell, has experience winemaking in France, and it shows in his attitude. He speaks of making wines that 'display signatures of vineyard provenance and vintage' and 'show regional typicity'. It's in line with the French concept of *terroir*, the sense of place and identity in a wine.

CURRENT RELEASE 2003 Made from old-vine shiraz and mataro (mourvèdre), this is an excellent example of the genre. The nose has syrupy dark-berry fruit aromas and earthy notes, with hints of spices and minerals, lightly dusted with oak. In the mouth there's lip-smacking flavour of rich concentration and lovely depth. It lasts long and finishes with ripe, fine tannins. An authentic regional red of handsome proportions. Try it with braised veal shank.

St Hallett Blackwell Shiraz

Quality 🍷🍷🍷🍷½
Value ★★★½
Grapes shiraz
Region Barossa Valley, SA
Cellar 🍾 2–8+
Alc./Vol. 14.5%
RRP $31.50

Winemaker Stuart Blackwell has had a lot to do with the re-emergence of the St Hallett brand, largely due to his skill with Barossa shirazes like this one. It's in the unashamedly full-throttle American-oaked type.

CURRENT RELEASE 2003 The nose has strong coconut and spice aromas with dark berries and chocolatey touches. It smells very smooth and complete, if somewhat oak-driven. In the mouth it's velvety and generously proportioned with mouth-filling, strongly vanillin-oaked Barossa shiraz flavour. Balance is excellent for such a young thing, and while it's very ripe, savoury tannins finish it off with a tasty bite. Try it with steak and kidney pie.

St Hallett Faith Shiraz

Faith is a step down the St Hallett ladder from Blackwell, a shiraz of less pronounced oakiness, and less impact. It boasts lovely drinkability though, and is very appealing in youth.
CURRENT RELEASE 2003   This has pure blackberry-like Barossa shiraz fruit on the nose, plus aromas of clay and chocolate and spice. It's a friendly, quietly interesting drop of medium body and sweet spice and juicy berry flavours. It has a seamless texture and is well balanced by soft tannins. A good match for a north Chinese-style beef hotpot.

Quality	♟♟♟♟♟
Value	★★★★
Grapes	shiraz
Region	Barossa Valley, SA
Cellar	5
Alc./Vol.	14.5%
RRP	$21.50

Stanton & Killeen Shiraz Durif

Stanton and Killeen have consistently made some of Rutherglen's best reds. They often have a touch of finesse that isn't common in the more traditional reds of the region.
CURRENT RELEASE 2003   A brilliant ruby-coloured young wine with an intense nose of spices, earth, dark berries and cedar. There's a slightly jammy, almost porty, regional touch to it, but it doesn't detract from this wine's satisfying make-up. The palate has good body and concentration of satisfying flavour with attractive grainy tannins behind it. Serve it with cotechino and lentils.

Quality	♟♟♟♟♟
Value	★★★★
Grapes	shiraz 66%; durif 34%
Region	Rutherglen, Vic.
Cellar	2–7
Alc./Vol.	13.5%
RRP	$22.00

Stella Bella Shiraz

The Stella Bella wines have a wonderfully eccentric feel to them, as do their Suckfizzle stablemates. Some use grape varieties and methods that are well outside the Margaret River mainstream, others are more traditional. Their quality is invariably good.
CURRENT RELEASE 2003   Margaret River shiraz isn't often spoken of in the same superlatives as the region's cabernet, but the best are superb wines, and they usually drink better as youngsters. This is a case in point, lovely young shiraz with an incredibly fragrant nose of raspberries, cherries, licorice, spices and old leather. The complex aromas lead seductively to a silky palate of long fine flavour that ends in agreeably soft tannins. Try it with coq au vin.

Quality	♟♟♟♟♟
Value	★★★★
Grapes	shiraz
Region	Margaret River, WA
Cellar	4
Alc./Vol.	14.0%
RRP	$26.00

Stonemason Shiraz

Quality 🍷🍷🍷½
Value ★★★★
Grapes shiraz
Region Fleurieu, SA
Cellar 1–4
Alc./Vol. 13.5%
RRP $15.00 $

Stonemason is a volume-priced brand from newcomers Ballast Stone Wines, owned by the Shaw Group. The Shaw Group is among South Australia's largest grape growers with a vast vineyard at Currency Creek and a smaller one at McLaren Vale, supplying other wine producers with grapes. Only lately have they started marketing wines of their own.

CURRENT RELEASE 2003 A wholesome young red with aromas of fruitcake, mulberries, earth and a little touch of vanillin oak. The palate is medium-bodied and smooth-tasting, but an extractive bit of hardness detracts slightly. As a result it finishes rather firmly, but it softens with food. It will be better in a year or so. A good-value red with surprising personality in a market slot where ho-hum wines abound. Enjoy it with hearty homemade lasagne.

Summerfield Reserve Shiraz

Quality 🍷🍷🍷🍷½
Value ★★★
Grapes shiraz
Region Pyrenees, Vic.
Cellar 2–10
Alc./Vol. 15.0%
RRP $50.00 🍷

Summerfield's specialities are strong regional Pyrenees reds like this. In recent years they've tended to be bigger and more alcoholic, but without any diminution in quality.

CURRENT RELEASE 2003 The deepest of purple colours introduces this formidable red as expected. The nose is rich and full with aromas of plum, loganberry, bitter chocolate, spices and herbs. A veneer of sweet oak seasons it without taking over. In the mouth it's ripe and full-bodied with black-cherry, plum and dark-chocolate flavours that last long and powerful, finishing with well-modulated dry tannins. A wine for heroes. Try it with roast rib of beef.

Tahbilk Reserve Shiraz

Quality 🍷🍷🍷🍷🍷
Value ★★★½
Grapes shiraz
Region Nagambie Lakes, Vic.
Cellar 🍾 14+
Alc./Vol. 14.0%
RRP $70.00 🍷

Tahbilk has a terrific heritage of old vines as well as famous National Trust classified buildings. The vines that produced this wine are old: the three blocks were planted in 1927, '33 and '36. The Tahbilk style is the antithesis of a 'show pony', but this one still managed a gold medal at Royal Melbourne.

CURRENT RELEASE 1999 A really lovely, mellow, aged wine, this may be a touch forward in development but it's very complex and stylish. Complex aged berry and meat-stock aromas also have touches of mint, tomato-leaf and crushed vine-leaf. The tannins are fine-grained and subtle. It comes out of its shell with breathing, and goes well with Cantonese roast duck.

Taltarni Heathcote Shiraz

Heathcote is emerging as yet another great region for Australian shiraz; indeed, the indications are that it could eventually be one of the very best. There is a happy combination of climate and soils that really suits shiraz. CURRENT RELEASE 2003 A new label for Taltarni, and an excellent debut wine. It has a deep purple–red colour, ripe plummy, blackberry fruit on both nose and palate well integrated with toasty, coconutty oak. It has serious depth of flavour in the mouth and a good backbone of tannin. All in all, it's a stand-out shiraz. It suits hard cheeses, such as reblochon.

Quality	🍷🍷🍷🍷🍷
Value	★★★⁺
Grapes	shiraz
Region	Heathcote, Vic.
Cellar	▬1–12+
Alc./Vol.	14.5%
RRP	$42.20

Three Brothers Reunion Shiraz

This is the cheapest wine in a range produced by Ben Riggs for Journeys End Vineyards. The price can drift as low as $10 on special. We think the '03 Reunion – like the previous vintage – offers extraordinary value for money. CURRENT RELEASE 2003 Fairly straightforward but ripe and ample aromas of plum pits, dried herbs and poached plums. The palate has some extractive astringency and alcohol heat, but the volume of flavour and richness more than compensates. The palate flavours suggest plum juice and blackberry jam. More guts than class, it's a real crowd-pleaser and would go well with grilled T-bone steak.

Quality	🍷🍷🍷🍷
Value	★★★★★
Grapes	shiraz
Region	not stated
Cellar	4+
Alc./Vol.	14.5%
RRP	$15.00 Ⓢ

Three Hills Shiraz

The Three Hills vineyard was established at Karridale in the southern part of Margaret River by Erl Happ of Happs at Dunsborough. He grows a wide range of grape varieties there. Winemaker is Mark Warren.
CURRENT RELEASE 2002 There are plenty of mint and eucalyptus aromas here, reminding us that '02 was a cool summer. There's also a lot of cool-grown spice plus a hint of camphor. The palate is medium-bodied, a trifle lean and lacking the fleshy richness we usually see in Margaret River reds. It's lively and intense with a suggestion of some underripe grapes. It drinks well with a gourmet hamburger with the lot.

Quality	🍷🍷🍷🍷
Value	★★⁺
Grapes	shiraz
Region	Margaret River, WA
Cellar	6+
Alc./Vol.	14.1%
RRP	$55.00
	(cellar door)

Tibooburra Yarra Valley Shiraz

Quality 🍷🍷🍷🍷
Value ★★★½
Grapes shiraz
Region Yarra Valley, Vic.
Cellar 🍾 4+
Alc./Vol. 14.5%
RRP $24.00 (cellar door)

Tibooburra is a little town in outback New South Wales, which has scant relevance to the Yarra Valley, we would have thought. The vineyard is located in the Seville area, one of the cooler parts of the valley. The makers claim the shiraz yielded just 1.3 tonnes to the acre, which is low.

CURRENT RELEASE 2003 There's a charry oak smokiness to the bouquet and it's a bit more complex than just simple fruit. The palate is elegant, with some attractive fruit sweetness, soft tannins and easy-drinking balance. There's a good deal of cool-climate style, but also properly ripe fruit, here. It drinks well with grilled ham steaks.

Tisdall Shiraz

Quality 🍷🍷🍷½
Value ★★★★
Grapes shiraz
Region central Vic.
Cellar 🍾 5
Alc./Vol. 14.5%
RRP $15.50 [$]

The Tisdall wines are based on the Rosbercon vineyard near Echuca in northern Victoria. The brand and vineyard were both established back in the early '80s by Dr Peter Tisdall, who sold out many years ago. Winemaker is the peripatetic Don Buchanan.

CURRENT RELEASE 2003 This is a straightforward but tasty red, well endowed with chocolate, vanilla and berry-jam flavours. It's very youthful and a touch raw, but the texture is soft and supple, possibly aided by a trace of sweetness, or it could be just the glycerol from high alcohol. It's medium- to full-bodied and drops slightly short at the finish. It would suit lamb chops.

Torbreck Descendant

Quality 🍷🍷🍷🍷
Value ★★
Grapes shiraz; viognier
Region Barossa Valley, SA
Cellar 🍾 5+
Alc./Vol. 14.5%
RRP $145.00 🍶

Descendant is made from a new vineyard, planted from cuttings taken from old vineyards that supply fruit for Runrig. It's also a shiraz-viognier, made in the image of Runrig. Hence the name Descendant.

CURRENT RELEASE 2003 A big, viscous, rich red that is more about guts than finesse. Dark-chocolate and vanillin-oak, spicy, plum-jam, raisin/prune fruit flavours with a decidedly cooked style. It's a big mouthful of flavour and bears a close resemblance to vintage port. It finishes with grainy tannins and the fruit character is very much in the shrivelled berry genre. It should go with aged parmesan.

Torbreck Runrig

This wine has established itself very quickly, in less than a decade, as a modern Australian cult wine, with a jaw-dropping price. But the authors are mystified at its appeal: it's not the sort of wine we enjoy, let alone at the price. CURRENT RELEASE 2002 The customary porty, raisiny, shrivelled-fruit aromas are there, coupled with lots of oak and a certain sweaty/meaty pong. It's a slightly lighter style, as you might expect in a cool year, but the palate is curiously deficient in depth. It lacks freshness and vibrancy – but that's the style its devotees apparently like. It does seem to lack the usual Runrig decadent richness. Try it with aged cheddar.

Quality	▼ ▼ ▼ ▼
Value	✶ ⟩
Grapes	shiraz; viognier
Region	Barossa Valley, SA
Cellar	▌5+
Alc./Vol.	14.5%
RRP	$299.00 ▮

Two Hands Angel's Share Shiraz

The angel's share (*le part des anges*) is the nickname given by France's Cognac producers to the shockingly large proportion of spirit that evaporates from the barrels during long-term oak maturation. A similar phenomenon applies to wine. Maker: Matt Wenk.
CURRENT RELEASE 2004 This is a baby, a touch raw and unformed at this stage but with lots of guts and promising to soften into a better wine with time. It's a dark purple–red hue and the aromas are of raw plum and coconut/vanilla American oak that sits slightly apart from the wine. The palate is sharp and raw, while it has good weight of fruit and flavour. Plenty of impact! Serve it with rare venison.

Quality	▼ ▼ ▼ ▼
Value	✶ ✶ ✶ ⟩
Grapes	shiraz
Region	McLaren Vale, SA
Cellar	⬤–2–6+
Alc./Vol.	14.5%
RRP	$25.00 ▨

Viking Wines Grand Shiraz Cabernet

Viking is yet another new name from the Barossa Valley, whose long established 9-hectare vineyard is at Marananga. As the name hints, it was set up by someone with Nordic connections: Thord Söderström. The wines are contract-made by Rolf Binder and Kym Teusner at Veritas; 500 cases of this were made.
CURRENT RELEASE 2004 We can see why Robert Parker likes Viking: it's a big, densely coloured and flavoured red with lots of oak and tannin, but is slightly on the porty side. The nose is big on dark chocolate and licorice, and reflects liberal contact with oak. The palate is tannic and somewhat aggressive, with high alcohol and some overripe characters. It needs age – or rare meat. Try a juicy rump steak.

Quality	▼ ▼ ▼ ▼
Value	✶ ✶ ✶
Grapes	shiraz; cabernet sauvignon
Region	Barossa Valley, SA
Cellar	⬤–2–10+
Alc./Vol.	14.5%
RRP	$40.00 ▮

Water Wheel Shiraz

Quality	♟ ♟ ♟ ♟
Value	★★★★
Grapes	shiraz
Region	Bendigo, Vic.
Cellar	♦ 5+
Alc./Vol.	15.5%
RRP	$22.00

Peter Cumming has always done the right thing by his customers, keeping the prices of his good Bendigo region reds very fair. The '03 is one of the biggest so far.
CURRENT RELEASE 2003   This has a dense, deep colour and a concentrated nose of raisiny blackberry with an almost floral, spirity angle to it. We thought the last vintage smelt of rum-and-raisin chocolate and this does a bit too. It is fruit/alcohol-sweet and very ripe, with a hint of dry tobacco adding a savoury element. The big, rich muscular palate is beefy and macho – wine for heroes! A potent Bendigo red wine to enjoy with a rare rump steak.

Whistling Eagle Eagles Blood Shiraz

Quality	♟ ♟ ♟ ♟ ♟
Value	★★★
Grapes	shiraz
Region	Heathcote, Vic.
Cellar	⊶ 2–8+
Alc./Vol.	15.5%
RRP	$46.95

Heathcote is prime shiraz country that even gets South Australian winemakers talking about its quality. The 500-million-year-old Cambrian soils in this Victorian region endow shiraz with great depth and richness.
CURRENT RELEASE 2003   Great name for an impressive young wine. It has a dense purplish colour and a ripe, alcoholic nose of jammy blackberry, aromatic spices, licorice and mocha. The full-bodied palate has velvety texture and ripe flavour of great presence and length. Alcoholic warmth and sweetness play a part, but the wine has the fruit substance to carry it, and soft ripe tannins pull everything into place. It's a red with a big 'wow' factor, but for these carping authors it would be easier to drink with a little less strength. Try it with braised oxtail.

Willandra Estate Leeton Selection Shiraz

Quality	♟ ♟ ♟ ♟
Value	★★★★★
Grapes	shiraz
Region	Riverina, NSW
Cellar	♦ 2
Alc./Vol.	14.0%
RRP	$8.00

The inexpensive Willandra Estate wines are sealed with those agglomerate corks with a disc of cork at either end, and several of our samples were tainted. We find agglomerate corks, with or without discs on their ends, are more prone to taint than one-piece corks.
CURRENT RELEASE 2004   This is a remarkably flavoursome shiraz at a very modest price. The colour is medium–deep purple–red and it smells sweetly ripe, with plummy aromas uppermost but also a hint of sweaty reductive character that won't bother $8-wine-drinkers at all. The palate has good depth and balance, with mild tannins to finish. A bargain. Serve it with meaty lasagne.

Wirra Wirra RSW Shiraz

These days Wirra Wirra's RSW follows the trend for wines of great significance to be sold in very heavy, toe-breaking bottles. Our advice is to be very careful not to drop one on your delicate little feet.
CURRENT RELEASE 2003 A solidly constructed customer, impenetrable in colour, this young shiraz smells of boiled-down dark fruits, vineyard soil, black chocolate, cedar and spice. In the mouth it's rich, firm, very long and powerful. A complex and impressively concentrated wine with a future. One of McLaren Vale's undoubted flagship red wines. Absolutely perfect with a sticky dish of slow-braised oxtail.

Quality 🍷🍷🍷🍷🍷
Value ★★★★
Grapes shiraz
Region McLaren Vale, SA
Cellar 🍾→2–12
Alc./Vol. 14.5%
RRP $48.00

Wirra Wirra Scrubby Rise

Wirra Wirra embraced the use of screw-caps on its wines with enthusiasm, but a few early wines were a little marred by a slight sulphide pong, possibly exacerbated by anaerobic conditions in the bottle. It might also have had a bit to do with earthy McLaren Vale regional character. The problem, common enough in European wines sealed with corks, worries some and not others, but it's under control, judging by the '02 Scrubby Rise.
CURRENT RELEASE 2002 On the nose there's a good measure of blackberry and a touch of McLaren Vale barnyard, dressed in smoky oak. In the mouth it has impressive palate weight, and quite firm, dry tannins. A solidly built regional red at a reasonable price that works well with a mixed grill.

Quality 🍷🍷🍷½
Value ★★★½
Grapes shiraz; cabernet sauvignon; petit verdot
Region McLaren Vale, SA
Cellar 🍾 3
Alc./Vol. 14.5%
RRP $17.00 [$] 🌀

Wirra Wirra Woodhenge Shiraz

What is 'Woodhenge?' Allow us to quote the label: 'To say Woodhenge, which greets visitors to Wirra Wirra, is a plain post-and-rail fence, is akin to saying Stonehenge is little more than a pile of rubble.' Wirra Wirra is a quirky place, largely due to its recently departed founder Greg Trott.
CURRENT RELEASE 2003 This McLaren Vale shiraz is a warts-and-all type with good concentration on the nose and some rather rustic meaty and slightly feral aromas, as well as spice and fruitcakey richness. It's very much a fruit-dominant red and has good mid-palate texture and some dry tannins backing it up. Its wildness may confront some drinkers, but those who like a bit of 'country' in their reds will love it. Try it with steak and kidney pie.

Quality 🍷🍷🍷🍷½
Value ★★★★
Grapes shiraz
Region McLaren Vale, SA
Cellar 🍾 2
Alc./Vol. 14.5%
RRP $29.00

Wolf Blass Gold Label Shiraz

Quality 🍷🍷🍷🍷
Value ★★★
Grapes shiraz
Region Barossa Valley, SA
Cellar 🍾8
Alc./Vol. 15.0%
RRP $23.00 [$] 🌀

The '03 Barossa reds often have a surfeit of alcohol, a legacy of a very hot vintage. This Gold Label Shiraz tips the scales at 15 per cent, but it doesn't quite show the fumy, soupy characters of some. Tread gently with it though.

CURRENT RELEASE 2003 The nose is sweet and ripe with a balanced interplay between strong dark fruits, a hint of portiness, well-measured oak and spicy notes. In the mouth it's full of flavour with heavy extract and chewy texture. Tannins are grainy and dry, giving some firmness to the palate. Reflecting the vintage, this is a big, warm Barossa red of good character. Try it with a northern Chinese-style lamb claypot dish.

Wolf Blass Gold Label Shiraz Viognier

Quality 🍷🍷🍷🍷½
Value ★★★★★
Grapes shiraz; viognier
Region Adelaide Hills, SA
Cellar 🍾3
Alc./Vol. 14.5%
RRP $22.00 [$] 🌀

The Wolf Blass Gold Label wines punch well above their weight in almost every category. They are symbolic of the contemporary, quality-driven approach that's taken hold of the Beringer-Blass empire in recent years.

CURRENT RELEASE 2003 Only a few short years ago it would have been unthinkable for a wine like this to wear a Wolf Blass label. It has a delicious, aromatic lushness that's very seductive, and lifts it well above its price tag. The nose has fruits-of-the-forest aromas, touches of sweet spice, violets and soft, subtle oak. In the mouth it has plump-fruit flavour, silky texture, and a long finish rides on soft, ripe tannins. Super value. Great with veal and ham pie.

Wolf Blass Grey Label Shiraz

Quality 🍷🍷🍷🍷
Value ★★★
Grapes shiraz
Region McLaren Vale, SA
Cellar 🍾6+
Alc./Vol. 15.0%
RRP $40.00

The Grey Label wines are the third tier of premium Wolf Blass wines. Until the last vintage or two the Grey and Black tended to look a bit old-fashioned compared to the Platinum, but the style is gradually changing to a more modern fruit-driven type.

CURRENT RELEASE 2003 This is a big, ripe, warm McLaren Vale shiraz that's full of blackberry jam, prune and spicy-varietal-fruit characters, with subtlety very much on hold. Oak is there, but it's not as overwhelming as it used to be. The palate is smooth and very concentrated, with jammy, chocolatey richness, alcoholic heat, and well-balanced, soft, ripe tannins. Drink it with steak and a reduced red-wine meat glaze.

Wolf Blass Platinum Label Shiraz

Platinum Label is the best Wolf Blass red wine by a country mile, and the excellent 2002 vintage has produced the finest example yet. Like the last edition, and unlike most other top-end reds, it's sealed with a screw-cap which we think is a big plus.

CURRENT RELEASE 2002   Deep in colour, this has a gorgeously ripe, fruitcake nose that's touched by sweet and savoury spices, and perfectly balanced mocha touches from high-quality oak. In the mouth it's lush and velvety; seamless complex flavours that end long and fragrant are supported by balanced fine-grained tannins. A lovely red that drinks extraordinarily well now, but we suspect that it has many years ahead of it. Enjoy it with venison.

Quality	🍷🍷🍷🍷🍷
Value	★★★
Grapes	shiraz
Region	Eden Valley & Barossa Valley, SA
Cellar	🍾 10
Alc./Vol.	14.0%
RRP	$180.00 🥂

Wood Park Kneebones Gap Shiraz

John Stokes originally sold much of the crop from his King Valley vineyard, but recent years have seen him developing a very good range of wines. His winemaking shows a skilled and assured hand, and his environmental credentials (he's an environmental scientist) have sent him well along the road of sustainability.

CURRENT RELEASE 2004   In the first flush of youth, this is a very minty, tangy wine with youthful aromas reminiscent of glacé cherries, chocolate and spice. The medium-bodied palate has good fleshy texture and a harmonious signature of soft tannins. Although the palate is agreeable now, it could do with some bottle-age, so keep your hands off it for a while, it should develop well short- to mid-term. Serve it with Arab-inspired lamb pastries.

Quality	🍷🍷🍷🍷🍷
Value	★★★★
Grapes	shiraz
Region	King Valley, Vic.
Cellar	🍾 5
Alc./Vol.	14.0%
RRP	$23.00

Wynns J Block Shiraz Cabernet

The J Block is a single vineyard in the heart of Coonawarra, part of the original parcel bought by Wynns in 1951. There are some 1920s vines in the plot, and back in the 1950s it had one of the largest cabernet plantings in Australia.

CURRENT RELEASE 2003   A more traditional Coonawarra style, somewhat removed from the bigger-is-better type that's been popular with some makers in recent years. The nose has spicy, peppery aromas of currants, small red and black berries, and cedar. The palate is tightly structured with good depth of flavour and attractively chewy texture, finishing long with ripe tannins. Serve it with minute steak.

Quality	🍷🍷🍷🍷🍷
Value	★★★★
Grapes	shiraz; cabernet sauvignon
Region	Coonawarra, SA
Cellar	➤ 1–10
Alc./Vol.	14.0%
RRP	$40.00

Wynns Shiraz

Quality 🍷🍷🍷🍷
Value ★★★½
Grapes shiraz
Region Coonawarra, SA
Cellar 3
Alc./Vol. 13.5%
RRP $19.50 (S)

This is one of the most recognisable labels in Australian wine, originally designed in the 1950s. As usual it's been tinkered with a little over the years (brand managers and marketing gurus have to make their mark don't they?) but essentially the clean, almost architectural draughtsmanship remains the same. Maker: Sue Hodder.

CURRENT RELEASE 2003 The nose has some peppery aromas with raspberry and plum-like fruit. It has an austerity that the best vintages don't have, making it a drier, less giving wine, but there's good intensity and medium body. The rather astringent finish is more angular than usual. A more savoury type of Wynns Shiraz. Great with pizza.

Yering Station Reserve Shiraz Viognier

Quality 🍷🍷🍷🍷🍷
Value ★★★
Grapes shiraz
Region Yarra Valley, Vic.
Cellar 5
Alc./Vol. 15.0%
RRP $58.00

One of Australia's best shiraz-viognier blends comes from this estimable enterprise in the Yarra Valley. Our advice is to have it with lunch at Yering Station's excellent restaurant, while looking out at the lovely pastoral landscape of the Yarra Valley.

CURRENT RELEASE 2003 More forceful than the '02 Shiraz Viognier, but still a lovely wine, this has a nose of chocolatey liqueur cherries and exotic floral/spicy notes. Cedary oak dresses it elegantly and the palate has silky-smooth texture and real elegance, despite 15 per cent alcohol. It's warm, harmonious and persistent on the palate with a touch of light astringency to give it structure. A great companion to beef fillet.

Yering Station Shiraz Viognier

Quality 🍷🍷🍷🍷
Value ★★★
Grapes shiraz; viognier
Region Yarra Valley, Vic.
Cellar 3
Alc./Vol. 14.0%
RRP $23.00

Viogner is jumping into bed with shiraz in wineries all over Australia. It's a trend that comes from the Rhône Valley's northern end, where interestingly some of the best syrah (shiraz)-based wines deliberately don't have this white grape blended in. Some of the Australian versions are very good indeed.

CURRENT RELEASE 2003 Viognier's fragrant contribution is immediately apparent on the nose here, giving a hint of apricot and musky spice to juicy berry aromas. In the mouth it's silky and mellow, not heavy, but well concentrated with light tannin astringency at the end. Very pleasant drinking with pork pie.

Other Reds and Blends

In the earliest days of Australian wine, growers often planted an enormous variety of grapes in their vineyards. After a while most of them learnt what went well, produced the best crops and made the best-quality wine. Slowly but surely the wide range of grape varieties used in Australia dwindled as growers increasingly played it safe with the most versatile types, and so it continued for the first three-quarters of the twentieth century. Then the wine boom arrived and experimentation became the order of the day. Thus gamay, petit verdot, nebbiolo, tempranillo and a score of other red grapes appeared in vineyards alongside shiraz, plus new blends of different varieties both familiar and arcane arrived – and an exciting new era dawned for Aussie wine consumers.

Bidgeebong Tempranillo

Tumbarumba may at first glance seem a little too cool a climate for tempranillo, the Spanish workhorse red variety. However, there are some quite cool parts of Navarra in the north of Spain that grow very good tempranillo. Maker: Andrew Birks.

CURRENT RELEASE 2003   Cherry is the dominant aroma in this fruit-driven style of tempranillo. There are some smoky, toasted oak aromas, too, and a twinge of volatility adding a balsamic-like note. The tannin/acid combination on the palate gives it a very firm finish, but the fruit is quite intense and the whole thing stays in good balance. A tidy, elegant red wine. It suits Wiener schnitzel.

Quality	♀♀♀♀
Value	★★★
Grapes	tempranillo
Region	Tumbarumba, NSW
Cellar	▮ 4+
Alc./Vol.	12.5%
RRP	$24.00

Brown Brothers Cellar Door Release Heathcote Durif

Brown Brothers has a large vineyard at Heathcote from which it is sourcing increasing quantities of red fruit in preference to the upper King Valley, which tends to be better suited to white and sparkling wines. Makers: Terry Barnett and Wendy Cameron.

CURRENT RELEASE 2003   You need to like monster reds! This is a whopper, in traditional durif style. The colour is very dense and purple, the aromas are inky and plum-essency. It's a concentrated, high-alcohol wine with some pruney, overripe fruit flavours, loads of tannin and guts. A robust but unsubtle red that lots of people will love. Cellar, then serve with rare steak and chips.

Quality	♀♀♀♀♀
Value	★★★★★
Grapes	durif
Region	Heathcote, Vic.
Cellar	▬ 2–12+
Alc./Vol.	14.5%
RRP	$18.90 ▮
	(cellar door)

Cape Mentelle Zinfandel

Quality	▲▲▲▲▼
Value	★★★
Grapes	zinfandel (or primitivo)
Region	Margaret River, WA
Cellar	▮ 10
Alc./Vol.	16.3%
RRP	$47.00

Australia's best-known zinfandel is a whopping, take-no-prisoners type of red, guaranteed to warm cockles of hearts, lower inhibitions and bring a glow to every cheek. Beware! CURRENT RELEASE 2003   This '03 is really too formidable to judge by normal red wine parameters. It's a big monster that smells of raisins, spices, sweet oak and herbs. The palate is jammy, warm, tannic and dry finishing. Despite the weight and alcohol there's a mystifying thread of green-herb character through it, suggesting that while some of the fruit was super-ripe, some was less so. If you like red wine that's an assault on the senses, this is it. It will probably score 100/100 with the American wine commentators, but can you drink more than a single glass? Probably not, but that's up to you. Try it with a brontosaurus burger.

Chrismont La Zona Marzemino

Quality	▲▲▲▲
Value	★★★
Grapes	marzemino
Region	King Valley, Vic.
Cellar	▮ 3
Alc./Vol.	13.5%
RRP	$23.00

Arnie Pizzini, proprietor of Chrismont, pioneered Italian grape varieties in Victoria's King Valley in 1984 when he planted barbera. Marzemino is a more recent addition to his range. This little-known red-grape variety originates in Italy's north-east. CURRENT RELEASE 2002   This has good depth of colour and a pleasant fragrance reminiscent of violets, tar and succulent currants and berries. It smells appetising and full of interest, and it tastes good too. In the mouth it's medium in body, but with a certain lightness of flavour. It's savoury rather than fruit-sweet, and it finishes with the gentle dryness of fine tannins. Try it with veal scallopine.

Cullen Mangan

Quality	▲▲▲▲
Value	★★★
Grapes	malbec 60%; petit verdot 40%
Region	Margaret River, WA
Cellar	▮ 4
Alc./Vol.	14.5%
RRP	$45.00 ▤

Cullen Mangan is at odds with the elegant cabernet blends from this premier Margaret River vineyard. It's a robust red. CURRENT RELEASE 2004   Mangan always has a striking, dense purplish colour, and the nose is very solid, miles away from the elegant, refined Cullen way with cabernet. The nose has minerally earth smells with a meaty touch and concentrated blackberry pastille at the core. In the mouth it's rich and dense in texture with hearty flavour and fine, soft tannins backing it up. Serve it with goulash.

Joseph Nebbiolo

The grapes came from Joe and Dina Grilli's one hectare of dry-grown vines in their Angel Gully vineyard above Clarendon. The label is so dark you can barely read the small black type, even in full sunlight. Not sure how you'd get on in a darkened restaurant! Maker: Joe Grilli.

CURRENT RELEASE 2002 Don't be put off by the tired-looking brick-red colour! That's the nature of nebbiolo. The wine is surprisingly good. It has earthy, herbal, mellowing aromas tinged with peppermint. The taste is savoury and mellowing. Developed savoury flavours of meat stock, dried herbs and soft-berry fruit, coupled with very drying tannins, mean it needs to be drunk with food. Try osso buco.

Quality	🍷🍷🍷🍷½
Value	★★★
Grapes	nebbiolo
Region	Adelaide Hills, SA
Cellar	🍾 3
Alc./Vol.	13.5%
RRP	$55.00 ⚱

Kingston Estate Empiric Durif

The Empiric name comes from the Greek 'to experiment' and Kingston Estate's Empiric range does just that, employing less well-known grape varieties that are uncommon in the Riverland. Maker: Bill Moularadellis.

CURRENT RELEASE 2002 This is a real tooth-stainer with impenetrable colour and a strong nose reminiscent of blackberry syrup, roasted spices and vanilla. It has a big warm palate that's solidly structured with plenty of tannic grip. A robust durif that shows the potential of the variety in the Murray Valley. Try it with braised oxtail.

Quality	🍷🍷🍷🍷
Value	★★★★
Grapes	durif
Region	Murray Valley, SA
Cellar	🍾 4+
Alc./Vol.	14.0%
RRP	$17.85 [$]

Morris Durif

Morris makes one of the grand-daddies of durifs. It's been enjoying a renaissance in popularity in recent years, and this hitherto obscure grape has found a new audience. The style is a little more modern than it once was, but there's still an old-worldy feel to it.

CURRENT RELEASE 2002 There's real rustic charm here, and a sort of timelessness. Despite a whisper more of oak influence than custom might dictate, this is probably the sort of flavoursome red wine our grandfathers might have sipped, if they ever sipped red wine of course! It smells and tastes of syrupy dark berries, spiced raisins and dark chocolate, with good palate lushness, weight and impact. Firm tannins follow along in power mode. Rutherglen red at its (almost) traditional best. Good with BBQ rump steak.

Quality	🍷🍷🍷🍷½
Value	★★★½
Grapes	durif
Region	Rutherglen, Vic.
Cellar	🍾 10
Alc./Vol.	14.0%
RRP	$25.00

Roundstone Gamay

Quality	♥♥♥♥
Value	★★★★
Grapes	gamay
Region	Yarra Valley, Vic.
Cellar	🍾 2+
Alc./Vol.	13.1%
RRP	$21.00 ⊗

There should be more high-quality light-bodied reds of this style. Our winemakers seem obsessed with making humungous reds in an effort to achieve fame and high scores from certain American critics. In doing this, they neglect the vast mass of people who just want a good wine that they can drink.
CURRENT RELEASE 2004   It's rare to find an Australian gamay, and this is a very good one. Like a light beaujolais, it has heaps of uncomplicated strawberry fruit and finishes with savoury flavours and just enough soft tannin to give it some authority. It's got stacks of charm and drinkability. It would suit steak tartare.

Vinifera Wines Tempranillo

Quality	♥♥♥♥
Value	★★★★
Grapes	tempranillo
Region	Mudgee, NSW
Cellar	🍾 3
Alc./Vol.	12.9%
RRP	$23.00

Vitis vinifera is the species of European grapevine used to make most of the wines we drink. There are many other species of the genus *Vitis*, some of which make pretty dreadful wine. Tempranillo, like shiraz and cabernet, is a cultivar of *Vitis vinifera*.
CURRENT RELEASE 2003   The aromas are fragrant and attractive in a black-cherry, almost pinot noir-ish way. There are hints of raspberry and mint as well. The palate is savoury, clean and dry and has some richness, density and length. It's an intriguing wine, and subtly different from other fare. Its tannins mean it's best with food. Try some gourmet sausages.

Wood Park Zinfandel

Quality	♥♥♥♥♥
Value	★★★★
Grapes	zinfandel
Region	King Valley, Vic.
Cellar	🍾 5
Alc./Vol.	14.0%
RRP	$30.00 ⊗

Despite a couple of very promising local wines, California's popular zinfandel grape (actually the southern Italian grape primitivo) is still only a bit player in this country. Wood Park's version is very hard to find, but it's worth trying if you ever see it.
CURRENT RELEASE 2003   An intense young zinfandel, and quite a civilised one. The nose has intense raspberry, cherry, floral and spice aromas. There are also touches of leather and dry herbs in the aromatic mix. It has a savoury Italian feel to it, which isn't surprising given zinfandel's Italian origins. The palate is intense with silky texture, excellent balance and great length. Ripe tannins are soft and friendly. A lovely, supple wine to drink right now, but it should do well with medium-term ageing.

Sweet Wines

Perhaps it's an obsession with diet, but we seem to be drinking less sweet wine (and maybe we're eating less of the sweet desserts or fatty cheeses they tend to be drunk with). Also there appear to be fewer 'stickies' around these days, the prolonged dry conditions in rural areas have probably not helped by keeping botrytis out of our vineyards. But the authors feel that there's still a place for a small glass of sweet wine at the dinner table. There's a variety of them: ranging from golden to syrupy Riverina botrytis semillons through to lighter, less domineering styles from cooler areas, often made from riesling, and non-botrytis late-picked whites such as frontignac.

Brown Brothers Moscato

The model for this kind of low-alcohol, lightly fizzy, semi-sweet muscat is in the Asti region of Italy's Piedmont. It's used as an aperitif or a digestif – but in fact it can be drunk pretty much any time you feel like it – like a beer substitute!
CURRENT RELEASE 2004   The '05 will probably be out by the time you read this but it's such a consistent style that similar comments will apply. And you need to drink it young and fresh. It has a very light yellow hue, a slight fizz when poured, and smells of clean, simple, aromatic muscat fruit. The palate is light and grapey, with noticeable spritz and a light fruity sweetness that doesn't cloy or weigh you down. It's delicious with sponge cake or a piece of fresh fruit.

Quality	♥♥♥♥
Value	★★★★┩
Grapes	muscat of Alexandria; muscat blanc à petits grains
Region	north-east Vic.
Cellar	▮ 1
Alc./Vol.	6.0%
RRP	$13.70 (cellar door)

Brown Brothers Patricia Late Harvested Noble Riesling

We reviewed the 2000 last year but it is still current, and still a delicious drop. Noble Riesling has been around for so long, heaven forbid we should take it for granted. It goes back to 1962 when it was labelled Spatlese Rhine Riesling. Maker: Terry Barnett and team.
CURRENT RELEASE 2000   At five years old, it's very rich and luscious for a riesling, with a bright, deep amber, aged colour and a bouquet of toffee, marmalade, vanilla and apricot compote. It's lusciously sweet, with finely balanced acidity, and shows lots of botrytis. While fully mature, it still has plenty of years ahead of it. It's just the thing to serve with crème brûlée.

Quality	♥♥♥♥♥
Value	★★★★
Grapes	riesling
Region	King Valley, Vic.
Cellar	▮ 4+
Alc./Vol.	9.5%
RRP	$49.00 (750 ml); $27.00 (375 ml) Ⓢ

Centennial Vineyards Finale Late Harvest Semillon

Quality	▼▼▼▼ï
Value	★★★★
Grapes	semillon
Region	Riverina, NSW
Cellar	▮3
Alc./Vol.	12.0%
RRP	$23.00 (375 ml)

Centennial Vineyards is at Bowral in the Southern Highlands of New South Wales, but many of their wines are made from grapes grown elsewhere, such as Orange, or in this case the Riverina. Naughtily, they don't usually state the source of their grapes on the packaging.
CURRENT RELEASE 2002   This is a very good wine, with plenty of botrytis character and a suggestion of oak that adds complexity. The colour is a brilliant deep golden yellow; it smells of vanilla, tea-leaf and apricotty botrytis that is quite exotic. It has good length and balance, with fruit and sweetness winning the tug-of-war against slightly firm acid and phenolics. Serve it with a fruity flan.

Cookoothama Botrytis Semillon

Quality	▼▼▼▼ï
Value	★★★
Grapes	semillon
Region	Riverina, NSW
Cellar	▮2
Alc./Vol.	12.5%
RRP	$22.95 (375 ml)

The Nugan family have a long history in the Griffith area of New South Wales, although their involvement in the local wine industry is fairly recent. They've made a lot of impact in a short time, and have expanded their vineyard holdings into Victoria's King Valley and South Australia's McLaren Vale.
CURRENT RELEASE 2003   This unctuous golden–amber coloured sweetie smells of honey, peach and orange marmalade, with touches of volatility and oak in the background. In the mouth it's made in a full-on Riverina botrytis style, luscious, very sweet and rich. A satisfying dessert wine that works well with soft blue cheese and biscuits.

De Bortoli Noble One Botrytis Semillon

Quality	▼▼▼▼▼
Value	★★★★
Grapes	semillon
Region	Riverina, NSW
Cellar	▮5+
Alc./Vol.	11.5%
RRP	$26.00 (375 ml); $49.00 (750 ml) $

This is the one that started it all – the craze to make botrytised sweet whites in the Riverina, we mean. In that sense, it is THE ONE. Hence the name. Darren De Bortoli was just new back at the ranch in 1982 when the first one was made. It was his idea. Now he's boss of the company.
CURRENT RELEASE 2002   This vintage is truly up to speed and one of the best of a distinguished lineage. Deep golden in colour, it has a very complex and tremendously fine bouquet, revealing rich toasted-nut, vanilla and honey characters, a lacing of barley sugar, and a whiff of toffee-topped crème brûlée. It's very sweet and luscious, deep and intense, loaded with character and, we fancy, has a touch more finesse than usual. Perfect with crème brûlée.

De Bortoli Windy Peak Spatlese Riesling

Spatlese riesling is dying out: it used to be very popular in the '70s and '80s. This style of wine was once labelled 'moselle' but that word can no longer be used.
CURRENT RELEASE 2004   The colour is light yellow and the aroma is very minerally – typical of young riesling. In the mouth it is light and lively, only slightly sweet, and finishes crisply with plenty of acid. It's somewhat developed for an '04 so don't cellar it too long. It's a clean, well-made wine of some charm. Enjoy it with a bunch of fresh grapes and some ice-cream.

Quality	♟ ♟ ♟ ♟
Value	★★★★
Grapes	riesling
Region	various, Vic.
Cellar	🍾 2
Alc./Vol.	11.0%
RRP	$14.00 Ⓢ ≋

Kabminye Au

Mmmm . . . what's an 'Au'? It's the chemical symbol for gold, of course, and it's entirely appropriate for this pricey bright golden wine.
CURRENT RELEASE 2004   A lot of countries make sweet muscats in this style and they're very popular as dessert wines. Au has a lemony yellow–gold colour, and an intensely varietal nose of floral aromas, ripe grapes, ginger and juicy stone-fruits. The palate is smooth and sweet-spicy with lush grapey flavours, a whisper of mint, and a long sweet palate. Try it with a selection of luscious summer fruits.

Quality	♟ ♟ ♟ ♟
Value	★ ★ ♪
Grapes	muscat à petits grains blanc
Region	Barossa Valley, SA
Cellar	🍾 2
Alc./Vol.	14.0%
RRP	$55.00 (375 ml) ≋

Lillypilly Noble Blend

'The 2002 vintage was one of the coolest on record in the Riverina and produced fruit with exceptional varietal intensity and balance,' says Robert Fiumara. He was worried the season was so cool and dry, the botrytis might not develop. 'But late in the season the morning mists moved in and provided the ideal environment for botrytis to work its usual magic, concentrating sugar, acid and flavour.'
CURRENT RELEASE 2002   An outstanding sweet wine, deep golden in colour and smelling very complex: floral, honeyed aromas mingle with butterscotch, spices, apricot, cumquat and mixed citrus peels. There's a lot of botrytis evident, and it's rich and quite viscous in the mouth – sweet, ample, almost luscious, with soft acidity. It would suit mango and strawberry millefeuille.

Quality	♟ ♟ ♟ ♟ ♟
Value	★ ★ ★ ★ ♪
Grapes	sauvignon blanc 80%; semillon 10%; riesling 5%; muscat of Alexandria 5%
Region	Riverina, NSW
Cellar	🍾 4+
Alc./Vol.	12.5%
RRP	$27.30 (375 ml) ≋

Lillypilly Noble Muscat of Alexandria

Quality	♟♟♟♟
Value	★★★★
Grapes	muscat of Alexandria
Region	Riverina, NSW
Cellar	🍾 4+
Alc./Vol.	11.0%
RRP	$22.50 (375 ml) 🍷

Tasting a selection of Robert Fiumara's sweet wines reminded HH of Austria, when he visited the famous Alois Kracher in Burgenland, where the Neusiedlersee raises humidity and promotes botrytis attack. In a great vintage like 1999, Kracher can show you 11 different botrytis wines, and they're all terrific. It's a bit like that at Lillypilly. CURRENT RELEASE 2003   This is a lighter-coloured wine than its siblings: medium gold, and smells of fragrant muscat grapes, bath-powdery and highly aromatic but perhaps with less botrytis character than the top wines. The palate, though, is very fine and restrained, at the same time intense and complex, with good sweetness and flavour. Its balance is a highlight and it retains liveliness at the finish. Serve with fruit salad and ice-cream.

Lillypilly Noble Riesling

Quality	♟♟♟♟♟
Value	★★★★
Grapes	riesling
Region	Riverina, NSW
Cellar	🍾 4
Alc./Vol.	12.5%
RRP	$18.75 (375 ml) 🍷

Lillypilly Estate's botrytis wines are all prefixed by the word 'noble'. This refers to noble rot, a common term for *Botrytis cinerea*, the special fungus that attacks the grapes, shrivelling and concentrating them and modifying flavour to produce these great, complex stickies. CURRENT RELEASE 2003   Deep golden amber coloured, this wine is heavily botrytised, resulting in a luscious, viscous and very rich wine. Apricot, spice and caramel are suggested by the complex aroma, and the palate is sweet and unctuous and perhaps lacks the cleansing acidity of some of the other wines. It goes well with pavlova.

Lillypilly Noble Sauvignon Blanc

Quality	♟♟♟♟♟
Value	★★★★★
Grapes	sauvignon blanc
Region	Riverina, NSW
Cellar	🍾 5+
Alc./Vol.	12.5%
RRP	$22.50 (375 ml) 🍷

This won a blue-gold medal and made the Top 100 at the 2004 Sydney International Wine Competition. We reckon it's pretty special, too. That's unusual because sauvignon blanc isn't often used for stickies in Australia. **CURRENT RELEASE 2002   This gorgeous deep golden wine has a fine, fresh flowery aroma with apricot and vanilla nuances from botrytis influence. The palate is a masterpiece. It's very fine, yet intense, and penetrating acidity keeps it light on its feet. There are honey, cumquat, caramel and mixed-peel flavours, with a hint of marmalade. It has a long, long finish, and maintains its great balance and harmony all the way. Yum! Delicious with crème brûlée.**

PENGUIN BEST SWEET WINE

Margan Botrytis Semillon

We thought the 2003 vintage of this delicious wine was one of the best Australian sweet whites we'd tasted in years, and this follow-up didn't disappoint us.
CURRENT RELEASE 2004   This is a lovely refined botrytised style with real elegance. The nose has rich barley-sugar-like sweet aromas and a whisper of European-accented minerally earthiness. Its combination of sweetness, lushness, long clean flavour, delicacy and finesse make it very seductive. Serve it with delicate patisserie.

Quality	♟♟♟♟♟
Value	★★★★
Grapes	semillon
Region	Hunter Valley, NSW
Cellar	▮ 3
Alc./Vol.	9.0%
RRP	$23.50 (375 ml)

Mount Horrocks Cordon Cut Riesling

While most high-quality Australian sweet whites rely on botrytis for their richness and intense sweetness, at Mount Horrocks they cordon-cut the fruit-bearing canes to allow the grapes to shrivel a little on the vine. The result is dehydrated grapes and great concentration.
CURRENT RELEASE 2004   A delicious young sweetie that shows recognisable varietal clues rather than just simple sweetness. It's a bright greenish lemon–yellow colour with a sweetly aromatic nose of flowers, lime and a delicious aroma that reminds us of pineapple doughnuts. The sweet, long palate has fine structure, luscious sweetness and a clean tangy finish. Delicious with crème brûlée.

Quality	♟♟♟♟♟
Value	★★★
Grapes	riesling
Region	Clare Valley, SA
Cellar	▮ 4
Alc./Vol.	10.5%
RRP	$32.75 (375 ml) 🍾

Punt Road Botrytis Semillon

Punt Road is a well-known street in central Melbourne. It's also the brand of Yarra Valley contract winery, The Yarra Hill. Winemaker is Kate Goodman.
CURRENT RELEASE 2003   This is really starting to show some age-development. The colour is old-gold–amber, and the bouquet is smoky and quite complex, showing some botrytis involvement. It's not very sweet, but does have richness. It dries off a bit towards the finish, where a phenolic grip chimes in. The tannins have a whisper of bitterness that doesn't mar it. It's not sweet enough for very sweet desserts: try it with a washed-rind cheese like Milawa Gold.

Quality	♟♟♟♟
Value	★★★
Grapes	semillon
Region	Riverina, NSW
Cellar	▮ 2
Alc./Vol.	13.0%
RRP	$30.00 (500 ml)

Southern Highland Wines Golden Vale Botrytis

Quality	❦❦❦❦❦
Value	★★★❦
Grapes	sauvignon blanc
Region	Southern Highlands, NSW
Cellar	▮3+
Alc./Vol.	10.5%
RRP	$35.00 (375 ml)

The label has both SHW and Southern Highland Wines, neither being an ideal brand name in our view. This is a very unusual 'sticky', by virtue of being made from sauvignon blanc – not a variety that's very susceptible to botrytis.

CURRENT RELEASE 2003   This is a delicious sweetie, with a deep golden–amber colour and a rich, mellow bouquet of glazed fruits, vanilla, toast and toffee. The palate has lots of sweetness and finishes with a lick of bitter citrus peels. It has a tight finish that dries the palate off nicely. The balance is good and it has some pleasing structure. It would suit mild blue cheese.

Stella Bella Pink Muscat

Quality	❦❦❦❦
Value	★★★
Grapes	red frontignac
Region	Margaret River, WA
Cellar	▮2
Alc./Vol.	7.5%
RRP	$18.00 (375 ml) ⛊

In keeping with Stella Bella's slightly unconventional approach compared to other Margaret River wines, this is made in a style that resembles the Italian moscatos, low in alcohol with a tingle of gas, sweetly fruity and so refreshing. The pink colour is a special feature.

CURRENT RELEASE 2004   A salmon-pink wine with a slight spritz on opening. The nose is grapey and floral-fragrant, and the palate is sweet, light and juicy with a little thread of firmness towards the back palate. A little whisper of sulphur may worry some, bit it didn't put us off at all. Try it with a fresh tropical fruit salad.

Trentham Murphy's Lore Spatlese Lexia

Quality	❦❦❦❦
Value	★★★★
Grapes	muscat gordo blanco
Region	Murray Valley, NSW
Cellar	▮1
Alc./Vol.	11.0%
RRP	$11.00 Ⓢ ⛊

Lexia is a common name for muscat gordo blanco, the 'fat white muscat', which has been grown in vast acreages for a long time in Australia's hotter irrigated regions.

CURRENT RELEASE 2004   The colour is pale yellow and the aroma is very fresh and muscaty, with herbal and spicy notes – like a fresh bunch of muscat grapes from the grocer's. It's quite sweet, and has a fresh, clean muscat fruit taste – simple and direct, with a slight bitter-peel taste at the finish. It goes well with any piece of fresh fruit.

Two Hands Brilliant Disguise Moscato

Two Hands uses quirky wine titles to great effect. They make your ears prick up and get you wondering what the story is. The label designs add to the sense of mystery. This one has a Groucho Marx theme.

CURRENT RELEASE 2004 This is a simple muscat style, which reminds us of a young Baumes-de-Venise (without the alcohol) rather than an Italian moscato. It has a lifted, high-toned fragrance. The aroma is pungent and spicy. The palate has searing acidity, while the sweetness level is moderate. Because of the low alcohol strength it fades quickly from the palate. It could cope well with washed-rind cheese.

Quality	🍷🍷🍷½
Value	★★★★
Grapes	muscat
Region	Barossa Valley, SA
Cellar	🍾 2
Alc./Vol.	5.0%
RRP	$13.50 (500 ml)

Fortified Wines

Some of Australia's greatest wines are fortifieds. Muscats and tokays from north-east Victoria, port styles from the Barossa and McLaren Vale, and a few dinosaur sherry styles. The market has shrunk so much that those players left in the game are the best, and the quality and value-for-money they offer are exceptional. What could be better than a glass of decadently rich port or muscat after a meal? All you need is a small glass, and the wine does you the unique favour of tasting just as good when you next access the bottle, days or even weeks later. We should all enjoy more of these great wines. As the boffins in the halls of economic rationalism say: use it or lose it!

All Saints Classic Rutherglen Muscat

Quality	♥♥♥♥♥
Value	★★★
Grapes	red frontignac
Region	Rutherglen, Vic.
Cellar	▮
Alc./Vol.	18.0%
RRP	$30.50

All Saints has long been a sensational source of north-east Victorian fortifieds. RK-P can remember 'liberating' glasses of his father's old All Saints Muscat as a young lout 30 years ago. The quality of the older wines remains superb.
CURRENT RELEASE *non-vintage* This is a grapier, less complex version of All Saints Muscat, but it does have some aged material in evidence. The colour is old mahogany and the nose suggests raisins, rosewater and vanilla. It tastes luxuriously sweet and intense with a long, syrupy, muscatel-perfumed finish. Serve it with cassata.

All Saints Grand Rutherglen Muscat

Quality	♥♥♥♥♥
Value	★★★
Grapes	red frontignac
Region	Rutherglen, Vic.
Cellar	▮
Alc./Vol.	18.0%
RRP	$55.00 (375 ml)

All Saints, one of the Rutherglen district's most significant wineries, was meandering when it was bought by Brown Brothers. Then Peter Brown took it over on his own in 1999, and today he and his family operate it with a strong emphasis on quality.
CURRENT RELEASE *non-vintage* This has an aged-mahogany colour with a hint of khaki at the edge, suggesting age. Our sample was perhaps a little less fresh than it could be, with a slightly feral quality to it, but it's well compensated for by the roasted, raisiny, burnt-sugar and toasted-nut aromas that mark all the older All Saints blends. The palate is very sweet, profound and very long with a delicious black-toffee aftertaste. Try it with blue cheese and muscatels.

All Saints Grand Rutherglen Tawny

All Saints fortified wines come in an encyclopaedic range of types, from ancient rarities in the muscat and tokay departments, to fresh young things, and forgotten styles like this tawny. Quality at the top end is outstanding. CURRENT RELEASE *non-vintage* Dense and autumnally russet-brown in colour, this is a classy aged fortified of real presence. It has tons of barrel-age and rancio character along with essency dried-fruit, caramel and leathery notes. In the mouth it starts out very sweet and intensely concentrated, then it dries out towards the finish, which is very long and fragrant. High acidity keeps it very tangy and clean tasting. Serve it with cloth-matured cheddar.

Quality	♛♛♛♛♕
Value	★★★
Grapes	shiraz
Region	Rutherglen, Vic.
Cellar	▮
Alc./Vol.	18.0%
RRP	$35.00 (375 ml)

All Saints Museum Release Rare Muscat

All Saints Museum Rare Muscat is one of the most concentrated and oldest Rutherglen fortifieds you can get. Is it worth $400-plus? We don't know your bank balance, but it *is* extremely rare, extremely delicious and very special. CURRENT RELEASE *non-vintage* Drawn from a solera of more than 70 years of age, this very old blend is an exquisitely aromatic, intense muscat. It has concentrated, ultra-complex, raisin syrup, toffee, orange peel, vanilla, and roasted almond rancio aromas, making up a voluminous bouquet. In the mouth it's unctuously sweet and luscious with extraordinary depth and a super-long raisin-nutty aftertaste. Sip it with espresso coffee.

Quality	♛♛♛♛♛
Value	★★⭒
Grapes	red frontignac
Region	Rutherglen, Vic.
Cellar	▮
Alc./Vol.	18.0%
RRP	$434.50 (500 ml)

All Saints Museum Release Rare Tokay

These unique Museum wines are the pinnacle of All Saints fortified wines. They are packaged in smart half-litre decanters shaped a little like the *pichet* of wine served to lone travellers at French bistros. CURRENT RELEASE *non-vintage* From a younger solera than All Saints Museum Muscat (at only 40 years, it's still no pup), this delectable wine still retains some tokay varietal cues, but the influence of long-age has almost submerged them in barrel-developed complexities. It's walnut-brown in colour with an olive rim, and the bouquet has concentrated malt, toffee, grilled nut and syrupy tea smells of extraordinary depth. The palate is syrupy, profound, unctuously textured and very long with a deliciously sweet, complex aftertaste. Delicious with caramels and coffee.

Quality	♛♛♛♛♛
Value	★★⭒
Grapes	muscadelle
Region	Rutherglen, Vic.
Cellar	▮
Alc./Vol.	18.0%
RRP	$434.50 (500 ml)

All Saints Rare Rutherglen Muscat

Quality 🍷🍷🍷🍷🍷
Value ★★★½
Grapes red frontignac
Region Rutherglen, Vic.
Cellar 🍾
Alc./Vol. 18.0%
RRP $107.50 (375 ml)

'Rare' is the rating given to Rutherglen's greatest examples of liqueur muscat and tokay. The decision as to what constitutes 'rare' is up to each individual winery, but they are regularly subject to scrutiny in a peer-group tasting to see how they measure up. While style, rather than great age, is the prime factor, the 'rare' wines are usually those with the greatest average age.

CURRENT RELEASE *non-vintage* A gorgeously concentrated old muscat. Some of the material in the blend is over 50 years old. It has aged-mahogany colour and a complex nose of raisined grapes, toffee, dried rose-petals and toasted nuts. The palate is superb, with deep, elaborate flavours finishing long, fine and aromatic. It's a wine for contemplation, to be enjoyed after a grand dinner.

All Saints Rare Rutherglen Tokay

Quality 🍷🍷🍷🍷½
Value ★★★
Grapes muscadelle
Region Rutherglen, Vic.
Cellar 🍾
Alc./Vol. 18.0%
RRP $107.50 (375 ml)

Rutherglen Tokay is named after the original Hungarian tokaji, but the two wines bear little resemblance to each other. The Hungarian wine is an unfortified, botrytised sweet white; Australian tokay is unique, a strong fortified wine made from the minor Bordeaux white grape muscadelle.

CURRENT RELEASE *non-vintage* A brownish-greenish colour and great viscosity appear very old here, and the nose confirms its age via very concentrated nut-toffee, malt and raisiny aromas. There was also a slight hint of staleness about our sample, maybe due to it having been in bottle a little too long, but all is redeemed on the palate. It tastes gorgeously deep and lusciously sweet, yet finishes clean with a long fragrant aftertaste. Serve it with some aged cheddar, muscatels and nuts.

Baileys Founder Muscat

Quality 🍷🍷🍷🍷
Value ★★★★
Grapes red frontignac
Region Glenrowan, Vic.
Cellar 🍾
Alc./Vol. 17.0%
RRP $20.00 [$]

The founder in question is Richard Bailey, who planted the first vines at this vineyard in the Warby Ranges outside Glenrowan in the 1870s. He would have been there when Ned Kelly's famous shoot-out occurred.

CURRENT RELEASE *non-vintage* This is the pick of the Founder Series trio, showing more depth, weight and complexity than the tawny or the tokay. It has a degree of complexity and good toffee-like muscat varietal fruit. A very drinkable, well-balanced muscat to sip with chocolates and coffee.

Baileys Founder Tokay

The owners, Beringer Blass, probably only keep this winery open because of the phylloxera quarantine regulations. They source a lot of fruit in north-east Victorian areas that are quarantined, and the law says you have to crush and de-juice those grapes inside the zone.

CURRENT RELEASE *non-vintage* This is a fresh fruity tokay of considerable charm, but it's very young and grapey and not at all complex. Loads of rosewater, Turkish delight, malt and honey aromas are enough to beguile the senses. The palate is very sweet, fruity and simple, without real evidence of wood-aged character, and it would make a great ice-cream topping.

Quality	🍷🍷🍷🍷
Value	★★★½
Grapes	muscadelle
Region	Glenrowan, Vic.
Cellar	🍾
Alc./Vol.	17.0%
RRP	$20.00 (S)

Campbells Classic Rutherglen Muscat

Campbells Rutherglen fortifieds often offer an elegant alternative to the ultra-lush Rutherglen producers' wines. They are sometimes a tad less powerful, yet they don't lose by the comparison. They have great purity and regional authenticity, and invariably very fine quality.

CURRENT RELEASE *non-vintage* A deep mahogany–red coloured muscat with a nose of intense raisiny varietal perfume. It doesn't have the ultra-complex nuances that come from plenty of old wood-aged material; it's all about luscious, smooth-textured muscat flavour that's clean, grapey and delicious, all with lovely depth and persistence of flavour. A fine partner to Turkish delight and strong coffee.

Quality	🍷🍷🍷🍷½
Value	★★★
Grapes	red frontignac
Region	Rutherglen, Vic.
Cellar	🍾
Alc./Vol.	17.5%
RRP	$41.70 (500 ml)

Campbells Grand Rutherglen Muscat

When new terminology was put in place a few years ago to grade Rutherglen's fortified wines into four classifications (Rutherglen, classic, grand and rare), Campbells had wines covering three of the four classifications. Now they have the fourth rating covered with this superb 'grand'.

CURRENT RELEASE *non-vintage* The colour shows wood-age with a deep brownish hue, edged in olive. The nose is intense and complex, reminiscent of boiled-down raisins, almonds, toffee, and clean grapey spirit. The palate is sweet, clean and long-tasting with tangy acidity behind it. A great example of the Campbells' muscat style, in its own elegant way every bit as good as bigger 'grand' muscats from other producers. Try it with nougat and coffee.

Quality	🍷🍷🍷🍷🍷
Value	★★★★
Grapes	red frontignac
Region	Rutherglen, Vic.
Cellar	🍾
Alc./Vol.	18.0%
RRP	$60.00 (375 ml)

Cheese and Wine Matching

There's an enduring mythology that cheese and wine are always perfect companions, but sublime cheese/wine pairings aren't as common or as straightforward as you might imagine. However, cheeses and wines *can* be friends and sometimes the combination is quite magical. Take, for example, a rich blue roquefort-type cheese and a very old blend of Rutherglen liqueur tokay: sublime, heavenly, so good we've run out of superlatives.

Here are a few tips to bear in mind when pairing cheese and wine:
- Tannins in red wine often clash with cheeses, so choose red wines with soft tannins, or mature wines with tannins that have mellowed with age.
- If you must serve a tannic red with cheese, choose a mature hard cheese like a good cheddar.
- A pinot noir usually works much better than cabernet sauvignon or shiraz.
- If you have an old red to round off a dinner with cheese, choose a mild firm cheese, perhaps something like Heidi gruyère.
- White wines are better companions to a wider range of cheeses than reds.
- Really smelly washed rind cheeses kill a lot of wines stone dead, but with the spice of gewürztraminer they find surprising harmony.
- Blue cheese is a perfect partner to botrytised sweet white wines, vintage port, liqueur muscat and liqueur tokay. We think these are just about the best cheese/wine combinations there are.
- Goat cheese's piercing acidity and feral qualities are difficult for most wines, but sauvignon blanc's penetrating personality works really well. And pinot noir can be good with goat cheese too.
- Brie and camembert type cheeses in perfect condition combine well with full-bodied whites like chardonnay, but if the cheese is very ripe it will wreck just about every wine there is.
- Chardonnay is one of the most cheese-friendly wines there is.
- When in doubt, you can't go wrong serving vintage port types or sweet fortified wines – they are very friendly to a wide range of cheeses.

Campbells Merchant Prince Rare Rutherglen Muscat

Quality	▼▼▼▼▼
Value	★★★★
Grapes	red frontignac
Region	Rutherglen, Vic.
Cellar	▮
Alc./Vol.	18.0%
RRP	$113.00 (375 ml)

This old muscat blend is one of Rutherglen's benchmark fortified wines and one of the rarest of the 'rare'. The name commemorates the sailing vessel *Merchant Prince* that brought John Campbell from Scotland to Australia in 1858. By 1870 he had planted vines at Rutherglen, founding one of the district's great winemaking dynasties.

CURRENT RELEASE *non-vintage* A simply lovely old muscat blend, epitomising Campbells elegant take on the best regional style. It's deep walnut in colour with aged-khaki notes, and the bouquet is driven by intense raisiny fruit, notes of burnt toffee and nutty rancio. The palate is exquisitely concentrated, plush and complex in flavour, yet it retains real freshness. Gorgeous. Serve it with florentines and coffee.

Campbells Rutherglen Tokay

Quality	▼▼▼▼▼
Value	★★★★★
Grapes	muscadelle
Region	Rutherglen, Vic.
Cellar	▮
Alc./Vol.	17.5%
RRP	$19.50 (375 ml)

Campbells wines boast some of the classiest packaging of all Rutherglen fortifieds, and the standard of the wines within more than measures up. This youngest of the tokays is delicious.

CURRENT RELEASE *non-vintage* A delightful young tokay, without the delectable complexities of great age perhaps, but with direct varietal and regional-fruit characters of great charm. Dark amber in colour, it smells of freshly opened tea-leaves and cream toffee. The palate is sweet and lush, but far from heavy, and it finishes sweet and lingering. Perfect with old-fashioned golden-syrup dumplings.

Cassegrain Cassae

Quality	▼▼▼▼
Value	★★★↓
Grapes	not stated
Region	Hastings Valley, NSW
Cellar	▮
Alc./Vol.	18.0%
RRP	$16.95 (375 ml)
	(cellar door)

The Cassegrain family hails from Cognac, and this wood-aged fortified grape-juice is modelled on a similar drink of Cognac called Pineau des Charentes. Maker: John Cassegrain.

CURRENT RELEASE *non-vintage* This is an oddity of the wine world. It has a medium-full amber colour and smells rather like an old oloroso sherry. There are definite oxidative aromas, with hints of old leather and dried citrus peel. The palate is very fiery and intense, with a lot of early sweetness, it then dries off with spirit and acid to finish. It's almost painfully intense. Refrigerate well as a pre-dinner aperitif or mixer.

Chambers Grand Rutherglen Muscat

Chambers' wines were among the fortifieds recently 'discovered' by American wine commentators. In a way it's unfortunate for us, as the Americans characteristically go for the rarest and most expensive wines and there's never enough of them to go around. Our advice is to grab 'em while you can.

CURRENT RELEASE *non-vintage* Chambers' wines are at the pinnacle of Rutherglen muscat, and their 'grand' version is absolutely superb. The nose has a sumptuous liqueurish richness of essency raisined aromas, hints of toffee, malt, and nutty nuances. In the mouth it shows perfect balance of satiny, luscious, tangy aged material in perfect harmony with the freshness that younger stuff brings. The finish goes on and on and on. Try it with orange crème brûlée.

Quality	🍷🍷🍷🍷🍷
Value	★★★★½
Grapes	red frontignac
Region	Rutherglen, Vic.
Cellar	🍾
Alc./Vol.	19.0%
RRP	$52.15 (375 ml)

Chambers Rutherglen Muscat

Time seems to stand still at the Chambers winery. It's a rustic unpretentious spot that's long been the source of some of Rutherglen's greatest fortified wines. And proprietor Bill Chambers is a living legend.

CURRENT RELEASE *non-vintage* A younger version of Chambers Muscat, and one of great charm. The nose has succulent grapey, raisiny aromas with a fragrant touch of Turkish delight. The palate follows the fresh, sweet, intense theme with attractive persistence, albeit painted with a lighter palette than the super-dooper oldies. A delicious wine to enjoy with good vanilla ice-cream.

Quality	🍷🍷🍷🍷½
Value	★★★★★
Grapes	red frontignac
Region	Rutherglen, Vic.
Cellar	🍾
Alc./Vol.	18.0%
RRP	$19.50

D'Arenberg Vintage Fortified Shiraz

D'Arenberg was one of the first wineries to switch from the soon-to-be-outlawed name of port to the alternative, fortified shiraz. D'Arenberg Vintage Ports of considerable age occupy a fond place in HH's memories of his first visits to the Vale, in 1980. Makers: Chester Osborn and Phillip Dean.

CURRENT RELEASE 2002 The colour is so dense and dark that it stains the glass. It smells of very ripe shiraz in the mulberry and blackberry style, while the palate is rich and sweet, backed by marvellously soft tannins. It's so smooth and easygoing you could drink it now, but it will be so much better in a few years. Serve with blue-vein cheese.

Quality	🍷🍷🍷🍷½
Value	★★★★
Grapes	shiraz
Region	McLaren Vale, SA
Cellar	🍾 2–22+
Alc./Vol.	18.5%
RRP	$23.00 (375 ml)

Grant Burge Aged Tawny

Quality	♥♥♥♥
Value	★★★★★
Grapes	grenache; shiraz; mataro
Region	Barossa Valley, SA
Cellar	▯
Alc./Vol.	19.0%
RRP	$13.25 Ⓢ

PENGUIN BEST-VALUE
FORTIFIED WINE

Grant Burge's family has been making port in the Barossa for yonks, so they have a pretty good stock of old wines to draw on when blending. This one seems to have gone up a peg since our last review of it.

CURRENT RELEASE *non-vintage* **This is a lovely port, showing good depth of aged character well above its price station. The colour is light tawny; it smells as though there's some sherry or 'old sweet white' material in it, and there's a dollop of rancio that you don't expect to find in a wine of its price. Underneath is a rich fruity palate with raisin, prune and chocolate flavours. The finish is mellow and clean, drying off nicely, and the complex flavours linger. A real bargain! Sip with chocolates and coffee.**

Knappstein Single Vineyard Fortified Shiraz

Quality	♥♥♥♥♥
Value	★★★↓
Grapes	shiraz
Region	Clare Valley, SA
Cellar	▯ 8+
Alc./Vol.	20.0%
RRP	$21.00 (375 ml)

This retro-type wine, packed in narrow hock bottles, was made from young vine fruit left very late on the vine. It was made by Andrew Hardy who, after ten years, left the Knappstein fold this year for a management position at Petaluma.

CURRENT RELEASE 1998 This is a bit like Clare Valley shiraz table wine on steroids. The nose has aromas of concentrated, juicy blackberry fruit, spice, mint, brandy spirit and vanillin oak. In the mouth it's full-bodied with the sort of lush, sweet, alcoholic personality guaranteed to warm the cockles of the heart. It finishes with a nutty aftertaste, and ripe, dry tannins give some macho firmness. Try it with soft blue cheese and crackers.

Morris Liqueur Muscat

Quality	♥♥♥♥♥
Value	★★★★★
Grapes	red frontignac
Region	Rutherglen, Vic.
Cellar	▯
Alc./Vol.	17.5%
RRP	$17.00 (500 ml)

The Morris family have yet to label their fortified wines in line with the Rutherglen classification, citing factors like the possible confusion customers might have with new names and labels. We have no doubt that this 'basic' wine would be graded as 'classic' at least, the quality is exemplary.

CURRENT RELEASE *non-vintage* We are always astonished by the quality of this Morris wine. It has a youthful red–tawny colour, and a nose that's pure and clean with delightful rose-petal and raisin aromas. In the mouth it has intense grapey flavours that are lusciously sweet, long and clean-finishing. Great with profiteroles and chocolate sauce.

Morris Liqueur Tokay

This wine and its muscat counterpart are known as the Morris 'canister' wines, due to the bottles being packed in cylindrical canisters. It makes a good gift pack, and Morris Rutherglen fortifieds always make a perfect gift.
CURRENT RELEASE *non-vintage* A wine of similar quality and value to the canister-packed muscat, this has a bright amber colour and classic Rutherglen tokay aromas of tea-leaves, butterscotch and malt extract. It tastes lush with silky sweetness that lingers long in the mouth, finishing fresh and zippy. Try it with Greek pastries.

Quality	🍷🍷🍷🍷🍷
Value	★★★★★
Grapes	muscadelle
Region	Rutherglen, Vic.
Cellar	🍴
Alc./Vol.	17.0%
RRP	$17.00 (500 ml)

Morris Old Premium Amontillado Sherry

It's hard to imagine there was a time when sherries were the holy grail of Australian winemakers, and they brought back all the grape varieties, yeasts and techniques from Spain to make the best sherries in Australia. Fashions changed, and few still persist, but those that do – like Morris – generally make great wines.
CURRENT RELEASE *non-vintage* The colour is full amber and the bouquet of new leather, chocolate and vanilla, with a slightly volatile lift from old blending material, sets the scene for a complex, satisfying sipper. It's a sweeter style of amontillado (some are bone-dry), and really fills the mouth with rich, mellow-aged flavours that recall sun-dried fruits and nuts. It goes well with French onion soup.

Quality	🍷🍷🍷🍷🍷
Value	★★★★
Grapes	palomino; pedro ximenez
Region	Rutherglen, Vic.
Cellar	🍴
Alc./Vol.	22.0%
RRP	$45.70 (500 ml) ⑨

Morris Old Premium Liqueur Muscat

At the Morris winery, Mick Morris and son David preside over a stash of old muscats in barrel that go back to the 1800s as a sort of Morris family reference library. Those oldest wines are so concentrated that they're almost like treacle, with flavour that's indescribably superb.
CURRENT RELEASE *non-vintage* Very old colour, typically deep with a greenish edge. The bouquet is beautifully concentrated with essency raisin, toffee, spicy-fruitcake and toasted-almond elements in lovely harmony. The palate reflects the blending genius that characterises great Rutherglen fortified makers like Morris and Chambers. It combines complexity and profound richness with great length of flavour, while retaining a lovely fresh tang. Outstanding muscat. Sip it alongside coffee and chocolates.

Quality	🍷🍷🍷🍷🍷
Value	★★★★★
Grapes	red frontignac
Region	Rutherglen, Vic.
Cellar	🍴
Alc./Vol.	17.5%
RRP	$57.00 (500 ml)

Morris Old Premium Liqueur Tokay

Quality 🍷🍷🍷🍷🍷
Value ★★★★★
Grapes muscadelle
Region Rutherglen, Vic.
Cellar 🍾
Alc./Vol. 18.0%
RRP $57.00 (500 ml)

This is always an extraordinary wine, reflecting the depth and breadth of material available to Mick and David Morris. Along with its companion wine, Old Premium Liqueur Muscat, it would easily rate the 'rare' classification in the modern Rutherglen scheme of things.

CURRENT RELEASE *non-vintage* A great old fortified blend with brown–olive colour, viscous appearance, and an ultra-complex nose that's like a delicious melange of malt extract, cold tea, vanilla, toffee apple and almond brittle. In the mouth it's deeply concentrated, very complex, and as long and lingering in flavour as any. Try it with ice-cream and caramel sauce.

Noon Winery Tawny

Quality 🍷🍷🍷🍷🍷
Value ★★★★★
Grapes not stated
Region McLaren Vale, SA
Cellar 🍾 5+
Alc./Vol. 20.5%
RRP $18.00 (500 ml) (cellar door)

Not port, just tawny. That's to keep the Europeans happy. In fact, the treaty between the EU and Australia that's been on the negotiating table for many years has still not been finalised or signed, so the phase-out of naughty names is still some way off. Maker: Drew Noon.

CURRENT RELEASE *non-vintage* This is a beautiful tawny in the traditional Australian style. In other words, rich and mellow, with a dense, fully sweet palate and lots of oak-matured rancio character. The colour is medium tawny–amber and the bouquet recalls old burnished timber, walnuts, dried fruits and drying rancio that carries through to the nicely aged character that lingers on the finish. Yum factor is high! Sip this with dried fruits and nuts.

Penfolds Bluestone 10-Year-Old Tawny

Quality 🍷🍷🍷🍷
Value ★★★
Grapes shiraz; mataro; muscadelle
Region Barossa Valley, SA
Cellar 🍾
Alc./Vol. 19.5%
RRP $22.00 [$]

Bluestone relates to the stone used in the old cellars at the Magill winery. It's a very hard type of stone and well suited to building purposes.

CURRENT RELEASE *non-vintage* The dark amber–tawny colour has some red glints and shows some youth as well as aged blending material. Leather, raisin and almost a hint of muscat feature in the bouquet, which has some cooked-fruit nuances. The palate has plenty of youthful fruitiness and some heat from the fortifying spirit. Serve with fruit-bread and aged cheeses.

Penfolds Grandfather Liqueur Tawny

The name says it all: Grandfather – something ancient and venerable with the mellowness of age and the complexity of time, but a fair way from 'past it'. This is special stuff, and comes in an appropriate clear-faced wooden box. CURRENT RELEASE *non-vintage*   Grandfather is always a sweeter, richer style of port, with great depth of character thanks to some very old blending material. The colour is amber–orange and the bouquet is a fascinating mix of walnut, dried citrus peel, raisins, vanilla and chocolate, all of which translates faithfully to the palate. It has great depth of lovely, mellow, rounded, rich flavour and sweetness. A luxurious fortified, to sip with chocolates and an espresso.

Quality	▮▮▮▮▮
Value	★★★
Grapes	shiraz; mourvèdre
Region	Barossa Valley, SA
Cellar	▮
Alc./Vol.	19.0%
RRP	$90.00

Peter Lehmann Fino Sherry Cellar Reserve

The story goes that Margaret Lehmann asked the winemakers to develop a sherry especially for her, and when the boss's wife asks for something, you don't say no. There's more in a barrel than Margaret can drink, so it's available at cellar door only. CURRENT RELEASE *non-vintage*   This is an individual interpretation of fino, with some floral and nutty-oak characters on the nose, and a richer, weightier palate than most Spanish wines. It's very dry with a slightly austere finish. It also has traditional aldehyde flor characters and a hint of bottle-age. A good aperitif that would suit whitebait.

Quality	▮▮▮▮
Value	★★★⁺
Grapes	not stated
Region	Barossa Valley, SA
Cellar	▮ 1
Alc./Vol.	16.0%
RRP	$20.00 ▨
	(cellar door)

Peter Lehmann The King AD 2017 Vintage Port

Peter Lehmann's vintage port nomenclature needs some explanation. The King relates to the playing cards seen on Lehmann labels, and harks back to fictional gambler Sky Masterson, with whom the gambler Peter Lehmann feels an affinity. AD 2017 is a hint as to when the winemakers reckon this vintage will peak. It's always 21 years from harvest. Maker: Andrew Wigan. CURRENT RELEASE 1996   The colour is deep red–purple with black tints. Super-ripe blackberry fruit plus brandy spirit dominate the bouquet, and the tannic pressings and taily spirit are also much in evidence on the palate. Chocolate and raisin flavours chime in. It's still a tad astringent and could use more time. Serve with stilton cheese and dry bikkies.

Quality	▮▮▮▮▮
Value	★★★★
Grapes	shiraz
Region	Barossa Valley, SA
Cellar	▮ 10+
Alc./Vol.	20.0%
RRP	$25.00 ▮

Queen Adelaide Fine Old Tawny Port

Quality	▯▯▯▯
Value	★★★★↓
Grapes	not stated
Region	not stated
Cellar	▮
Alc./Vol.	18.5%
RRP	$8.00 Ⓢ

The title 'fine old' seems to be an exaggeration, but there are no rules relating to the use of those words on a fortified wine, as far as we know. There should be!

CURRENT RELEASE *non-vintage* The colour shows lots of red that indicates youth, while the nose offers a lot of peppery, floral spirit and spicy red-fruit aromas. The spirit is quite dominant, giving a fairly hot finish while the fruit is a bit light-on and simple. But it's a decent sweet red and remarkable value at the price. Use it in a fruitcake, or sip with a strong cigar.

Seppelt Grand Rutherglen Muscat DP63

Quality	▯▯▯▯▯
Value	★★★★★
Grapes	red frontignac
Region	Rutherglen, Vic.
Cellar	▮
Alc./Vol.	17.0%
RRP	$28.50

The revamp of Seppelt's fortified range has brought us some commendable bargains. This is one of them. Blender/winemaker is Gentleman James Godfrey.

CURRENT RELEASE *non-vintage* A delicious, deep-coloured Rutherglen muscat and, in common with most Seppelt fortified wines, it's a bargain at the price. The nose is very seductive with deep raisiny aromas that are clean and fresh, yet age makes its mark as well. There are touches of spice and malt toffee adding delicious interest, and the palate is very sweet, succulent and long flavoured. Great with a cheese selection.

Seppelt Grand Rutherglen Tokay DP57

Quality	▯▯▯▯▯
Value	★★★★
Grapes	muscadelle
Region	Rutherglen, Vic.
Cellar	▮
Alc./Vol.	17.5%
RRP	$28.50

Liqueur tokay is one of the only wines we can actually call uniquely Australian. As far as we know, there isn't another aged fortified sweet wine made from the muscadelle grape anywhere. And it's one of the greatest fortified wines in the world. Aussies should dip their lids to wines like these.

CURRENT RELEASE *non-vintage* At the less luscious but more focused end of the Rutherglen tokay scale, this has a pure, penetrating aged personality that's very lovely. The nose has burnt-toffee and roasted-almond aromas with a light touch of varietal tea and honey. The palate is sweet and essency with a touch of syrupy tea flavour on the very long aftertaste. Try it with plum pud.

Seppelt Para 100-Year-Old Vintage Tawny

How many single vintage wines in the world are released every year after one hundred years in wood? We think this is the only one. It's a breathtaking testament to Australian wine's rich history, and it comes from a unique treasure trove of outstanding fortified wines, the living museum of Seppeltsfield in the Barossa Valley. It's amazing to recall that the now discredited, rationalist Southcorp management of a few years ago wanted to sell Seppeltsfield off. Blender: James Godfrey.

CURRENT RELEASE 1905   Tasting these wines is always an extraordinary experience. This has a treacly dark, glass-staining, viscous appearance, almost like motor oil, and in bouquet and flavour it has amazing power and complexity. It's hard to fit descriptors to it, and last year HH came up with the idea that the 1904 had something in common with very old balsamic vinegar, and it really did! What's the '05 like? Molasses, dark chocolate, vanillin oak, old furniture, burnt toffee, leather upholstery, spices, coffee grounds, tar and cough mixture. It's very sweet, and the acidity is very penetrating, especially the volatile component, yet few wines could possibly be so memorable. Sip it on its own, and marvel. And although its price tag is very high, its real value would be many times more.

Quality	♥ ♥ ♥ ♥ ♥
Value	★ ★ ★
Grapes	grenache; shiraz; mataro
Region	Barossa Valley, SA
Cellar	▮
Alc./Vol.	23.0%
RRP	$1045.00 (750 ml)
	$528.50 (375 ml)

Seppelt Para Liqueur Aged Tawny No. 123

A wine nicknamed 'Purple Para' was once a favourite, and slightly notorious, tipple back in the days when wine was plonk and fortified wine sales dominated the Australian scene. Para Liqueur has always been a rather different critter, an aged blend of liqueurish intensity and very high quality. It remains an excellent thing indeed.

CURRENT RELEASE *non-vintage*   Classical Para Liqueur: pale orange–amber colour, nose and flavours of nuts, raisins, honey and subtle toasty rancio. Very sweet yet not cloying, with richness and balance, and an extremely long aftertaste that's simply delicious. An Australian classic. Serve it with cream-filled brandy snaps.

Quality	♥ ♥ ♥ ♥ ♥
Value	★ ★ ★ ★ ★
Grapes	grenache; shiraz; mataro
Region	Barossa Valley, SA
Cellar	▮
Alc./Vol.	20.9%
RRP	$19.95

Seppelt Para Liqueur Single Vintage Tawny

Quality	🍷🍷🍷🍷◗
Value	★★★◗
Grapes	grenache; shiraz; mataro
Region	Barossa Valley, SA
Cellar	▮
Alc./Vol.	19.0%
RRP	$43.95

PENGUIN BEST FORTIFIED WINE

The fad of people hoarding wine in the hope of making a huge profit reached its absurd pinnacle 30 years ago, when people, most with no real wine knowledge, stashed away heaps of vintage-dated Para Liqueur. It fizzled out as it was always going to. This is a wine to drink, not a wine to keep! **CURRENT RELEASE 1984 Amber-hued with a little more depth of colour than the 'standard' Para, this has a lovely complex bouquet that's very refined. It smells of burnished timber, old leather chesterfields, crushed dried fruits and roasted nuts. In the mouth it's sweet enough with delicious, lush flavour, but there's also a dry thread through it that keeps it mouth-wateringly appetising. It's easy to drink too much of this old fortified. Exercise caution and sip it with coffee and dried fruit.**

Seppelt Rare Rutherglen Muscat GR113

Quality	🍷🍷🍷🍷🍷
Value	★★★★
Grapes	red frontignac
Region	Rutherglen, Vic.
Cellar	▮
Alc./Vol.	17.5%
RRP	$65.95

This gorgeous blend is based on a superb parcel of 1983 vintage muscat that achieved an extraordinary level of ripeness, blended with more recent material.
CURRENT RELEASE *non-vintage* How do you describe a wine of such dazzling flavour? Well, here goes . . . the colour is deep brown turning to olive on the edge, it smells of muscatels, pot-pourri, toasted almond and exotic spices. The sumptuous palate has exquisite lush flavour that's raisin-sweet and ultra-complex, with piercing acidity to keep balance. The aftertaste lingers forever. A great Rutherglen muscat. Serve it with vanilla ice-cream.

Seppelt Rare Rutherglen Tokay DP59

Quality	🍷🍷🍷🍷◗
Value	★★★◗
Grapes	muscadelle
Region	Rutherglen, Vic.
Cellar	▮
Alc./Vol.	17.5%
RRP	$65.95

Some of the Seppelt Rutherglen fortifieds are a shade less alcoholic than their peers from other makers; however, they lack nothing in terms of luscious richness though. Their 'rare' grade wines are authentic examples of the region's best.
CURRENT RELEASE *non-vintage* The colour shows great age with a touch of olive to it. The bouquet is ultra-concentrated. Dark toffee, almond and vanillin characters overtake simple varietals on the nose, but our sample was just a whisper less fresh than we would like. The palate was ultra-sweet and very deeply flavoured with great persistence of burnt sugar and roasted-nut aftertaste.

Seppelt Rare Tawny DP90

This wonderful old fortified blend shows just what superb tawny port styles Australia is capable of producing. We don't call it port any more, and only a handful of people drink it anyway, but in its way it's one of Australia's greatest wines.

CURRENT RELEASE *non-vintage* The colour is deep amber with almost no red tones left. It smells delicate, yet quite heady, with aromas of dry spirit, scorched nuts, spices, old drawing rooms – all very complex and mysteriously savoury. In the mouth it's very long, and subtly flavoured with an exquisitely fine texture. The finish lingers for ages. Try it with fresh almonds and walnuts.

Quality	♟ ♟ ♟ ♟ ♟
Value	★★★★
Grapes	mostly shiraz & grenache
Region	Barossa Valley, SA
Cellar	▮
Alc./Vol.	20.5%
RRP	$65.95

Seppelt Rutherglen Muscat DP33

Seppelt once had a winery and vineyard at Rutherglen but it was sold off years ago. These days they buy grapes for their excellent fortified wines from contract sources, and the wines are matured and blended at Seppeltsfield by their famous fortified guru James Godfrey.

CURRENT RELEASE *non-vintage* A bargain in anyone's language, this is a 750 ml bottle of Rutherglen muscat priced the same as other makers' 375 ml bottles. And there's no problem with the quality. It has a grapey nose with some delicious raisiny overtones, giving an impression of purity and freshness. It doesn't show any real age, instead it offers immediate luscious fruit that's relatively light and uncomplicated, yet admirably long flavoured. Delicious sipped with a casual cheese platter.

Quality	♟ ♟ ♟ ♟ ♟
Value	★★★★★
Grapes	red frontignac
Region	Rutherglen, Vic.
Cellar	▮
Alc./Vol.	17.0%
RRP	$16.95

Seppelt Rutherglen Tokay DP37

The Seppelt Rutherglen fortifieds aren't just bargains; in each quality grade they stand comparison with the best. This is the basic 'Rutherglen' tokay. It doesn't have pretensions to greatness, but it is an excellent example of the type.

CURRENT RELEASE *non-vintage* This has a bright coppery amber colour and a pure varietal nose reminiscent of cold sweet tea, honey and toffee. The syrupy palate is lush in texture and flavour yet relatively light and fresh, and it finishes sweet, nutty and long. Delicious with mild blue cheese.

Quality	♟ ♟ ♟ ♟
Value	★★★★★
Grapes	muscadelle
Region	Rutherglen, Vic.
Cellar	▮
Alc./Vol.	17.0%
RRP	$16.95

Seppelt Show Amontillado DP116

Quality	♟♟♟♟♟
Value	★★★★★
Grapes	palomino
Region	Barossa Valley, SA
Cellar	▮
Alc./Vol.	22.0%
RRP	$20.95

Another sherry style whose bottle was doubled in size a few years back, while staying the same price. Such generosity is rare in the modern wine world, but it deserves loud applause. For the record, this amontillado is fino sherry, which is wood-aged after the flor yeast has been removed; complexity and depth are enhanced by that time in cask. CURRENT RELEASE *non-vintage* Glittering old gold in colour, this has a complex, subtle bouquet of mixed nuts, candied peel, toffee and vanilla. In the mouth there's a slight hint of sweetness, but the current blend seems somewhat drier than it used to be. The flavour lingers long and appetising with a bracing backbone of acidity. It could be used as an aperitif, it's dry and zesty enough, but we think its best place is with a soup based on strong beef or veal stock. Another great bargain in the Seppelt portfolio.

Seppelt Show Fino DP117

Quality	♟♟♟♟♟
Value	★★★★★
Grapes	palomino
Region	Barossa Valley, SA
Cellar	▮
Alc./Vol.	15.5%
RRP	$20.95

We have both bouquets and brickbats for Seppelt when it comes to their repackaging of these outstanding sherry styles. Praise is due in great measure for doubling the size of the bottle while keeping the price the same. On the down side, they've removed the bottling date from the labels, an odd move with a wine like this 15.5 per cent alcohol fino that needs to be as fresh as possible. CURRENT RELEASE *non-vintage* Pale and shiny, this fino has a wonderfully more-ish flor aroma that gives a yeasty, nutty, sour-apple sort of smell that's so mysteriously savoury. The flavour is dry and piercing with a slight biscuity touch and a desert-dry, sea-salty finish. Serve it chilled pre-dinner with some olives, and make sure the bottle doesn't hang around forever; once opened it goes stale in a matter of days.

Seppelt Show Oloroso DP38

Seppelt's James Godfrey is one of the most significant winemakers in Australia. Fortifieds are his thing, and the range of wines he's responsible for includes classics in almost every style imaginable, some being unique. This oloroso is one of his masterpieces.

CURRENT RELEASE *non-vintage*   Oloroso is the sweetest and richest of the Seppelt sherry-type wines, a majestic thing indeed. The colour is a brilliant amber, and the nose is super-complex with aromas ranging from vanilla through spice, burnt toffee, dried fruits and nuts. The palate is a delicious interplay between sweetness, nutty complexity and mouth-watering acidity. The delicious toasted almond aftertaste seems to go on forever. Delicious with a fairly plain dessert cake.

Quality	♟♟♟♟♟
Value	★★★★★
Grapes	palomino
Region	Barossa Valley, SA
Cellar	▮
Alc./Vol.	21.0%
RRP	$20.95

Seppelt Vintage Fortified GR27

Port is a Portuguese fortified wine and international agreements will soon prevent Australian ports being called port any more. What's the alternative? Some local producers are calling them 'fortified' which we think is a bit clumsy. Can any readers suggest alternatives?

CURRENT RELEASE 1997   Praise must go to Seppelt for releasing these wines with some bottle-age. Bottle-development is a necessary component of the style. This '97 smells of dark berries, currants, spices, mint and clean spirit. The palate is smooth and round with great depth of sweet cherry, marzipan, liquorice, mint and liqueur-chocolate flavours that last long and aromatic. A complex-port style with a persistent, fine finish, and an absolute bargain to boot! Serve it with cheese.

Quality	♟♟♟♟♟
Value	★★★★★
Grapes	shiraz; tinta molle
Region	Barossa Valley, SA
Cellar	▮ 5+
Alc./Vol.	19.0%
RRP	$13.00 (375ml)

Stanton & Killeen Classic Rutherglen Muscat

Stanton and Killeen's fortified wines aren't quite as powerfully luscious as the super-dooper Rutherglens. From one of Rutherglen's most thoughtful winemakers, Chris Killeen, these have a real charm of their own.

CURRENT RELEASE *non-vintage*   An intense muscat of 12 years average age with aromas of raisins and muscatels, and rather earthy spirit. In the mouth it has intense sweetness, yet it's slightly lighter in texture and body than the big syrupy Rutherglen muscats. That said, its exquisitely focused sweet grapiness is hard to resist. Try it with steamed golden-syrup pudding.

Quality	♟♟♟♟♟
Value	★★★♩
Grapes	red frontignac
Region	Rutherglen, Vic.
Cellar	▮
Alc./Vol.	18.0%
RRP	$28.00 (500ml)

Stanton & Killeen Rutherglen Ruby Port

Quality	♥♥♥♥
Value	★★★
Grapes	not stated
Region	Rutherglen, Vic.
Cellar	♦
Alc./Vol.	18.0%
RRP	$19.00 (500 ml)

In Portuguese terminology, Ruby is a name given to younger port wines bottled without the long wood-ageing that turns them into tawny. Stanton & Killeen's ruby follows a similar pattern.

CURRENT RELEASE *non-vintage*   More brick-red than ruby in colour, this young port style has an attractively intense nose reminiscent of prunes, licorice and polished leather. In the mouth it's sweet and fresh with rather delicate fruit and spirit characters that lead to a dry appetising finish. Sip it with plain cake.

Stanton & Killeen Vintage Port

Quality	♥♥♥♥♦
Value	★★★★
Grapes	touriga 38%; tinta cao 24%; tinta barrocca 18%; shiraz 14%; durif 6%
Region	Rutherglen, Vic.
Cellar	♦ 6
Alc./Vol.	17.7%
RRP	$33.00 (750 ml) $25.00 (375 ml)

When the authors first visited the Stanton and Killeen winery, some decades ago, old Jack Stanton presided over the tasting room with good humour and generosity. Jack has passed on, but the feel of the place hasn't changed all that much. This vintage port, made with large input from the classic Portuguese port grapes, is a classic of the region. CURRENT RELEASE 2000   Although a shade less powerful than some predecessors, this retains the complexity and classical personality. The nose has black-cherry, orange-peel, blackcurrant-jam and spice aromas with an earthy-spirit edge. In the mouth it's ripe enough, yet the flavours are almost delicate, and underpinned by ripe tannins. A lighter Stanton & Killeen VP that will probably be earlier maturing than usual. Try it with soft cheeses.

Turkey Flat Pedro Ximenez

Quality	♥♥♥♥
Value	★★★
Grapes	pedro ximenez
Region	Barossa Valley, SA
Cellar	♦
Alc./Vol.	17.2%
RRP	$25.00 (350 ml) (cellar door)

This wine doesn't fit any of the usual fortified wine categories, hence the varietal title. It's probably more like a ruby port than anything. Pedro ximenez is a little-used grape these days. Maker: Peter Schulz.

CURRENT RELEASE *non-vintage*   The colour is dark amber shot through with red. The aromas are of shrivelled, raisined grapes, sweet and fairly youthful without a lot of wood-aged character. The palate is very sweet and lacks a definite varietal signature, but is clean and well-made, and would be enjoyed by a lot of people. It would go well with stilton cheese.

Wine Terms

The following are commonly used winemaking terms.

Acid   There are many acids that occur naturally in grapes and it's in the winemaker's interest to retain the favourable ones because these promote freshness and longevity.

Agrafe   A metal clip used to secure champagne corks during secondary bottle fermentation.

Alcohol   Ethyl alcohol (C_2H_5OH) is a by-product of fermentation of sugars. It's the stuff that makes people happy and it adds warmth and texture to wine.

Alcohol by Volume (A/V)   The measurement of the amount of alcohol in a wine. It's expressed as a percentage, e.g. 13.0% A/V means there is 13.0% pure alcohol as a percentage of the total volume.

Aldehyde   An unwanted and unpleasant organic compound formed between acid and alcohol by oxidation. It's removed by sulfur dioxide.

Allier   A type of oak harvested in the French forest of the same name.

Aperitif   A wine that stimulates the appetite.

Aromatic   A family of grape varieties that have a high terpene content. Riesling and gewürztraminer are examples, and terpenes produce their floral qualities.

Autolysis   A Vegemite or freshly baked bread taste and smell imparted by spent yeast cells in sparkling wines.

Back Blend   To add unfermented grape juice to wine or to add young wine to old wine in fortifieds.

Barrel Fermentation   The process of fermenting a red or white wine in a small barrel, thereby adding a creamy texture and toasty or nutty characters, and better integrating the wood and fruit flavours.

Barrique   A 225-litre barrel.

Baumé   The measure of sugar in grape juice used to estimate potential alcohol content. It's usually expressed as a degree, e.g. 12 degrees Baumé juice will produce approximately 12.0% A/V if it's fermented to dryness. The alternative brix scale is approximately double Baumé and must be divided by 1.8 to estimate potential alcohol.

Bentonite   A fine clay (drillers mud) used as a clarifying (fining) agent.

Blend   A combination of two or more grape varieties and/or vintages. *See also* Cuvée.

Botrytis Cinerea   A mould that thrives on grapevines in humid conditions and sucks out the water of the grapes thereby concentrating the flavour. Good in white wine but not so good in red. (There is also a loss in quantity.)

Breathing   Uncorking a wine and allowing it to stand for a couple of hours before serving. This introduces oxygen and dissipates bottle odours. Decanting aids breathing.

Brix *see* Baumé.

Brut The second lowest level of sweetness in sparkling wine; it does not mean there is no added sugar.

Bush Vine Although pruned the vine is self-supporting in a low-to-the-ground bush. (Still common in the Barossa Valley.)

Carbonic Maceration Fermentation in whole (uncrushed) bunches. This is a popular technique in Beaujolais. It produces bright colour and soften tannins.

Charmat Process A process for making sparkling wine where the wine is fermented in a tank rather than in a bottle.

Clone (Clonal) A recognisable subspecies of vine within a varietal family, e.g. there are numerous clones of pinot noir and these all have subtle character differences.

Cold Fermentation (Also Controlled Temperature Fermentation) Usually applied to white wines where the ferment is kept at a low temperature (10–12 degrees Centigrade).

Cordon The arms of the trained grapevine that bear the fruit.

Cordon Cut A technique of cutting the fruit-bearing arms and allowing the berries to dehydrate to concentrate the flavour.

Crush Crushing the berries to liberate the free-run juice (*q.v.*). Also used as an expression of a wine company's output: 'This winery has a 1000-tonne crush'.

Cuvée A Champagne term meaning a selected blend or batch.

Disgorge The process of removing the yeast lees from a sparkling wine. It involves freezing the neck of the bottle and firing out a plug of ice and yeast. The bottle is then topped up and recorked.

Dosage Sweetened wine added to a sparkling wine after disgorgement.

Downy Mildew A disease that attacks vine leaves and fruit. It's associated with humidity and lack of air circulation.

Drip Irrigation An accurate way of watering a vineyard. Each vine has its own dripper and a controlled amount of water is applied.

Dryland Vineyard A vineyard that has no irrigation.

Esters Volatile compounds that can occur during fermentation or maturation. They impart a distinctive chemical taste.

Fermentation The process by which yeast converts sugar to alcohol with a by-product of carbon dioxide.

Fining The process of removing solids from wine to make it clear. There are several methods used.

Fortify The addition of spirit to increase the amount of alcohol in a wine.

Free-run Juice The first juice to come out of the press or drainer (as opposed to pressings).

Generic Wines labelled after their district of origin rather than their grape variety, e.g. Burgundy, Chablis, Champagne etc. These terms can no longer legally be used on Australian labels. *Cf.* Varietal.

Graft Changing the nature/variety of a vine by grafting a different variety onto a root stock.

Imperial A 6-litre bottle (contains eight 750-ml bottles).

Jeroboam A 4.5-litre champagne bottle.

Laccase   A milky condition on the surface of red wine caused by noble rot. The wine is usually pasteurised.

Lactic Acid   One of the acids found in grape juice; as the name suggests, it's milky and soft.

Lactobacillus   A micro-organism that ferments carbohydrates (glucose) or malic acid to produce lactic acid.

Lees   The sediment left after fermentation. It consists mainly of dead yeast cells.

Malic Acid   One of the acids found in grape juice. It has a hard/sharp taste like a Granny Smith apple.

Malolactic Fermentation   A secondary process that converts malic acid into lactic acid. It's encouraged in red wines when they are in barrel. If it occurs after bottling, the wine will be fizzy and cloudy.

Mercaptan   Ethyl mercaptan is a sulfur compound with a smell like garlic, burnt rubber or asparagus water.

Méthode Champenoise   The French method for producing effervescence in the bottle; a secondary fermentation process where the carbon dioxide produced is dissolved into the wine.

Methoxypyrazines   Substances that give sauvignon blanc and cabernet sauvignon that added herbaceousness when the grapes aren't fully ripe.

Mousse   The froth or head on sparkling wines.

Must   *see* Free-run juice.

Negociant   A French word that describes a person or organisation that produces and sells wine from grapes and/or bulk wine bought-in from other people.

Noble Rot   *see* Botrytis cinerea.

Non-vintage   A wine that is a blend of two or more years.

Oak   The least porous wood, genus *Quercus*, and used for wine storage containers.

Oenology   The science of winemaking.

Organic Viticulture   Growing grapes without the use of pesticides, fungicides or chemical fertilisers. Certain chemicals, e.g. copper sulfate, are permitted.

Organic Wines   Wines made from organically grown fruit without the addition of chemicals.

Oxidation   Browning and dullness of aroma and flavour caused by excessive exposure to air.

pH   The measure of the strength of acidity. The higher the pH the higher the alkalinity and the lower the acidity. Wines with high pH values should not be cellared.

Phenolics   A group of chemical compounds which includes the tannins and colour pigments of grapes. A white wine described as 'phenolic' has an excess of tannin, making it taste coarse.

Phylloxera   A louse that attacks the roots of a vine, eventually killing the plant.

Pigeage   To foot-press the grapes.

Pressings   The juice extracted by applying pressure to the skins after the free-run juice has been drained.

Pricked   A wine that is spoilt and smells of vinegar, due to excessive volatile acidity. *Cf.* Volatile.

Puncheon   A 500-litre barrel.

Racking   Draining off wine from the lees or other sediment to clarify it.

Saignée   French for bleeding: the winemaker has run off part of the juice of a red fermentation to concentrate what's left.

Skin Contact   Allowing the free-run juice to remain in contact with the skins; in the case of white wines, usually for a very short time.

Solero System   Usually a stack of barrels used for blending maturing wines. The oldest material is at the bottom and is topped up with younger material from the top barrels.

Solids   Minute particles suspended in a wine.

Sulfur Dioxide (SO₂)   (Code 220) A chemical added since Roman times to wine as a preservative and a bactericide.

Sur Lie   Wine that has been kept on lees and not racked or filtered before bottling.

Taché   A French term that means 'stained', usually by the addition of a small amount of red wine to sparkling wine to turn it pink.

Tannin   A complex substance derived from skins, pips and stalks of grapes as well as the oak casks. It has a preservative function and imparts dryness and grip to the finish.

Terroir   Arcane French expression that describes the complete growing environment of the vine, including climate, aspect, soil, etc., and the direct effect this has on the character of its wine.

Varietal   An industry-coined term used to refer to a wine by its grape variety, e.g. 'a shiraz'. *Cf.* Generic.

Véraison   The moment when the grapes change colour and gain sugar.

Vertical Tasting   A tasting of consecutive vintages of one wine.

Vigneron   A grapegrower or vineyard worker.

Vinegar   Acetic acid produced from fruit.

Vinify   The process of turning grapes into wine.

Vintage   The year of harvest, and the produce of a particular yeast.

Volatile   Excessive volatile acids in a wine.

Yeast   The micro-organism that converts sugar into alcohol.

Tasting Terms

The following terms refer to the sensory evaluation of wine.

Aftertaste   The taste (sensation) after the wine has been swallowed. It's usually called the finish.

Astringent (Astringency)   Applies to the finish of a wine. Astringency is caused by tannins that produce a mouth-puckering sensation and coat the teeth with dryness.

Balance   'The state of . . .'; the harmony between components of a wine.

Bilgy   An unfortunate aroma like the bilge of a ship. Usually caused by mouldy old oak.

Bitterness   A sensation detected at the back of the tongue. It's not correct in wine but is desirable in beer.

Bouquet   The aroma of a finished or mature wine.

Brettanomyces (Brett)   A spoilage yeast that produces chemical compounds that are present in most red wines but usually at small concentrations. In large doses, these cause aromas reminiscent of bandaids, sweaty horses and other unappetising things, as well as a metallic taste and bitter tannins on the palate. A recent scourge of the Australian wine industry.

Broad   A wine that lacks fruit definition; usually qualified as soft or coarse.

Burnt Match   A sulfide-related odour, often associated with wild or indigenous yeast fermentations in chardonnay. In small doses, can be a positive factor, adding complexity.

Cassis   A blackcurrant flavour common in cabernet sauvignon. It refers to a liqueur produced in France.

Chalky   An extremely dry sensation on the finish.

Cheesy   A dairy character sometimes found in wine, particularly sherries.

Cigar Box   A smell of tobacco and wood found in cabernet sauvignon.

Cloudiness   A fault in wine that is caued by suspended solids that make it look dull.

Cloying   Excessive sweetness that clogs the palate.

Corked   Spoiled wine that has reacted with a tainted cork, and smells like wet cardboard. (The taint is caused by trichloroanisole.)

Creamy   The feeling of cream in the mouth, a texture.

Crisp   Clean acid on the finish of a white wine.

Depth   The amount of fruit on the palate.

Dry   A wine that does not register sugar in the mouth.

Dull   Pertaining to colour; the wine is not bright or shining.

Dumb   Lacking nose or flavour on the palate.

Dusty   Applies to a very dry tannic finish; a sensation.

Earthy   Not as bad as it sounds, this is a loamy/mineral character that can add interest to the palate.

Finesse   The state of a wine. It refers to balance and style.

Finish   *see* Aftertaste.

Firm   Wine with strong, unyielding tannins.

Flabby   Wine with insufficient acid to balance ripe fruit flavours.

Fleshy   Wines of substance with plenty of fruit.

Flinty   A character on the finish that is akin to sucking dry creek pebbles.

Flor yeast   A yeast that grows on the surface of young sherry in partly filled barrels, producing aldehydes that are a key part of the flavour and aroma of fino and manzanilla sherries.

Garlic   *see* Mercaptan (in Wine Terms).

Grassy   A cut-grass odour, usually found in semillon and sauvignon blancs.

Grip   The effect on the mouth of tannin on the finish; a puckering sensation.

Hard   More tannin or acid than fruit flavour.

Herbaceous   Herbal smells or flavour in wine.

Hollow   A wine with a lack of flavour in the middle palate.

Hot   Wines high in alcohol that give a feeling of warmth and a slippery texture.

Hydrogen Sulfide   A rotten-egg-like character, usually created by yeasts during fermentation.

Implicit Sweetness   A just detectable sweetness from the presence of glycerin (rather than residual sugar).

Inky   Tannate of iron present in a wine which imparts a metallic taste.

Integrated (Well)   The component parts of a wine fit together without gaps or disorders.

Jammy   Ripe fruit that takes on the character of stewed jam.

Leathery   A smell like old leather, not necessarily bad if it's in balance.

Length (Long)   The measure of the registration of flavour in the mouth. (The longer the better.)

Lifted   The wine is given a lift by the presence of either volatile acid or wood tannins, e.g. vanillin oak lift.

Limpid   A colour term usually applied to star-bright white wine.

Madeirised   Wine that has aged to the point where it tastes like a madeira.

Mouldy   Smells like bathroom mould; dank.

Mouth-feel   The sensation the wine causes in the mouth; a textural term.

Musty   Stale, flat, out-of-condition wine.

Pepper   A component in either the nose or the palate that smells or tastes like cracked pepper.

Pungent   Wine with a strong nose.

Rancio   A nutty character found in aged fortifieds that is imparted by time on wood.

Reductive   *see* Hydrogen Sulfide.

Residual Sugar   The presence of unfermented grape sugar on the palate; common in sweet wines.

Rough Unpleasant, aggressive wines.

Round A full-bodied wine with plenty of mouth-feel (*q.v.*).

Sappy A herbaceous character that resembles sap.

Short A wine lacking in taste and structure. *See also* Length.

Sous-bois The French word for undergrowth. Used in describing some pinot noirs, especially those made with stalks included in the fermentation.

Spicy A wine with a high aromatic content; spicy character can also be imparted by wood.

Stalky Exposure to stalks, e.g. during fermentation. Leaves a bitter character in the wine.

Tart A lively wine with a lot of fresh acid.

Toasty A smell of cooked bread.

Vanillin The smell and taste of vanilla beans; usually imparted by oak ageing.

Varietal Refers to the distinguishing qualities of the grape variety used in the wine.

PRINCIPAL WINE REGIONS

WESTERN AUSTRALIA
1 Swan Valley
2 Perth Hills
3 Geographe
4 Margaret River
5 Pemberton/Manjimup
6 Great Southern

SOUTH AUSTRALIA
7 Riverland
8 Clare Valley
9 Barossa Valley
10 Eden Valley
11 Adelaide Hills
12 McLaren Vale
13 Langhorne Creek
14 Coonawarra

TASMANIA
15 Tamar Valley
16 Derwent Valley
17 Coal River
18 East Coast
19 Piper's River

VICTORIA
20 Henty/Drumborg
21 Murray Valley
22 Sunraysia
23 Gippsland
24 Mornington Peninsula

25 Yarra Valley
26 Sunbury
27 Geelong/Bellarine
   Peninsula
28 Grampians/Great Western
29 Macedon Ranges
30 Heathcote
31 Bendigo
32 Pyrenees
33 Rutherglen
34 King Valley
35 Beechworth
36 Goulburn Valley

NEW SOUTH WALES
37 Murray Valley
38 Tumbarumba
39 Riverina
40 Canberra District
41 Hilltops/Young
42 Cowra
43 Shoalhaven
44 Southern Highlands
45 Orange
46 Mudgee
47 Hunter Valley
48 Hastings Valley

QUEENSLAND
49 Granite Belt
50 South Burnett

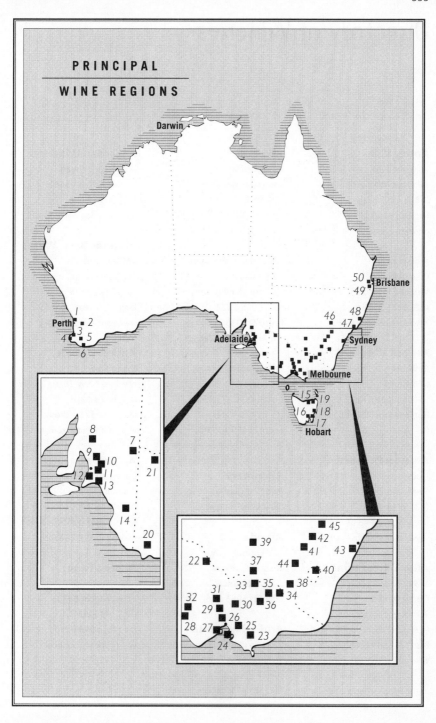

PRINCIPAL

WINE REGIONS

Darwin

Perth

Adelaide

Melbourne

Sydney

Brisbane

Hobart

Directory of Wineries

Abbey Vale
Wildwood Rd
Yallingup WA 6282
(08) 9755 2121
fax (08) 9755 2286
www.abbeyvale.com.au

Abercorn
Cassilis Rd
Mudgee NSW 2850
(02) 6373 3106
www.abercornwine.com.au

Affleck Vineyard
RMB 244
Millynn Rd
(off Gundaroo Rd)
Bungendore NSW 2651
(02) 6236 9276

Ainsworth Estate
Ducks Lane
Seville Vic. 3139
(03) 5964 4711
fax (03) 5964 4311
www.ainsworth-estate.com.au

Albert River Wines
1–117 Mundoolun
Connection Rd
Tamborine Qld 4270
(07) 5543 6622
fax (07) 5543 6627
www.albertriverwines.com.au

Alkoomi
Wingebellup Rd
Frankland WA 6396
(08) 9855 2229
fax (08) 9855 2284
www.alkoomiwines.com.au

All Saints Estate
All Saints Rd
Wahgunyah Vic. 3687
(02) 6035 2222
fax (02) 6035 2200
www.allsaintswine.com.au

Allandale
Lovedale Rd
Pokolbin NSW 2320
(02) 4990 4526
fax (02) 4990 1714
www.allandalewinery.com.au

Allanmere
(see First Creek)
www.allanmere.com.au

Allinda
119 Lorimer's Lane
Dixon's Creek Vic. 3775
(03) 5965 2450
fax (03) 5965 2467

Amberley Estate
Wildwood & Thornton Rds
Yallingup WA 6282
(08) 9755 2288
fax (08) 9755 2171
www.amberleyestate.com.au

Anderson Winery
Lot 13 Chiltern Rd
Rutherglen Vic. 3685
(03) 6032 8111
www.andersonwinery.com.au

Andraos Bros. Wines
150 Vineyard Rd
Sunbury Vic. 3429
(03) 9740 9703
fax (03) 9740 9795
www.andraosbros.com.au

Andrew Harris
Sydney Rd
Mudgee NSW 2850
(02) 6373 1213
fax (02) 6373 1296
www.andrewharris.com.au

Angove's
Bookmark Ave
Renmark SA 5341
(08) 8580 3100
fax (08) 8580 3155
www.angoves.com.au

Annie's Lane
Main North Rd
Watervale SA 5452
(08) 8843 0003
fax (08) 8843 0096
www.annieslane.com.au

Annvers
(no cellar door)
(08) 8374 1787
fax (08) 8374 2102
www.annvers.com.au

Antcliffe's Chase
RMB 4510
Caveat
via Seymour Vic. 3660
(03) 5790 4333

Apsley Gorge
'The Gulch'
Bicheno Tas. 7215
(03) 6375 1221
fax (03) 6375 1589

Arakoon
229 Main Rd
McLaren Vale SA 5171
(08) 8323 7339
fax (02) 6566 6288

Arlewood
Harmans South Rd
Wilyabrup WA 6284
Phone/fax (08) 9755 6267
www.arlewood.com.au

Armstrong Vineyards
(not open to public)
(08) 8277 6073
fax (08) 8277 6035

Arrowfield
Golden Hwy
Jerry's Plains NSW 2330
(02) 6576 4041
fax (02) 6576 4144
www.arrowfieldwines.com.au

Arthurs Creek Estate
(not open to public)
(03) 9714 8202

Ashton Hills
Tregarthen Rd
Ashton SA 5137
(08) 8390 1243
fax (08) 8390 1243

Ashwood Grove
(not open to public)
(03) 5030 5291

Auldstone
Booth's Rd
Taminick via Glenrowan
Vic. 3675
(03) 5766 2237
www.auldstone.com.au

Austins Barrabool
870 Steiglitz Rd
Sutherlands Creek Vic. 3331
(03) 5281 1799
fax (03) 5281 1673
www.abwines.com.au

Avalon
4480 Wangaratta–Whitfield Rd
Whitfield Vic. 3733
(03) 5729 3629
www.avalonwines.com.au

Baileys
Taminick Gap Rd
Glenrowan Vic. 3675
(03) 5766 2392
fax (03) 5766 2596
www.baileysofglenrowan.com.au

Baldivis Estate
(see Palandri)

Balgownie
Hermitage Rd
Maiden Gully Vic. 3551
(03) 5449 6222
fax (03) 5449 6506
www.balgownieestate.com

Balnaves
Main Rd
Coonawarra SA 5263
(08) 8737 2946
fax (08) 8737 2945
www.balnaves.com.au

Bannockburn
(not open to public)
Midland Hwy
Bannockburn Vic. 3331
tel/fax (03) 5243 7094
www.bannockburnvineyards.com

Banrock Station
(see Hardys)

Barak's Bridge
(see Yering Station)

Barambah Ridge
79 Goschnicks Rd
Redgate via Murgon
Qld 4605
(07) 4168 4766
fax (07) 4168 4770
www.barambahridge.com.au

Barossa Settlers
Trial Hill Rd
Lyndoch SA 5351
(08) 8524 4017

Barossa Valley Estate
Seppeltsfield Rd
Marananga SA 5355
(08) 8562 3599
fax (08) 8562 4255
www.brlhardy.com.au

Barratt
(not open to public)
PO Box 204
Summertown SA 5141
tel/fax (08) 8390 1788
www.barrattwines.com.au

Barwang
(see McWilliams)

Bass Phillip
(by appointment)
Cnr Tosch's & Hunts Rds
Leongatha South Vic. 3953
(03) 5664 3341

Batista
Franklin Rd
Middlesex WA 6258
tel/fax (08) 9772 3530

Bay of Fires
(see Hardys)

Belgenny
Level 8, 261 George St
Sydney NSW 2000
(02) 9247 5577
fax (02) 9247 7273
www.belgenny.com.au

Beresford
26 Kangarilla Rd
McLaren Vale SA 5171
(08) 8323 8899
fax (08) 8323 7911
www.beresfordwines.com.au

Beringer Blass
77 Southbank Blvd
Southbank Vic. 3000
(03) 8626 3300
fax (03) 8626 3450
www.beringerblass.com.au

Berrys Bridge
633 Carapooee Rd
St Arnaud Vic. 3478
(03) 5496 3220
fax (03) 5496 3322
www.berrysbridge.com.au

Best's Great Western
Western Hwy
Great Western Vic. 3377
(03) 5356 2250
fax (03) 5356 2430

Bethany
Bethany Rd
Bethany
via Tanunda SA 5352
(08) 8563 2086
fax (08) 8563 2086
www.bethany.com.au

Bianchet
187 Victoria Rd
Lilydale Vic. 3140
(03) 9739 1779
fax (03) 9739 1277
www.bianchet.com

Bidgeebong
(no cellar door)
PO Box 5393
Wagga Wagga NSW 2650
(02) 6931 9955
www.bidgeebong.com

Bindi
(not open to public)
343 Melton Rd
Gisborne Vic. 3437
(03) 5428 2564
fax (03) 5428 2564

Bird in Hand
Pfeiffer & Bird In Hand Rds
Woodside SA 5244
(08) 8389 9488
fax (08) 8389 9511
www.olivesoilwine.com

Birdwood Estate
Mannum Rd
Birdwood SA 5234
(08) 8263 0986

Blackjack Vineyard
Calder Hwy
Harcourt Vic. 3452
tel/fax (03) 5474 2355
www.blackjackwines.com.au

Bleasdale
Wellington Rd
Langhorne Creek SA 5255
(08) 8537 3001
www.bleasdale.com.au

Blewitt Springs
Recreational Rd
McLaren Vale SA 5171
(08) 8323 8689
www.hillsview.com.au

Bloodwood Estate
4 Griffin Rd
via Orange NSW 2800
(02) 6362 5631
www.bloodwood.com.au

Blue Pyrenees Estate
Vinoca Rd
Avoca Vic. 3467
(03) 5465 3202
fax (03) 5465 3529
www.bluepyrenees.com.au

Bookpurnong Hill
Bookpurnong Rd
Bookpurnong Hill
Loxton SA 5333
(08) 8584 1333
fax (08) 8584 1388
www.salenaestate.com.au

Boston Bay
Lincoln Hwy
Port Lincoln SA 5605
(08) 8684 3600
www.bostonbaywines.com.au

Botobolar
Botobolar Lane
PO Box 212
Mudgee NSW 2850
(02) 6373 3840
fax (02) 6373 3789
www.botobolar.com

Bowen Estate
Riddoch Hwy
Coonawarra SA 5263
(08) 8737 2229
fax (08) 8737 2173

Boyntons of Bright
Great Alpine Rd
Porepunkah Vic. 3740
(03) 5756 2356

Brands of Coonawarra
Naracoorte Hwy
Coonawarra SA 5263
(08) 8736 3260
fax (08) 8736 3208
www.mcwilliams.com.au

Brangayne
49 Pinnacle Rd
Orange NSW 2800
(02) 6365 3229
www.brangaynewines.com

Bremerton
Strathalbyn Rd
Langhorne Creek SA 5255
(08) 8537 3093
fax (08) 8537 3109
www.bremerton.com.au

Briagolong Estate
Valencia-Briagalong Rd
Briagalong Vic. 3860
tel/fax (03) 5147 2322

Brian Barry
(not open to public)
(08) 8363 6211

Briar Ridge
593 Mount View Rd
Mt View NSW 2321
tel/fax (02) 4990 3670
www.briarridge.com.au

Bridgewater Mill
(see Petaluma)

Brindabella Hills
Woodgrove Cl.
via Hall ACT 2618
(02) 6230 2583

Broke Estate
(see Ryan Family Wines)

Brokenwood
McDonalds Rd
Pokolbin NSW 2321
(02) 4998 7559
fax (02) 4998 7893
www.brokenwood.com.au

Brookland Valley
Caves Rd
Wilyabrup WA 6280
(08) 9755 6042
fax (08) 9755 6038
www.brooklandvalley.com.au

Brown Brothers
Meadow Crk Rd
(off the Snow Rd)
Milawa Vic. 3678
(03) 5720 5500
fax (03) 5720 5511
www.brown-brothers.com.au

Browns of Padthaway
PMB 196
Naracoorte SA 5271
(08) 8765 6040
fax (08) 8765 6003
www.browns-of-padthaway.com

Buller & Sons, R.L.
Three Chain Rd
Rutherglen Vic. 3685
(02) 6032 9660
www.rlbullerandson.com.au

Burge Family Winemakers
Barossa Hwy
Lyndoch SA 5351
(08) 8524 4644
fax (08) 8524 4444
www.burgefamily.com.au

Burnbrae
Hargraves Rd
Erudgere
Mudgee NSW 2850
(02) 6373 3504
fax (02) 6373 3435

By Farr
(no cellar door)
101 Kelly Lane
Bannockburn Vic. 3331
(03) 5281 1733
tel/fax (03) 5281 1433

Calais Estate
Palmers Lane
Pokolbin NSW 2321
(02) 4998 7654
fax (02) 4998 7813

Cambewarra Estate
520 Illaroo Rd
Cambewarra NSW 2541
(02) 4446 0170
fax (02) 4446 0170

Campbells
Murray Valley Hwy
Rutherglen Vic. 3685
(02) 6032 9458
fax (02) 6032 9870
www.campbellswines.com.au

Cannibal Creek
260 Tynong North Rd
Tynong North Vic. 3813
(03) 5942 8380
fax (03) 5942 8202

Canobolas-Smith
Boree Lane (off Cargo Rd)
Orange NSW 2800
tel/fax (02) 6365 6113

Canonbah Bridge
Merryanbone Station
Warren NSW 2824
(02) 6833 9966
www.canonbah.com.au

Cape Clairault
via Caves Rd
or Bussell Hwy
CMB Carbunup River
WA 6280
(08) 9755 6225
fax (08) 9755 6229

Cape Mentelle
Wallcliffe Rd
Margaret River WA 6285
(08) 9757 0888
fax (08) 9757 3233
www.capementelle.com.au

Capel Vale
Lot 5 Capel North West Rd
Capel WA 6271
(08) 9727 0111
fax (08) 9727 0136
www.capelvale.com

Capercaillie
Londons Rd
Lovedale NSW 2325
(02) 4990 2904
fax (02) 4991 1886
www.capercailliewine.com.au

Carlei Green Vineyards
1 Albers Rd
Upper Beaconsfield Vic. 3808
(03) 5944 4599
www.carlei.com.au

Carlyle
(see Pfeiffer)

Casa Freschi
Ridge Rd
Summertown SA 5141
tel/fax (08) 8536 4569
www.casafreschi.com.au

Cascabel
Rogers Rd
Willunga SA 5172
(08) 8557 4434
fax (08) 8557 4435

Casella Carramar Estate
Wakley Rd
Yenda NSW 2681
(02) 6961 3000
www.casellawines.com.au

Cassegrain
Fern Bank Crk Rd
Port Macquarie NSW 2444
(02) 6583 7777
fax (02) 6584 0353
www.cassegrainwines.com.au

Castagna
(by appointment)
88 Ressom Lane
Beechworth Vic. 3747
(03) 5728 2888
fax (03) 5728 2898
www.castagna.com.au

Castle Rock Estate
Porongurup Rd
Porongurup WA 6324
(08) 9853 1035
fax (08) 9853 1010
www.castlerockestate.com.au

Chain of Ponds
Main Adelaide Rd
Gumeracha SA 5233
(08) 8389 1415
fax (08) 8389 1877
www.chainofpondswines.com.au

Chalkers Crossing
387 Grenfell Rd
Young NSW 2594
(02) 6382 6900
fax (02) 6382 5068
www.chalkerscrossing.com.au

Chambers Rosewood
Corowa–Rutherglen Rd
Rutherglen Vic. 3685
(02) 6032 8641
fax (02) 6032 8101

Chandon
Maroondah Hwy
Coldstream Vic. 3770
(03) 9739 1110
fax (03) 9739 1095
www.chandon.com.au

Chapel Hill
Chapel Hill Rd
McLaren Vale SA 5171
(08) 8323 8429
fax (08) 8323 9245
www.chapelhillwine.com.au

Charles Cimicky
Hermann Thumm Dve
Lyndoch SA 5351
(08) 8524 4025
fax (08) 8524 4772

Charles Melton
Krondorf Rd
Tanunda SA 5352
(08) 8563 3606
fax (08) 8563 3422
www.charlesmeltonwines.com.au

Charles Sturt University
Boorooma St
North Wagga Wagga
NSW 2678
(02) 6933 2435
fax (02) 6933 4072
www.csu.edu.au/winery

Chateau Leamon
5528 Calder Hwy
Bendigo Vic. 3550
(03) 5447 7995
www.chateauleamon.com.au

Chatsfield
O'Neill Rd
Mount Barker WA 6324
tel/fax (08) 9851 2660
www.chatsfield.com.au

Chatto
(see First Creek)

Chestnut Grove
Perup Rd
Manjimup WA 6258
(08) 9772 4255
fax (08) 9772 4543
www.chestnutgrove.com.au

Cheviot Bridge
(no cellar door)
(03) 9820 9080
fax (03) 9820 9070
www.cheviotbridge.com.au

Chrismont
Upper King Valley Rd
Cheshunt Vic. 3678
(03) 5729 8220
fax (03) 5729 8253
www.chrismontwines.com.au

Clarendon Hills
(not open to public)
(08) 8364 1484
www.clarendonhills.com.au

Classic McLaren
PO Box 245
McLaren Vale SA 5171
tel/fax (08) 8323 9551

Cleveland
Shannons Rd
Lancefield Vic. 3435
(03) 5429 9000
fax (03) 5429 2143
www.clevelandwinery.com.au

Clonakilla
Crisps Lane
Murrumbateman NSW 2582
(02) 6227 5877
www.clonakilla.com.au

Cloudy Bay
(see Cape Mentelle)

Clover Hill
(see Taltarni Vineyards)

Cobaw Ridge
Perc Boyer's Lane
East Pastoria
via Kyneton Vic. 3444
tel/fax (03) 5423 5227
www.cobawridge.com.au

Cockfighter's Ghost
(see Poole's Rock)

Cofield
Distillery Rd
Wahgunyah Vic. 3687
(03) 6033 3798
www.cofieldwines.com

Coldstream Hills
31 Maddens Lane
Coldstream Vic. 3770
(03) 5964 9410
fax (03) 5964 9389
www.coldstreamhills.com.au

Connor Park
59 Connor Road
Leichardt Vic. 3516
(03) 5437 5234
fax (03) 5437 5204
www.bendigowine.com.au

Constable Hershon
1 Gillards Rd
Pokolbin NSW 2320
(02) 4998 7887
fax (02) 4998 6555
www.constablehershon.com.au

Cookoothama
(see Nugan Estate)

Coolangatta Estate
1355 Bolong Rd
Shoalhaven Heads NSW 2535
(02) 4448 7131
fax (02) 4448 7997
www.coolangattaestate.com.au

Coombend
Swansea Tas. 7190
(03) 6257 8256
fax (03) 6257 8484

Cope-Williams
Glenfern Rd
Romsey Vic. 3434
(03) 5429 5428
fax (03) 5429 5655
www.cope-williams.com.au

Coriole
Chaffeys Rd
McLaren Vale SA 5171
(08) 8323 8305
fax (08) 8323 9136
www.coriole.com

Cowra Estate
Boorowa Rd
Cowra NSW 2794
(02) 6342 3650

Crabtree of Watervale
North Tce
Watervale SA 5452
(08) 8843 0069
fax (08) 8843 0144

Craig Avon
Craig Avon Lane
Merricks North Vic. 3926
(03) 5989 7465

Craigie Knowe
Cranbrook Tas. 7190
(03) 6223 5620

Craiglee
Sunbury Rd
Sunbury Vic. 3429
(03) 9744 4489
fax (03) 9744 4489

Craigmoor
Craigmoor Rd
Mudgee NSW 2850
(02) 6372 2208

Craigow
Richmond Rd
Cambridge Tas. 7170
(03) 6248 5482

Craneford
Moorundie St
Truro SA 5356
(08) 8564 0003
fax (08) 8564 0008
www.cranefordwines.com

Cranswick Estate
(see Evans & Tate)

Crawford River
Condah Vic. 3303
(03) 5578 2267

Crittenden at Dromana
25 Harrisons Rd
Dromana Vic. 3936
(03) 5981 8322
fax (03) 5981 8366

Crofters
(see Houghton)

Cullens

Caves Rd
Wilyabrup
via Cowaramup WA 6284
tel/fax (08) 9755 5277
www.cullenwines.com.au

Currency Creek

Winery Rd
Currency Creek SA 5214
(08) 8555 4069
www.currencycreekwines.com.au

Dalfarras

(see Tahbilk)

Dalrymple

Pipers Brook Rd
Pipers Brook Tas. 7254
(03) 6382 7222

Dalwhinnie

Taltarni Rd
Moonambel Vic. 3478
(03) 5467 2388
www.dalwhinnie.com.au

Dal Zotto

Edi Rd
Cheshunt Vic. 3678
(03) 5729 8321
fax (03) 5729 8490

D'Arenberg

Osborn Rd
McLaren Vale SA 5171
(08) 8323 8206
www.darenberg.com.au

Darling Estate

(by appointment only)
Whitfield Rd
Cheshunt Vic. 3678
(03) 5729 8396
fax (03) 5729 8396

Darling Park

232 Red Hill Rd
Red Hill 3937
tel/fax (03) 5989 2324
www.darlingparkwinery.com

David Traeger

139 High St
Nagambie Vic. 3608
(03) 5794 2514

Deakin Estate

(see Katnook Estate)

De Bortoli

De Bortoli Rd
Bibul NSW 2680
(02) 6966 0100
fax (02) 6966 0199
or
Pinnacle Lane
Dixons Creek Vic. 3775
(03) 5965 2423
Fax (03) 5965 2464
www.debortoli.com.au

De Iuliis

Lot 21 Broke Rd
Pokolbin NSW 2320
(02) 4993 8000
fax (02) 4998 7168

Delamere

4238 Bridport Rd
Pipers Brook Tas. 7254
(03) 6382 7190

Delatite

Stoney's Rd
Mansfield Vic. 3722
(03) 5775 2922
fax (03) 5775 2911
www.delatitewinery.com.au

Dennis

Kangarilla Rd
McLaren Vale SA 5171
(08) 8323 8665
fax (08) 8323 9121
www.daringacellars.com.au

Devil's Lair

(not open to public)
PO Box 212
Margaret River WA 6285
(08) 9757 7573
fax (08) 9757 7533
www.devilslair.com.au

Diamond Valley Vineyards

Kinglake Rd
St Andrews Vic. 3761
(03) 9722 0840
fax (03) 9722 2373
www.diamondvalley.com.au

Dominion Wines

Upton Rd, via Avenel
Strathbogie Ranges Vic. 3664
(03) 5796 2718
fax (03) 5796 2719
www.dominionwines.com

Doonkuna Estate

Barton Hwy
Murrumbateman NSW 2582
(02) 6227 5811
fax (02) 6227 5085
www.doonkuna.com.au

Dowie Doole
182 Main Rd
McLaren Vale SA 5171
(08) 8323 7314
fax (08) 8323 7305

Drayton's Bellevue
Oakey Creek Rd
Pokolbin NSW 2320
(02) 4998 7513
fax (02) 4998 7743
www.draytonswines.com.au

Dromana Estate
RMB 555 Old Moorooduc Rd
Tuerong Vic. 3933
office (03) 5974 3899
fax (03) 5974 1155
www.dromanaestate.com.au

Elderton
3 Tanunda Rd
Nuriootpa SA 5355
(08) 8568 7878
fax (08) 8568 7879
www.eldertonwines.com.au

Eldridge Estate
120 Arthurs Seat Rd
Red Hill Vic. 3937
(03) 5989 2644
fax (03) 5989 2089
www.eldridge-estate.com.au

Elgee Park
(no cellar door)
Junction Rd
Merricks Nth Vic. 3926
(03) 5989 7338
fax (03) 5989 7553
www.elgeeparkwines.com.au

Eppalock Ridge
Metcalfe Pool Rd
Redesdale Vic. 3444
(03) 5425 3135

Evans & Tate
Lionel's Vineyard
Payne Rd
Jindong WA 6280
(08) 9755 8855
fax (08) 9755 4362
www.evansandtate.com.au

Evans Family
Palmers Lane
Pokolbin NSW 2320
(02) 4998 7333

Fergusson's
84 Wills Rd
Yarra Glen Vic. 3775
(03) 5965 2237
www.fergussonwinery.com.au

Fermoy Estate
Metricup Rd
Wilyabrup WA 6284
(08) 9755 6285
fax (08) 9755 6251
www.fermoy.com.au

Fern Hill Estate
Ingoldby Rd
McLaren Flat SA 5171
(08) 8323 9666
fax (08) 8323 9280
www.fernhillestate.com.au

Ferngrove
Ferngrove Rd
Frankland WA 6396
(08) 9855 2378
fax (08) 9855 2368
www.ferngrove.com.au

Fettler's Rest
(see Jindalee)

Fire Gully
(see Pierro)

First Creek
Monarch Wines
McDonalds Rd
Pokolbin NSW 2320
(02) 4998 7293
fax (02) 4998 7294
www.firstcreekwines.com.au

Fleur De Lys
(see Seppelt)

Flinders Bay
(see Old Station)

Fontys Pool
(see Cape Mentelle)

Fox Creek
Malpas Rd
Willunga SA 5172
(08) 8556 2403
fax (08) 8556 2104
www.foxcreekwines.com.au

Fox River
(see Goundrey)

Frankland Estate
Frankland Rd
Frankland WA 6396
(08) 9855 1544
fax (08) 9855 1549
www.franklandestate.com.au

Freycinet Vineyard
Tasman Hwy
Bicheno Tas. 7215
(03) 6257 8574
fax (03) 6257 8454

Gabriel's Paddocks
Deasy's Rd
Pokolbin NSW 2321
(02) 4998 7650
fax (02) 4998 7603
www.gabrielspaddocks.com.au

Galafrey
Quangellup Rd
Mount Barker WA 6324
(08) 9851 2022
fax (08) 9851 2324

Galah Wines
Box 231
Ashton SA 5137
(08) 8390 1243

Gapsted Wines
Great Alpine Rd
Gapsted Vic. 3737
(03) 5751 1383
fax (03) 5751 1368
www.gapstedwines.com

Garden Gully
Western Hwy
Great Western Vic. 3377
(03) 5356 2400
www.gardengully.com.au

Gartelmann
Lovedale Rd
Lovedale NSW 2321
(02) 4930 7113
fax (02) 4930 7114
www.gartelmann.com.au

Gembrook Hill
(by appointment only)
Launching Place Rd
Gemrook Vic. 3783
(03) 5968 1622
fax (03) 5968 1699

Gemtree
Kangarilla Rd
McLaren Vale SA 5171
(08) 8323 8199
fax (08) 8323 7889
www.gemtreevineyards.com.au

Geoff Merrill
291 Pimpala Rd
Woodcroft SA 5162
(08) 8381 6877
fax (08) 8322 2244
www.geoffmerrillwines.com.au

Geoff Weaver
(not open to public)
2 Gilpin Lane
Mitcham SA 5062
(08) 8272 2105
fax (08) 8271 0177
www.geoffweaver.com.au

Giaconda
(not open to public)
Beechworth Vic.
(03) 5727 0246
www.giaconda.com.au

Gilbert Wines
Albany Hwy
Kendenup WA 6323
(08) 9851 4028
(08) 9851 4021

Glaetzer
34 Barossa Valley Way
Tanunda SA 5352
(08) 8563 0288
fax (08) 8563 0218
www.glaetzer.com

Glenara
126 Range Rd Nth
Upper Hermitage SA 5131
(08) 8380 5277
fax (08) 8380 5056
www.glenara.com.au

Glenguin
Boutique Wine Centre
Broke NSW 2330
tel/fax (02) 4998 7474

Golden Grove Estate
Sundown Rd
Ballandean Qld 4382
(07) 4684 1291
www.goldengrove.com.au

Goona Warra
790 Sunbury Rd
Sunbury Vic. 3429
(03) 9740 7766
fax (03) 9744 7648
www.goonawarra.com.au

The Gorge
(see Pothana Vineyard)

Goundrey
Muir Hwy
Mount Barker WA 6324
(08) 9892 1777
fax (08) 9851 1997
www.goundrey.com

Gramp's
(see Orlando)

Grand Cru Estate
Ross Dewell's Rd
Springton SA 5235
(08) 8568 2378

Granite Hills
Burke and Wills Track
Baynton
via Kyneton Vic. 3444
(03) 5423 7273
fax (03) 5423 7288
www.granitehills.com.au

Grant Burge
Jacobs Creek
Barossa Valley Hwy
Tanunda SA 5352
(08) 8563 3700
Fax (08) 8563 2807
www.grantburgewines.com.au

Green Point
(see Chandon)

Greenock Creek
Radford Rd
Seppeltsfield SA 5360
(08) 8562 8103
fax (08) 8562 8259

Grosset
King St
Auburn SA 5451
(08) 8849 2175
fax (08) 8849 2292
www.grosset.com.au

Grove Estate
Murringo Rd
Young NSW 2594
(02) 6382 6999
fax (02) 6382 4527
www.groveestate.com.au

Gulf Station
(see De Bortoli)

Hainault
255 Walnut Road
Bickley WA 6076
(08) 9293 8339
fax (08) 9293 8339
www.hainault.com.au

Half Mile Creek
(see Beringer Blass)

Hamilton
Willunga Vineyards
Main South Rd
Willunga SA 5172
(08) 8556 2288
fax (08) 8556 2868
www.hamiltonwinegroup.com.au

Hamilton's Ewell
Barossa Valley Way
Nuriootpa SA 5355
(08) 8562 4600
fax (08) 8562 4611
www.hamiltonewell.com.au

Hanging Rock
Jim Rd
Newham Vic. 3442
(03) 5427 0542
fax (03) 5427 0310
www.hangingrock.com.au

Hanson Wines
'Oolorong'
49 Cleveland Ave
Lower Plenty Vic. 3093
(03) 9439 7425

Happs
Commonage Rd
Dunsborough WA 6281
(08) 9755 3300
fax (08) 9755 3846
www.happs.com.au

Harcourt Valley
Calder Hwy
Harcourt Vic. 3453
(03) 5474 2223

Hardys
Reynella Rd
Reynella SA 5161
(08) 8392 2222
fax (08) 8392 2202
www.hardywines.com.au

Harewood Estate
Scotsdale Rd
Denmark WA 6333
(08) 9840 9078
fax (08) 9840 9053

Haselgrove Wines
Sand Rd
McLaren Vale SA 5171
(08) 8323 8706
fax (08) 8323 8049
www.haselgrove.com.au

Hay Shed Hill
Harmans Mill Rd
Wilyabrup WA 6285
(08) 9755 6046
fax (08) 9758 5988
www.hayshedhill.com.au

Heathcote Winery
183 High St
Heathcote Vic. 3523
(03) 5433 2595
fax (03) 5433 3081
www.heathcotewinery.com.au

Heathfield Ridge
Caves Rd
Naracoorte SA 5271
(08) 8363 5800
fax (08) 8363 1980
www.heathfieldridgewines.com.au

Heggies
(see Yalumba)

Helm's
Yass River Rd
Murrumbateman NSW 2582
(02) 6227 5953
fax (02) 6227 0207
www.helmwines.com.au

Henschke
Moculta Rd
Keyneton SA 5353
(08) 8564 8223
fax (08) 8564 8294
www.henschke.com.au

Heritage Wines
Seppeltsfield Rd
Marananga
via Tununda SA 5352
(08) 8562 2880

Hewitson
16 McGowan Ave
Unley SA 5061
(08) 8271 5755
fax (08) 8271 5570
www.hewitson.com.au

Hickinbotham
Nepean Hwy
Dromana Vic. 3936
(03) 5981 0355
fax (03) 5987 0692
www.hickinbotham.biz

Highbank
Riddoch Hwy
Coonawarra SA 5263
(08) 8736 3311
www.highbank.com.au

Highwood
(see Beresford)

Hill Smith Estate
(see Yalumba)

Hillstowe Wines
104 Main Rd
Hahndorf SA 5245
(08) 8388 1400
fax (08) 8388 1411
www.hillstowe.com.au

Hollick
Racecourse Rd
Coonawarra SA 5263
(08) 8737 2318
fax (08) 8737 2952
www.hollick.com

Holm Oak
11 West Bay Rd
Rowella, Tas. 7270
(03) 6394 7577
fax (03) 6394 7350
www.holm-oak.com

Home Hill
38 Nairn St
Ranelagh Tas. 7109
(03) 6264 1200
fax (03) 6264 1069
www.homehillwines.com.au

Homes
(see Massoni Home)

Honeytree
130 Gillards Rd
Pokolbin NSW 2321
tel/fax (02) 4998 7693
www.honeytree.wines.com

Hope Estate
Cobcroft Rd
Broke NSW 2330
(02) 6579 1161
fax (02) 6579 1373

Horseshoe Vineyard
Horseshoe Rd
Horseshoe Valley
Denman NSW 2328
(02) 6541 3512

Houghton
Dale Rd
Middle Swan WA 6056
(08) 9274 5100
fax (08) 9250 3872
www.houghton-wines.com.au

House of Certain Views
(see Margan)

Howard Park
Scotsdale Rd
Denmark WA 6333
(08) 9848 2345
fax (08) 9848 2064
www.howardparkwines.com.au

Hugh Hamilton Wines
McMurtrie Rd
McLaren Vale SA 5171
(08) 8323 8689
fax (08) 8323 9488
www.hamiltonwines.com.au

Hugo
Elliott Rd
McLaren Flat SA 5171
(08) 8383 0098
fax (08) 8383 0446

Hungerford Hill
(see Cassegrain)

Huntington Estate
Cassilis Rd
Mudgee NSW 2850
(02) 6373 3825
fax (02) 6373 3730

Ingoldby
Kangarilla Rd
McLaren Vale SA 5171
(08) 8383 0005
www.beringerblass.com.au

Innisfail
(not open to public)
(03) 5276 1258

Ivanhoe
Marrowbone Rd
Pokolbin NSW 2320
(02) 4998 7325
www.ivanhoewines.com.au

James Irvine
Roeslers Rd
Eden Valley SA 5235
PO Box 308
Angaston SA 5353
(08) 8564 1046
fax (08) 8564 1314
www.irvinewines.com.au

Jamiesons Run
(see Beringer Blass)

Jane Brook
Toodyay Rd
Middle Swan WA 6056
(08) 9274 1432
fax (08) 9274 1211
www.janebrook.com.au

Jansz
(see Yalumba)

Jasper Hill
Drummonds Lane
Heathcote Vic. 3523
(03) 5433 2528
fax (03) 5433 3143

Jeanneret
Jeanneret Rd
Sevenhill SA 5453
(08) 8843 4308
fax (08) 8843 4251
www.ascl.com/j-wines

Jeir Creek Wines
Gooda Creek Rd
Murrumbateman NSW 2582
(02) 6227 5999

Jenke Vineyards
Jenke Rd
Rowland Flat SA 5352
(08) 8524 4154
fax (08) 8524 4154
www.jenkevineyards.com

Jim Barry
Main North Rd
Clare SA 5453
(08) 8842 2261
fax (08) 8842 3752

Jindalee
(not open to public)
(03) 5276 1280
fax 5276 1537
www.jindaleewines.com.au

Jingalla
Bolganup Dam Rd
Porongurup WA 6324
(08) 9853 1023
fax (08) 9853 1023
www.jingallawines.com.au

John Gehrig
80 Gehrig's Lane
Oxley Vic. 3678
(03) 5727 3395
www.johngehrigwines.com.au

Joseph
(see Primo Estate)

Juniper Estate
Harmans Rd Sth
Cowaramup WA 6284
(08) 9755 9000
fax (08) 9755 9100
www.juniperestate.com.au

Kangarilla Road Winery
Kangarilla Rd
McLaren Flat SA 5171
(08) 8383 0533
fax (08) 8383 0044
www.kangarillaroad.com.au

Kara Kara
Sunraysia Hwy
St Arnaud Vic. 3478
tel/fax (03) 5496 3294
www.pyrenees.org.au/karakara.htm

Karina Vineyards
35 Harrisons Rd
Dromana Vic. 3936
(03) 5981 0137

Karl Seppelt
(see Grand Cru Estate)

Karrivale
Woodlands Rd
Porongurup WA 6324
(08) 9853 1009
fax (08) 9853 1129

Karriview
RMB 913
Roberts Rd
Denmark WA 6333
(08) 9840 9381
www.karriviewwines.com.au

Katnook Estate
Riddoch Hwy
Coonawarra SA 5263
(08) 8737 2394
fax (08) 8737 2397
www.katnookestate.com.au

Kays Amery
Kay's Rd
McLaren Vale SA 5171
(08) 8323 8201
fax (08) 8323 9199
www.kaybrothersamerywines.com

Keith Tulloch
Hunter Ridge Winery
Hermitage Rd
Pokolbin NSW 2320
(02) 4998 7500
fax (02) 4998 7211
www.keithtullochwine.com.au

Kies Estate
Barossa Valley Way
Lyndoch SA 5351
(08) 8524 4110
www.kieswines.com.au

Kilikanoon
PO Box 205
Auburn SA 5451
tel/fax (08) 8843 4377
www.kilikanoon.com.au

Killawarra
(see Southcorp Wines)

Killerby
Minnimup Rd
Gelorup WA 6230
(08) 9795 7222
fax (08) 9795 7835
www.killerby.com.au

Kingston Estate
Sturt Hwy
Kingston-on-Murray SA 5331
(08) 8583 0500
fax (08) 8583 0304
www.kingstonestatewines.com

Kirrihill Estates
Farrell Flat Rd
Clare SA 5453
(08) 8842 1233
fax (08) 8842 1556
www.kirrihillestates.com.au

Knappstein Wines
2 Pioneer Ave
Clare SA 5453
(08) 8842 2600
fax (08) 8842 3831
www.knappsteinwines.com.au

Kooyong
110 Hunts Rd
Tuerong Vic. 3933
(03) 5989 7355
fax (03) 5989 7677
www.kooyong.com

Koppamurra
(no cellar door)
PO Box 110
Blackwood SA 5051
(08) 8271 4127
fax (08) 8271 0726
www.koppamurrawines.com.au

Kulkunbulla
Brokenback Estate
1595 Broke Rd
Pokolbin NSW 2320
(02) 4998 7140
fax (02) 4998 7142
www.kulkunbulla.com.au

Kyeema
(not open to public)
PO Box 282
Belconnen ACT 2616
(02) 6254 7557

Laanecoorie
(cellar door by arrangement)
RMB 1330
Dunolly Vic. 3472
(03) 5468 7260

Lake Breeze
Step Rd
Langhorne Creek SA 5255
(08) 8537 3017
fax (08) 8537 3267
www.lakebreeze.com.au

Lake's Folly
Broke Rd
Pokolbin NSW 2320
(02) 4998 7507
fax (02) 4998 7322
www.lakesfolly.com.au

Lamont's
Bisdee Rd
Millendon WA 6056
(08) 9296 4485
fax (08) 9296 1663
www.lamonts.com.au

Lancefield Winery
Woodend Rd
Lancefield Vic. 3435
(03) 5433 5292

The Lane
Ravenswood Lane
Hahndorf SA 5245
(08) 8388 1250
fax (08) 8388 7233
www.ravenswoodlane.com.au

Langmeil
Cnr Langmeil & Para Rds
Tanunda SA 5352
(08) 8563 2595
fax (08) 8563 3622
www.langmeilwinery.com.au

Lark Hill
521 Bungendore Rd
Bungendore NSW 2621
(02) 6238 1393
www.larkhillwine.com.au

Laurel Bank
(by appointment only)
130 Black Snake Lane
Granton Tas. 7030
(03) 6263 5977
fax (03) 6263 3117

Leasingham
7 Dominic St
Clare SA 5453
(08) 8842 2555
fax (08) 8842 3293
www.leasingham-wines.com.au

Leconfield
Riddoch Hwy
Coonawarra SA 5263
(08) 8737 2326
fax (08) 8737 2285
www.leconfield.com.au

Leeuwin Estate
Stevens Rd
Margaret River WA 6285
(08) 9757 0000
fax (08) 9757 0001
www.leeuwinestate.com.au

Leland Estate
PO Lenswood SA 5240
(08) 8389 6928
www.lelandestate.com.au

Lengs & Cooter
24 Lindsay Tce
Belair SA 5052
tel/fax (08) 8278 3998
www.lengscooter.com.au

Lenswood Vineyards
3 Cyril John Crt
Athelstone SA 5076
tel/fax (08) 8365 3766
www.knappsteinlenswood.com.au

Lenton Brae
Caves Rd
Wilyabrup WA 6280
(08) 9755 6255
fax (08) 9755 6268
www.lentonbrae.com

Leo Buring
(see Southcorp Wines)

Lillydale Vineyards
Davross Crt
Seville Vic. 3139
(03) 5964 2016
www.mcwilliams.com.au

Lillypilly Estate
Farm 16, Lilly Pilly Rd
Leeton NSW 2705
(02) 6953 4069
fax (02) 6953 4980
www.lillypilly.com

Lindemans
McDonalds Rd
Pokolbin NSW 2320
(02) 4998 7501
fax (02) 4998 7682
www.southcorp.com.au

The Little Wine Company
824 Milbrodale Rd
Broke NSW 2330
(02) 6579 1111
fax (02) 6579 1440
www.thelittlewinecompany.
com.au

Logan
(not open to public)
(02) 9958 6844
www.loganwines.com.au

Long Gully
Long Gully Rd
Healesville Vic. 3777
tel/fax (03) 5962 3663
www.longgullyestate.com

Longleat
Old Weir Rd
Murchison Vic. 3610
(03) 5826 2294
fax (03) 5826 2510
www.longleatwines.com

Lovegrove
Heidelberg–Kinglake Road
Cottlesbridge Vic. 3099
(03) 9718 1569
fax (03) 9718 1028

Lowe Family
Ashbourne Vineyard
Tinja Lane
Mudgee NSW 2850
(02) 6372 0800
fax (02) 6372 0811
www.lowewine.com.au

Madew
Westering Vineyard
Federal Hwy
Lake George NSW 2581
(02) 4848 0026
fax (02) 4848 0026
www.madewwines.com.au

Madfish
(see Howard Park)

Maglieri
RSD 295 Douglas Gully Rd
McLaren Flat SA 5171
(08) 8383 2211
fax (08) 8383 0735
www.beringerblass.com.au

Main Ridge
Lot 48 Williams Rd
Red Hill Vic. 3937
(03) 5989 2686
www.mre.com.au

Majella
Lynn Rd
Coonawarra SA 5263
(08) 8736 3055
fax (08) 8736 3057
www.majellawines.com.au

Malcolm Creek
(open weekends and public
holidays)
Bonython Rd
Kersbrook SA 5231
tel/fax (08) 8389 3235

Margan Family
1238 Milbrodale Rd
Broke NSW 2330
tel/fax (02) 6579 1317
www.margan.com.au

Maritime Estate
Tuck's Rd
Red Hill Vic. 3937
(03) 5989 2735

Massoni Home
(by appointment only)
Mornington–Flinders Rd
Red Hill Vic. 3937
(03) 5981 8008
fax (03) 5981 2014
www.massoniwines.com

Maxwell
Cnr Olivers & Chalkhill Rds
McLaren Vale SA 5171
(08) 8323 8200
www.maxwellwines.com.au

McAlister
(not open to public)
RMB 6810
Longford Vic. 3851
(03) 5149 7229

McGuigan
Cnr Broke & McDonalds Rds
Pokolbin NSW 2320
(02) 4998 7700
fax (02) 4998 7401
www.mcguiganwines.com.au

McWilliams
Hanwood NSW 2680
(02) 6963 0001
fax (02) 6963 0002
www.mcwilliams.com.au

Meadowbank
Denholms Rd
Cambridge Tas. 7170
(03) 6248 4484
fax (03) 6248 4485
www.meadowbankwines.com.au

Meerea Park
Lot 3 Palmers Lane
Pokolbin NSW 2320
(02) 4998 7006
fax (02) 4998 7005
www.meereapark.com.au

Merricks Estate
Cnr Thompsons Lane &
Frankston–Flinders Rd
Merricks Vic. 3916
(03) 5989 8416
fax (03) 9613 4242

Miceli
60 Main Creek Rd
Arthur's Seat Vic. 3936
(03) 5989 2755

Middleton Estate
Flagstaff Hill Rd
Middleton SA 5213
(08) 8555 4136
fax (08) 8555 4108

The Mill
(see Windowrie Estate)

Mintaro Cellars
Leasingham Rd
Mintaro SA 5415
(08) 8843 9150
www.mintarowines.com.au

Miramar
Henry Lawson Dr.
Mudgee NSW 2850
(02) 6960 3000
www.miramarwines.com.au

Miranda Wines
57 Jordaryan Ave
Griffith NSW 2680
(02) 6960 3000
fax (02) 6962 6944
www.mirandawines.com.au

Mirrool Creek
(see Miranda Wines)

Mitchell
Hughes Park Rd
Sevenhill via Clare SA 5453
(08) 8843 4258
www.mitchellwines.com

Mitchelton Wines
Mitcheltstown
Nagambie 3608
(03) 5736 2222
fax (03) 5736 2266
www.mitchelton.com.au

Molly Morgan
Talga Rd
Lovedale NSW 2321
(02) 4930 7695
fax (02) 9816 2680
www.mollymorgan.com

Monichino
70 Berry's Rd
Katunga Vic. 3640
(03) 5864 6452
fax (03) 5864 6538

Montalto
33 Shoreham Rd
Red Hill South Vic. 3937
(03) 5989 8412
fax (03) 5989 8417
www.montalto.com.au

Montara
Chalambar Rd
Ararat Vic. 3377
(03) 5352 3868
fax (03) 5352 4968
www.montara.com.au

Montrose/Poets Corner
Henry Lawson Dr.
Mudgee NSW 2850
(02) 6372 2208
www.poetscornerwines.com.au

Moondah Brook
(see Houghton)

Moorilla Estate
655 Main Rd
Berridale Tas. 7011
(03) 6277 9900
www.moorilla.com.au

Moorooduc Estate
Derril Rd
Moorooduc Vic. 3933
(03) 5971 8506
www.moorooducestate.com.au

**Mornington Vineyards
Estate**
(see Dromana Estate)

Morris
off Murray Valley Hwy
Mia Mia Vineyards
Rutherglen Vic. 3685
(02) 6026 7303
fax (02) 6026 7445
www.orlandowyndhamgroup.com

Moss Brothers
Caves Rd
Wilyabrup WA 6280
(08) 9755 6270
fax (08) 9755 6298
www.mossbrothers.com.au

Moss Wood
Metricup Rd
Wilyabrup WA 6284
(08) 9755 6266
fax (08) 9755 6303
www.mosswood.com.au

Mount Avoca
Moates Lane
Avoca Vic. 3467
(03) 5465 3282
www.mountavoca.com

Mount Horrocks
Curling St
Auburn SA 5451
(08) 8849 2202
fax (08) 8849 2265
www.mounthorrocks.com

Mount Hurtle
(see Geoff Merrill)

Mount Ida
(see Beringer Blass)

Mount Langi Ghiran
Warrak Rd
Buangor Vic. 3375
(03) 5354 3207
fax (03) 5354 3277
www.langi.com.au

Mount Mary
(not open to public)
(03) 9739 1761
fax (03) 9739 0137

Mount Pleasant
Marrowbone Rd
Pokolbin NSW 2321
(02) 4998 7505
fax (02) 4998 7761
www.mcwilliams.com.au

Mount Prior Vineyard
Cnr River Rd & Popes Lane
Rutherglen Vic. 3685
(02) 6026 5591
fax (02) 6026 5590

Mount William Winery
Mount William Rd
Tantaraboo Vic. 3764
(03) 5429 1595
fax (03) 5429 1998
www.mtwilliamwinery.com.au

Mountadam
High Eden Ridge
Eden Valley SA 5235
(08) 8564 1900
www.mountadam.com

Mulyan
North Logan Rd
Cowra NSW 2794
(02) 6342 1336
fax (02) 6341 1015
www.mulyan.com.au

Murrindindi
(not open to public)
(03) 5797 8217

Neagle's Rock
Main North Rd
Clare SA 5453
(08) 8843 4020
www.neaglesrock.com

Nepenthe Vineyards
(not open to public)
(08) 8389 8218
www.nepenthe.com.au

Nicholson River
Liddells Rd
Nicholson Vic. 3882
(03) 5156 8241
www.nicholsonriverwinery.com.au

Ninth Island
(see Pipers Brook)

Noon Winery
(cellar door seasonal)
Rifle Range Rd
McLaren Vale SA 5171
tel/fax (08) 8323 8290

Normans
(see Xanadu)

Notley Gorge
(see Rosevears Estate)

Nugan Estate
Darlington Point Rd
Wilbriggie NSW 2680
(02) 6968 5311
fax (02) 6962 5399

Oakridge Estate
864 Maroondah Hwy
Coldstream Vic. 3770
(03) 9739 1920
fax (03) 9739 1923
www.oakridgeestate.com.au

Oakvale Winery
1596 Broke Rd
Pokolbin NSW 2320
(02) 4998 7088
www.oakvalewines.com.au

Old Kent River
Turpin Rd
Rocky Gully WA 6397
(08) 9855 1589
fax (08) 9855 1589

Old Station
PO Box 40
Watervale SA 5452
(02) 9144 1925

O'Leary Walker
Main Rd
Leasingham SA 5452
(08) 8843 0022
fax 08 8843 0004
www.olearywalkerwines.com

Olivine
(see The Little Wine
Company)

Orlando
Barossa Valley Way
Rowland Flat SA 5352
(08) 8521 3111
fax (08) 8521 3102
www.orlandowyndhamgroup.com

Osborns
166 Foxeys Rd
Merricks North Vic. 3926
(03) 5989 7417
fax (03) 5989 7510

Padthaway Estate
Riddoch Hwy
Padthaway SA 5271
(08) 8765 5235
fax (08) 8765 5294
www.padthawayestate.com

Palandri
Cnr Boundary Rd & Bussell
Hwy
Margaret River WA 6285
(08) 9756 5100
fax (08) 9755 5722
www.palandri.com.au

Palmer Wines
Caves Rd
Wilyabrup WA 6280
(08) 9756 7388
fax (08) 9756 7399

Pankhurst Wines
Woodgrove Rd
Hall ACT 2618
(02) 6230 2592
www.pankhurstwines.com.au

Panorama
1848 Cygnet Coast Rd
Cradoc Tas. 7109
Tel/fax (03) 6266 3409
www.panoramavineyard.com.au

Paracombe
Paracombe Rd
Paracombe SA 5132
(08) 8380 5058
fax (08) 8380 5488
www.paracombewines.com

Paradise Enough
(weekends & holidays only)
Stewarts Rd
Kongwak Vic. 3951
(03) 5657 4241
www.paradiseenough.com.au

Paringa Estate
44 Paringa Rd
Red Hill South Vic. 3937
(03) 5989 2669
www.paringaestate.com.au

Parker Coonawarra Estate
Riddoch Hwy
Coonawarra SA 5263
(08) 8737 3525
fax (08) 8737 3527
www.parkercoonawarraestate.com.au

Passing Clouds
Powlett Rd
via Inglewood
Kingower Vic. 3517
(03) 5438 8257

Pattersons
St Werburghs Rd
Mount Barker WA 6324
tel/fax (08) 9851 2063

Paul Conti
529 Wanneroo Rd
Woodvale WA 6026
(08) 9409 9160
fax (08) 9309 1634
www.paulcontiwines.com.au

Paul Osicka
Majors Creek Vineyard
Graytown Vic. 3608
(03) 5794 9235
fax (03) 5794 9288

Paulett Wines
Polish Hill River Rd
Sevenhill SA 5453
(08) 8843 4328
fax (08) 8843 4202
www.paulettwines.com.au

Peel Estate
Fletcher Rd
Baldivis WA 6171
(08) 9524 1221
www.peelwine.com.au

Pendarves Estate
110 Old North Rd
Belford NSW 2335
(02) 6574 7222

Penfolds
(see Southcorp Wines)

Penley Estate
McLean's Rd
Coonawarra 5263
(08) 8736 3211
fax (08) 8736 3124
www.penley.com.au

Penny's Hill
Main Rd
McLaren Vale SA 5171
(08) 8556 4460
fax (08) 8556 4462
www.pennyshill.com.au

Pepper Tree Wines
Halls Rd
Pokolbin NSW 2320
(02) 4998 7539
fax (02) 4998 7746
www.peppertreewines.com.au

Pepperjack
(see Beringer Blass)

Peppers Creek
Cnr Ekerts & Broke Rds
Pokolbin NSW 2321
(02) 4998 7532

Petaluma
Spring Valley Rd
Piccadilly SA 5151
(08) 8339 9300
fax (08) 8339 9301
www.petaluma.com.au

Peter Lehmann
Para Rd
Tanunda SA 5352
(08) 8563 2500
fax (08) 8563 3402
www.peterlehmannwines.com.au

Petersons
Lot 21 Mount View Rd
Mount View NSW 2325
(02) 4990 1704
www.petersonswines.com.au

Pewsey Vale
(see Yalumba)

Pfeiffer
Distillery Rd
Wahgunyah Vic. 3687
(02) 6033 2805
www.pfeifferwines.com.au

Phillip Island Wines
Lot 1 Berrys Beach Rd
Phillip Island Vic. 3922
(03) 5956 8465
www.phillipislandwines.com.au

Pibbin Farm
Greenhill Rd
Balhannah SA 5242
(08) 8388 4794

Picardy
(not open to public)
tel/fax (08) 9776 0036
www.picardy.com.au

Pierro
Caves Rd
Wilyabrup WA 6280
(08) 9755 6220
fax (08) 9755 6308

Pikes
Polish Hill River Rd
Seven Hill SA 5453
(08) 8843 4370
fax (08) 8843 4353
www.pikeswines.com.au

Pipers Brook
3959 Bridport Hwy
Pipers Brook Tas. 7254
(03) 6332 4444
fax (03) 6334 9112
www.pbv.com.au

Pirramimma
Johnston Rd
McLaren Vale SA 5171
(08) 8323 8205
fax (08) 8323 9224
www.pirramimma.com.au

Pizzini
King Valley Rd
Whitfield Vic. 3678
(03) 5729 8278
fax (03) 5729 8495
www.pizzini.com.au

Plantagenet
Albany Hwy
Mount Barker WA 6324
(08) 9851 2150
fax (08) 9851 1839

Plunkett's
Cnr Lambing Gully Rd &
Hume Fwy
Avenel Vic. 3664
(03) 5796 2150
fax (03) 5796 2147
www.plunkett.com.au

Poole's Rock
McDonalds Rd
Pokolbin NSW 2320
(02) 4998 7501
fax (02) 4998 7682
www.poolesrock.com.au

Port Phillip Estate
261 Red Hill Rd
Red Hill Vic. 3937
(03) 5989 2708
fax (03) 5989 2891
www.portphillip.net

Portree Vineyard
72 Powell's Track
Lancefield Vic. 3435
(03) 5429 1422
fax (03) 5429 2205
www.portreevineyard.com.au

Pothana Vineyard
Pothana Lane
Belford NSW 2335
(02) 6574 7164
fax (02) 6574 7209

Preece
(see Mitchelton Wines)

Prentice
(see Tuck's Ridge)

Preston Peak
31 Preston Peak Lane
Preston Qld 4352
tel/fax (07) 4630 9499
www.prestonpeak.com

Primo Estate
Cnr Old Port Wakefield &
Angle Vale Rds
Virginia SA 5120
(08) 8380 9442
fax (08) 8380 9696
www.primoestate.com.au

Prince Albert
Lemins Rd
Waurn Ponds Vic. 3221
(03) 5243 5091
fax (03) 5241 8091

Provenance
(by appointment)
PO Box 74
Bannockburn Vic. 3331
(03) 5265 6055
fax (03) 5265 6077
www.provenancewines.com.au

Providence
236 Lalla Rd
Lalla Tas. 7267
(03) 6395 1290
fax (03) 6395 2088
www.providence-vineyards.com.au

Punt Road
St Huberts Rd
Coldstream Vic. 3770
(03) 9739 0666
fax (03) 9739 0633
www.puntroadwines.com.au

Punters Corner
Cnr Riddoch Hwy &
Racecourse Rd
Coonawarra SA 5263
(08) 8737 2007
www.punterscorner.com.au

Queen Adelaide
(see Southcorp)

Radenti
(see Freycinet Vineyard)

Ralph Fowler
Lot 101 Limestone Coast Rd
Mount Benson SA 5275
tel/fax (08) 8768 5008
www.ralphfowlerwines.com.au

Red Edge
(not open to public)
Heathcote Vic. 3523
(03) 9337 5695

Red Hill Estate
53 Shoreham Rd
Red Hill South Vic. 3937
(03) 5989 2838
www.redhillestate.com.au

Redbank Winery
1 Sally's Lane
Redbank Vic. 3478
(03) 5467 7255
www.sallyspaddock.com.au

Redgate
Cnr Caves & Boodjidup Rds
Margaret River WA 6285
(08) 9757 6488
fax (08) 9757 6308
www.redgatewines.com.au

Redman
Riddoch Hwy
Coonawarra SA 5263
(08) 8736 3331
fax (08) 8736 3013

Renmano
Renmark Ave
Renmark SA 5341
(08) 8586 6771
fax (08) 8586 5939
www.hardywines.com.au

Reynell
(see Hardys)

Ribbon Vale Estate
(see Moss Wood)

Richmond Grove
(see Orlando)

Riddoch
(see Katnook Estate)

Rimfire
via Bismarck St
Maclagan Qld 4352
(07) 4692 1129
www.rimfirewinery.com.au

Riverina Estate
700 Kidman Way
Griffith NSW 2680
(02) 6963 8300
fax (02) 6962 4628

Robinvale Wines
Sealake Rd
Robinvale Vic. 3549
(03) 5026 3955
fax (03) 5026 1123
www.organicwines.com

Rochford
Cnr Maroondah Hwy & Hill Rd
Coldstream Vic. 3770
(03) 5962 2119
www.rochfordwines.com.au

Rockford
Krondorf Rd
Tanunda SA 5352
(08) 8563 2720
info@rockfordwines.com.au

Rosabrook Estate
Rosa Brook Rd
Margaret River WA 6285
(08) 9758 2286
fax (08) 9758 8226
www.rosabrook.com

Rosemount
Rosemount Rd
Denman NSW 2328
(02) 6549 6450
fax (02) 6549 6588
www.rosemountestate.com.au

Rosevears Estate
1A Waldhorn Dve
Rosevears Tas. 7277
(03) 6330 1800
fax (03) 6330 1810
www.rosevearsestate.com.au

Rosily Vineyard
Yelverton Rd
Wilyabrup WA 6280
tel/fax (08) 9755 6336
www.rosily.com.au

Rothbury Estate
Broke Rd
Pokolbin NSW 2321
(02) 4998 7555
fax (02) 4998 7553
www.beringerblass.com.au

Rothvale
Deasy's Rd
Pokolbin NSW 2321
(02) 4998 7290
www.rothvale.com.au

Rufus Stone
(see Tyrrell's)

Rumball
(no cellar door)
(08) 8332 2761
fax (08) 8364 0188

Ryan Family Wines
Broke Estate
Broke Rd
Broke NSW 2330
tel/fax (02) 6579 1065
www.ryanwines.com.au

Ryecroft
Ingoldby Rd
McLaren Flat SA 5171
(08) 8383 0001
www.southcorp.com.au

Rymill
The Riddoch Run Vineyards
(off Main Rd)
Coonawarra SA 5263
(08) 8736 5001
fax (08) 8736 5040
www.rymill.com.au

Saddlers Creek
Marrowbone Rd
Pokolbin NSW 2321
(02) 4991 1770
fax (02) 4991 2482
www.saddlerscreekwines.com.au

Salisbury
(see Evans & Tate)

Salitage
Vasse Hwy
Pemberton WA 6260
(08) 9776 1771
fax (08) 9776 1772
www.salitage.com.au

Saltram
Nuriootpa Rd
Angaston SA 5353
(08) 8564 3355
www.saltramwines.com.au

Sandalford
West Swan Rd
Caversham WA 6055
(08) 9374 9374
fax (08) 9274 2154
www.sandalford.com

Sandhurst Ridge
156 Forest Dve
Marong Vic. 3515
(03) 5435 2534
fax (03) 5435 2548
www.sandhurstridge.com

Sandstone Vineyard
(cellar door by appointment)
Caves & Johnson Rds
Wilyabrup WA 6280
(08) 9755 6271
fax (08) 9755 6292

Scarborough Wines
Gillards Rd
Pokolbin NSW 2321
(02) 4998 7563
www.scarboroughwine.com.au

Scarpantoni
Scarpantoni Dve
McLaren Flat SA 5171
(08) 8383 0186
fax (08) 8383 0490
www.scarpantoni-wines.com.au

Schinus
(see Crittenden at Dromana)

Scotchman's Hill
Scotchmans Rd
Drysdale Vic. 3222
(03) 5251 3176
fax (03) 5253 1743
www.scotchmanshill.com.au

Seaview
Chaffeys Rd
McLaren Vale SA 5171
(08) 8323 8250
www.southcorp.com.au

Seppelt
Seppeltsfield
via Tanunda SA 5352
(08) 8562 8028
fax (08) 8562 8333
www.southcorp.com.au

Sevenhill
College Rd
Sevenhill
via Clare SA 5453
(08) 8843 4222
fax (08) 8843 4382
www.sevenhillcellars.com.au

Seville Estate
Linwood Rd
Seville Vic. 3139
(03) 5964 2622
fax (03) 5964 2633
www.sevilleestate.com.au

Shadowfax
K Road
Werribee Vic. 3030
(03) 9731 4420
fax (03) 9731 4421
www.shadowfax.com.au

Shantell
Melba Hwy
Dixons Creek Vic. 3775
(03) 5965 2155
fax (03) 5965 2331
www.shantellvineyard.com.au

Sharefarmers
(see Petaluma)

Shaw and Smith
(weekends only)
Lot 4 Jones Rd
Balhannah SA 5242
(08) 8398 0500
fax (08) 8398 0600
www.shawandsmith.com.au

Shottesbrooke
1 Bagshaws Rd
McLaren Flat SA 5171
(08) 8383 0002
fax (08) 8383 0222
www.shottesbrooke.com.au

Simon Hackett
(not open to public)
(08) 8331 7348

Skillogalee
Skillogalee Rd
via Sevenhill SA 5453
(08) 8843 4311
fax (08) 8843 4343
www.skillogalee.com.au

Smithbrook
(not open to public)
(08) 9772 3557
fax (08) 9772 3579
www.smithbrook.com.au

Sorrenberg
Alma Rd
Beechworth Vic. 3747
(03) 5728 2278
www.sorrenberg.com

Southcorp Wines
Tanunda Rd
Nuriootpa SA 5355
(08) 8568 9389
fax (08) 8568 9489
www.southcorp.com.au

St Hallett
St Halletts Rd
Tanunda SA 5352
(08) 8563 7000
fax (08) 8563 7001
www.sthallett.com.au

St Huberts
Maroondah Hwy
Coldstream Vic. 3770
(03) 9739 1118
fax (03) 9739 1096
www.sthuberts.com.au

St Leonards
St Leonard Rd
Wahgunyah Vic. 3687
(02) 6033 1004
fax (02) 6033 3636
www.stleonardswine.com.au

St Mary's Vineyard
V and A Lane
via Coonawarra SA 5263
(08) 8736 6070
fax (08) 8736 6045
www.stmaryswines.com.au

St Matthias
(see Moorilla Estate)

Stanley Brothers
Barossa Valley Way
Tanunda SA 5352
(08) 8563 3375
fax (08) 8563 3758
www.stanleybrothers.com.au

Stanton & Killeen
Murray Valley Hwy
Rutherglen Vic. 3685
(02) 6032 9457
www.stantonandkilleenwines.
com.au

Starvedog Lane
(see Hardys)

Stein's Wines
Pipeclay Rd
Mudgee NSW 2850
(02) 6373 3991
fax (02) 6373 3709

Stella Bella/Suckfizzle
(no cellar door)
PO Box 536
Margaret River WA 6285
(08) 9757 6377
fax (08) 9757 6022
www.stellabella.com.au

Stephen John Wines
Government Rd
Watervale SA 5452
tel/fax (08) 8843 0105

Stonehaven
(see Hardys)

**Stoney Vineyard/
Domaine A**
Teatree Rd
Campania Tas. 7026
(03) 6260 4174
fax (03) 6260 4390

Stonier
362 Frankston–Flinders Rd
Merricks Vic. 3916
(03) 5989 8300
fax (03) 5989 8709
www.stoniers.com.au

Stumpy Gully
1247 Stumpy Gully Rd
Moorooduc Vic. 3933
(03) 5978 8429
fax (03) 5978 8419

Summerfield
Main Rd
Moonambel Vic. 3478
(03) 5467 2264
fax (03) 5467 2380
www.summerfieldwines.com.au

Tahbilk
Tahbilk Vic. 3607
via Nagambie
(03) 5794 2555
fax (03) 5794 2360
www.tahbilk.com.au

Talijancich
26 Hyem Rd
Herne Hill WA 6056
(08) 9296 4289
fax (08) 9296 1762

Tallarook
(not open to public)
(03) 9818 3455
www.tallarook.com

Taltarni Vineyards
Taltarni Rd
Moonambel Vic. 3478
(03) 5459 7900
fax (03) 5467 2306
www.taltarni.com.au

Talunga
Lot 101 Adelaide-Mannum Rd
Gumeracha SA 5233
(08) 8389 1222
fax (08) 8389 1233
www.talunga.com.au

Tamar Ridge
Auburn Rd
Kayena Tas. 7270
(03) 6394 7002
fax (03) 6394 7003

Tamburlaine Wines
McDonalds Rd
Pokolbin NSW 2321
(02) 4998 7570
fax (02) 4998 7763
www.tamburlaine.com.au

Tanglewood Downs
Bulldog Creek Rd
Merricks North
(03) 5974 3325
www.tanglewoodestate.com.au

Tapestry
Merrivale Wines
Olivers Rd
McLaren Vale SA 5171
(08) 8323 9196
fax (08) 8323 9746
www.merrivale.com.au

TarraWarra
Healesville Rd
Yarra Glen Vic. 3775
(03) 5962 3311
fax (03) 5962 3887
www.tarrawarra.com.au

Tatachilla Winery
151 Main Rd
McLaren Vale SA 5171
(08) 8323 8656
fax (08) 8323 9096
www.tatachillawinery.com.au

Taylors
Mintaro Rd
Auburn SA 5451
(08) 8849 2008
www.taylorswines.com.au

Temple Bruer
Angas River Delta
via Strathalbyn SA 5255
(08) 8537 0203
fax (08) 8537 0131
www.templebruer.net.au

Tempus Two
(see McGuigan)

T'Gallant
1385 Mornington-Flinders Rd
Main Ridge Vic. 3937
(03) 5989 6565
fax (03) 5989 6577

Thalgara Estate
De Beyers Rd
Pokolbin NSW 2321
(02) 4998 7717
www.thalgara.com.au

Thomas Wines
PO Box 606
Cessnock NSW 2325
tel/fax (02) 6574 7371
www.thomaswines.com.au

Thorn-Clarke
PO Box 402
Angaston SA 5353
(08) 8564 3373
fax (08) 8564 3255
www.thornclarkewines.com.au

Tim Adams
Warenda Rd
Clare SA 5453
(08) 8842 2429
fax (08) 8842 3550
www.timadamswines.com.au

Tim Gramp
Mintaro/Leasingham Rd
Watervale SA 5452
(08) 8843 0199
fax (08) 8843 0299
www.timgrampwines.com.au

Tin Cows
(see TarraWarra)

Tintilla
Hermitage Rd
Pokolbin NSW 2335
(02) 6574 7093
fax (02) 6574 7094
www.tintilla.com

Tisdall
Cornelia Creek Rd
Echuca Vic. 3564
(03) 5482 1911
fax (03) 5482 2516

Torbreck
Roennfeldt Rd
Marananga SA 5360
(08) 8562 4155
fax (08) 8562 3418
www.torbreck.com

Torresan Estate
Estate Dve
Flagstaff Hill SA 5159
(08) 8270 2500

Tower Estate
Cnr Broke & Halls Rds
Pokolbin NSW 2321
(02) 4998 7989
www.towerestatewines.com.au

Trentham Estate
Sturt Hwy
Trentham Cliffs
via Gol Gol NSW 2738
(03) 5024 8888
fax (03) 5024 8800
www.trenthamestate.com.au

Tuck's Ridge
37 Red Hill-Shoreham Rd
Red Hill South Vic. 3937
(03) 5989 8660
fax (03) 5989 8579
www.tucksridge.com.au

Turkey Flat
Bethany Rd
Tanunda SA 5352
(08) 8563 2851
fax (08) 8563 3610
www.turkeyflat.com.au

Turramurra Estate
295 Wallaces Rd
Dromana Vic. 3936
(03) 5987 1146
fax (03) 5987 1286
www.turramurraestate.com.au

Two Hands
Neldner Rd
Marananga SA 5355
(08) 8562 4566
fax (08) 8562 4744
www.twohandswines.com

Two Rivers
18 Craig Street
Artarmon NSW 2064
(02) 9436 3022
fax (02) 9439 7930

Tyrrell's
Broke Rd
Pokolbin NSW 2321
(02) 4993 7000
fax (02) 4998 7723
www.winefutures.com.au

Vasse Felix
Cnr Caves & Harmans Rds
Cowaramup WA 6284
(08) 9756 5000
fax (08) 9755 5425
www.vassefelix.com.au

Veritas
Cnr Seppeltsfield & Stelzer Rds
Dorrien SA 5355
(08) 8562 3300
www.veritaswinery.com

Virgin Hills
(not open to public)
(03) 5422 3032
www.virginhills.com.au

Voyager Estate
Stevens Rd
Margaret River WA 6285
(08) 9757 6354
fax (08) 9757 6494
www.voyagerestate.com.au

Wandin Valley Estate
Wilderness Rd
Lovedale NSW 2320
(02) 4930 7317
fax (02) 4930 7814
www.wandinvalley.com.au

Wantirna Estate
(not open to public)
(03) 9801 2367
www.wantirnaestate.com.au

Warburn Estate
(see Riverina Estate)

Wards Gateway Cellars
Barossa Valley Hwy
Lyndoch SA 5351
(08) 8524 4138

Warrabilla
Murray Valley Hwy
Rutherglen Vic. 3687
tel/fax (02) 6035 7242
www.warrabillawines.com.au

Warramate
27 Maddens Lane
Gruyere Vic. 3770
(03) 5964 9219

Warrenmang
Mountain Ck Rd
Moonambel Vic. 3478
(03) 5467 2233
fax (03) 5467 2309
www.bazzani.com.au/warrenmang

Waterwheel Vineyards
Raywood Rd
Bridgewater Vic. 3516
(03) 5437 3060
fax (03) 5437 3082
www.waterwheelwine.com

Wedgetail
(not open to public)
(03) 9714 8661
www.wedgetailestate.com.au

Wellington
(Hood Wines)
489 Richmond Rd
Cambridge Tas. 7170
(03) 6248 5844
fax (03) 6248 5855

Wendouree
Wendouree Rd
Clare SA 5453
(08) 8842 2896

Westend
1283 Brayne Rd
Griffith NSW 2680
(02) 6964 1506
fax (02) 6962 1673

Westfield
Memorial Ave
Baskerville WA 6056
(08) 9296 4356

Wetherall
Naracoorte Rd
Coonawarra SA 5263
(08) 8737 2104
fax (08) 8737 2105

Wignalls
Chester Pass Rd
Albany WA 6330
(08) 9841 2848
www.wignallswines.com.au

Wild Duck Creek
(by appointment only)
Springflat Rd
Heathcote Vic. 3523
(03) 5433 3133

Wildwood
St Johns Lane
via Wildwood Vic. 3428
(03) 9307 1118
www.wildwoodvineyards.com.au

Will Taylor
1 Simpson Pde
Goodwood SA 5034
(08) 8271 6122

Willespie
Harmans Mill Rd
Wilyabrup WA 6280
(08) 9755 6248
fax (08) 9755 6210
www.willespie.com.au

Willow Creek
166 Balnarring Rd
Merricks North Vic. 3926
(03) 5989 7448
fax (03) 5989 7584
www.willow-creek.com

The Willows Vineyard
Light Pass Rd
Barossa Valley SA 5355
(08) 8562 1080
www.thewillowsvineyard.com.au

The Wilson Vineyard
Polish Hill River
via Clare SA 5453
(08) 8843 4310
www.wilsonvineyard.com.au

Winchelsea Estate
C/- Nicks Wine Merchants
(03) 9639 0696

Windowrie Estate
Windowrie Rd
Canowindra NSW 2804
(02) 6344 3598
fax (02) 6344 3597
www.windowrie.com.au

Winstead
Winstead Rd
Bagdad Tas. 7030
(03) 6268 6417

Wirilda Creek
Lot 32 McMurtrie Rd
McLaren Vale SA 5171
(08) 8323 9688

Wirra Wirra
McMurtrie Rd
McLaren Vale SA 5171
(08) 8323 8414
fax (08) 8323 8596
www.wirra.com.au

Wolf Blass
Sturt Hwy
Nuriootpa SA 5355
(08) 8568 7300
fax (08) 8568 7380
www.wolfblass.com.au

Wood Park
Kneebones Gap Rd
Bobinawarrah Vic. 3678
(03) 5727 3367
fax (03) 5727 3682
www.woodpark.com.au

Woodstock
Douglas Gully Rd
McLaren Flat SA 5171
(08) 8383 0156
fax (08) 8383 0437
www.woodstockwine.com.au

Woody Nook
Metricup Rd
Metricup WA 6280
(08) 9755 7547
fax (08) 9755 7007
www.woodynook.com.au

Wyanga Park
Baades Rd
Lakes Entrance Vic. 3909
(03) 5155 1508
fax (03) 5155 1443

Wyndham Estate
Dalwood Rd
Dalwood NSW 2321
(02) 4938 3444
fax (02) 4938 3555
www.wyndhamestate.com.au

Wynns
Memorial Dve
Coonawarra SA 5263
(08) 8736 3266
fax (08) 8736 3202
www.wynns.com.au

Xanadu
Boodjidup Rd
Margaret River WA 6285
(08) 9757 2581
fax (08) 9757 3389
www.xanaduwines.com.au

Yabby Lake
(no cellar door)
(03) 9667 6644
fax (03) 9639 0540
www.yabbylake.com

Yaldara
Gomersal Rd
Lyndoch SA 5351
(08) 8524 0200
fax (08) 8524 0240
www.yaldara.com.au

Yalumba
Eden Valley Rd
Angaston SA 5353
(08) 8561 3200
fax (08) 8561 3393
www.yalumba.com

Yarra Burn
Settlement Rd
Yarra Junction Vic. 3797
(03) 5967 1428
fax (03) 5967 1146
www.hardywines.com.au

Yarra Ridge
Glenview Rd
Yarra Glen Vic. 3775
(03) 9730 1022
fax (03) 9730 1131
www.beringerblass.com.au

Yarra Valley Hills
(see Dromana Estate)

Yarra Yering
Briarty Rd
Gruyere Vic. 3770
(03) 5964 9267

Yarraman Estate
700 Yarraman Rd
Wybong NSW 2333
(02) 6547 8118
fax (02) 6547 8039
www.yarramanestate.com.au

Yellowglen
White's Rd
Smythesdale Vic. 3351
(03) 5342 8617
www.yellowglen.com.au

Yellow Tail
(see Casella)

Yeringberg
(not open to public)
(03) 9739 1453
fax (03) 9739 0048

Yering Station
Melba Hwy
Yering Vic. 3775
(03) 9730 0100
fax (03) 9739 0135
www.yering.com

Zarephath
Moorialup Rd
East Porongurup WA 6324
tel/fax (08) 9853 1152
www.zarephathwines.com

Zema Estate
Riddoch Hwy
Coonawarra SA 5263
(08) 8736 3219
fax (08) 8736 3280
www.zema.com.au

Zilzie
Lot 66 Kulkyne Way
Karadoc Vic. 3496
(03) 5025 8100
fax (03) 5025 8116
www.zilziewines.com

Index